Consumer Alternative Dispute Resolution in Emerging Economies

This book provides a comprehensive guide to consumer Alternative Dispute Resolution (ADRs) and the unconventional challenges they pose for emerging economies, aiming to advance their growth within developing nations.

Written in response to the increasing number of transactions between consumers and traders in the digital age, and the accompanying rise in consumer disputes, the book details ADR systems which have come to the fore to settle complaints. Covering ADR techniques including arbitration, mediation, and ombudsman services, it provides a guide to efficient dispute resolution and its application to emerging economies worldwide. The book also examines the role of technology in shaping ADR processes, given the prevalence of digital transactions in consumer markets.

Thoughtfully explaining the challenges faced in implementing these systems suggests how governments and businesses can encourage the use of ADR, alongside providing practical case studies detailing past integrations into emerging economies.

Practical, thorough, and internationally focused, this book will be of interest to researchers in the fields of dispute resolution, consumer law, and technology.

Eda Sahin-Sengül is a senior lecturer in law, Bath Spa University, UK. She received her LLM degree from the University of East Anglia and her PhD from Queen Mary University of London, UK. Her research interests include class actions, competition law, and consumer law.

Serkan Kaya is an assistant professor in law, Boğaziçi University in Istanbul, Turkey. He received his PhD and LLM degrees from Brunel Law School at Brunel University London, UK. His research interests include civil procedure law, alternative dispute resolution, and online dispute resolution.

Consumer Alternative Dispute Resolution in Emerging Economies

Edited by Eda Sahin-Sengül and Serkan Kaya

Routledge
Taylor & Francis Group
LONDON AND NEW YORK

First published 2025
by Routledge
4 Park Square, Milton Park, Abingdon, Oxon OX14 4RN

and by Routledge
605 Third Avenue, New York, NY 10158

Routledge is an imprint of the Taylor & Francis Group, an informa business

British Library Cataloguing-in-Publication Data
A catalogue record for this book is available from the British Library

ISBN: 978-1-032-66098-1 (hbk)
ISBN: 978-1-032-68971-5 (pbk)
ISBN: 978-1-032-68973-9 (ebk)

DOI: 10.4324/9781032689739

Typeset in Times New Roman
by Apex CoVantage, LLC

Contents

Contributors

Hani Abdulghani Alharbi Assistant Professor and Vice Dean Jeddah College of Law (JCL) at the University of Business and Technology (UBT). Dr Hani is a legal expert in different aspects and his interests include commercial law and alternative dispute resolution (ADR), Saudi labour law, and international law in the Kingdom of Saudi Arabia.

Giorgi Amiranashvili, PhD in law (TSU), is an assistant professor in private law and a senior specialist at the Faculty of Law, Ivane Javakhishvili Tbilisi State University. He is a member of the Contemporary Private Law Institute and the International Association of Consumer Law. His research experience includes fellowships at the Max Planck Institute, Harvard Law School Library, Swiss Institute of Comparative Law, and UNIDROIT.

Arushi Bajpai is an assistant professor and fellow of the Centre for Alternative Dispute Resolution at Jindal Global Law School where she teaches the Indian Penal Code and Code of Criminal Procedure. She completed her higher studies in international criminal law at the University of Kent at Canterbury, United Kingdom. She graduated from the National University of Study and Research in Law, Ranchi, where she majored in criminal law. She has also completed a course in public international law from the Hague Academy of Public International Law with a full scholarship.

Dr. Luca Dal Pubel is a conflict resolution and ADR expert, blending practical experience with cutting-edge research. He teaches ADR, negotiation, and conflict resolution at San Diego State University (SDSU) and Point Loma Nazarene University (PLNU). He's a visiting lecturer at Portugal's National Defence Institute (IDN), a member of the International Council for Online Dispute Resolution (ICODR), and an editorial board member of the Law Journal *Consensual Justice*. His research focuses on conflict resolution, international mediation, ADR, and ODR.

Fatih Buğra Erdem (LLM, PhD, University of London, post-doctorate, Trinity College Dublin) is an associate professor of commercial law at the Social Sciences University of Ankara. As of 2021, Dr Erdem joined Ankara Social Sciences University Faculty of Law and has been awarded a professorship in competition law by Freie Berlin University since the same period. He is also practising law at his own law firm, SAPIENTI, as well as acting as an expert in the NATO DIANA program. His academic research especially focuses on insurance law and corporate governance in public companies and investor transactions in the capital markets.

Akash Gupta is an assistant professor and assistant director of the Centre for Alternative Dispute Resolution at Jindal Global Law School, where he specialises in teaching arbitration courses. Additionally, he is a Visiting Faculty at the National Law School of India University, Bengaluru. He has attended summer and winter schools at the Paris Arbitration Academy and the Hague Academy of International Law, respectively, both on full scholarship and full sponsorship. Recognised for his contributions to the field, Akash was awarded the "Young ADR Academic of the Year" by the Asia Pacific Centre for Arbitration and Mediation in May 2023.

Muhammad Danyal Khan, a lecturer at Liverpool Hope University, holds a PhD in law, specialising in intellectual property rights, human rights law, and medical negligence. With nearly 13 years of academic experience, he is a published researcher and has presented his work internationally. Recognised for his engaging teaching, Dr. Khan received the 2019 Teaching Excellence Award from Brunel Pathway College. He is also involved in community initiatives, volunteering to provide legal advice to those lacking access to legal services.

Yi Lu, Senior Lecturer at Peking University, holds JSD and LLM degrees from Yale Law School and JD and JM degrees from Peking University School of Transnational Law. As a licensed attorney, Dr. Lu has also practised at TransAsia Lawyers, Clifford Chance LLP, and Morrison Foerster LLP. Her academic interests include commercial law, administrative law, environmental law, food law, and international trade law.

Andrea Marighetto is an international lawyer specialising in international contracts and ADR, with expertise in civil law systems in Europe and Latin America, particularly Brazil. He holds two PhD degrees, one in comparative and uniform commercial law (University of Roma I La Sapienza) and the other in private law (UFRGS). He serves as legal counsel and board member for multinational companies and is a member of various legal organisations. Dr. Marighetto is based in Brazil, Italy, and the Netherlands.

Maizatul Farisah Mohd Mokhtar is a lecturer at Universiti Sains Islam Malaysia (USIM) with extensive experience in law and Syariah since 2008. An expert in alternative dispute resolution (ADR), including mediation, arbitration, sulh, and tahkim, as well as consumer law, she specialises in medical law, ethics, and AI in medicine. Her PhD research at Brunel University London (2017) focused on medical law and ADR, reflecting her strong multidisciplinary legal research background.

Rodrigo Momberg is a professor of private and consumer law at the Pontificia Universidad Católica de Valparaíso, Chile. He holds an LLM in European private law and a PhD from the University of Utrecht, the Netherlands. He is also a visiting research fellow at the Institute of European and Comparative Law of the University of Oxford. Rodrigo Momberg has published extensively in the fields of contract, consumer, and comparative private law.

María Elisa Morales is an associate professor of the Department of Private Law and Law Sciences at the Universidad Austral de Chile. She holds a PhD in law from the University of Chile. Her research interests are private law, consumer law, and comparative law. She has published numerous articles and books on law in these areas and is a permanent member of the group of lecturers of the Doctorate in Law at the Universidad Austral de Chile.

Tjakie Naude is a professor of private law at the University of Cape Town, South Africa. She is a co-editor of the book, *Commentary on the Consumer Protection Act*, published by Juta (Naude and Eiselen (eds)) and updated annually. She has also published articles and chapters on consumer law and the Law of Contracts. She obtained the degrees BA (cum laude), LLB (cum laude), and LLD from the University of Stellenbosch, South Africa.

Alberto Pino-Emhart is an associate professor at Universidad Adolfo Ibañez, Viña del Mar, Chile. He holds a D.Phil in law degree from the University of Oxford, an LLM degree from Duke University, a master in law and a bachelor in law degree from Universidad de Chile. His research interests are jurisprudence and the law of obligations, focusing his main area of interest in the philosophy of tort law.

Janani Sivaraman holds a bachelor's degree in commerce from the University of Mumbai. She is currently a law researcher at Jindal Global Law School, O.P. Jindal Global University, with a keen interest in private international law, dispute resolution, and arbitration law.

Cătălin Gabriel Stănescu is Associate Professor in law at the Faculty for Business and Social Sciences, University of Southern Denmark (Denmark). His current research focuses on topics related to consumer financial protection, informal debt collection regulation, and digital law. Cătălin has been a visiting scholar at several renowned research institutions such as the Institute for Advanced Legal Studies (London), the Centre for Commercial Law Studies of Queen Mary University (London); Max Planck Institute for Comparative and Private International Law (Hamburg); the European University Institute (Florence) and the Centre for Banking and Finance Law (Singapore).

Henry C. Uzokwe is a lecturer, consumer protection attorney, and associate research fellow at Brunel University Law School, London. He holds degrees in English, law, diplomacy, and a PhD in consumer protection law. His research focuses on consumer financial literacy, commercial law, and consumer protection in Africa. He has been a visiting research fellow at the Max Plank Institute and served as a legal consultant for the Consumer Protection Council and NGOs in Africa.

1 Introduction

Eda Sahin-Sengül and Serkan Kaya

Background

Consumers, who usually have low-value claims, are the weaker party and need protection included in the institutions meant to protect them.[1] Although redress was recognised as one of the consumer rights early on, efforts initially concentrated on creating rights for consumers without giving much thought to how those rights would be upheld.[2] Particularly, legal systems of emerging economies are ill-prepared to safeguard consumer rights and leave them unprotected. In the upcoming years, alternative dispute resolution (ADR) systems, as a fast-growing phenomenon, may develop into a legitimate method for providing consumers with access to justice globally. Therefore, this book, the first to focus solely on consumer ADR systems in emerging economies, strives to close a significant gap in the legal literature by utilising technology to increase consumers' access to justice.

The digital age we live in gives rise to the continuously increasing number of transactions between consumers and traders, which raises the probability of the occurrence of consumer disputes. In parallel, in order to minimise the number of consumer disputes, substantive consumer rights are developing, especially for online consumers, who paradoxically have much more comprehensive protection than traditional offline consumers. However, if consumers do not have an effective means to ensure that these rights are complied with, their rights can only be considered wet paper.[3] In other words, consumer rights are effective only when they are enforceable in practice. In today's digitalised society, the resolution of disputes through traditional litigation is not only costly, time-consuming, and slow but also much more complicated than ADR systems.

This book aims to provide an introduction to consumer ADRs and offers analyses of the novel challenges they pose for emerging economies. In the last decades, ADR systems have become increasingly popular as a means of settling consumer

1 Mary O'Hara, 'Foreword' in Christine Riefa and Séverine Saintier (eds) *Vulnerable Consumers and the Law* (Routledge 2021) xv

2 Christine Riefa and Séverine Saintier, 'In Search of (Access to) Justice for Vulnerable Consumers' in Christine Riefa and Séverine Saintier (eds) *Vulnerable Consumers and the Law* (Routledge 2021) 3

3 Pablo Cortés, *The Law of Consumer Redress in an Evolving Digital Market: Upgrading From Alternative to Online Dispute Resolution* (Cambridge University Press 2017) 272

DOI: 10.4324/9781032689739-1

complaints. ADR techniques, including arbitration, mediation, and ombudsman services, provide an efficient way for dispute resolution that is faster, less formal, and frequently more cost-effective than traditional legal procedures. The average duration of a case in consumer courts is 425 days for the first-instance courts in Turkey.[4] In comparison, the average time typically needed to resolve cases in a court is 559 days in the United Arab Emirates (UAE).[5] Moreover, some countries' litigation systems are expensive compared to other ADR options.[6] According to a study conducted by the CMS Research Programme on Civil Justice Systems at the Centre for Socio-Legal Studies at the University of Oxford, the cost to the claimant is not proportionate to the sum obtained in dispute in a significant number of countries.[7]

A survey published in 2023 by the European Commission entitled "Survey of consumers' attitudes towards cross-border trade and consumer-related issues 2023" pointed out that a fourth of consumers in the European Union (EU) had a problem with their purchase over the past 12 months. Almost six out of seven consumers who had experienced a problem purchasing online goods or services did not take any action to resolve the problem.[8] The survey showed that the main reasons for not taking action were that it would take too much time (49%), the value of goods or services is too low (42%), and that a satisfactory solution cannot be reached (36%).[9] All these statistics show that even though action has been taken to protect consumers, disputes are inevitable in the course of business. The value of a claim in these disputes is often low, which is why traditional dispute resolution methods are often inconvenient, impractical, time-consuming, and expensive.

Particularly for low-value claims, the high cost and long time associated with the litigation and a lack of awareness and trust towards the dispute resolution process are among the numerous barriers to consumers' access to justice via traditional litigation.[10] Rationally, if the claimant makes his or her decision based on risk and cost-benefit analysis and considers that the dispute is not worthy of pursuing, then

4 Republic of Turkey Ministry of Justice Statistics, <https://adlisicil.adalet.gov.tr/Resimler/SayfaDokuman/22420211427211062020170359HizmeteOzel-2019-baskı-İSA.pdf> accessed 20 December 2023

5 Saifaldeen Najim Al-Azzawi, 'Access to Justice for Consumers in the United Arab Emirates' in Serkan Kaya (ed) *Access to Justice in Emerging Economies* (Adalet 2021) 122

6 Christopher Hodges, Stefan Vogenauer and Magdalena Tulibacka, 'The Oxford Study on Costs and Funding of Civil Litigation' in Christopher Hodges, Stefan Vogenauer and Magdalena Tulibacka (eds) *The Costs and Funding of Civil Litigation: A Comparative Perspective* (Hart Publishing 2010) 4

7 Christopher Hodges, Stefan Vogenauer and Magdalena Tulibacka, 'The Oxford Study on Costs and Funding of Civil Litigation' in Christopher Hodges, Stefan Vogenauer and Magdalena Tulibacka (eds) *The Costs and Funding of Civil Litigation: A Comparative Perspective* (Hart Publishing 2010) 35

8 DG Justice and Consumers, *Survey of Consumers' Attitudes Towards Cross-Border Trade and Consumer-Related Issues 2023* (Publications Office of the European Union 2023) 13

9 DG Justice and Consumers, *Survey of Consumers' Attitudes Towards Cross-Border Trade and Consumer-Related Issues 2023* (Publications Office of the European Union 2023) 14

10 Katalin J. Cseres, 'Harmonising Private Enforcement of Competition Law in Central and Eastern Europe: The Effectiveness of Legal Transplants Through Consumer Collective Actions' (2015) 8(12) *Yearbook of Antitrust and Regulatory Studies* 33, 42

the consumer's legal right will be undefended.[11] In the cases where the consumers do not even make an attempt to get redress, this actually results in injustice to them. For those reasons, consumer ADR mechanisms have emerged in many countries. Many governments are interested in developing consumer ADR as an out-of-court system for enhancing access to justice and overcoming the problems of costs, time, and formality of traditional litigation mechanisms.

ADR mechanisms have the potential to play a vital role in ensuring that consumers in emerging economies have access to justice, particularly in contexts where access to the courts is restricted, and the legal system is susceptible to being delayed and corrupt. In recent years, there has been an increasing interest in using ADR in emerging economies to address consumer disputes.[12] Despite this increased interest, there still needs to be more awareness of the specific obstacles and opportunities that occur in implementing ADR. (Even in the European Union, only about 6% of consumers have brought their issue to an ADR body,[13] and this is mainly due to their lack of awareness about this option.[14]) Additionally, there needs to be more research on the effectiveness of consumer ADR in these economies and how it can be used to benefit consumers.

Chapters of the Book

As most of the legal studies are conducted in developed nations, consumer ADR is an understudied area in developing countries. No comprehensive study to date has been conducted on consumer ADR in emerging economies. However, there is evidence that ADR is still at an early stage of evolution in these economies as it faces legal and cultural challenges. The book, therefore, seeks to contribute to the knowledge and literature on the establishment and development of ADR methods for consumer disputes in the legal context of developing nations.

There are 152 developing countries in the world with a current population of around 6.77 billion, which constitutes 85.49% of the world's population.[15] Among those, the book includes countries with high populations, as high populations give rise to high consumer disputes in practice. The book also contains countries with economic and geopolitical importance in the region and chooses one country

11 Sutatip Yuthayotin, *Access to Justice in Transnational B2C E-Commerce: A Multidimensional Analysis of Consumer Protection Mechanisms* (Springer International Publishing 2015) 94

12 United Nations Conference on Trade and Development, *Strengthening consumer protection and competition in the digital economy* (19–23 October 2020) TD/RBP/CONF.9/4 <https://unctad.org/system/files/official-document/tdrbpconf9d4_en.pdf> accessed 2 November 2024

13 DG Justice and Consumers, *Consumer Conditions Scoreboard 2023* (Publications Office of the European Union 2023) 28

14 Approximately 45% of consumers do not know any ADR entities and not surprisingly, nearly seven out of ten consumers who had used ADR mechanisms expressed their satisfactions See DG Justice and Consumers, *Consumer Conditions Scoreboard 2023* (Publications Office of the European Union 2023) 28

15 World Data, <https://www.worlddata.info/developing-countries.php#:~:text=According%20to%20the%20IMF%20definition,proportion%20of%20the%20world's%20population> accessed 13 July 2024

among the countries which have similar regimes. The book has chapters written on the following developing countries: Georgia, China, Chile, Pakistan, Turkey, Romania, India, South Africa, Saudi Arabia, and the United Arab Emirates.

Each chapter examines the various forms of ADR, the challenges of implementing them, and the opportunities they present for improving access to justice for consumers in emerging economies. Each chapter also explores the role of the government, private sector, and civil society in promoting the use of ADR in these countries. Additionally, the authors provide practical examples of how ADR has been successfully implemented in developed jurisdictions to be used in their jurisdiction. Each essay on emerging economies assesses the enforcement mechanisms and the effectiveness of consumer laws in their jurisdictions, explains the existing consumer dispute resolution systems, provides an overview of Consumer ADR mechanisms, discusses the use of technology, and reflects on the challenges and opportunities in implementing Consumer ADR in these regions. Accordingly, the book explains how consumer ADR operates in developing jurisdictions and offers a comparative analysis of such an under-researched area with the aim of making an important contribution to the development of consumer ADR in the selected developing countries.

In addition to the developing jurisdictions, the book analyses consumer ADRs in developed countries, which are the European Union and the United Kingdom, in order to identify what can be learned from them and how these can be used in developing countries so that an effective redress system can be offered to consumers in developing jurisdictions as well. The chapter on the European Union includes an overview of consumer protection, enforcement mechanisms of consumer law, availability of consumer ADR and online dispute resolution (ODR) mechanisms, summary, and assessment. The United Kingdom was chosen as a jurisdiction to reflect on its consumer protection system as a developed and non-EU jurisdiction. This chapter includes an overview of the legal system, the institutional landscape for consumer claims, enforcement of consumer law, availability of consumer ADR and ODR mechanisms, and a summary and assessment. These chapters are later used to draw lessons from their experiences and propose recommendations to the emerging economies to the extent that they fit the legal system of the country in question. Accordingly, this book intends to draw lessons from the experience of the developed jurisdictions and the well-established practices in the field of consumer ADR internationally that could thereafter be considered by developing jurisdictions in order to ensure more effective resolution of consumer disputes. The collected essays, which have not been published before, offer a combination of theoretical and empirical analysis. In addition to presenting the trends in this growing area of litigation, the essays will provide procedural difficulties unique to consumer claims and implementation challenges of ADRs in emerging economies by benefiting from the experiences of the developed jurisdictions.

The conclusion chapter offers a comparative analysis of the jurisdictions discussed in the book. This chapter aims to analyse running themes and findings from the book. As a concluding chapter, it reflects on the results of the book and identifies common challenges facing emerging economies in promoting consumer ADR.

References

Cortés P, *The Law of Consumer Redress in an Evolving Digital Market: Upgrading from Alternative to Online Dispute Resolution* (Cambridge University Press 2017)

Cseres KJ, 'Harmonising Private Enforcement of Competition Law in Central and Eastern Europe: The Effectiveness of Legal Transplants Through Consumer Collective Actions' (2015) 8(12) Yearbook of Antitrust and Regulatory Studies

DG Justice and Consumers, *Consumer Conditions Scoreboard 2023* (Publications Office of the European Union 2023)

DG Justice and Consumers, *Survey of Consumers' Attitudes Towards Cross-Border Trade and Consumer-Related Issues 2023* (Publications Office of the European Union 2023)

Hodges C, Vogenauer S and Tulibacka M, 'The Oxford Study on Costs and Funding of Civil Litigation' in Christopher Hodges, Stefan Vogenauer and Magdalena Tulibacka (eds) *The Costs and Funding of Civil Litigation: A Comparative Perspective* (Hart Publishing 2010)

Najim Al-Azzawi S, 'Access to Justice for Consumers in the United Arab Emirates' in Serkan Kaya (ed) *Access to Justice in Emerging Economies* (Adalet 2021)

O'Hara M, 'Foreword' in Christine Riefa and Séverine Saintier (eds) *Vulnerable Consumers and the Law* (Routledge 2021)

Republic of Turkey Ministry of Justice Statistics, <https://adlisicil.adalet.gov.tr/Resimler/SayfaDokuman/2242021142721106202017O359HizmeteOzel-2019-baskı-İSA.pdf> accessed 20 December 2023

Riefa C and Saintier S, 'In Search of (Access to) Justice for Vulnerable Consumers' in Christine Riefa and Séverine Saintier (eds) *Vulnerable Consumers and the Law* (Routledge 2021)

United Nations Conference on Trade and Development, *Strengthening consumer protection and competition in the digital economy* (19–23 October 2020) TD/RBP/CONF.9/4 <https://unctad.org/system/files/official-document/tdrbpconf9d4_en.pdf> accessed 2 November 2024

World Data, <https://www.worlddata.info/developing-countries.php#:~:text=According%20to%20the%20IMF%20definition,proportion%20of%20the%20world's%20population> accessed 13 July 2024

Yuthayotin S, *Access to Justice in Transnational B2C E-Commerce: A Multidimensional Analysis of Consumer Protection Mechanisms* (Springer International Publishing 2015)

2 Consumer ADR in the EU

Serkan Kaya and Eda Sahin-Sengül

Introduction

The European Union, inhabiting 448.4 million consumers,[1] is unique in its multi-tiered system, where consumer law is primarily established at the EU level but enforced by the Member States. Consumer spending has recently become the dominant component of the GDP. In the European Union, consumer expenditure represents 52.3% of the total GDP.[2] Consequently, a growing focus has been on regulating consumer protection within the European Union. The rationale behind these regulations is the belief that consumer policies are essential for the proper functioning of markets.[3] Business-to-consumer (B2C) transactions in the European Union reached €899 billion in 2022, reflecting a growth rate of 6%.[4] Approximately 76% of the EU population shopped online, and over 31% of consumers in the European Union purchased goods or services from retailers across borders.[5]

In 2023, the European Commission released a survey titled 'Survey of Consumers' Attitudes towards Cross-border Trade and Consumer-related Issues 2023', revealing that one-fourth of consumers in the European Union encountered issues with their purchases in the past year.[6] Alarmingly, nearly six out of seven consumers who faced problems with online purchases did not take any steps to resolve them. The survey identified that the primary reasons for not taking action included concerns about the time involved (49%), the perceived low value of the goods or

1 EU Demographics, <https://european-union.europa.eu/principles-countries-history/key-facts-and-figures/life-eu_en> accessed 9 July 2024

2 Eurostat Statistics Explained, (Eurostat 2024) <https://ec.europa.eu/eurostat/statistics-explained/index.php?title=National_accounts_and_GDP#:~:text=In%20current%20price%20terms%2C%20consumption,general%20government%20expenditure%20was%2021.1%25> accessed 14 July 2024

3 Mark Armstrong, 'Interactions Between Competition and Consumer Policy' (2008) 4(1) *Competition Policy International* 97, 144

4 European E-commerce Report 2023, <https://ecommerce-europe.eu/wp-content/uploads/2023/11/European-Ecommerce-Report-2023-Light-Version.pdf> accessed 14 July 2024

5 European E-commerce Report 2023, <https://ecommerce-europe.eu/wp-content/uploads/2023/11/European-Ecommerce-Report-2023-Light-Version.pdf> accessed 14 July 2024

6 DG Justice and Consumers, *Survey of Consumers' Attitudes Towards Cross-Border Trade and Consumer-Related Issues 2023* (Publications Office of the European Union 2023) 13

DOI: 10.4324/9781032689739-2

services (42%), and doubts about achieving a satisfactory resolution (36%).[7] These statistics underscore that disputes remain inevitable in B2C transactions despite efforts to safeguard consumers.

In the European Union, fostering consumer trust in B2C transactions has become a key political objective of the European Commission. To build this trust and provide an effective dispute resolution system, the European Parliament and the Council adopted the EU Directive on Consumer ADR and the EU Regulation on Consumer ODR on 21 May 2013. The EU Directive on Consumer ADR mandates that Member States ensure the availability of high-quality ADR entities that adhere to consumer procedural standards. In February 2016, the EU Regulation on Consumer ODR established an online platform (EU ODR Platform) that allows for the submission of complaints online and their transmission to nationally approved ADR entities in the Member States. These two pieces of legislation have initiated a process that institutionalises and professionalises consumer ADR, making it a central component of EU consumer redress law.

Legal Framework for Consumer Protection

The pursuit of a high level of consumer protection is one of the EU's goals.[8] Although not explicitly stated, it is embedded within the EU's objective to establish a highly competitive social market economy, as outlined in Article 3(3) of the TEU. Article 12 of the Treaty on the Functioning of the European Union (TFEU) mandates the integration of consumer protection requirements into other EU policies.[9] Furthermore, Article 38 of the Charter of Fundamental Rights of the European Union stipulates that 'Union policies shall ensure a high level of consumer protection'. Consumer protection is a vital component of EU law and policy, aimed at ensuring consumers have access to safe products, accurate and relevant information about goods and services, and protection from unfair and misleading practices.[10]

Over time, the European Union has created an increasingly comprehensive legal framework for Member States to enforce consumer law.[11] According to the TFEU, consumer protection is a shared competence, meaning after EU legislation in this area is passed through the ordinary legislative procedure, it is the Member States' duty to implement and enforce EU laws.[12] The EU's consumer protection framework, referred to as the Consumer Acquis, is a comprehensive set of rules and regulations

7 DG Justice and Consumers, *Survey of Consumers' Attitudes Towards Cross-Border Trade and Consumer-Related Issues 2023* (Publications Office of the European Union 2023) 14

8 Vanessa Mak, *Consumer Protection* (The Oxford Encylopedia of EU Law 2022) 5

9 Stephen Weatherill, *Law and Values in the European Union* (Oxford 2016) 137

10 Elena Mainardi and Barbara Martinello, 'EU Mapping: Overview of Internal Market and Consumer Protection Related Legislation' PE 754.211 (July 2024) 39

11 Peter Rott, 'The EU Legal Framework for the Enforcement of Consumer Law' in Hans-W Micklitz and Geneviève Saumier (eds) *Enforcement and Effectiveness of Consumer Law* (Springer 2018) 249

12 Jana Valant, *Consumer Protection in the EU – Policy Overview* (EPRS 2015) 3 <http://aei.pitt.edu/96092/1/consumer.1.pdf> accessed 9 July 2024

developed over the years to defend consumer rights and interests.[13] This framework encompasses a wide array of measures, including regulations, directives, and decisions, covering multiple aspects of consumer protection, such as product safety, distance selling, and unfair commercial practices.[14] The European Parliament has implemented various measures to safeguard consumers. These include regulations on product safety, labelling, and advertising. Additionally, there are provisions for consumer rights, dispute resolution, and access to information. The goal is to ensure fair and transparent transactions while empowering consumers in the digital age.[15]

The General Design of the Enforcement Mechanism

For a long time, the EU has concentrated on enhancing consumer rights but recently realised that effective consumer rights require strong sanctions. Since most consumers are not legal experts, the enforcement mechanisms must not only be straightforward for non-professionals to use but also be tailored to the consumers' needs. Reflecting this, the latest EU consumer protection laws emphasise creating efficient enforcement mechanisms for consumer rights in Europe.[16] One of the important legislative acts is the Regulation (EU) 2017/2394[17] (the CPC Regulation), replacing Regulation (EC) No 2006/2004.[18] The CPC Regulation establishes a framework for national authorities in the European Economic Area to address breaches of consumer protection laws within the European Union collaboratively. This creates a European enforcement network known as the 'CPC Network'. National authorities within this network possess robust powers to combat illegal practices and identify rogue traders. They can gather information from domain registrars and banks to identify responsible traders, perform mystery shopping to investigate issues like geographical discrimination or after-sales conditions and immediately remove scam websites. The European Commission oversees the cooperation among these authorities, ensuring that consumer rights legislation is consistently applied and enforced throughout the single market.[19]

13 Jana Valant, *Consumer Protection in the EU – Policy Overview* (EPRS 2015) 3 <http://aei.pitt.edu/96092/1/consumer.1.pdf> accessed 9 July 2024

14 Jana Valant, *Consumer Protection in the EU – Policy Overview* (EPRS 2015) 3 <http://aei.pitt.edu/96092/1/consumer.1.pdf> accessed 9 July 2024

15 Fact Sheets on the European Union, <https://www.europarl.europa.eu/factsheets/en/sheet/47/consumer-protection-measures> accessed 24 July 2024

16 Horst Eidenmller and Martin Engel, 'Against False Settlement: Designing Efficient Consumer Rights Enforcement Systems in Europe' (2014) 29(2) *Ohio State Journal on Dispute Resolution* 261, 262

17 Regulation (EU) 2017/2394 of the European Parliament and of the Council of 12 December 2017 on cooperation between national authorities responsible for the enforcement of consumer protection laws and repealing Regulation (EC) No 2006/2004, OJ L 345, 27 December 2017, 1–26

18 Regulation (EC) No 2006/2004 of the European Parliament and of the Council of 27 October 2004 on cooperation between national authorities responsible for the enforcement of consumer protection laws (the Regulation on consumer protection cooperation) OJ L 364, 9 December 2004, 1–11

19 European Commission, 'Consumer Protection Cooperation Regulation' <https://commission.europa.eu/law/law-topic/consumer-protection-law/consumer-protection-cooperation-regulation_en> accessed 31 July 2024

The other two important legislative acts are the Directive 2013/11/EU on Consumer Alternative Dispute Resolution (The ADR Directive)[20] and Regulation 524/2013 on EU Online Dispute Resolution (ODR Regulation).[21] The ADR sets the criteria for qualifying an entity as an ADR body and the procedural rules for resolving disputes arising from sales or service contracts between traders and consumers within the European Union outside of court.[22] The ODR Regulation establishes an ODR platform which allows consumers and traders to resolve disputes related to products or services purchased anywhere in the European Union.[23] The ODR Regulation requires online traders selling goods or services to consumers via a website or other electronic means to include an easily accessible link to the ODR platform on their sales platform. They must also provide consumers with a direct contact email address. The goal is to offer an easy and low-cost method for resolving consumer disputes without needing to go to court.[24]

Current Consumer Dispute Resolution Processes

Small Claims Procedures

When a dispute arises between a consumer and a trader, the first step is typically negotiation for an amicable resolution. If no agreement is reached, the consumer can pursue rights in court or drop the claim. Given the high costs and complexities of traditional civil litigation for small claims, many legal systems offer simplified, affordable judicial processes – often termed Small Claims Procedures (SCP) or Courts. These aim to swiftly resolve low-value disputes less formally. SCPs serve as an alternative to standard civil procedures designed to ensure that the cost and duration of resolving disputes are proportional to the claim's value.[25]

20 Directive 2013/11/EU of the European Parliament and of the Council of 21 May 2013 on alternative dispute resolution for consumer disputes and amending Regulation (EC) No 2006/2004 and Directive 2009/22/EC OJ L 165, 18.6.2013, 63–79 (The ADR Directive)

21 Regulation (EU) No 524/2013 of the European Parliament and of the Council of 21 May 2013 on online dispute resolution for consumer disputes and amending Regulation (EC) No 2006/2004 and Directive 2009/22/EC OJ L 165, 18.6.2013, 1–12 (The ODR Regulation)

22 European Parliament, 'Briefing – EU Legislation in Progress – Alternative Dispute Resolution' (March 2024) <https://www.europarl.europa.eu/RegData/etudes/BRIE/2024/757639/EPRS_BRI(2024)757639_EN.pdf> accessed 31 July 2024

23 EU Monitor, 'Regulation 2013/524 – Online Dispute Resolution for Consumer Disputes and Amending Regulation (EC) No 2006/2004 and Directive 2009/22/EC (Regulation on Consumer ODR)' <https://www.eumonitor.eu/9353000/1/j4nvk6yhcbpeywk_j9vvik7m1c3gyxp/vjs5ga5ai5ot#:~:text=Summary%20of%20Legislation,-Solving%20consumer%E2%80%93trader&text=It%20aims%20to%20create%20an,the%20European%20Union%20(EU)> accessed 31 July 2024

24 Victoria Hobbs and Louise Lanzkron, 'EU Online Dispute Resolution – All Bark and No Bite?' <https://www.twobirds.com/en/insights/2017/global/eu-online-dispute-resolution-all-bark-and-no-bite> accessed 31 July 2024

25 Pablo Cortés, *Online Dispute Resolution for Consumers in the European Union* (Routledge 2011) 17

According to Baldwin, SCPs generally share five key characteristics.[26] First, SCPs are typically more straightforward and less formal than traditional civil court procedures. Second, legal representation is usually discouraged or not required, with parties often not needing to make formal legal arguments. Third, judges or adjudicators frequently assist unrepresented litigants with procedural matters. Fourth, SCPs allow litigants to present evidence freely and give judges considerable discretion in conducting hearings and making decisions. Lastly, litigants are responsible for their own legal costs regardless of the judgment's outcome.

Many countries have national SCP; for example, in England and Wales, under the current Civil Procedure Rules, there are three tracks: small, fast, and multi-track. Cases valued over £10,000 can be heard under the SCP if both parties agree.[27] Similarly in Spain, the Civil Procedure Act distinguishes between the Ordinary and Oral procedures. The Oral Procedure is used for claims up to €6,000 and shares similarities with SCPs but with some distinctions.[28] For instance, attending court without a lawyer and public prosecutor is not permitted if the claim exceeds €2,000.[29]

The European Small Claims Procedure (ESCP) was established by regulation on 11 July 2007 and became effective in all EU Member States (except Denmark) on 1 January 2009.[30] It aims to expedite the resolution of small-value cross-border civil and commercial disputes. Initially applicable to claims up to €2,000, the threshold was raised to €5,000 on 14 July 2017.[31] The ESCP eliminates the requirement for legal representation[32] and is conducted entirely in writing, utilising standardised forms accessible online in all EU languages.[33] It serves as an alternative to traditional procedures provided by Member State laws.[34]

26 John Baldwin, 'Is There a Limit to Expansion of Small Claims?' in Michael Freeman (ed) *Current Legal Problems Vol 56* (Oxford University Press 2014) 313, 317

27 Citizen Advice, 'Making Small Claim' (2024) <https://www.citizensadvice.org.uk/law-and-courts/legal-system/small-claims/making-a-small-claim/> accessed 20 June 2024

28 See European e-Justice, 'Small Claims: Spain' (2024) <https://e-justice.europa.eu/42/EN/small_claims?SPAIN&member=1> accessed 20 July 2024

29 European e-Justice, 'Small Claims: Spain' (2024) <https://e-justice.europa.eu/42/EN/small_claims?SPAIN&member=1> accessed 20 July 2024

30 Regulation (EC) 861/2007 of the European Parliament and of the Council of 11 July 2007 establishing a European Small Claims Procedure [2007] OJ L199, 31 July 2007

31 Your Europe, 'European Small Claims Procedure' (2024) <https://europa.eu/youreurope/business/dealing-with-customers/solving-disputes/european-small-claims-procedure/index_en.htm> accessed 20 July 2024

32 Regulation (EC) 861/2007 establishing a European Small Claims Procedure, OJ L 1999/. The ESCP Regulation was amended on 16 December 2015, and it entered into application on 14 July 2017 – See Regulation (EU) 2015/2421

33 Pablo Cortés and Rafał Mańko, 'Developments in European Civil Procedures' in Pablo Cortés (ed) *The New Regulatory Framework for Consumer Dispute Resolution* (Oxford University Press 2016) 41, 50

34 Rafał Mańko, 'European Small Claims Procedure: Commission Proposal to Remedy Weaknesses in the Current System' European Parliamentary Research Service, In-Depth Analysis' PE 542.137 (November 2014) 7

The ESCP aims to cut litigation costs, simplify and speed up procedures, bypass intermediate steps, and facilitate recognition and enforcement.[35] According to the European Commission, it has reduced the cost of cross-border low-value dispute resolution by up to 40% on average and shortened the duration from over two years to just five months.[36] However, for many litigants seeking quicker and less formal resolutions, the process still falls short in terms of speed and cost-effectiveness. Nonetheless, more than 60% of ESCP users express satisfaction with the procedure.[37] One of its key advantages is the uniform, fast-track process with strict deadlines, applied consistently across all EU Member States.[38]

The ESCP was designed to improve access to justice for low-value cross-border disputes significantly. However, its initial usage fell short of expectations, with only an estimated 3,500 cases in 2012.[39] The European Commission identified three key barriers hindering the ESCP's efficiency: limited awareness of its existence, high costs (including translation, court fees, service of documents, and oral hearings), and uncertainty about litigation fees and payment systems.[40] To address these barriers and enhance the effectiveness of reducing litigation costs for cross-border low-value claims, the ESCP was amended on 3 December 2015, with the amended Regulation taking effect on 14 July 2017.[41] The amendments aimed to clarify and expedite the process, improve transparency regarding litigation costs, shorten the search time for relevant information, and raise awareness among stakeholders involved in the ESCP.[42]

The primary reform introduced by the ESCP Regulation was raising the threshold from €2,000 to €5,000.[43] This increase was significant, but the estimated cost of a €5,000 claim is comparable to that of a €10,000 claim, suggesting a justification for further threshold adjustments in future revisions of the Regulation, such as those expected in 2021.[44] The previous €2,000 threshold was deemed too low, lim-

35 Deloitte, 'An Assessment of the Socio-Economic Impacts of the Policy Options for the Future of the European Small Claims Regulation' Final Report (19 July 2013) 5

36 European Commission, Report from the Commission to the European Parliament, the Council and the European Economic and Social Committee on the application of Regulation (EC) 861/2007 of the European Parliament and the Council establishing a European Small Claims Procedure COM (2013) 795 Final, 2 (European Small Claims Procedure Report)

37 Special Eurobarometer 395, 'European Small Claims Procedure' (April 2013) <http://ec.europa.eu/public_opinion/archives/ebs/ebs_395_en.pdf> accessed 20 July 2024

38 Cortés and Mańko (n 33) 51

39 Deloitte (n 35) v. The Deloitte Report also stated that every year, the number of problematic cross-border transactions with a value below 2,000 euros is 14.7 million

40 Deloitte (n 35) v. According to EEC-Net, 47% of the courts and judges in all Member States are not aware of the existence of the ESCP, while 53% had knowledge regarding the application of this procedure, ECC-Net, 'European Small Claims Procedure Report' (2012) 22

41 Regulation (EU) 2015/2421 of the European Parliament and of the Council of 16 December 2015 Amending Regulation (EC) No 861/2007 Establishing a European Small Claims Procedure and Regulation (EC) No 1896/2006 Creating a European Order for Payment Procedure

42 Regulation (EU) 2015/2421 (n 41) vii

43 Article 2(1) of the ESCP as amended by Regulation 2015/2421

44 Deloitte (n 35) 10. These thresholds vary greatly in all the Member States, from €600 in Germany to €25,000 in the Netherlands. See European Small Claims Procedure Report (n 36) 3

iting access to the procedure, especially for SMEs. Around 30% of business claims fall within the €2,000 to €10,000 range, prompting many businesses to resort to national small claims procedures, which can lead to higher and more prolonged litigation costs.[45]

The amended ESCP Regulation aims to reduce costs and streamline procedures by mandating the use of electronic communications where appropriate. While the ESCP primarily operates as a written procedure, there are cases where reaching a decision based solely on written evidence is challenging or where parties request an oral hearing.[46] The European Commission reports that the average cost of travelling to attend an oral hearing ranges from €300 to €700, with a minimum travel time of nine hours.[47] Therefore, the amended Regulation limits the use of oral hearings and encourages the use of remote communication technologies, such as video conferencing or teleconferencing.[48] Furthermore, the Regulation permits parties to submit their claims directly to the court or tribunal by post or any other acceptable means of communication (such as fax or email) as determined by the Member State where the competent court is located.[49]

Currently, the 2007 ESCP Regulation mandates Member States to assist parties with information on jurisdiction, appeal possibilities, languages for enforcement, and practical form-filling assistance.[50] However, a significant gap existed in practice, with 41% of courts across the Member States failing to provide this required assistance, as noted in the ECC-Net Report.[51] Eurobarometer 395 further revealed that 17% of parties were unaware of the system, 16% struggled with form completion, and 10% requested but did not receive help with their applications.[52] To address these issues, the amended Regulation expands Member States' obligations. Now, they must also furnish information on court fees, payment methods, and competent authorities or organisations offering practical assistance.[53] Previously, some Member States did not accept electronic payments like credit cards, requiring in-person payments or financial stamps.[54] The amended text now mandates Member States to offer at least one of three electronic payment options: bank transfer, credit/debit card, or direct debit from the claimant's bank account.[55]

45 Alexia Maniaki-Griva, 'European Small Claims Procedure: Initial Appraisal of the Commission's Impact Assessment, European Parliamentary Research Service' PE 514.109 (March 2014) 1
46 Article 5(1a) of the ESCP as amended by Regulation 2015/2421
47 Maniaki-Griva (n 45) 5
48 Article 8(1) of the ESCP as amended by Regulation 2015/2421
49 Article 13 of the ESCP as amended by Regulation 2015/2421
50 Article 25 of the ESCP as amended by Regulation 2015/2421
51 ECC-Net (n 40) 22
52 Special Eurobarometer 395, 'European Small Claims Procedure' (April 2013) <http://ec.europa.eu/public_opinion/archives/ebs/ebs_395_en.pdf> accessed 20 June 2024
53 Article 25 of the ESCP as amended by Regulation 2015/2421
54 Rafał Mańko, 'Reform of the European Small Claims Procedure System' European Parliamentary Research Service, PE 557.014 (May 2015) 2
55 Article 15(2) of the ESCP as amended by Regulation 2015/2421

EU Representative Actions

The protection of consumers' collective interests has been a priority for EU institutions since the 1980s.[56] Discussions about creating a directive to defend these interests in court began in 1985 with the EU Commission's memorandum on consumer redress,[57] which led to the enactment of the Injunctions Directive.[58] However, no legal tools offered compensatory relief to consumers. In 2005, the Green Paper on damages actions for breaches of EC antitrust rules highlighted the need for collective actions to improve consumer access to justice and facilitate compensation in competition cases.[59] In 2007, the Commission's six-year consumer strategy emphasised the necessity for collective actions for violations of consumer law.[60]

In 2013, the Commission issued a set of common but non-binding principles for injunctive and compensatory collective redress actions across all areas of law.[61] The Recommendation urged Member States to adopt these principles in their national systems by July 2015.[62] A 2018 Commission report gathered data on the implementation of these principles and found that while all Member States offered some form of collective redress through injunctive relief, compensatory collective redress was only available in 19 Member States, with significant variations in design.[63] Consequently, the Recommendation failed to ensure compliance with the common principles or provide an effective tool for consumers to seek redress.

56 European Economic and Social Committee (2008) 442nd Plenary Session Held on 13 and 14 February 2008 Opinion of the European Economic and Social Committee on Defining the Collective Actions System and Its Role in the Context of Community Consumer Law (Own-Initiative Opinion) [2008/C] OJ L 162/01, para 3.7 <https://eur-lex.europa.eu/LexUriServ/LexUriServ.do?uri=OJ:C:2008:162:0001:0019:EN:PDF> accessed 31 July 2024

57 European Commission (1985) Consumer Redress Commission Memorandum to the Council transmitted on 4 January 1985 (Bulletin of the European Communities Supplement 2/85) (1984, COM (84) 629) <http://aei.pitt.edu/1597/1/1597.pdf> accessed 31 July 2024

58 European Commission (1990), 'Three Year Action Plan of Consumer Policy in the EEC (1990 1992)' (COM (90) 98 Final) <https://eur-lex.europa.eu/legal-content/EN/TXT/PDF/?uri=CELEX:51990DC0098&from=nl> accessed 31 July 2024

59 European Commission (2005), 'Green Paper – Damages Actions for Breach of the EC Antitrust Rules' (SEC (2005) 1732/COM/2005/0672 Final)

60 European Commission (2007), Communication from the Commission to the Council, the European Parliament and the European Economic and Social Committee: EU Consumer Policy strategy 2007–2013, 'Empowering Consumers, Enhancing Their Welfare, Effectively Protecting Them' (COM (2007) 99 Final) 11 <https://eur-lex.europa.eu/legal-content/EN/TXT/PDF/?uri=CELEX:52007DC0099&from=EN> accessed 31 July 2024

61 European Commission (2013), Recommendation of 11 June 2013 on common principles for injunctive and compensatory collective redress mechanisms in the Member States concerning violations of rights granted under Union Law (2013/396/EU) [2013] OJ L201/60

62 European Commission (2013) (n 61) para 38

63 European Commission (2018), Report from the Commission to the European Parliament, the Council and the European Economic and Social Committee on the implementation of the Commission Recommendation of 11 June 2013 on common principles for injunctive and compensatory collective redress mechanisms in the Member States concerning violations of rights granted under Union law (2013/396/EU) (COM/2018/040 final) para 2.1.1

In 2018, a proposal for a directive on representative actions for protecting consumers' collective interests was introduced. It argued that globalisation and digitalisation increase the risk of large numbers of consumers being affected by the same unlawful conduct, necessitating an effective enforcement mechanism for collective compensation.[64] In 2020, this proposal was enacted into law, resulting in the Directive on representative actions for protecting consumers' collective interests.[65] The Directive mandates that Member States provide at least one effective and efficient representative action for both injunctions and redress for consumers.[66]

The Directive permits qualified entities to initiate collective actions. According to Article 4 of the Directive, the representative party must be a qualified entity, which includes consumer organisations and public bodies. The Directive allows collective actions to be brought before administrative national authorities and courts (Directive Article 7(1)). The qualified entity must provide the authority or court with adequate information about the group of consumers represented in the collective action (Directive Article 7(2)). The entity can seek monetary damages, injunctions, or both, either in a single proceeding or in separate proceedings (Directive Article 7(5)). The Directive allows collective actions to seek injunctive and redress measures (Directive Articles 8–9). Article 9 of the Directive permits both opt-out and opt-in actions. This allows Member States, based on their legal traditions, to implement either an opt-in or opt-out mechanism or a combination of both. Regardless of the chosen approach, national laws must ensure that consumers have a sufficient opportunity to explicitly or tacitly express their desire to be bound by the case's outcome (Directive Article 9(2)).

Article 10 of the Directive requires full transparency regarding the funding of collective actions, particularly if a third-party funder is involved. Indirect funding sources can include equal contributions from the organisation's members, crowdfunding, donations, and contributions related to corporate social responsibility.[67] Article 12 of the Directive implements the loser-pays rule to deter abusive litigation. Under this rule, the party that loses the collective action is responsible for covering the litigation costs. Affected consumers benefit from the outcome of the action but are not responsible for the costs of the proceedings unless their own intentional or negligent actions lead to additional expenses (Directive Article 12).

64 European Commission (2018), Proposal for a Directive of the European Parliament and of the Council on representative actions for the protection of the collective interests of consumers, and repealing Directive 2009/22/EC 2018/0089 (COD)

65 European Commission (2020), Directive (EU) 2020/1828 of the European Parliament and of the Council of 25 November 2020 on representative actions for the protection of the collective interests of consumers and repealing Directive 2009/22/EC, OJ L 409/1

66 European Commission (2020) (n 65) para 7

67 European Commission (2020) (n 65) para 53

Alternative Dispute Resolution for Consumer Disputes

The ADR Directive and ODR Regulation

According to the 2023 consumer attitudes survey by the European Commission, just 6% of EU consumers who faced problems when buying a product or service and pursued action reported the issue to an ADR body.[68] ADR is a method for resolving complaints about contract breaches outside the courtroom, involving impartial and neutral entities that offer mediation, arbitration, or conciliation. Therefore, ADR serves as an alternative to or a supplement for litigation under consumer and contract law.[69]

On 21 May 2013, the European Parliament and the European Council enacted two significant legislative measures concerning consumer dispute resolution: the ADR Directive and the ODR Regulation. These pieces of legislation became effective in July 2013.[70] The ADR Directive establishes a legislative framework to guarantee consumers access to high-quality ADR procedures for resolving disputes with traders.[71] The primary objective of the ADR Directive is to resolve B2C disputes out of court more quickly, affordably, and straightforwardly than traditional court proceedings.[72] Under the Directive, Member States are responsible for enabling EU consumers to access ADR services and ensuring that consumers can use quality-certified ADR entities to resolve disputes with EU traders regarding the purchase of products or services. ADR should be available to consumers across all economic sectors, covering both online and offline purchases and domestic and cross-border disputes, except for disputes related to health services and higher education.[73]

The current ADR Directive adopts a minimum harmonisation approach in defining the criteria for qualifying an entity as an ADR body and establishing procedural rules. This approach requires that individuals handling cases demonstrate expertise, independence, and impartiality.[74] Additionally, specific requirements ensure that the procedural rules and ADR organisations operate transparently, effectively, and fairly.[75] The primary goal of the ODR Regulation is to enhance the use of ADR entities to resolve national and cross-border consumer disputes originating from

68 DG Justice and Consumers, *Survey of Consumers' Attitudes Towards Cross-Border Trade and Consumer-Related Issues 2023* (Publications Office of the European Union 2023) 14

69 Clément Evroux, 'Alternative Dispute Resolution' European Parliamentary Research Service, PE 757.639 (March 2024) 1

70 See Directive 2013/11/EU (n 20); Regulation (EU) No 524/2013 (n 21)

71 Report from the Commission to the European Parliament, the Council and the European Economic and Social Committee on the application of Directive 2013/11/EU of the European Parliament and of the Council on alternative dispute resolution for consumer disputes and Regulation (EU) No. 524/2013 of the European Parliament and of the Council on online dispute resolution for consumer disputes, COM (2023) 648 Final, 1 (ADR/ODR Report 2023)

72 The ADR Directive, Recital 5

73 The ADR Directive, Article 2(2)

74 The ADR Directive, Article 6

75 Evroux (n 69) 1

online purchases of goods or services.[76] To this end, the Regulation ensures the quality of ADR schemes by setting minimum standards and launched the EU ODR Platform, which provides a forum for resolving online disputes efficiently with the help of advanced technologies.[77] The ODR Platform is described in Article 5(2) as

> a single point of entry for consumers and traders seeking the out-of-court resolution of disputes covered by this Regulation. It shall be an interactive website which can be accessed electronically and free of charge in all the official languages of the institutions of the Union.[78]

Article 2 of the ODR Regulation specifies that it applies to contractual obligations arising from online sales or service contracts between a consumer living in the European Union and a trader based in the European Union. Recital 14 further clarifies that an online sales or service contract involves a trader or their intermediary offering goods or services via a website or other electronic means, with the consumer placing their order through the same electronic channels. Consequently, this regulation does not cover offline contracts, and offline claims cannot be submitted to the EU ODR platform.[79]

Consumers complete an online complaint form, available in all EU languages, on the EU ODR platform's website. Once submitted, the form is automatically forwarded to the trader. The trader then has three choices: resolve the claim directly with the consumer, use the ODR platform to address the claim or opt out of participating. If both parties agree to use the ODR platform (within a 30-day timeframe), the complaint is forwarded to a consumer ADR/ODR entity chosen by both parties. This entity then has 90 days to resolve the dispute.[80] According to Article 9 of the ODR Regulation, the online dispute resolution process starts when the complainant fills out the necessary information in the complaint form and sends it, along with other required data about the ADR business, to the respondent. This information is automatically and promptly forwarded to the ADR body chosen by the parties through the platform. If the parties do not agree on an ADR body within 30 days of submitting the complaint form, or if the ADR body refuses to handle the dispute, the complaint is rejected. In such cases, ODR consultants may inform the disputing parties about alternative redress options.[81]

76 The ODR Regulation, Recital 8

77 Serkan Kaya, *Consumer Dispute Resolution in the Digital Age: Online Dispute Resolution* (Oniki Levha 2020) 85

78 The ODR Regulation, Article 5(2)

79 Emma van Gelder, 'The EU Approach to Consumer ODR' (2019) 6(2) *International Journal of Online Dispute Resolution* 219, 222

80 Emma van Gelder, 'The EU Approach to Consumer ODR' (2019) 6(2) *International Journal of Online Dispute Resolution* 219, 222

81 Mokhinur Bakhramova, 'Theoretical and Legal Regulation of ODR in the European Union Countries' (2022) 2(1) *European Journal of Innovation in Nonformal Education* 299, 301

Member States are tasked with setting up and maintaining national ODR contact points, which include two national ODR advisers.[82] It is up to each Member State to choose who will fulfil this role. Typically, this responsibility is assigned to a European Consumer Centre (ECC), except in three Member States (Lithuania, Slovenia, and Poland), where a national authority takes on this function.[83] According to Article 7(2) of the ODR Regulation, the contact points assist parties (consumers, traders, ADR entities) in using the platform and providing general information about applicable consumer rights and redress options. According to Article 26 of the ADR Directive, every four years,

> the Commission shall submit to the European Parliament, the Council, and the European Economic and Social Committee a report on the application of this Directive. This report shall assess the development and utilisation of ADR entities and the impact of this Directive on both consumers and traders, particularly regarding consumer awareness and trader adoption levels. If necessary, this report shall accompany proposals for amending the Directive.

The 2019 implementation report on the ADR/ODR framework concluded that the ADR Directive has enabled EU consumers to access high-quality ADR procedures throughout the Union.[84] This accessibility extends across virtually all retail sectors, regardless of whether the dispute is domestic or cross-border and whether the purchase was made online or offline.[85] The statistics noted that the ODR platform has developed into a multilingual centre, handling 222,000 dispute submissions.[86] A list of around 430 qualified ADR entities in the EEA (European Union, Iceland, Liechtenstein, and Norway), available on the ODR Platform, reveals a wide disparity in the number of entities per Member State.[87] For instance, Finland and Romania each have three entities, whereas France has 82 qualified ADR entities.[88]

While ADR mechanisms have marked a notable improvement for consumers, the evolving digital landscape, procedural complexity, and insufficient awareness challenge the ADR framework established in 2013.[89] Despite several updates, the ODR platform has reportedly failed to meet its goals.[90] On 17 October 2023, the

82 ADR/ODR Report 2023 (n 71) 6
83 ADR/ODR Report 2023 (n 71) 6
84 ADR/ODR Report 2023 (n 71) 1
85 ADR/ODR Report 2023 (n 71) 1
86 EU Online Dispute Resolution Platform, 'Reports and Statistics' (2024) <https://ec.europa.eu/consumers/odr/main/?event=main.statistics.show> accessed 31 July 2024
87 Susanna Tenhunen and Jonathan Blanckaert, 'EU Framework on Alternative Dispute Resolution for Consumers' European Parliamentary Research Service, PE 757.788 (February 2024) 3
88 Susanna Tenhunen and Jonathan Blanckaert, 'EU Framework on Alternative Dispute Resolution for Consumers' European Parliamentary Research Service, PE 757.788 (February 2024) 3
89 Susanna Tenhunen and Jonathan Blanckaert, 'EU Framework on Alternative Dispute Resolution for Consumers' European Parliamentary Research Service, PE 757.788 (February 2024) 3
90 Susanna Tenhunen and Jonathan Blanckaert, 'EU Framework on Alternative Dispute Resolution for Consumers' European Parliamentary Research Service, PE 757.788 (February 2024) 3

European Commission proposed specific amendments to the ADR Directive and recommended the repeal of the ODR Regulation.[91] It also presented a new recommendation to establish quality standards for online marketplaces and EU trade associations offering dispute resolution services.[92] These proposed revisions aim to modernise the ADR system and align with Better Regulation goals focused on simplification and reducing administrative burdens.[93]

Mediation

To encourage peaceful resolution of disputes by improving mediation effectiveness and balancing its relationship with judicial processes, the Mediation Directive 2008/52/EC was adopted by the European Parliament and Council in May 2008.[94] All Member States incorporated this Directive into national law by May 2011.[95] Despite more than thirteen years since its adoption, mediation and ADR methods in Europe remain significantly underutilised. A 2016 study commissioned by the European Parliament, known as 'The Implementation of the Mediation Directive Workshop' (The Workshop),[96] confirms that mediation is not fully utilised across most Member States.[97]

Both the Rebooting Study and the Workshop recommended that Member States require an initial mediation session with a mediator before commencing court proceedings in all civil and commercial disputes.[98] The Rebooting Study argues that a direct and efficient mechanism requires amendments to the Directive. A proposed revision of Article 5(2) could state:

> Member States must integrate mediation sessions into the judicial process for civil and commercial cases, except where mediation is deemed unsuitable by Member States. Minimum requirements for such sessions include parties

91 ADR/ODR Report 2023 (n 71) 6
92 ADR/ODR Report 2023 (n 71) 6
93 Tenhunen and Blanckaert (n 84) 3
94 Directive 2008/52 of the European Parliament and of the Council of 21 May 2008 on Certain Aspects of Mediation in Civil and Commercial Matters, 2008 OJ (L 136)
95 Directive 2008/52 of the European Parliament and of the Council of 21 May 2008 on Certain Aspects of Mediation in Civil and Commercial Matters, 2008 OJ (L 136)
96 Giuseppe De Palo and Leonardo D'Urso, 'Achieving a Balanced Relationship Between Mediation and Judicial Proceedings' in Monika Laura Lazaruk (ed) *The Implementation of the Mediation Directive Workshop* (Policy Department C: Citizens' Rights and Constitutional Affairs 2016) 98; PE 571.395 (November 2016) 96
97 Similarly, it is confirmed by a study called 'Rebooting the Mediation Directive: Assessing the Limited Impact of Its Implementation and Proposing Legislative and Non-Legislative Measures to Increase the Number of Mediations in the EU'. See Giuseppe De Palo, Leonardo D'Urso, Mary Trevor, Bryan Branon, Romina Canessa, Beverly Cawyer and L. Reagan Florence, 'Rebooting the Mediation Directive: Assessing the Limited Impact of Its Implementation and Proposing Legislative and Non- Legislative Measures to Increase the Number of Mediations in the EU' PE 493.042 (January 2014) <http://www.europarl.europa.eu/RegData/etudes/etudes/join/2014/493042/IPOLJURI_ET(2014)493042_EN.pdf> accessed 31 July 2024
98 De Palo and D'Urso (n 96) 96. See also The Rebooting Study (n 97) 7

meeting with a mediator, with the procedure being non-binding, swift, suspending time limits for claims, and being free or low-cost if any party opts out at the initial session.[99]

Initially appearing applicable only to cross-border disputes, such amendments could impact the mediation process by promoting regularity.[100] The Mediation Directive aims to enhance ADR accessibility and promote mediation while ensuring a balanced relationship with court proceedings.[101] The Directive includes five key rules: a) Requiring each Member State to enhance mediator training and uphold high mediation standards. b) Granting judges the authority to recommend mediation as the initial step in dispute resolution. c) Ensuring that mediated settlement agreements are enforceable upon mutual agreement of both parties. d) Maintaining mediation confidentiality, with mediators prohibited from disclosing mediation details in subsequent disputes. e) Ensuring parties retain their right to pursue court action regardless of time spent in mediation.[102] In 2017, the European Parliament adopted a 'Resolution' on the implementation of the Mediation Directive.[103] Based on a 2016 Commission report, the Resolution aims to enhance the effectiveness of mediation in EU civil and commercial cases.[104]

Arbitration

In the EU, while each Member State's laws vary, EU law primarily considers consumer interests as interpreted by the Court of Justice of the European Union (CJEU) regarding consumers' deliberate choice to enter into arbitration agreements. Consequently, it establishes specific provisions in this context. Concerning pre-dispute agreements in consumer contracts, Member States typically adopt one of three approaches:

a. Some Member States prohibit consumers from entering into arbitration agreements altogether. Under this approach, consumers are not permitted to resolve disputes through arbitration, either before or after a dispute arises. Any arbitration clause entered into by a consumer would be deemed null and void. For instance,

99 De Palo and D'Urso (n 96) 96

100 Giuseppe De Palo and Romina Canessa, 'New Trends for ADR in the European Union' in Pablo Cortés (ed) *The New Regulatory Framework for Consumer Dispute Resolution* (Oxford University Press 2016) 407, 420

101 EU Press Release Reference: Mediation in Civil and Commercial Matters, MEMO/08/263, Brussels, 23 April 2008

102 The Mediation Directive (n 91)

103 See the European Parliament resolution of 12 September 2017 on the implementation of Directive 2008/52/EC of the European Parliament and of the Council of 21 May 2008 on certain aspects of mediation in civil and commercial matters (2016/2066(INI)), C 337/2

104 Report from the Commission to the European Parliament, the Council and the European Economic and Social Committee on the application of Directive 2008/52/EC of the European Parliament and of the Council on certain aspects of mediation in civil and commercial matters, COM (2016) 542 Final, 26 August 2016

in France, Article 2061 of the French Civil Code specifies that 'an arbitration clause is valid in contracts concluded for professional purposes',[105] thereby excluding contracts between businesses and consumers from arbitration.[106]

b. In some EU Member States like Sweden, Austria, Lithuania, Denmark, Finland, Slovenia, and Ireland, consumers are initially barred from entering arbitration agreements before a dispute arises. However, once a dispute does occur, consumers have the option to agree to arbitration.
c. In other Member States, consumers have the freedom to negotiate arbitration agreements before any disputes arise, but these agreements must be individually tailored. For instance, in the Czech Republic, an arbitration clause is considered valid if consumers are fully informed about the legal implications of consenting to arbitration.[107] This requirement stems from Article 3 of Council Directive 93/13/EEC on Unfair Terms in Consumer Contracts, which states that a contractual term not individually negotiated is unfair if it significantly disadvantages the consumer, contrary to the principle of good faith.[108]

This principle was affirmed in the case of *Elisa María Mostaza Claro v Centro Móvil Milenium SL*,[109] which referenced the precedent set *by Océano Grupo Editorial v Roció Murciano Quintero.*[110] In particular, the Court emphasised that 'the protection system established by the Directive rests on the premise that consumers are in a disadvantaged position compared to sellers or suppliers, both in terms of bargaining power and knowledge'.[111]

Challenges and Opportunities

At the EU level, a 2019 report[112] on the ADR/ODR framework's implementation, which was issued one year after achieving complete ADR coverage and three and a half years following the launch of the ODR platform, highlighted that consumer ADR is not widely used due to a lack of awareness, the complexity and variety of

105 French Civil Code Article 2061

106 Some scholars argued that provision that this provision concerning arbitration agreements was negotiated before the new law came into force. See Alexander J Bělohlávek, *B2C Arbitration Consumer Protection in Arbitration* (Juris Net 2012) 292

107 Some scholars argued that provision that this provision concerning arbitration agreements was negotiated before the new law came into force. See Alexander J Bělohlávek, *B2C Arbitration Consumer Protection in Arbitration* (Juris Net 2012) 292

108 The Council Directive 93/13/EEC on Unfair Terms in Consumer Contracts, Article 3

109 Case C-168/05 *Elisa María Mostaza Claro v Centro Móvil Milenium SL* (2006)

110 *Case C-240 Océano Grupo Editorial SA v Roció Murciano Quintero (1998)*

111 Case C-240 *Océano Grupo Editorial SA v Roció Murciano Quintero* (1998)

112 Report from the Commission to the European Parliament, the Council and the European Economic and Social Committee on the application of Directive 2013/11/EU of the European Parliament and of the Council on alternative dispute resolution for consumer disputes and Regulation (EU) No 524/2013 of the European Parliament and of the Council on online dispute resolution for consumer disputes COM/2019/425 final (ADR/ODR Report 2019)

the ADR system, and the general unwillingness of traders to participate.[113] With regard to the ODR platform, it was observed that, despite significant traffic, there was limited consumer engagement in requesting ADR procedures from traders.[114] In many instances, traders either did not respond or suggested resolving the dispute outside the platform. As a result, only around 2% of ADR requests were actually directed to an ADR entity.[115]

The latest application report, published in 2023 alongside the amending proposal, concluded that the ADR system had established a foundation for accessible and high-quality consumer redress throughout the EU. This applies to all retail sectors in the single market, both online and offline, and covers domestic and cross-border disputes. While the 2019 report recognised the European ODR platform as a 'centralised and multilingual hub for resolving online disputes', it also highlighted that it only partially meets user needs. The challenges noted in the 2019 report persisted and were reiterated in the 2023 report. Despite efforts, the ADR/ODR framework remained underutilised; navigating the national ADR landscape was difficult due to significant variations between Member States; and awareness of ADR among both consumers and traders remained low, particularly regarding traders' participation.[116]

The 2023 report and its supporting study indicate that ADR usage has remained relatively stable since 2018. However, 2020 was an exception due to the COVID-19 pandemic, which led to numerous travel service cancellations and subsequent reimbursement disputes with airlines and tourism service providers. Between 2019 and 2021, the top four areas for ADR cases were financial services, transport services, consumer goods, and energy and water. The report also revealed that only 30% of EU retailers were willing and able to use ADR, while 43% were unaware of its existence. Despite this, most traders in EU Member States are willing to engage in ADR if approached by an ADR entity, with only 10% or fewer refusing to participate. Although data on ADR entities' resolution rates are incomplete, it is clear that the number of resolved disputes varies significantly across Member States, with most reporting a resolution rate of 50% or higher. The 2023 application report evaluates the practical implementation of the ODR Regulation and highlights the platform's limited use. While digital marketplaces have become key channels for dispute resolution, the ODR platform, despite attracting two to three million visits annually, facilitates only about 200 ADR outcomes across the European Union each year. The report concludes that the performance of the ODR system does not justify its costs, both for the Commission in terms of maintenance and for public administration and online businesses in compliance expenses.[117]

While this chapter acknowledges the positive aspects of the legal advancements made to date, it argues that certain objectives outlined by the Commission still

113 Report on the application of Directive 2013/11/EU (n 112) 1

114 ADR/ODR Report 2023 (n 71) 1

115 ADR/ODR Report 2023 (n 71) 1

116 European Parliament, Briefing – Implementation Appraisal (n 110) 3

117 European Parliament, Briefing – Implementation Appraisal (n 110) 3

need to be met for the EU ADR Directive and ODR Regulation to achieve their full potential. The proposed revisions to modernise the ADR framework and minimise unnecessary administrative burdens are aligned with the new consumer agenda,[118] which is the EU's strategy for guiding consumer policy from 2020 to 2025. For instance, although online traders established in the European Union are required to inform consumers about the EU ODR Platform by providing a link on their websites, they are not obligated to participate in the process. Consequently, many consumer disputes remain unresolved. To address this, the chapter suggests that disputes not resolved through online negotiation should be escalated to the appropriate dispute resolution body. Furthermore, the paper proposes that the EU ODR Platform should serve more than just a referral function. It should also include an issue identification and dispute prevention function that encourages early resolution by automatically providing tailored information about consumer rights and obligations.[119]

Conclusion

The analysis of the consumer ADR and ODR frameworks within the European Union highlights both the progress and the persisting challenges in ensuring accessible and effective consumer redress. Despite the establishment of a comprehensive ADR system and the introduction of the ODR platform, usage remains limited due to factors such as lack of awareness, the complexity of the ADR landscape, and the reluctance of traders to engage in these processes. The 2023 application report underscores that while the ADR system has laid a foundation for high-quality dispute resolution across the European Union, significant disparities and underutilisation persist. This is evident in the low engagement rates with the ODR platform and the varied resolution rates across Member States. The report's findings suggest that despite efforts to improve the framework, consumer disputes are frequently unresolved due to traders' non-participation and consumers' lack of awareness about available ADR options.

To address these issues, the proposed revisions to the ADR framework aim to modernise the system and reduce administrative burdens, aligning with the EU's broader consumer policy goals outlined in the new consumer agenda. Key recommendations include making participation in ADR processes mandatory for traders and enhancing the functionality of the ODR platform to not only serve as a referral hub but also actively facilitate early dispute resolution through tailored information about consumer rights. Overall, while the European Union has made significant strides in institutionalising consumer ADR, the ongoing challenges necessitate further refinements to realise these frameworks' potential fully. Continued efforts to raise awareness, simplify procedures, and ensure trader compliance are crucial for

118 Nikolina Šajn, 'New Consumer Agenda' European Parliamentary Research Service, PE 679.079 (February 2021)

119 Pablo Cortes, *The Law of Consumer Redress in an Evolving Digital Market: Upgrading From Alternative to Online Dispute Resolution* (Cambridge University Press 2018) 99

achieving a more effective and widely utilised consumer dispute resolution system in the European Union.

References

Armstrong M, 'Interactions Between Competition and Consumer Policy' (2008) 4(1) Competition Policy International 97, 147

Bakhramova M, 'Theoretical and Legal Regulation of ODR in the European Union Countries' (2022) 2(1) European Journal of Innovation in Nonformal Education 299, 304

Baldwin J, 'Is There a Limit to Expansion of Small Claims?' in Michael Freeman (ed) *Current Legal Problems Vol. 56* (Oxford University Press 2014)

Bělohlávek AJ, *B2C Arbitration Consumer Protection in Arbitration* (Juris Net 2012)

Citizen Advice, 'Making Small Claim' (2024) <https://www.citizensadvice.org.uk/law-and-courts/legal-system/small-claims/making-a-small-claim/> accessed 20 June 2024

Cortés P, *Online Dispute Resolution for Consumers in the European Union* (Routledge 2011)

Cortés P, *The Law of Consumer Redress in an Evolving Digital Market: Upgrading from Alternative to Online Dispute Resolution* (Cambridge University Press 2018)

Cortés P and Mańko R, 'Developments in European Civil Procedures' in Pablo Cortés (ed) *The New Regulatory Framework for Consumer Dispute Resolution* (Oxford University Press 2016)

De Palo G and Canessa R, 'New Trends for ADR in the European Union' in Pablo Cortés (ed) *The New Regulatory Framework for Consumer Dispute Resolution* (Oxford University Press 2016)

De Palo G and D'Urso L, 'Achieving a Balanced Relationship Between Mediation and Judicial Proceedings' in Monika Laura Lazaruk (ed) *The Implementation of the Mediation Directive Workshop* (Policy Department C: Citizens' Rights and Constitutional Affairs 2016), 98, PE 571.395 (November 2016)

De Palo G, D'Urso L, Trevor M, Branon B, Canessa R, Cawyer B and Florence LR, 'Rebooting the Mediation Directive: Assessing the Limited Impact of Its Implementation and Proposing Legislative and Non-Legislative Measures to Increase the Number of Mediations in the EU' PE 493.042 (January 2014)

Deloitte, 'An Assessment of the Socio-Economic Impacts of the Policy Options for the Future of the European Small Claims Regulation' Final Report (19 July 2013)

Eidenmller H and Engel M, 'Against False Settlement: Designing Efficient Consumer Rights Enforcement Systems in Europe' (2014) 29(2) Ohio State Journal on Dispute Resolution

Evroux C, 'Alternative Dispute Resolution' European Parliamentary Research Service, PE 757.639 (March 2024)

Hobbs V and Lanzkron L, 'EU Online Dispute Resolution – All Bark and No Bite?' <https://www.twobirds.com/en/insights/2017/global/eu-online-dispute-resolution-all-bark-and-no-bite> accessed 31 July 2024

Kaya S, *Consumer Dispute Resolution in the Digital Age: Online Dispute Resolution* (Oniki Levha 2020)

Mainardi E and Martinello B, 'EU Mapping: Overview of Internal Market and Consumer Protection Related Legislation' PE 754.211 (July 2024)

Mak V, *Consumer Protection* (The Oxford Encyclopedia of EU Law 2022)

Maniaki-Griva A, 'European Small Claims Procedure: Initial Appraisal of the Commission's Impact Assessment, European Parliamentary Research Service' PE 514.109 (March 2014)

Mańko R, 'European Small Claims Procedure: Commission Proposal to Remedy Weaknesses in the Current System' European Parliamentary Research Service, In-Depth Analysis, PE 542.137 (November 2014)

Mańko R, 'Reform of the European Small Claims Procedure System' European Parliamentary Research Service, PE 557.014 (May 2015)

Rott P, 'The EU Legal Framework for the Enforcement of Consumer Law' in Hans-W Micklitz and Geneviève Saumier (eds) *Enforcement and Effectiveness of Consumer Law* (Springer 2018)
Šajn N, 'New Consumer Agenda' European Parliamentary Research Service, PE 679.079 (February 2021)
Tenhunen S and Blanckaert J, 'EU Framework on Alternative Dispute Resolution for Consumers' European Parliamentary Research Service, PE 757.788 (February 2024)
Valant J, *Consumer Protection in the EU – Policy Overview* (EPRS 2015) <http://aei.pitt.edu/96092/1/consumer.1.pdf> accessed 9 July 2024
van Gelder E, 'The EU Approach to Consumer ODR' (2019) 6(2) International Journal of Online Dispute Resolution 219, 226
Weatherill S, *Law and Values in the European Union* (Oxford 2016)

3 Consumer ADR in the UK

Eda Sahin-Sengül and Serkan Kaya

Introduction

In recent years, the landscape of consumer dispute resolution in England and Wales has undergone significant transformation, influenced by technological advancements and legislative changes. The departure of the United Kingdom from the European Union, that is to say, Brexit, has particularly marked a pivotal shift in how consumer disputes are managed and resolved. This chapter delves into the evolving framework of consumer ADR within this context, emphasising the necessity for adaptive measures post-Brexit.

Historically, consumer protection in the United Kingdom has been guided by a rich legal tradition, evolving from the early principles of 'caveat emptor' to comprehensive legislation like the Sale of Goods Act and the Consumer Rights Act 2015. The chapter explores the current mechanisms of consumer dispute resolution, highlighting the role of traditional and modern ADR methods. With the increasing complexity of consumer transactions and the corresponding disputes, there is a growing reliance on ADR processes such as mediation, arbitration, and ODR. The shift towards ODR is particularly notable, as it promises to offer more accessible and cost-effective solutions for resolving consumer disputes, especially in the digital age.

This chapter aims to provide a comprehensive overview of the current state of consumer ADR in the United Kingdom, discussing the challenges and opportunities ahead. It offers insights into the ongoing efforts to harmonise consumer protection laws, the effectiveness of various ADR mechanisms, and the potential for technological innovations to reshape the future of consumer dispute resolution. Through this exploration, the chapter underscores the importance of developing a responsive and efficient ADR system that meets the needs of modern consumers in a post-Brexit era.

Legal Framework for Consumer Protection

The United Kingdom (referring to England and Wales) has a long tradition of defending consumer rights.[1] Until the nineteenth century, fewer products were

1 Department for Exiting the European Union, EU Withdrawal Bill, 'Factsheet 9: Consumer Protection' <https://assets.publishing.service.gov.uk/government/uploads/system/uploads/attachment_data/file/714380/9.pdf> accessed 18 April 2024

DOI: 10.4324/9781032689739-3

available, and people consumed fewer things than now. Therefore, the concept of '*caveat emptor*', meaning 'let the buyer beware', was applied. However, with the Industrial Revolution, a sizable body of case law was developed to deal with the buyer/seller relationship, and that led to the adoption of the Sale of Goods Act in 1893,[2] which codified the prior common law of sales.[3] The mid-twentieth century witnessed the enactment of the Unfair Contract Terms Act 1977 and the Sale of Goods Act 1979.

Although the history of criminal law regulating weights and measures, food safety, and other topics dates back a thousand years,[4] no civil or commercial single code for the protection of consumers was adopted.[5] Instead, there was a wide range of legislation addressing various elements of consumer protection,[6] making consumer law unnecessarily complex.[7] Its membership to the European Union had added to this complexity through the transposition of several EU regulations and directives into national law.[8] English consumer law became fragmented and, at times, ambiguous, containing overlaps and contradictions between changes brought about by adopting EU legislation and pre-existing national legislation that has not been altered.[9] This complex legal framework caused consumer misunderstanding, inconsistencies, and conflicts. All these problems ultimately called for a unified regime dealing with consumer rights.[10]

2 Muhammad Akbar Khan, 'The Origin and Development of Consumer Protection Laws in the United Kingdom' (2017) 3(3) *Journal of Asian and African Social Science and Humanities* 38–52; 40–42

3 Christine Riefa and Chris Willett, 'Enforcement and Effectiveness of Consumer Law in the UK' in Hans-W Micklitz and Geneviève Saumier (eds) *Enforcement and Effectiveness of Consumer Law* (Springer 2018) 673

4 Christine Riefa and Chris Willett, 'Enforcement and Effectiveness of Consumer Law in the UK' in Hans-W Micklitz and Geneviève Saumier (eds) *Enforcement and Effectiveness of Consumer Law* (Springer 2018) 673

5 Christine Riefa and Chris Willett, 'Enforcement and Effectiveness of Consumer Law in the UK' in Hans-W Micklitz and Geneviève Saumier (eds) *Enforcement and Effectiveness of Consumer Law* (Springer 2018) 673; Christine Riefa, 'Codification: The Future of English Consumer Law? [2015] *European Journal of Consumer and Market Law* 1–2; 12–19; 16

6 Khan (n 2) 44. These were Supply of Goods (Implied Terms) Act 1973, Sale of Goods Act 1979, Supply of Goods and Services Act 1982, Sale and Supply of Goods Act 1994, Sale and Supply of Goods to Consumers Regulations 2002, Unfair Contract Terms Act 1977, Unfair Terms in Consumer Contracts Regulations 1999, Unfair Terms in Consumer Contracts (Amendment) Regulations 2001, Competition Act 1998 and Enterprise Act 2002, see Consumer Rights Act 2015, Background, para 8

7 Consumer Rights Act 2015, Background, para 5

8 House of Commons, 'Brexit: UK Consumer Protection Law' Briefing Paper Number 9126 (21 May 2021) 1–23; 5 <https://researchbriefings.files.parliament.uk/documents/CBP-9126/CBP-9126.pdf> accessed 18 April 2024

9 Consumer Rights Act 2015, Background, para 5. See similarly that the law was vague and unclear, The Law Commission (LAW COM No 332) and The Scottish Law Commission (SCOT LAW COM No 226), 'Consumer Redress for Misleading and Aggressive Practices' (Cm 8323 SG/2012/21, March 2012), para 4.45 <https://www.scotlawcom.gov.uk/files/3213/3189/7313/rep226.pdf> accessed 18 April 2024

10 Khan (n 2) 44; The Law Commission (LAW COM No. 292) and The Scottish Law Commission (SCOT LAW COM No. 199), 'Unfair Terms in Contracts' Report on a reference under section 3(1)(e)

The proposals discussing the adoption of unified key legislation aimed to bring resources closer to the point of interaction with consumers, lower the complexity of the consumer legislation, enhance the efficiency of consumer enforcement, and boost cost-effectiveness.[11] The Government then set its consumer protection policy, focusing on misleading and aggressive selling, delivery charges for online orders, recall of unsafe products, giving more power to consumers regarding personal data, community buying, food information, and alternative and online dispute resolution systems.[12] With these aims in mind, the Consumer Rights Act 2015 (CRA 2015) was enacted to harmonise and consolidate a wide range of consumer protection legislation and, therefore, to protect the interests of consumers effectively.[13] The CRA, which is now the cornerstone of the consumer protection regime, involves features of both EU law and former national legislation.[14]

Although the CRA 2015 combined many previous consumer protection legislation, other laws and regulations are still in force to protect consumers. The Consumer Protection from Unfair Trading Regulations 2008 (CPUTRs) impose a general duty on traders not to trade unfairly and ban deceptive and aggressive behaviour. The Consumer Contracts (Information, Cancellation, and Additional Charges) Regulations 2013 require dealers to provide various information and other criteria when selling to consumers. The Consumer Protection Act 1987 (CPA) and General Product Safety Regulations 2005 (GPSR) include consumer health and safety protections.[15]

The General Design of the Enforcement Mechanism

Enforcement of consumer protection in England relies on administrative and civil enforcement. Concerning administrative enforcement, the principal authority is the Competition and Markets Authority (CMA)[16] (Section 30 of the CRA 2015).

---

of the Law Commissions Act 1965 (Cm 6464 SE/2005/13, February 2005) <https://www.scotlawcom.gov.uk/files/2512/7989/6621/rep199.pdf> accessed 18 April 2024

11 National Audit Office, 'Protecting Consumers – The System for Enforcing Consumer Law' (15 June 2011) <https://www.nao.org.uk/reports/protecting-consumers-the-system-for-enforcing-consumer-law/> accessed 18 April 2024

12 UK Government Policy Paper, '2010 to 2015 Government Policy: Consumer Protection' (8 May 2015) <https://www.gov.uk/government/publications/2010-to-2015-government-policy-consumer-protection/2010-to-2015-government-policy-consumer-protection> accessed 18 April 2024

13 Khan (n 2) 44, 45

14 House of Commons (n 8) 5

15 Nigel Parr and Christopher Eberhardt, 'ICLG – Consumer Protection Laws and Regulations – United Kingdom Chapter' (28 April 2023) <https://iclg.com/practice-areas/consumer-protection-laws-and-regulations/united-kingdom#:~:text=Consumers%20may%20seek%20to%20enforce,delivery%20date%20under%20the%20contract)> accessed 18 April 2024

16 See the UK government seeks to enhance the enforcement powers of the CMA, Department for Business, Energy & Industrial Strategy, 'Reforming Competition and Consumer Policy: Government Response' (April 2022, CP 656, E02666137 04/22) <https://www.gov.uk/government/consultations/reforming-competition-and-consumer-policy/outcome/reforming-competition-and-consumer-policy-government-response#ministerial-foreword> accessed 18 April 2024 ('Reform')

The Trading Standards Service (TSS), which is in charge of the majority of consumer law enforcement, and sectoral regulators like the Office of Communications (Ofcom), the Financial Conduct Authority (FCA), the Civil Aviation Authority (CAA), Water Services Regulation Authority (OFWAT), the Office of Gas and Electricity Markets (Ofgem), and the Office of Rail and Road (ORR) share the CMA's authority to enforce consumer laws.[17]

Consumer enforcement powers shared by the CMA and other regulatory bodies are civil powers, criminal powers, investigatory powers, and the capacity to ask for an injunction to prevent companies from using deceptive terms or notifications with customers. Civil powers include ending violations of specific consumer regulations or pursuing a civil court enforcement action against traders who breach laws like the CPUTRs and the CRA 2015. Criminal powers include bringing legal action against traders who engage in unfair practices violating the CPUTRs (for example, dealers who use aggressive, threatening, or coercive tactics on purpose or carelessly). Investigatory powers include requesting information from an individual or company and seeking a court order mandating compliance if the infringing individual or company refuses to comply with the law.[18] The CMA use these powers, particularly where legal violations point to systemic market failures, where there is a chance to establish a significant legal precedent, where there is a need to obtain compensation for consumers and maintain the efficacy of the CRA's unfair contract terms regime.[19]

Current Consumer Dispute Resolution Processes

Civil enforcement contains consumer disputes to be filed before the High Court or the County Court (Section 30 of the CRA 2015). Typically, civil lawsuits will begin in the County Court. Subsequently, the High Court and then the Court of Appeal will hear appeals; however, they will be heard by different divisions of those courts.[20] Civil disputes of up to £25,000 are handled by county courts; they will also consider greater value claims with the approval of a designated civil judge.[21] The High Court deals with all high-value and high-importance civil law cases in the first instance and, aside from a few legislative exceptions, has

17 See Reform (n 16)

18 Mark Jephcott, Duncan Green, and Alice Lauterjung, 'Enhanced UK Consumer Protection Enforcement Expected Soon' (14 February 2023) <https://www.simmons-simmons.com/en/publications/cle3ls0ft00p2tsmsl4pggwhc/enhanced-uk-consumer-protection-enforcement-expected-soon> accessed 18 April 2024

19 Mark Jephcott, Duncan Green, and Alice Lauterjung, 'Enhanced UK Consumer Protection Enforcement Expected Soon' (14 February 2023) <https://www.simmons-simmons.com/en/publications/cle3ls0ft00p2tsmsl4pggwhc/enhanced-uk-consumer-protection-enforcement-expected-soon> accessed 18 April 2024

20 Courts and Tribunals Judiciary, 'The Justice System' <https://www.judiciary.uk/about-the-judiciary/our-justice-system/court-structure/> accessed 18 April 2024

21 Courts and Tribunals Judiciary, 'County Court' <https://www.judiciary.uk/courts-and-tribunals/county-court/> accessed 18 April 2024

supervisory authority over all inferior courts and tribunals.[22] The Court of Appeal hears appeals from, *inter alia*, all divisions of the High Court.[23]

No specialised tribunal for consumer claims exists, so the civil procedure system addresses these claims.[24] Although the government does not agree, a specialised tribunal is favoured by some who see consumer laws as a specialised field that requires insight into consumer behaviour, market dynamics, and business economics.[25]

Consumer claims can also follow three tracks, the small claims track,[26] fast track, and multi-track,[27] which are based on their financial worth and legal character.[28] Small-claims track applies to lower-value and less complicated claims with a value of up to £10,000. Fast track is available for claims with a value of between £10,000 and £25,000. Multi-track is used in complicated claims valued at £25,000 or more.[29]

On the one hand, generalist courts have rendered clear and reasonable rulings so far. These courts had the discretion to assign cases to judges with appropriate expertise to ensure efficient handling of cases.[30] As consumer law is broad in scope, the court system has been the more cost-effective way of resolving complex issues.[31] On the other hand, civil actions are generally expensive, time-consuming, and too complicated for consumers to handle without the help of a legal professional.[32] Another downside is that consumer disputes do not qualify for legal aid.[33]

Alternative Dispute Resolution for Consumer Disputes

Overview

The 1980s saw the widespread use of the term ADR, and consequently, the first ADR institutions started to appear around the end of this decade.[34] In 1994, the

22 Courts and Tribunals Judiciary, 'High Court' <https://www.judiciary.uk/courts-and-tribunals/high-court/> accessed 18 April 2024
23 Court of Appeal Civil Division, <https://www.gov.uk/courts-tribunals/court-of-appeal-civil-division> accessed 18 April 2024
24 Riefa and Willett (n 3) 682
25 Reform (n 16)
26 See for Small Claims Track in the Civil Courts, <https://assets.publishing.service.gov.uk/government/uploads/system/uploads/attachment_data/file/725675/ex306-eng.pdf> accessed 18 April 2024
27 See for Fast-Track and Multi-Track in the Civil Courts, <https://assets.publishing.service.gov.uk/government/uploads/system/uploads/attachment_data/file/725673/ex305-eng.pdf> accessed 18 April 2024
28 Riefa and Willett (n 3) 682
29 Small claims track (n 26)
30 Reform (n 16)
31 Department for Business, Innovation and Skills, 'Government Response to Call for Evidence – EU Proposals on Alternative Dispute Resolution' (May 2012) 9 <https://assets.publishing.service.gov.uk/government/uploads/system/uploads/attachment_data/file/190192/12–674-government-respons e-eu-proposals-alternative-dispute-resolution_1_.pdf> accessed 18 April 2024
32 Riefa and Willett (n 3) 683
33 Riefa and Willett (n 3) 683; Legal Aid, <https://www.gov.uk/legal-aid/eligibility> accessed 18 April 2024
34 Loukas A Mistelis, 'ADR in England and Wales: A Successful Case of Public Private Partnership' [2003] The ADR Bulletin 1–45; 6

Commercial Court issued a practice note emphasising the consideration of ADR methods by lawyers.[35] This required lawyers to discuss the possibility of resolving disputes through mediation, conciliation, or other means with their clients and other parties involved. The goal was to inform parties about cost-effective dispute resolution methods.[36] This approach resulted in higher take-up rates and higher client satisfaction. Additionally, the commercial courts played a leading role in using orders to support ADR.[37] In 1995, the High Court's practice note on civil litigation and case management[38] further enhanced judicial control over cases, emphasising discussions on ADR between legal advisers and clients and promoting consideration of ADR for issue resolution.[39]

These developments were followed by the Woolf Inquiry on 'Access to Justice', prompted by the rising expenses of civil litigation and the time it took to resolve cases. Lord Woolf emphasised the advantages of mediation and ADR in his reports on intermediate and final findings in 1995 and 1996.[40] In response to Woolf's reports, the Civil Procedure Rules 1998 (CPR 1998)[41] was adopted, and one of its aims was to promote alternatives to court procedure.[42] In accordance with this aim, CPR 1998 encouraged the use of ADR both before and after litigation begins, with potential consequences in suitable circumstances where an ADR procedure was not followed.[43]

The Final Report issued in December 2009 of Lord Justice Jackson's 'Review of Civil Litigation Costs' went further in embedding the use of ADR, stating all litigation lawyers should be properly informed of the functioning of ADRs and the benefits that it can bring. The Jackson Review also suggested changes to the CPR to encourage the use of ADR, the majority of which were enacted as a package in April 2013.[44] Particularly, the use of ADR is encouraged in low-value matters where the expenses of litigation might quickly grow disproportionate to the amount in dispute.[45]

35 The Commercial Court, 'Practice Note: Commercial Court: Alternative Dispute Resolution' [1994] 1 All ER 34

36 The Commercial Court, 'Practice Note: Commercial Court: Alternative Dispute Resolution' [1994] 1 All ER 34

37 Blake, Browne, and Sime (n 38) 8

38 'The High Court Practice Note *(Civil Litigation: Case Management)*' (1995) 1 All ER 385

39 Blake, Browne, and Sime (n 38) 8

40 Marian Liebmann, 'Introduction' in Marian Liebmann (ed) *Mediation in Context* (Jessica Kingsley Publishers 2000) 13

41 Civil Procedure Rules 1998, <https://www.legislation.gov.uk/uksi/1998/3132/contents> accessed 18 April 2024

42 Mistelis (n 34) 13

43 Susan Blake, Julie Browne, and Stuart Sime, *A Practical Approach to Alternative Dispute Resolution* (5th edn, OUP 2022) 4

44 Susan Blake, Julie Browne, and Stuart Sime, *A Practical Approach to Alternative Dispute Resolution* (5th edn, OUP 2022) 4

45 Susan Blake, Julie Browne, and Stuart Sime, *A Practical Approach to Alternative Dispute Resolution* (5th edn, OUP 2022) 11

Under the CPR 1998, the courts' duty to manage cases involves encouraging parties to adopt an ADR method and facilitating its use if the court finds it suitable for the resolution of the dispute (Rule 1.4(2)(e)). The courts are also entitled to halt the proceedings if the parties request it in order to try to settle the case by ADR or if the judge deems it necessary to facilitate a settlement through ADR (Rule 26.4). The courts may also impose sanctions on a party that fails to employ ADR when it would have been appropriate (Rule 44.5), but the parties cannot be forced to adopt this form of dispute settlement as it would amount to a breach of their Article 6 right to a fair trial under the European Convention of Human Rights.[46] However, courts consider ADR as a helpful means of conciliation for disputing parties.[47] Therefore, a party's total and unjustified refusal to participate in ADR will result in a sanction in the form of a payment of subsequent court costs spent by the opposing party.[48]

Consumer ADR

A consumer can seek redress through an ADR system only after they have attempted to address their complaint directly with the trader. To put it another way, the consumer must have reached a 'deadlock' with the trader after going through its own customer service and internal complaints system. Traders are not required to agree to utilise ADR for a consumer complaint (unless required by law, scheme membership, or contract). Traders, however, must offer specific information regarding ADR to consumers under the Alternative Dispute Resolution for Consumer Disputes (Competent Authorities and Information) Regulations 2015 (ADR 2015) (as modified by the Consumer Protection (Amendment etc.) (EU Exit) Regulations 2018). The trader must supply the consumer with the contact information for an ADR supplier but is not required to agree to utilise ADR.[49] The trader, hence, must provide the name and website address of the ADR provider or scheme on their own website and in their general contract terms (ADR 2015, s.19).

There is not a single mechanism in place to provide ADR.[50] Consumer ADR is divided into two main categories: adjudicative and non-adjudicative. In adjudicative types of ADR, the procedure is not about reaching an agreement, but rather, it is about somebody making a decision about the dispute.[51] The term 'adjudicative' refers to a person sitting as an adjudicator, this is to say a person independent of the parties who will hear from the other parties and make a decision on the dispute and, in most cases, decide on the remedy. Even though there is a third party making a decision as to the dispute, the adjudicative forms of ADR, with its less formal, less expensive, and less time-consuming features, differ from litigating

46 *Halsey v Milton Keynes General NHS Trust* [2004] EWCA Civ 57
47 James Marson and Katy Ferris, *Business Law* (6th edn, OUP 2020) 82
48 *PGF II SA v OMFS Company 1 Limited* [2013] EWCA Civ 1288; Marson and Ferris (n 47) 82
49 Lorraine Conway, 'Consumer Disputes: Alternative Dispute Resolution (ADR)' Research Briefing No 7336 (12 May 2022) 10 <https://commonslibrary.parliament.uk/research-briefings/cbp-7336/> accessed 18 April 2024
50 Blake, Browne, and Sime (n 43) 24
51 Alisdair Gillespie and Siobhan Weare, *The English Legal System* (9th edn, OUP 2023) 688

in court.[52] Adjudicative forms of ADR are arbitration, expert determination, and adjudication.[53]

Arbitration[54] is the most common and formal form of adjudicative ADR, recognised by the Arbitration Act 1996, and is one of the oldest and most common dispute resolution methods.[55] An arbitration procedure is similar to a trial, where both parties present their case to an arbitrator for a decision.[56] There are extremely few opportunities for the parties to contest the arbitration's decision, or the award, which is final and binding on them.[57] If the contract has a clause allowing for it, there is a chance that consumer issues will be resolved through alternative dispute resolution procedures like arbitration. Since 1988, laws have been in place to restrict the unfair operation of such provisions. In the law of England, an arbitration clause in a consumer contract is deemed unfair if the claim is under £5,000.[58] Therefore, for claims below this threshold, pre-dispute arbitration clauses are automatically non-binding under the Unfair Contract Terms Directive. For claims exceeding £5,000, the fairness of the clause is assessed according to the Consumer Rights Act 2015.[59] Prior to this Act, the Unfair Terms in Consumer Contracts Regulation provided the relevant test, with Schedule 2(1) offering examples of unfair terms for guidance.[60] The binding nature of an arbitration clause can vary.[61] For instance, English courts, in cases such as *Allen Wilson v Buckingham*[62] and *Westminster Building Company v Beckingham*,[63] have ruled that an arbitration clause is fair when the consumer has received professional advice. Presently, arbitration clauses in business-to-consumer (B2C) contracts for claims over £5,000 may still be deemed unfair under the Consumer Rights Act 2015.[64]

There are also private, independent and online arbitration schemes, such as Consumer Arbitration, that deal with consumer-trader issues. Consumer Dispute Resolution Limited (CDRL), one of the main ADR providers in the United Kingdom,

52 Gillespie and Weare (n 51) 683
53 Gillespie and Weare (n 51) 687
54 Arbitration remains unregulated by the EU and unaffected by Brexit. In England, Wales, and Northern Ireland, arbitration proceedings continue to be governed by the Arbitration Act 1996
55 Gillespie and Weare (n 51) 688
56 Blake, Browne, and Sime (n 43) 63
57 Conway (n 49) 12
58 UK Arbitration Act 1996, Section 91(1)
59 The UK Consumer Rights Act 2015
60 The Unfair Terms in Consumer Contracts Regulations 1999, Article 5. Section 5(5), Schedule 2 to these Regulations contains an indicative and non-exhaustive list of the terms which may be regarded as unfair
61 Pablo Cortés, 'The Consumer Arbitration Conundrum: A Matter of Statutory Interpretation or Time for Reform?' in Pablo Cortés (ed) *The New Regulatory Framework for Consumer Dispute Resolution* (Oxford University Press 2016) 69
62 *Allen Wilson v Buckingham [2005] EWHC 1165 (TCC), para 43*
63 *Westminster Building Company v Beckingham* [2004] BLR 508 (QB) para 45
64 Paragraph 20 of Schedule 2 and s 63(a) of the Consumer Rights Act 2015 states 'excluding or hindering the consumer's right to take legal action or exercise any other legal remedy, particularly by requiring the consumer to take disputes exclusively to arbitration not covered by legal provisions'

operates the Consumer Arbitration scheme, which is certified by the Chartered Trading Standards Institute, the Civil Aviation Authority, and Ofcom.[65]

The expert determination procedure is used in disputes involving extremely technical matters where an independent expert resolves the factual circumstances and provides a binding opinion of a fact.[66] For instance, self-funded organisations in specific sectors[67] or public bodies like Ofgem provide an expert determination procedure to resolve consumer disputes.[68] Adjudication includes an expert deciding on highly technical matters. It is frequently mentioned in contracts where an adjudicator will decide on performance issues. Failure to utilise the adjudicator would be regarded as a breach of contract and might result in legal action.[69] Typically, adjudication results in a ruling that is only legally enforceable against the business, not the consumer.[70]

Non-adjudicative forms do not necessitate the participation of a third party and can be completed by the parties themselves through the exchange of communications.[71] A third party may still be present, but their duty is not to be decisive but rather to try to bring the two sides together, to understand their points of view, and to strive towards a solution that both parties are content with. Non-adjudicative forms can occasionally produce situations in which a party does not believe they have 'won' or 'lost' since it is about establishing a solution that both parties are comfortable with and which avoids the need to spend significant sums of money on litigation.[72] Non-adjudicative forms include mediation, neutral/expert evaluation, and conciliation.[73]

Through the process of mediation, parties identify the issues at hand, consider potential solutions, and make an effort to come to a mutually agreeable conclusion with the assistance of a mediator, who is a neutral third party. There are two types of mediation, facilitative mediation and evaluative mediation.[74] However, a solution cannot be imposed by the mediator who can only assist the disputing parties in reaching an agreement.[75] There are also independent schemes that offer online mediation services to consumers. For instance, ProMediate (UK) Limited, which

65 Consumer Arbitration, 'About Us' <https://consumerarbitration.co.uk/about/> accessed 18 April 2024

66 Gillespie and Weare (n 51) 689

67 Qasss, 'About Us' <https://www.qasss.co.uk/about-us> accessed 18 April 2024

68 Ofgem, 'Guidance on the Determination of Disputes for Use of System or Connection to Energy Networks' (13 April 2017) No 117/12 <https://www.ofgem.gov.uk/sites/default/files/docs/2017/05/ofgems_guidance_on_determinations.pdf> accessed 18 April 2024

69 Gillespie and Weare (n 51) 689

70 Conway (n 49) 7

71 Gillespie and Weare (n 51) 689; Blake, Browne, and Sime (n 43) 27

72 Gillespie and Weare (n 51) 683

73 Gillespie and Weare (n 51) 687

74 Conway (n 49) 11

75 BIS, Resolving Consumer Disputes – Alternative Dispute Resolution and the Court System, Final Report (April 2018) 11 <https://assets.publishing.service.gov.uk/government/uploads/system/uploads/attachment_data/file/698442/Final_report_-_Resolving_consumer_disputes.pdf> accessed 18 April 2024

consists of a panel of expert mediators registered with the Civil Mediation Council, is an ADR body certified by the Chartered Trading Standards Institute to deal with consumer complaints about goods and services.[76] Neutral/expert evaluation, which is similar to expert determination, is used in cases where the disagreement stems from the parties' differing perspectives of a certain factual situation. In that instance, bringing in an impartial expert to analyse the problem might sometimes help resolve it. Unlike adjudicative expert assessments, the parties are not obligated to adopt the expert's opinion; rather, it is used to urge the parties to negotiate a suitable settlement based on the third party's perspective.[77] Similar to mediation, conciliation involves a more active suggestion from an impartial third party on what should be agreed upon.[78] There are independent conciliation online services for consumers as well. For instance, the National Conciliation Service (NCS), which operates in the retail motor industry, handles disputes between a consumer and a trader that have not been resolved to the consumer's satisfaction or have reached an impasse.[79]

An ombudsman, who provides an impartial service that can assist a consumer with an unresolved complaint with a firm, often incorporates fact-finding, mediation, and adjudication.[80] Most ombudsmen are members of the Ombudsman Association, which gives information about public and commercial sector ombudsman systems.[81] Ombudsmen are regularly called upon to deal with more challenging concerns that cannot be handled through an organisation's internal complaints procedure. The Ombudsman Association's guide to Principles of Good Complaint Handling[82] outlines good practices for how complaints are examined under ombudsman systems. Two major aims are that complaints be evaluated impartially and on their merits, and that independent judgement be adopted.[83] Online ombudsman schemes are available for a variety of consumer services, including various professions, such as property or furniture ombudsman,[84] private parking,[85] public utility companies such as energy, water, and telecommunications, and financial institutions such as banks and insurance firms. The Financial Services and Markets Act 2000, Sections 225–234A, has a legislative ombudsman programme for the financial industry.[86]

76 ProMediate, 'Who We Are' <https://www.promediate.co.uk/who-we-are/> accessed 18 April 2024
77 Gillespie and Weare (n 51) 690
78 BIS (n 67) 11
79 National Conciliation Service, 'Who We Are' <https://www.nationalconciliationservice.co.uk/about-us/who-we-are/> accessed 18 April 2024
80 Conway (n 49) 6
81 Blake, Browne, and Sime (n 43) 357
82 Ombudsman Association, 'Principles of Good Complaint Handling' <https://www.ombudsmanassociation.org/best-practice-and-publications/principles-good-complaint-handling> accessed 18 April 2024
83 Blake, Browne, and Sime (n 43) 357
84 BIS (n 67) 56
85 Ombudsman Services, <https://www.ombudsman-services.org/> accessed 18 April 2024
86 Blake, Browne, and Sime (n 43) 357

Role of Technology in Consumer ADR – Online Dispute Resolution for Consumer Disputes

In 2015, the Civil Justice Council's Online Dispute Resolution Advisory Group issued a report titled Online Dispute Resolution for Low-Value Civil Claims, proposing the formation of a new internet-based court service known as HM Online Court to assist in the resolution of all civil disputes worth less than £25,000.[87] According to the report, ODR has the immense potential to offer two significant improvements to the judicial system: decreased court costs and increased access to justice. Therefore, the advisory group believed that ODR could provide more economical and accessible conflict resolution in suitable instances.[88]

In 2016, the European Commission established, in accordance with the EU Regulation on Online Dispute Resolution (Regulation (EU) 524/2013), a free Online Dispute Resolution portal (ODRp) via which traders and consumers in member countries can attempt to settle consumer disputes and have access to recognised EU ADR providers. Like all EU businesses that conduct online sales, service contracts, or online marketplaces English businesses must have provided a link to the ODR platform on their website. However, after Brexit, the Consumer Protection (Amendment etc.) (EU Exit) Regulations of 2018 repealed the Online Dispute Resolution Regulation in England. Since 2021, English companies and consumers have not been able to view the ODR dashboard or utilise the ODRp to connect with EU ADR providers. Furthermore, there is no longer a requirement for online retailers selling in the UK to link to the ODRp on their websites. Though not via the ODRp, UK consumers can still access ADR entities in EU countries.[89] Therefore, Brexit has affected the resolution of consumer disputes, as it is no longer possible to raise a complaint on the ODRp in the European Union.

In 2023, the Ministry of Justice launched a new Online Procedure Rule Committee under the Judicial Review and Courts Act 2022 to assist judges, legal counsel, and litigants in navigating online court proceedings. Before cases are taken before a court or tribunal, the Committee will supervise the establishment of regulations for online proceedings across the Civil, Family, and Tribunals jurisdictions, as well as data and behavioural requirements for ODR. The Committee, as an advisory non-departmental public body, will have six members, including the heads of the civil, family, and tribunal domains.[90] The use of ODR for consumer claims is also within the realm of this committee.

87 Civil Justice Council, 'Online Dispute Resolution for Low Value Civil Claims – Online Dispute Resolution Advisory Group' <https://www.judiciary.uk/wp-content/uploads/2015/02/Online-Dispute-Resolution-Final-Web-Version1.pdf> accessed 18 April 2024; Blake, Browne, and Sime (n 43) 77

88 Civil Justice Council (n 76) para 1.10

89 Conway (n 49) 19–20

90 Ministry of Justice, 'New Online Procedure Rule Committee Launched' (12 June 2023) <https://www.gov.uk/government/news/new-online-procedure-rule-committee-launched#:~:text=The%20OPRC%20will%20oversee%20the,Review%20and%20Courts%20Act%202022> accessed 18 April 2024

Challenges and Opportunities

The Brexit and the end of the UK's membership to the European Union have affected English consumers' access to ODRp in the European Union. Now a new challenge is awaiting the parliament and the judiciary to pave the way for the resolution of consumer disputes through ODR. Currently, there are studies for utilising ODR for consumer disputes in England. Traditional ADR methods like mediation and arbitration are often conducted partially or entirely online. New purely online processes, not strictly fitting conventional ADR definitions, are being discussed at the national level, particularly for lower-value disputes. The push for efficient and reasonably fair resolution of smaller-scale disputes is the driving force behind the development of software systems for ODR. However, challenges may arise regarding precise legal rights and accessibility for those without easy online access. ODR is anticipated to increasingly serve as a triage facility, settling simpler claims online to reserve court resources for more complex disputes.[91]

Technological advancements are altering communication, interaction, and knowledge management, resulting in unavoidable changes in how conflicts are resolved. The transition away from traditional courtrooms is expected to go beyond just transferring current processes online with the introduction of whole new systems. ODR is regarded as a 'fourth party' because of its ability to contribute to conflict resolution independently of the two sides and an unbiased third party. While there is scepticism regarding technology's capacity to handle complicated disputes, existing software can duplicate mediation and negotiating procedures, with additional improvement possible. Secure websites provide participants with virtual collaboration spaces in which they may share messages and documents while engaging in real-time or delayed talks. Multifaceted programmes may combine information and produce choices, employing virtual reality and avatars to speed up talks, particularly in difficult or emotionally challenging circumstances.[92]

Conclusion

The landscape of Consumer ADR in England and Wales is at a crucial juncture, influenced by the twin forces of technological advancement and significant legislative changes, notably Brexit. As consumer transactions become increasingly complex and digital, the necessity for a robust and adaptable ADR system has never been more apparent. This chapter has explored the evolution of consumer dispute resolution from its historical roots to its current state, examining both traditional and modern methods. The interplay between national legislation and EU directives has shaped a unique framework that, despite its strengths, has faced challenges in coherence and accessibility. Post-Brexit, the United Kingdom is presented with the opportunity to refine its ADR processes, ensuring they are tailored to its consumers' specific needs while maintaining high fairness and efficiency standards.

91 Blake, Browne, and Sime (n 43) 80
92 Blake, Browne, and Sime (n 43) 80–81

The transition towards ODR is particularly promising, offering potential solutions that are not only more accessible but also more efficient in resolving disputes. The establishment of the Online Procedure Rule Committee signifies a forward-thinking approach by the judiciary, embracing digital innovation to enhance the civil justice system. As these digital processes are integrated, it is crucial to ensure they are user-friendly, equitable, and capable of handling the diversity of consumer disputes. Looking ahead, the United Kingdom must foster an environment that protects consumer rights while promoting confidence in the market. To address emerging challenges and leverage new opportunities, continuous evaluation and adaptation of ADR mechanisms will be essential.

References

BIS, 'Resolving Consumer Disputes – Alternative Dispute Resolution and the Court System' Final Report (April 2018) <https://assets.publishing.service.gov.uk/government/uploads/system/uploads/attachment_data/file/698442/Final_report_-_Resolving_consumer_disputes.pdf> accessed 18 April 2024

Blake S, Browne J and Sime S, *A Practical Approach to Alternative Dispute Resolution* (5th edn, OUP 2022).

Civil Justice Council, 'Online Dispute Resolution for Low Value Civil Claims – Online Dispute Resolution Advisory Group' <https://www.judiciary.uk/wp-content/uploads/2015/02/Online-Dispute-Resolution-Final-Web-Version1.pdf> accessed 18 April 2024

Conway L, 'Consumer Disputes: Alternative Dispute Resolution (ADR)' Research Briefing No 7336 (12 May 2022) <https://commonslibrary.parliament.uk/research-briefings/cbp-7336/> accessed 18 April 2024

Court of Appeal Civil Division, <https://www.gov.uk/courts-tribunals/court-of-appeal-civil-division> accessed 18 April 2024

Courts and Tribunals Judiciary, <https://www.judiciary.uk/about-the-judiciary/our-justice-system/court-structure/> accessed 18 April 2024

Department for Business, Energy & Industrial Strategy, 'Reforming Competition and Consumer Policy: Government Response' (April 2022, CP 656, E02666137 04/22) <https://www.gov.uk/government/consultations/reforming-competition-and-consumer-policy/outcome/reforming-competition-and-consumer-policy-government-response#ministerial-foreword> accessed 18 April 2024 ('Reform')

Department for Business, Innovation and Skills, 'Government Response to Call for Evidence – EU Proposals on Alternative Dispute Resolution' (May 2012) <https://assets.publishing.service.gov.uk/government/uploads/system/uploads/attachment_data/file/190192/12–674-government-response-eu-proposals-alternative-dispute-resolution_1_.pdf> accessed 18 April 2024

Department for Exiting the European Union, 'EU Withdrawal Bill, Factsheet 9: Consumer Protection' <https://assets.publishing.service.gov.uk/government/uploads/system/uploads/attachment_data/file/714380/9.pdf> accessed 18 April 2024

Fast-Track and Multi-Track in the Civil Courts, <https://assets.publishing.service.gov.uk/government/uploads/system/uploads/attachment_data/file/725673/ex305-eng.pdf> accessed 18 April 2024

Gillespie A and Weare S, *The English Legal System* (9th edn, OUP 2023)

House of Commons, 'Brexit: UK Consumer Protection Law' Briefing Paper Number 9126 (21 May 2021), 1–23, 5 <https://researchbriefings.files.parliament.uk/documents/CBP-9126/CBP-9126.pdf> accessed 18 April 2024

Jephcott M, Green D and Lauterjung A, 'Enhanced UK Consumer Protection Enforcement Expected Soon' (14 February 2023) <https://www.simmons-simmons.com/en/publications/

cle3ls0ft00p2tsmsl4pggwhc/enhanced-uk-consumer-protection-enforcement-expected-soon> accessed 18 April 2024

Khan MA, 'The Origin and Development of Consumer Protection Laws in United Kingdom' (2017) 3(3) Journal of Asian and African Social Science and Humanities 38, 52

Legal Aid, <https://www.gov.uk/legal-aid/eligibility> accessed 18 April 2024

Liebmann M, 'Introduction' in Marian Liebmann (ed) *Mediation in Context* (Jessica Kingsley Publishers 2000)

Marson J and Ferris K, *Business Law* (6th edn, OUP 2020)

Ministry of Justice, 'New Online Procedure Rule Committee Launched' (12 June 2023) <https://www.gov.uk/government/news/new-online-procedure-rule-committee-launched#:~:text=The%20OPRC%20will%20oversee%20the,Review%20and%20Courts%20Act%202022> accessed 18 April 2024

Mistelis LA, 'ADR in England and Wales: A Successful Case of Public Private Partnership' [2003] The ADR Bulletin 1, 45

National Audit Office, 'Protecting Consumers – The System for Enforcing Consumer Law' (15 June 2011) <https://www.nao.org.uk/reports/protecting-consumers-the-system-for-enforcing-consumer-law/> accessed 18 April 2024

National Conciliation Service, 'Who We Are' <https://www.nationalconciliationservice.co.uk/about-us/who-we-are/> accessed 18 April 2024

Ofgem, 'Guidance on the Determination of Disputes for Use of System or Connection to Energy Networks' (13 April 2017) No. 117/12 <https://www.ofgem.gov.uk/sites/default/files/docs/2017/05/ofgems_guidance_on_determinations.pdf> accessed 18 April 2024

Ombudsman Association, 'Principles of Good Complaint Handling' <https://www.ombudsmanassociation.org/best-practice-and-publications/principles-good-complaint-handling> accessed 18 April 2024

Ombudsman Services, <https://www.ombudsman-services.org/> accessed 18 April 2024

Parr N and Eberhardt C, 'ICLG – Consumer Protection Laws and Regulations – United Kingdom Chapter' (28 April 2023) <https://iclg.com/practice-areas/consumer-protection-laws-and-regulations/united-kingdom#:~:text=Consumers%20may%20seek%20to%20enforce,delivery%20date%20under%20the%20contract)> accessed 18 April 2024

ProMediate, 'Who We Are' <https://www.promediate.co.uk/who-we-are/> accessed 18 April 2024

Qasss, 'About Us' <https://www.qasss.co.uk/about-us> accessed 18 April 2024

Riefa C, 'Codification: The Future of English Consumer Law?' (2015) 1–2 European Journal of Consumer and Market Law 12, 19

Riefa C and Willett C, 'Enforcement and Effectiveness of Consumer Law in the UK' in Hans-W Micklitz and Geneviève Saumier (eds) *Enforcement and Effectiveness of Consumer Law* (Springer 2018)

Small Claims Track in the Civil Courts, <https://assets.publishing.service.gov.uk/government/uploads/system/uploads/attachment_data/file/725675/ex306-eng.pdf> accessed 18 April 2024

The Commercial Court, 'Practice Note: Commercial Court: Alternative Dispute Resolution' (1994) 1 All ER 34

The High Court Practice Note, 'Civil Litigation: Case Management' (1995) 1 All ER 385

The Law Commission (LAW COM No 332) and The Scottish Law Commission (SCOT LAW COM No 226), 'Consumer Redress for Misleading and Aggressive Practices' (Cm 8323 SG/2012/21, March 2012) <https://www.scotlawcom.gov.uk/files/3213/3189/7313/rep226.pdf> accessed 18 April 2024

The Law Commission (LAW COM No 292) and The Scottish Law Commission (SCOT LAW COM No 199), 'Unfair Terms in Contracts' Report on a Reference Under Section 3(1)(e) of the Law Commissions Act 1965 (Cm 6464 SE/2005/13, February 2005) <https://www.scotlawcom.gov.uk/files/2512/7989/6621/rep199.pdf> accessed 18 April 2024

UK Government Policy Paper, '2010 to 2015 Government Policy: Consumer Protection' (8 May 2015) <https://www.gov.uk/government/publications/2010-to-2015-government-policy-consumer-protection/2010-to-2015-government-policy-consumer-protection> accessed 18 April 2024

Cases

Allen Wilson v Buckingham [2005] EWHC 1165 (TCC)
Halsey v Milton Keynes General NHS Trust [2004] EWCA Civ 57
PGF II SA v OMFS Company 1 Limited [2013] EWCA Civ 1288
Westminster Building Company v Beckingham [2004] BLR 508 (QB)

4 Consumer ADR in Turkey

Serkan Kaya and Eda Sahin-Sengül

Introduction

Consumer protection is a fundamental aspect of public policy that ensures the safeguarding of individuals' economic interests, health, and safety. The Turkish Constitution of 1982 was a significant milestone, marking the first official recognition of consumer protection as a public policy concern. This pivotal inclusion granted the government the authority to implement necessary measures to protect consumers and support related initiatives.

In the subsequent years, the legal framework for consumer protection in Turkey evolved, culminating in enacting the Consumer Protection Law (CPL) in 2013, which replaced the earlier Law No. 4077. The CPL, which came into force in 2014, aims to address practical challenges consumers face and align with European Union regulations and directives. The law's primary objectives include protecting consumers' health, safety, and economic interests, providing redress for losses, and promoting consumer education and self-protection initiatives.

This chapter delves into the intricate legal framework established for consumer protection in Turkey, exploring the roles of consumer arbitration boards and consumer courts. It also discusses the importance of ADR mechanisms, particularly in handling low-value claims, and highlights the ongoing need for improvements to ensure these mechanisms are accessible and effective for all consumers.

Legal Framework for Consumer Protection

Article 172 of the Turkish Constitution 1982 marked the initial acknowledgement of consumer protection as a public policy, granting the State the authority to enact necessary measures to safeguard consumers and promote initiatives for their protection.[1] This provision not only laid the groundwork for state-sponsored consumer protection but also afforded individuals the opportunity to form consumer organisations. The CPL was enacted in 2013 to replace the Consumer Protection Law

1 Constitution of the Republic of Turkey, Article 172

DOI: 10.4324/9781032689739-4

No. 4077 and entered into force in 2014. Article 1 of the CPL states its purpose as follows:

> The purpose of this Law is to take measures that protect the health, safety and economic interests of the consumer, to compensate the loss of the consumers, to ensure the protection of the consumers from environmental hazards, which inform and educate the consumers by the public interest; to promote self-protecting initiatives by the consumers and to regulate particulars on the promotion of the voluntary organisations for establishing policies regarding this matter.[2]

The CPL aims to address practical challenges and align with EU Regulations and Directives. It specifically addresses the evolution of sales methods and the emergence of new types of sales. Recognising that existing punitive measures often fail to achieve their intended goals, CPL emphasises the significance of effectively informing consumers rather than solely relying on punishment.[3]

The term 'consumer' is defined by CPL as 'a natural person or legal entity acting with non-commercial or non-professional purposes'.[4] The CPL stipulates that if a natural or legal entity engages in activities for commercial or professional purposes, they are not classified as consumers.[5] According to this description, all contracts and legal transactions, such as contracts of employment, contracts of carriage, brokerage contracts, and insurance contracts, between consumers and natural or legal entities – whether public or private – engaging in commercial or professional activities within the goods or services markets fall under the purview of consumer transactions and are governed by the CPL.[6] Additionally, Article 83(2) of the CPL states that transactions involving consumers as one of the parties, regardless of being regulated by other laws, remain classified as consumer transactions and are subject to the provisions outlined therein.[7]

Section 2 of the CPL outlines the fundamental legal principles governing consumer contracts. Article 4 of the CPL underscores the essential principles, which include defining the substantive content and form of consumer contracts, emphasising that the terms of a consumer contract cannot be altered to the detriment of

2 CPL, Article 1

3 The CPL contains provisions in favour of consumers on: credit cards, early payment of house and consumer loans, complex contracts, interest rate in consumer transactions, right of retraction, time-share property sales, real estate sales on the basis of architectural models, door-to-door sales, defective goods, online shopping and distance contracts, distance sales of financial services, termination of subscriptions, promotional campaigns organised by newspapers and journals, and pyramid sales

4 CPL, Article 3

5 CPL Article 3(n): 'Consumer: Real Person or Legal Entity Acting With Non-Commercial or Non-Professional Purposes'

6 CPL Article 3(n): 'Consumer: Real Person or Legal Entity Acting With Non-Commercial or Non-Professional Purposes'

7 CPL Article 3(n): 'Consumer: Real Person or Legal Entity Acting With Non-Commercial or Non-Professional Purposes' Article 83(2)

the consumer during the contract's duration, prohibiting compound interest, and bars unfair terms in consumer contracts. Furthermore, the CPL delineates the rights afforded to consumers in the event of issues concerning unfair terms in contracts, refusal to sell, unordered goods or services, as well as defective goods and services. It is important to note that, to enhance consumer protection, various related and subsidiary legislations exist as well.[8]

The General Design of the Enforcement Mechanism

It is evident that access to justice and the availability of suitable mechanisms for resolving disputes are fundamental rights of consumers.[9] In the Turkish legal system, the Code of Civil Procedure serves as the primary law, outlining the redress system for resolving disputes and specifying the scope, subjects, and procedures for dispute resolution. The procedural rules and principles concerning consumer disputes are outlined in the CPL.[10] Articles 66 to 72 of the CPL govern the establishment and operation of consumer arbitration boards overseen by the Ministry of Trade. These boards have the jurisdiction to settle disputes up to a specified economic threshold[11] and have the power to issue binding decisions in these matters. On the other hand, Articles 73 and 74 address the establishment and functions of consumer courts. These courts are authorised to adjudicate disputes that exceed the aforementioned economic threshold. Additionally, consumer courts serve as appellate bodies for decisions made by the consumer arbitration boards. In 2020, the Law Amending the Civil Procedure Law and Certain Laws number 7251 added 'Article 73(A)', 'Mediation as a prerequisite', to the CPL, stating that going to mediation is a prerequisite to file lawsuits for consumer disputes involving

8 No. 6563 Electronic Commerce Law 2014; No. 5411 Banking Law 2005; Regulation on Warranty Deed 2014; Regulation on After-Sale Services 2014; Regulation on Prospectus and Instruction for Use 2014; Regulation on Unfair Terms in Consumer Contracts 2014; Regulation on Travel Agencies 2017; Regulation on Price Tags 2014; Regulation on Consumer Arbitration Board 2014; Regulation on Consumer Arbitration Board Rapporteur 2014; Regulation on Pre-Paid Housing Sales 2014; Regulation on Distance Contracts 2014; Regulation on Board of Advertising 2014; Regulation on Commercial Advertising and Unfair Trade Practices 2015; Regulation on Outside-of-Work Contracts 2015; Regulation on Package Tours 2015; Regulation on Instalment Sales Contracts 2015; Regulation on Subscription Agreements 2015; Regulation on Distance Financial Services Contracts 2015

9 This point was stated by the 'Council resolution of 14 April 1975 on a preliminary programme of the European Economic Community for a consumer protection and information policy OJ 1975, No. C92/1'. The 1975 Preliminary Programme identified four more basic rights of consumers as follow: the right to protection of health and safety, the right to protection of economic interests, the right to information and education, and the right of representation

10 Consumer protection as a public policy was first recognised by the Article 172 of the 1982 Constitution which granted the State the authority to take all necessary measures for the protection of consumers. In 1995, Law on Consumer Protection, No. 4077, which specifically addressed consumer protection, was entered into force

11 This monetary threshold is determined and announced each year in the Official Gazette by the Ministry of Custom and Trade. See CPL Article 68, and the Regulation on Consumer Arbitration Board Article 6

monetary claims of TRY 104,000 and above.[12] However, going to the mediation is not mandatory in the following situations[13]:

- Consumer disputes that are in the scope of the Consumer Arbitration Board's duty (disputes involving monetary claims under TRY 104,000);
- Objections made against the Consumer Arbitration Board decisions;
- Lawsuits in order to impose an interim injunction to prevent or suspend a threat that may arise in a contradiction to Law or to detect, prevent or suspend the unlawful condition;
- Lawsuits to detect whether a series of goods offered for sale are defective, to suspend the production and sale of such, to remedy the defect and to recall such from those who are holding such goods for sale;
- The dispute whose nature is a consumer action and arising from absolute rights regarding real estate.

Current Consumer Dispute Resolution Processes

In the Turkish legal system, there is not a single comprehensive regulation that governs ADR with all its principles. Instead, various laws and regulations address specific aspects of ADR. The Code of Civil Procedure 2011 and the Code of International Arbitration 2011 predominantly address arbitration, the most frequently utilised form of ADR. Furthermore, various legal instruments such as the Attorneyship Law 1969, the CPL, the Code of Labour Court 2017, the Code of Criminal Procedure 2004, the Code of Tax Procedure 1961, the Code of Civil Procedure 2011, and the Law on Mediation in Civil Disputes 2012 contain provisions directly pertaining to ADR.

In Turkish law, the first provision supporting ADR can be found in the Attorneyship Law. Article 35 of this law permits lawyers to engage in conciliation processes.[14] This provision encourages lawyers to facilitate the resolution of disputes between parties through conciliation. According to Article 35 of the Attorneyship Law, lawyers are empowered to propose conciliation either before initiating legal action or during ongoing court proceedings, provided the parties have the discretion to settle. If the other party agrees to conciliation, and by the conclusion of the conciliation process both parties reach an agreement on the dispute, they and their respective lawyers sign a written agreement known as a 'conciliation protocol' that effectively resolves the dispute. The conciliation protocol must outline the details of the disputes, the date, and the obligations owed by each party. This protocol carries the same legal weight as court decisions and is binding and enforceable.[15] Another example of conciliation in Turkish law can be found in Article 253 of the Code of Criminal Procedure and Article 73 of the Code of Criminal Procedure. These provisions stipulate that, upon the decision of the judge and the prosecutor,

12 CPL Article 68, and the Regulation on Consumer Arbitration Board Article 6
13 CPL Article 68, and the Regulation on Consumer Arbitration Board Article 6
14 The Attorneyship Law, Article 35
15 The Code of Execution and Insolvency, Article 38

both the offender and the victim have the opportunity to engage in conciliation in cases involving offences prosecuted upon complaint.[16]

The Turkish Civil Procedure Code 6100 mandates that the judge, prior to trial or during the preliminary examination, must actively encourage both parties to seek an amicable resolution of their disputes or pursue mediation, particularly in cases where the parties have the option to settle.[17] This is not a discretionary authority granted to the judge, rather, it is an obligation the judge must fulfil. If the judge believes an amicable settlement is feasible, they may adjourn the hearing and set a new date. Article 139 of the Turkish Civil Procedure Code specifies that parties are informed about the necessary preparations for peace through the invitation sent to them for the preliminary hearing.[18]

The Law on Mediation in Civil Disputes, No. 6325, marked the establishment of the first legislation governing mediation. This law delineates the procedures and principles to be adhered to in resolving civil disputes through mediation. Additionally, it outlines the rights and responsibilities of mediators, the mediation service, requirements for mediator registration, and the establishment of mediation training institutions. The law exclusively applies to disputes where parties have the option to settle, stemming from civil matters and proceedings, including those with a foreign element. Until 2018, mediation operated as a voluntary dispute resolution method involving the engagement of an impartial and independent third party in Turkey.

The Code of Labour Courts, No. 7036, was officially published in the Official Gazette on 25 October 2017, with its primary provisions coming into effect on 1 January 2018. This code is designed to alleviate the workload of labour courts by mandating that parties pursue mediation before initiating legal proceedings in disputes arising from employee or employer claims and compensation related to individual and collective labour agreements. Article 3(2) of the Code stipulates that applying for mediation is a prerequisite before initiating legal action. Failure to engage in mediation prior to filing a lawsuit may result in the court lawfully rejecting the application without further action, citing lack of cause for action.

Following the implementation of mandatory mediation regulations for labour disputes, the Turkish Parliament ratified Law No. 7155, which mandates mediation for commercial disputes related to monetary claims, compensation, annulment of objection, negative clearance, and restitution litigation.[19] This legislation came into force on 1 January 2019. The passage of Law No. 7251, amending the Civil Procedure Law and Certain Laws, marked the introduction of 'Article 73(A)' titled 'Mediation as a prerequisite' to the CPL Law, No. 6502, on 28 July 2020.[20]

16 The Code of Criminal Procedure, Article 253 and the Code of Criminal, Article 73

17 The Code of Civil Procedure 2011, Article 137

18 The Code of Civil Procedure 2011, Article 140

19 Serkan Kaya and Meltem Karatepe Kaya, 'Emerging Trends of Resolving Commercial Disputes Through Mandatory Mediation in Turkey' (2021) 32(11) *International Company and Commercial Law Review* 591, 593

20 Serkan Kaya and Çağatay Serdar Şahin, 'Mandatory Mediation for Consumer Disputes: Unintended Consequences of Mandatory Mediation' (2023) 34(1) *International Company and Commercial Law Review* 26, 27

Finally, since 1 September 2023, with the seventh judicial package, Article 18(B) added to the Law on Mediation in Civil Disputes, excluding disputes regarding the eviction of immovables, disputes arising from the rental relationship, disputes involving the sharing of movable and immovable property, and the dissolution of a partnership, disputes arising from condominium ownership, disputes deriving from neighbour rights, and disputes arising from agricultural production contract have been subject to mandatory mediation.[21]

Alternative Dispute Resolution for Consumer Disputes

Overview

The CPL establishes a monetary threshold and allocates judicial authority to consumer arbitration boards and consumer courts. Disputes exceeding 104,000 Turkish lira fall under the jurisdiction of consumer courts, while consumer arbitration boards typically handle lower-value disputes. If a dispute falls below the monetary threshold, it is mandatory to first apply to the consumer arbitration board before seeking resolution in the Consumer Court. Conversely, a claim exceeding the specified limit must be brought directly to the consumer courts.[22] According to the CPL, both consumer arbitration boards and consumer courts are authorised to resolve disputes arising from consumer transactions and implementation of the CPL.[23]

Before delving into the nature of consumer arbitration boards, examining and determining their legal character is essential, as this matter is disputed from a doctrinal perspective.[24] Indeed, the dispute settlement method of consumer arbitration boards appears to be an extrajudicial (out-of-court) form of dispute resolution, as it is not presided over by individuals possessing the authority and independence of judges. Therefore, it is debatable whether this extrajudicial method of dispute resolution qualifies as arbitration or falls within the realm of ADR.[25]

21 Seventh Judicial Package <https://www.barobirlik.org.tr/Haberler/kamuoyunda-7-yargi-paketi-olarak-bilinen-kanun-resmi-gazetede-yayimlanmistir-83703> accessed 19 March 2024

22 CPL Article 68

23 CPL Articles 2 and 66

24 For a detailed review of this discussion see Evrim Erişir, 'Tüketici İşlemlerinden Doğan Uyuşmazlıkların Çözümü Usûlü' in M. Murat İnceoğlu (Derleyen) *Yeni Tüketici Hukuku Konferansı* (On İki Levha Yayıncılık 2015); İbrahim Ermenek, 'Yargı Kararları Işığında Tüketici Sorunları Hakem Heyetleri ve Bu Alanda Ortaya Çıkan Sorunlara İlişkin Çözüm Önerileri/Arbitration Committees for Consumer Problems in the Light of Judicial Decisions and Recommendations for Problems That Arose in this Field' (2013) C17 Gazi Üniversitesi Hukuk Fakültesi Dergisi 574; Bilgehan Yeşilova, '6502 sayılı Yeni Tüketicinin Korunması Hakkında Kanun'a Göre Tüketici Uyuşmazlıklarının Çözümü Usulü ve Yargılama Kuralları'/Dispute Resolution Procedure and Jurisdictional Issues in Consumer Matters Under the New Law of Consumer Protection No. 6502 (2014) C9 Terazi Hukuk Dergisi 107

25 Hakan Pekcanıtez, 'Tüketici Sorunları Hakem Heyeti/Arbiration Committee for Consumer Problems' (1996) Izmir Barosu Dergisi 41–42; Mehmet Akif Tutumlu, *Tüketici Sorunları Hakem Heyetlerinin Yapısı, İşleyişi, Sorunları ve Çözüm Önerileri/Structure, Functioning of Arbitration Committee for Consumer Problems and Problems and Solutions* (Seckin Yayıncılık 2006) 37–39

The answer to this question holds practical significance in determining which resources can be utilised for interpreting the provisions related to consumer arbitration boards and addressing any gaps in the legal framework.[26] Some scholars argue that consumer arbitration boards serve as a model for compulsory arbitration.[27] They assert that the decisions rendered by these boards are binding and enforceable, thus resembling compulsory arbitration.[28] Conversely, other scholars contend that consumer arbitration boards should be categorised as part of ADR methods.[29] The main arguments supporting this view are that the CPL regime does not guarantee the principle of fair trial in the operation of consumer arbitration boards. A third perspective posits that consumer arbitration boards do not fit neatly into categories such as courts, compulsory arbitration systems, or ADR mechanisms.[30] Instead, they represent a unique and distinct form of dispute resolution known as sui generis.[31] We argue that consumer arbitration boards cannot be regarded as arbitration in the broader sense. This is primarily because parties are not allowed to submit to the boards voluntarily, nor do they have the authority to choose arbitrators. Moreover, given their affiliation with the Ministry of Trade, which establishes and finances the boards, they lack independence. The activities of consumer arbitration boards share similarities with judicial proceedings of state courts, making them a sui generis form of dispute resolution that is extrajudicial. Therefore, it would be appropriate to reference provisions governing judicial proceedings of state courts to address any gaps in legislation concerning the operation of the boards.

Referring back to the jurisdiction of consumer arbitration boards, as stipulated in Article 66 of the CPL, the Ministry of Trade is required to establish a minimum of one Consumer Arbitration Board in the capital of every province and district. These boards are tasked with resolving disputes stemming from consumer transactions and consumer-oriented practices.[32] Currently, 81 provincial and 921 district Arbitration Boards for Consumers are functioning across Turkey.

26 For example, Article 30(23) of the Insurance Law entitled ‘Arbitration in Insurance’ states that in cases where there is no provision in the Insurance Law concerning arbitration, the provisions of the Civil Procedure Code related to arbitration also apply to the arbitration in insurance disputes

27 For a detailed review of this discussion, see Aydın Zevkliler/Murat Aydoğdu, *Tüketicinin Korunması Hukuku* (Seçkin Yayıncılık 2004) 426; Ermenek (n 24) 580; Yahya Deryal, *Tüketici Hukuku* (Seçkin Yayıncılık 2008) 208

28 Zevkliler and Aydoğdu (n 27) 426; Ermenek (n 24) 580; Deryal (n 27) 208

29 Melis Taşpolat Tuğsavul, *Türk Hukukunda Arabuluculuk/Mediation in Turkish Law* (Yetkin Yayıncılık 2012) 344; Erişir (n 24) 56

30 Ali Cem Budak, ‘6502 s. TKHK’ya göre Tüketici Hakem Heyetleri/Consumer Arbitration Board According to the Turkish Consumer Law Numbered 6502’ (2014) 16 Dokuz Eylül Üniversitesi Hukuk Fakültesi Dergisi 80

31 Ali Cem Budak, ‘6502 s. TKHK’ya göre Tüketici Hakem Heyetleri/Consumer Arbitration Board According to the Turkish Consumer Law Numbered 6502’ (2014) 16 Dokuz Eylül Üniversitesi Hukuk Fakültesi Dergisi 80

32 CPL Article 66. Moreover, the principles and procedures regarding the establishment and management of the Arbitration Board for Consumers are included in the Regulation on Consumer Arbitration Committee for Consumers. See the Regulation on Consumer Arbitration Boards Article 1

The decisions rendered by the boards are obligatory for the involved parties and can be enforced in accordance with the regulations outlined in the Enforcement and Bankruptcy Code 2004.[33] Parties have the right to challenge the decisions of the boards by appealing to consumer courts within fifteen days of receiving notification.[34] It is important to note that appealing does not automatically halt the execution of the decision. However, parties have the option to request a suspension of execution.[35]

As previously mentioned, Law No. 7251 introduced Article 73(A) to the CPL, expanding the scope of mandatory mediation to include consumer disputes. However, Article 73(A) of the CPL does not mandate mediation for all disputes arising from consumer transactions; it excludes certain disputes. Notably, mandatory mediation does not apply to collective legal protection. Therefore, consumers and consumer organisations are not required to engage in mediation before initiating a collective action in consumer courts (CPL, Article 73(6); 74(1)). Mandatory mediation is also restricted to cases of personal legal protection. In resolving consumer disputes, two distinct authorities exist: consumer arbitration boards and consumer courts. Provisions requiring mediation as a prerequisite for litigation do not apply to disputes falling under the jurisdiction of consumer arbitration boards.

Consumer ADR

The scope and concept of arbitrability are generally regulated by Article 1(4) of the Code of International Arbitration, No. 4686, and Article 408 of the Code of Civil Procedure in Turkey. According to Article 408 of the Code of Civil Procedure, disputes arising from 'rights in rem' on immovable property and disputes governed by areas of law not subject to the will of the parties, such as family law disputes, are considered non-arbitrable. Turkish courts have interpreted this provision in a highly restrictive manner.[36] Similarly, the Code of International Arbitration contains a similar statement, specifying that 'this Code shall not apply to disputes concerning in rem rights of immovable properties located in Turkey or to disputes that are not subject to the parties' wills'.[37]

According to some scholars[38] and established case law, the phrase 'disputes not subject to parties' choice' encompasses disputes related to public interest. Therefore, consumer disputes associated with public interest are deemed incapable of settlement through arbitration. In 2008, the Turkish Court of Cassation affirmed this viewpoint as well.[39] The Court cited Law No. 4077, former legislation aimed

33 CPL Article 70
34 CPL Article 70(3)
35 CPL Article 70(3)
36 Decision of the Court of Cassation 15th Civil Chamber, dated 31 May 1979 (E. 1979/1195, K. 1979/1330)
37 The Code of International Arbitration, Article 1
38 Gülen Sinem Tek, 'Tüketici Mahkemelerinin Görevi, Yetkisi ve Tüketici Mahkemelerinde Yapılan Yargılamanın Usulü/Jurisdiction and Competency of Consumer Courts and Procedure of Consumer Courts' Proceedings' (2015) *Kazancı Hukuk Araştırmaları Dergisi* 138
39 CC.13/CD, 25.09.2008, D.2008/3492, F.2008/11120

at safeguarding consumer rights, which mandated the establishment of arbitration boards under Article 22. Furthermore, Article 23 of the former consumer protection law explicitly states that disputes regarding its application must be exclusively resolved by either consumer courts or arbitration board committees, depending on the claim amount. Consequently, the legislature implicitly prohibited private arbitration for consumer disputes. The Court determined that a dispute arising from a package tour holiday contract fell within the ambit of this law.[40] Thus, since consumer courts are designated to handle such disputes, any arbitration clause included in the contract was deemed invalid.[41]

It is clear that there is no legal obstacle in the Turkish legal system, apart from the Court of Cassation's case law, that does not allow the resort to private arbitration for consumer disputes.[42] The Court of Cassation's case law indicates that consumer disputes are closely tied to public policy, thereby rendering them non-arbitrable. Additionally, it has been argued that consumer disputes do not fall within the purview of arbitration per the specific criteria outlined by the Code of Civil Procedure and the Law on Mediation in Civil Disputes. However, it is essential to note that in the Turkish legal system, the validity of an arbitration agreement is often conflated with the arbitrability of consumer disputes. There is no legal impediment to the validity of post-dispute consumer arbitration agreements or pre-dispute arbitration clauses negotiated individually by the parties. Consequently, consumer disputes should be arbitrable if they align with the consumer's preferences and have been individually negotiated with the trader.

The Retail Customer Arbitration Board is established as a part of the Bank Association to resolve disputes arising from banking products and services, such as debit cards, credit cards, consumer loans, and insurance transactions between banks and their retail or individual customers. The activities of the arbitral tribunal cover only retail or individual banking transactions, and only natural persons' applications are assessed. Both applications of legal entities and applications of natural persons related to commercial and agricultural activities are rejected. The complaint must be submitted to the Arbitration Board for examination within a period of two years following the date of occurrence of the transaction or action underlying the complaint. Services provided by the Arbitration Board are free of charge. The awards of the Arbitration Board with regard to disputes of an amount of up to 66,000[43] Turkish lira must be enforced and executed by the banks. Customers must apply to their bank for disputes before applying to the arbitration

40 Decision of the Court of Cassation 13th Civil Chamber, dated 20 October 2008 (2008/6195 K. 2008/12026); Decision of the Court of Cassation 13th Civil Chamber, dated 25 September 2008 (E.2008/3492, K.2008/11120)

41 Decision of the Court of Cassation 13th Civil Chamber, dated 20 October 2008 (2008/6195 K. 2008/12026); Decision of the Court of Cassation 13th Civil Chamber, dated 25 September 2008 (E.2008/3492, K.2008/11120)

42 Gökçe Kurtulan, 'Türk Hukukunda Tüketici Uyuşmazliklarinin Tahkime Elverişliliği/The Arbitrability of Consumer Disputes Under Turkish Law' (2017) 131 *Türkiye Barolar Birliği Dergisi* 254

43 This amount is valid for the year 2023 and is amended on the basis of the rate of variation in the annual consumer price index published by the Turkish Statistics Institute every year

board. If the bank does not resolve the dispute, customers can apply with a fully completed application form and all related documents to the arbitration board via e-Government Gateway or by ordinary mail, fax, or electronic mail. Applications made personally to the Banks Association of Turkey are not accepted.[44]

The Telecommunication Authority, which was established with Telegraph and Telephone Law No. 4502 to carry out the regulation and supervision function of the telecommunication sector by an independent administrative authority, established a competitive telecommunication sector and can observe effectively and productively the developments within this industry which are influenced by the rapid emergence of globalisation. It is a special budgeted institution with administrative and financial autonomy, which has a public legal personality to perform the duties given by the law.

The Electronic Communication Law No. 5809, authorises the Authority to operate the resolution of disputes, especially through the conciliation method, which is one of the non-judicial remedies.[45] In this context, Article 2(1) of Electronic Communications Law states that the implementation and execution of resolution procedures are performed under this Law.[46] In addition, Article 6 of this Law explicitly points to the competence of the Authority to settle the disputes between the operators when necessary and to take the measures required that are binding on parties unless otherwise agreed by parties.[47] In 2012, the Authority launched an 'Online Complaint Notification System' to enable consumers to submit their complaints electronically and monitor all procedures and steps of applications. Thanks to this system, the Authority can analyse the complaints and carry out necessary audit activities on the areas where the claims are submitted. The system transmits consumer complaints to service providers within one working day, records the applications submitted, and consumers receive a response within an electronic environment. The system only accepts complaints related to the information sector, such as broadband, landline mobile lines, mobile phones, and satellite platforms.[48]

Consumer complaints can be transmitted to the Authority through the Online Complaint Notification System with a username and password created at 'tuketici.btk.gov.tr' website. The Authority analyses the responses, and the ones that comply with the legislation are delivered to the consumer. Inadequate responses are sent back to the relevant service providers or taken back to the Authority for further evaluation. If the recorded complaints cannot be resolved, an examination, or even an investigation, about service providers can be initiated. Lastly, in addition to the 'Online Complaints Notification System', since 1 July 2014, all service providers are obliged to establish their own 'online consumer complaints systems'.

44 The Banks Association of Turkey Customer Complaints Arbitration Panel, <https://www.tbb.org.tr/en/Content/Upload/Dokuman/148/BMHH_Brosuru_31_Ocak_2017_Internet_Ingilizce.pdf> accessed 19 March 2024

45 Electronic Communications Law No. 5809, Article 2

46 Electronic Communications Law No. 5809, Article 2

47 Electronic Communications Law No. 5809, Article 6

48 Electronic Communications Law No. 5809, Article 6

Role of Technology in Consumer ADR – Online Dispute Resolution for Consumer Disputes

The Turkish Ministry of Justice has developed a National Judiciary Informatics System (UYAP) since 1998 to perform a particularly driving information system between the courts and all other judicial institutions, including prisons, to improve the speed, reliability, and performance of the judicial service offered to citizens in the digital age. UYAP has been implemented by these institutions with ICT, giving them access to all the legislation, the judicial decision of the Cassation Court, judicial records, police and military records, and judicial data. In this way, UYAP builds a computerised system incorporating all courts, prosecutorial offices, and law enforcement agencies, along with the Central Organisation of the Ministry of Justice. Thanks to UYAP, both lawyers and citizens who can connect to UYAP Lawyer or Citizen Portal using their e-signature or mobile signature,[49] can file a suit in civil courts, examine all their judicial and administrative cases, pay their case fees, commence execution proceedings, submit any related documents, and question the situation of the cases in the Court of Cassation and Council of State through online.

With regards to consumer disputes falling within the remit of consumer courts, consumers can file a suit to consumer courts online by using their e-signature or m-signature since 2015. Citizens who want to submit or follow their case in an electronic environment can access the UYAP Citizen Portal Information System.[50] Consumers who wish to log in to the Portal via e-signature or m-signature can access the cases and enforcement proceedings in consumer courts, examine the contents of all the submitted documents in the case, and calculate the fees and expenses related to the lawsuit. Citizens who do not have an e-signature or a mobile signature can use the e-government gateway to view only the primary safeguard information of the case files in the consumer courts under UYAP and cannot submit a case to courts through the Internet. Thus, an e-signature or m-signature is required to file a suit or take action online.

Lastly, applications to Consumer Arbitration Boards that can be made personally or by mail have been quickly done electronically since 2017.[51] It has become possible for consumers to submit their applications from the relevant screen after logging in with the e-Government passwords. Users can access the 'Consumer Complaints Application' and 'Consumer Complaints Applications' steps. As a result of this application, consumers are no longer obliged to apply to courts or arbitration boards in person for low-value claims, and they can make their applications

49 While electronic signature is presented by Electronic Certificate Service Providers approved by Information Technologies and Communication Authority, mobile signature is serviced by mobile network operators in Turkey

50 The system is accessible through <https://vatandas.uyap.gov.tr/vatandas/index.jsp.> accessed 19 March 2024

51 The Regulation on the Amendment of the Law on Consumer Arbitration Boards was published in the Official Gazette and entered into force on 11 August 2017 <http://www.resmigazete.gov.tr/eskiler/2017/08/20170811–1.htm> accessed 2 March 2024

online. This possibility encourages consumers who think that it is not time-efficient to go to court in person for low-value claims to defend their rights.

Finally, the introduction of e-hearing to the Turkish legal system with Law No. 7251 marks a significant advancement. The implementation of e-Hearing, which commenced on 15 September 2020, is rapidly gaining popularity across Turkey. Lawyers seeking to utilise the system first check their hearings on the UYAP Lawyer Portal and then submit an e-hearing request along with their justification.[52] The lawyer can connect to the hearing via video conference if the judge approves the request through the system. E-hearing commences upon activation by the court. The e-hearing application is paramount as it facilitates access to justice services and saves time for lawyers. The system, allowing lawyers to participate in hearings online in civil courts, including consumer courts, has garnered considerable interest, particularly during the pandemic. With its activation in all civil courts across 81 provincial centres, lawyers now have the opportunity to attend hearings in civil courts with audio and video from anywhere they are.[53]

Challenges and Opportunities

As previously outlined, consumers in Turkey typically resort to consumer arbitration boards or consumer courts to resolve their disputes. Despite the positive outcomes achieved by the consumer redress system and other legislative measures, there are still issues hindering its full efficiency. One such issue is the unpredictability of the time required to resolve low-value disputes. The Law on Consumer Arbitration Boards stipulates that after the submission of a dispute, the boards must initiate resolution procedures within six months. Similarly, a report conducted by the Ministry of Justice revealed that the average duration of a case in consumer courts is more than 300 days. This timeframe may be deemed excessive, particularly for certain types of consumer disputes, such as low-value disputes arising from e-commerce.[54]

Compared to the swift resolution times achieved by some established Online Dispute Resolution (ODR) schemes, such as eBay's Resolution Centre or Modria, where disputes are typically handled and resolved in less than ten days, the disparity is evident. Therefore, it is imperative to amend the Consumer Protection Law to mandate that both the boards and the courts resolve disputes within a maximum of 90 days. This adjustment would enhance efficiency and consumer confidence in the dispute resolution process.

52 e-Duruşma 81 İlde 3042 Hukuk Mahkemesinde Uygulanıyor (E-Duruşma Bilgilendirme, 2023) <https://edurusmabilgi.adalet.gov.tr/e-durusma-81-ilde-3042-hukuk-mahkemesinde-uygulaniyor> accessed 20 March 2024

53 e-Duruşma (n 52)

54 Graham Ross, 'The Possible Unintended Consequences of the European Directive on Alternative Dispute Resolution and the Regulation on Online Dispute Resolution' (2014) 10 Revista Democracia Digital e Governo Electrônico 206, 218. For instance, if a consumer files a complaint about a pair of shoes worth 700 Turkish lira with the Consumer Arbitration Board, the Board is expected to resolve the dispute within 180 days. However, this extended period for dispute resolution may deter consumers from utilising the system for low-value disputes

Another issue with the system is that the Turkish Consumer Protection Law mandates that the Board consists of five members. This abundance of board members for resolving low-value disputes may delay delivering justice. Larger boards often struggle to convene regularly due to difficulties coordinating all members' busy schedules. Additionally, discussions within larger boards tend to be longer and less focused than those of smaller boards, resulting in slower decision-making processes. In practice, the number of arbitrators in commercial disputes usually ranges from one to three. Therefore, it raises questions about whether it is reasonable to expect five board members to handle submitted consumer disputes, which are typically less complex than commercial disputes. To address this issue, it is suggested that the number of board members be reduced and capped at a maximum of one or two. This adjustment would streamline the decision-making process, enhance efficiency, and expedite the resolution of consumer disputes.

Another barrier identified by research is the lack of awareness about the process of applying to consumer arbitration boards and consumer courts. As mentioned in the preceding section, complaints to the Consumer Arbitration Boards have been quickly submitted electronically since 2017, and consumers have been able to file suits to consumer courts online since 2015. However, parties often face challenges related to travel time and encounter a lack of transparency regarding procedural details. Consequently, vulnerable consumers and a significant portion of society may not perceive the system as an accessible means of redress. Similar to the EU ODR Regulation 2013, online merchants should be legally mandated to inform consumers about consumer arbitration boards and courts to enhance consumer awareness regarding the use of electronic communications for submitting complaints to either the boards or courts. They should also provide consumers with a link to access the Consumer Information System and Citizen Portal. This measure would promote accessibility to consumer dispute resolution mechanisms and empower consumers to exercise their rights effectively.

Conclusion

This chapter analysed the existing Turkish legislation on consumer redress mechanisms. While it can be generally acknowledged that the consumer redress system and other legislative measures have yielded positive outcomes, it is evident that new challenges persist. Urgent improvements are required to establish a readily accessible mechanism ADR in practice. It is essential to note that courts remain indispensable; they cannot be replaced by extra-judicial mechanisms, particularly in criminal proceedings. However, for numerous online cases where the value of the claim is lower than court expenses, and both parties enter into the contract in good faith, alternative options are necessary. An effective mechanism for resolving online consumer disputes can facilitate complaint resolution and foster consumer trust, thereby making e-commerce more reliable. Lengthy proceedings, whether judicial or administrative, pose the primary obstacle to consumers seeking redress. Consequently, non-judicial mechanisms of dispute resolution such as ODR are gaining importance.

References

Budak AC, '6502 s. TKHK'ya göre Tüketici Hakem Heyetleri/Consumer Arbitration Board According to the Turkish Consumer Law Numbered 6502' (2014) 16 Dokuz Eylül Üniversitesi Hukuk Fakültesi Dergisi 80

Deryal Y, *Tüketici Hukuku* (Seçkin Yayıncılık 2008)

Erişir E, 'Tüketici İşlemlerinden Doğan Uyuşmazlıkların Çözümü Usûlü' in M Murat İnceoğlu (Derleyen) *Yeni Tüketici Hukuku Konferansı* (On İki Levha Yayıncılık 2015)

Ermenek İ, 'Yargı Kararları Işığında Tüketici Sorunları Hakem Heyetleri ve Bu Alanda Ortaya Çıkan Sorunlara İlişkin Çözüm Önerileri/Arbitration Committees for Consumer Problems in the Light of Judicial Decisions and Recommendations for Problems That Arose in This Field' (2013) C17 Gazi Üniversitesi Hukuk Fakültesi Dergisi 574

Kaya S and Karatepe Kaya M, 'Emerging Trends of Resolving Commercial Disputes Through Mandatory Mediation in Turkey' (2021) 32(11) International Company and Commercial Law Review 591

Kaya S and Şahin ÇS, 'Mandatory Mediation for Consumer Disputes: Unintended Consequences of Mandatory Mediation' (2023) 34(1) International Company and Commercial Law Review 26

Kurtulan G, 'Türk Hukukunda Tüketici Uyuşmazliklarinin Tahkime Elverişliliği/The Arbitrability of Consumer Disputes Under Turkish Law' (2017) 131 Türkiye Barolar Birliği Dergisi 254

Pekcanıtez H, 'Tüketici Sorunları Hakem Heyeti/Arbiration Committee for Consumer Problems' (1996) Izmir Barosu Dergisi 41, 42

Ross G, 'The Possible Unintended Consequences of the European Directive on Alternative Dispute Resolution and the Regulation on Online Dispute Resolution' (2014) 10 Revista Democracia Digital e Governo Electrônico 206

Seventh Judicial Package, <https://www.barobirlik.org.tr/Haberler/kamuoyunda-7-yargi-paketi-olarak-bilinen-kanun-resmi-gazetede-yayimlanmistir-83703> accessed 19 March 2024

Taşpolat Tuğsavul M, *Türk Hukukunda Arabuluculuk* (Yetkin Yayıncılık 2012)

Tek GS, 'Tüketici Mahkemelerinin Görevi, Yetkisi ve Tüketici Mahkemelerinde Yapılan Yargılamanın Usulü/Jurisdiction and Competency of Consumer Courts and Procedure of Consumer Courts' Proceedings' (2015) Kazancı Hukuk Araştırmaları Dergisi 138

The Banks Association of Turkey Customer Complaints Arbitration Panel, <https://www.tbb.org.tr/en/Content/Upload/Dokuman/148/BMHH_Brosuru_31_Ocak_2017_Internet_Ingilizce.pdf> accessed 19 March 2024

Tutumlu MA, *Tüketici Sorunları Hakem Heyetlerinin Yapısı, İşleyişi, Sorunları ve Çözüm Önerileri/Structure, Functioning of Arbitration Committee for Consumer Problems and Problems and Solutions* (Seckin Yayıncılık 2006)

Yeşilova B, '6502 sayılı Yeni Tüketicinin Korunması Hakkında Kanun'a Göre Tüketici Uyuşmazlıklarının Çözümü Usulü ve Yargılama Kuralları'/Dispue Resolution Procedure and Jurisdicional Issues in Consumer Matters Under the New Law of Consumer Protection No:6502 (2014) C9 Terazi Hukuk Dergisi 107

Zevkliler A and Aydoğdu M, *Tüketicinin Korunması Hukuku* (Seçkin Yayıncılık 2004)

5 Consumer ADR in Chile

Rodrigo Momberg, María Elisa Morales, and Alberto Pino-Emhart

Introduction

This chapter is intended to provide an overview and assessment of the ADR mechanisms in Consumer Law in Chile. To that end, not only are the legal and administrative regulations described, but empirical data are also included, where available. The chapter will first provide a general account of the legal framework for consumer protection in Chile, followed by a description of the enforcement mechanisms. In this context, enforcement by administrative authorities and courts will be analysed. Then, the chapter will assess the ADR mechanisms currently in force in Chile, namely the SERNAC's seal, the individual complaints procedure and the recently reformed PVC mechanism. In addition, a brief account of ADR mechanisms outside the Protection Consumer Act (Law No. 19.496) will be provided. The chapter will then put forward some reflections regarding the role of technology in the context of consumer ADR mechanisms. Some challenges and opportunities for the Chilean legal system in this aspect will also be identified. Finally, the chapter will end with our conclusions.

Legal Framework for Consumer Protection

The milestone for consumer protection in Chile was the enactment of the Consumer Protection Act in 1997 (Ley N° 19.496 sobre protección de los derechos de los consumidores, hereon CPA). The enactment of the Act entailed the development of consumer policies by the State, particularly with the institutional strengthening of the National Service of the Consumer (Servicio Nacional del Consumidor – SERNAC) as the public agency responsible for the enforcement of consumer law, the promotion of consumer rights and the development of actions for the information and education of the consumer.

Although the President's message, which introduced the CPA into Parliament for discussion, did not expressly mention the sources of inspiration for the Act, the influence of comparative sources is evident in significant aspects of the Act and its subsequent amendments. Thus, it is clear that an important source of inspiration was the now-repealed Spanish Ley 26/1984 General para la Defensa de los Consumidores. In particular, the rules on unfair terms were heavily influenced by EU

DOI: 10.4324/9781032689739-5

consumer law via Council Directive (EEC) 93/13 of 5 April 1993 on unfair terms in consumer contracts [1993] OJ L95/29. Likewise, the introduction and regulation of collective actions were influenced by U.S. and Brazilian consumer law. For instance, the distinction between collective and diffuse interests was adopted in light of Brazilian consumer law.[1]

The Act is technically "special legislation"; therefore, the Civil Code applies as default law, particularly in matters related to consumer contract law and damages (tort). With regard to other instruments of special legislation, although they may include some provisions relevant to consumers, the trend is to incorporate the regulation of consumer protection in specific areas (e.g. financial services) in the CPA. Additionally, courts have interpreted the scope of application of the Act very broadly, including a wide range of issues under its sphere of protection, even when they are regulated in other pieces of specific legislation. Thus, it has been decided that the Act applies to claims related to public utilities, transport, educational services, medical services, and insurance.[2]

Even when Chile does not have an official national consumer policy, SERNAC's Institutional Strategic Objectives include[3]:

- Ensure compliance with consumer rights protection regulations through developing timely and effective control actions and applying voluntary and/or judicial procedures to compensate those affected, make practices transparent and establish fair consumer relations.
- Reduce information asymmetries through the elaboration and dissemination of studies, research, and the application of behavioural sciences to promote balanced consumer relations between consumers and providers, leading to more transparent markets.
- Promote responsible and sustainable consumption through the development of educational actions to increase consumer knowledge, with the aim of preventing over-indebtedness and incorporating sustainable consumption practices.

The General Design of the Enforcement Mechanism

To analyse the enforcement mechanisms in consumer law, it is helpful to distinguish between public, private and mixed mechanisms.[4] Thus, public enforcement

1 See especially Maite Aguirrezabal Grünstein, *Defensa de los consumidores y acceso a la justicia. Un análisis del procedimiento colectivo en la legislación chilena* (Thomson Reuters 2006)

2 Rodrigo Momberg Uribe, 'Leyes especiales y aplicación de la Ley No. 19.496 sobre protección de los derechos de los consumidores. Análisis de casos' in María Elisa Morales and Pamela Mendoza (eds) *Derecho del consumo: Ley, doctrina y jurisprudencia* (Der Ediciones)

3 Ministerio de Economía, Fomento y Turismo, 'Definiciones estratégicas año 2023–2026. SERNAC: Objetivos Estratégicos Institucionales' <https://www.dipres.gob.cl/597/articles-302576_doc_pdf.pdf> accessed 21 June 2024

4 Jens-Uwe Franck, 'Private Enforcement versus Public Enforcement' in Franz Hofmann and Franziska Kurz (eds) *Law of Remedies: A European Perspective* (Intersentia 2019) 107–131

is characterised by the state agency enforcing or encouraging compliance with the law, either by taking legal action, acting directly through a desist request, or imposing a sanction, among others; private enforcement is characterised by the absence of state agency intervention, either because individuals sue themselves, or because the law is enforced through an ADR mechanism without public intervention; and is mixed if both private and state agency enforcement is involved, where it is commonly also an ADR. The CPA establishes several enforcement mechanisms. Nevertheless, some of these mechanisms exist outside the CPA. In the following, we will map the enforcement mechanisms in Chilean consumer law, starting with those in the Consumer Protection Act and then those outside it.

The main administrative authority responsible for the enforcement of consumer law is the National Service of the Consumer (SERNAC). The legal basis for the establishment of SERNAC is the CPA (Arts. 57 to 60). According to this regulation, SERNAC is a specialised agency that enforces consumer law. Its main functions are to supervise compliance with the CPA and other legal provisions related to consumer protection, promote, and inform consumers of their rights and duties, and perform information and education activities for consumers. SERNAC is exclusively responsible for enforcing consumer law and has no competence in other areas of law, for instance, competition law, insurance law, environmental law, etc.

Before the 2018 reform, the CPA only authorised SERNAC to receive individual consumer complaints against providers, establishing a special administrative procedure. In this procedure, SERNAC acts as a mediator, which is voluntary for the provider. SERNAC notifies the supplier of the complaint, and if the provider responds to the complaint, SERNAC proposes a settlement. The administrative procedure described previously is one of Chile's main tools for consumer redress. According to SERNAC's Public Report 2023, 628,645 claims were filed during 2022, of which 52.4% obtained a favourable solution.[5]

In the field of financial services, what is the CPA? Established the figure of financial mediators and arbitrators, who have the authority to deal with complaints from financial consumers when the internal customer services of the banks or financial institutions have not dealt satisfactorily with the consumer's complaint. Again, however, these mechanisms are voluntary for financial service providers and have only been used once, in the so-called "La Polar affair", to deal with the massive complaints related to this financial scandal. This case has been relevant to the point that it will be used as a guide for similar cases in the future.[6]

There are a number of public agencies or bodies responsible for the supervision of specific economic sectors. However, although most have the power to impose fines on providers for breaches of legal or regulatory provisions, which may include provisions dealing with consumer issues, they are not specifically designed and organised to deal with consumer enforcement.

5 SERNAC, 'Cuenta Pública Participativa. Gestión Institucional 2022' <https://www.sernac.cl/portal/604/articles-71808_recurso_1.pdf> accessed 21 June 2024

6 See <https://www.sernac.cl/portal/604/w3-article-3191.html> accessed 21 June 2024

The main characteristics of these agencies are that they are public and autonomous and that their directors are appointed by the Executive. Their main function is supervising the activities of companies and providers within their scope of competence.[7] However, some ADR mechanisms have been implemented in these economic sectors. We provide a brief overview of these mechanisms in section about "Consumer Law Mechanisms of Enforcement Outside the CPA".

Current Consumer Dispute Resolution Processes

Structure of the Chilean Judicial System

The structure of the judicial system in Chile is based on a Supreme Court ("Corte Suprema"), 17 Courts of Appeal ("Cortes de Apelaciones"), and a Constitutional Court ("Tribunal Constitucional") as superior courts. The Supreme Court is based in Santiago, has 21 judges, and operates in three or four separate panels. It is the court of last resort and Chile's highest court of appeal. The Constitutional Court is an autonomous court that does not report to the Supreme Court. It has ten judges, and its primary function is to control and review the constitutionality of laws.[8]

At the lower levels of the hierarchy, there are "Juzgados de Letras", which generally hear non-criminal disputes, and specialised criminal courts ("Juzgados de Garantía" and "Tribunales Orales en lo Penal"). There are also specialised courts for family law ("Juzgados de Familia"), labour law ("Juzgados de Letras del Trabajo" and "Juzgados de Cobranza Laboral y Provisional"), and tax law ("Tribunales Tributarios y Aduaneros").[9]

Individual Consumer Disputes

In Chile, individual consumer disputes are heard by "Juzgados de Policía Local" (JPL). These courts are not part of the judicial system ("Poder Judicial") but are supervised by the competent Court of Appeal. Juzgados de Policía Local are non-specialised courts. These courts generally deal with traffic offences and infringements of other municipal regulations.[10] The Consumer Protection Act states explicitly that all individual actions arising from the Act shall be heard by these courts (Art. 50 A). If the amount in dispute (according to the claim) is less than 10 UTM (approximately 650 USD at current exchange rates), there is no appeal

7 The main supervisory agencies are the Comisión para el Mercado Financiero (CMF – Commision for the Financial Market), the Superintendencia de Electricidad y Combustibles (SEC – Superintendence of Electricity and Fuels), the Superintendencia de Servicios Sanitarios (SISS – Superintendence of Sanitary Services), and the Subsecretaría de Telecomunicaciones (Subtel – Sub Secretariat of Telecommunications)

8 Chilean Constitution Art. 93 <https://constituteproject.org/constitution/Chile_2021www.constituteproject.org/constitution/Chile_2015?lang=en> accessed 31 March 2024

9 Código Orgánico de Tribunales Art. 5

10 Law No. 15.231 of 1978 Art. 13

against the court's decision (Art. 50 G of Law No. 19.496); if the amount is more than ten UTM, the court's decision can be appealed to the Court of Appeal.

Article 50 of Law No. 19.496 provides that a consumer whose rights have been infringed may, in the same procedure, request the imposition of a sanction on the seller or supplier, the nullity of any unfair term in the contract, the performance of the contract, a judicial order to cease the infringement and adequate damages compensation. The Act provides a simplified procedure for consumer disputes, in which the consumer can apply directly to the court (JPL). The assistance of a lawyer is not required to file a claim or to participate in the proceedings, except in the case of collective actions (Art. 50 C). In principle, no court fees or taxes are payable. However, the court may consider the claim "frivolous" (*temeraria*), in which case the consumer will be fined (Art. 50 E).

There are no court fees or taxes, nor is the assistance of a lawyer required to bring a claim to court. Therefore, legal aid is not explicitly offered to consumers. However, applying for legal aid from the Corporación de Asistencia Judicial is possible if the consumer has financial difficulty. This institution provides free legal aid for non-criminal cases. Law graduates who are trained to become lawyers offer the assistance.

Advantages and Limitations of Judicial Enforcement: Individual Consumer Disputes

The system offers two main advantages for individual claims. First, the procedure is simplified and should take less time to resolve than an ordinary legal claim. Second, the fact that the procedure does not require the assistance of a lawyer makes it easier for consumers to access the courts to bring a claim.

Paradoxically, however, the advantage of a simplified procedure could also turn out to be its main disadvantage, mainly because the JPLs are not specialised consumer courts. Even today, when in practice, all JPL judges are lawyers, no professional training is required for appointment to the position, and most are appointed on a part-time basis. Also, the fact that no legal assistance is required to appear before the court can be detrimental to the consumer if, on the other side, the provider is assisted by a lawyer. Furthermore, if the dispute reaches the Court of Appeal, the length of the proceedings may increase considerably. At the same time, it has been suggested that SERNAC should have more prerogatives, as many consumers are reluctant to go to court if the supplier has not settled the case during the previous conciliation procedure.

Collective Redress Mechanism for Consumers

Articles 51 to 54 of Law No. 19.496 provide for a form of collective redress. It was introduced in 2004 (Law No. 19.955) and later amended in 2011 and 2018 (Law No. 20.543 and No. 21.081). The regulation follows the Brazilian model of the protection of collective and diffuse interests (Law No. 8.078 of 1990), or supra-individual interests. The CPA now provides for a special procedure for collective redress. The competent court for these disputes is not the Juzgado de Policía Local but the ordinary civil courts ("Juzgados de Letras").

According to Article 51, the procedure is applied in cases where the collective or diffuse interest of consumers is involved and can be initiated by SERNAC, a consumers' association or a group of 50 or more consumers having the same collective interest. The court will examine the admissibility of the collective action in relation to its formal requirements. If the court deems the collective action admissible, the plaintiff(s) must publish a notice informing the public that the collective action has been brought. Any consumer concerned must be allowed to participate in the proceedings (Art. 53).[11] The judgement of the court has an *erga omnes* effect, in the sense that any consumer affected by the same facts can claim the damages or other remedies ordered by the court (Art. 54).

One of the main innovations introduced by the 2018 reform of the CPA is the recognition of so-called "collective moral damage". To be recoverable, such moral damage must "affect the physical or psychological integrity or dignity of consumers" (Art. 51(2)). Legal scholarship has been critical of this provision, and there is still some uncertainty as to how the courts will interpret the legal text.[12]

In recent years, collective actions have been extended to certain economic sectors where consumer rights may be seriously affected. Thus, Decreto con Fuerza de Ley No. 458 of 1975 (Ley General de Urbanismo y Construcciones) Article 19 and Law No. 20.945 of 2016, which amended various legal provisions on competition law, have introduced the possibility for consumers to bring collective actions for infringement and damages in matters related to construction, housing, and competition.

The number of cases opened each year shows that the procedure is used relatively frequently (e.g., 12 cases were opened in 2022) and is increasing. Moreover, according to information on the institution's official website, more than 133 cases have been in process since 2015.[13] The results of collective actions can generally be considered satisfactory for consumer interests. The main drawback is that the procedure can be lengthy, with some cases taking more than five years to reach the Supreme Court.

11 See Maite Aguirrezabal Grünstein, 'La extensión de los efectos de la sentencia dictada en procesos promovidos para la defensa de los intereses colectivos y difusos de consumidores y usuarios: Régimen en la ley chilena de protección al consumidor' (2010) 16 Ius et Praxis 99

12 Rodrigo Momberg Uribe and Alberto Pino-Emhart, 'Algunos aspectos relevantes para el ejercicio de acciones indemnizatorias en procedimientos colectivos' in Francisca Barrientos and Lucas del Villar (eds) *Interés general, las negociaciones extrajudiciales y juicios colectivos en el derecho del consumo* (Thomson Reuters 2021) 313–316

13 See <https://www.sernac.cl/portal/609/w3-propertyvalue-59114.html#recuadros_articulo_1394_group_pvid_67500> accessed 21 June 2024

Alternative Dispute Resolution for Consumer Disputes

The ADRs in the CPA

Three mixed mechanisms exist: "SERNAC's seal", the individual complaint, and the Collective Voluntary Procedures (PVC). There are two exciting things about them. First, all of them are ADR, and second, one is powerful since, as we will see further, it is a collective mechanism with an erga omnes effect. In general, ADRs "describe a multitude of techniques (arbitration, conciliation, mediation, and settlement, for example) that aim to assist in reaching an outcome for a dispute without involving a court".[14] ADRs for consumer disputes are typically associated with small-value complaints about goods and services that would usually not make it into a courtroom. However, in Chile, as we have just anticipated, there is a collective mechanism that covers significant value issues that concern many consumers. We will now describe each mixed enforcement mechanism in the CPA, focusing on their role as ADR.

SERNAC's Seal

According to Title V of the CPA, there is a mechanism by which SERNAC can grant a "seal" to the standard contracts of financial service providers. This seal is a kind of legal certification of the standard financial services contracts.[15] It is a mixed enforcement mechanism because, despite the administrative procedure carried out by SERNAC, the providers also participate voluntarily. In fact, according to Articles 55 to 56 H of the CPA, obtaining the seal is undertaken at the request of the financial provider, who voluntarily decides to submit all its standard contracts to the control of SERNAC. After checking each contract, SERNAC gives the contract a sort of stamp. At the same time, this procedure is considered a preventive control of unfair terms, as SERNAC verifies the legality of the general terms and conditions.[16]

Although SERNAC's Seal is an ADR, the CPA provides an alternative dispute resolution system applicable only in cases where the seal has been granted. The law requires providers to have a customer service department to deal with consumers' queries and complaints about any financial product or service offered through a standard contract as a qualifying requirement for obtaining the seal.

If customer service does not respond satisfactorily to consumers' queries, they can turn to a mediator or financial arbitrator to resolve the dispute, who can only act if the case has not been brought before the courts. This ADR system aims to avoid disputes being brought before the courts. It is a private enforcement mechanism since the intervention of the public authority is only involved at the beginning of

14 Naomi Creutzfeldt, 'An Introduction to Alternative Dispute Resolution (ADR) for Consumers in Europe' in Caroline Cauffman and Jan M Smits (eds) *The Citizen in European Private Law: Norm-Setting, Enforcement and Choice* (Intersentia 2016) 141

15 María Elisa Morales, *Control Preventivo de Cláusulas Abusivas* (Der Ediciones 2018) 101–102

16 María Elisa Morales, *Control Preventivo de Cláusulas Abusivas* (Der Ediciones 2018) 101

the mechanism and not in the negotiation process that could take place afterwards between providers and consumers in customer service, mediation, or financial arbitration.

Unfortunately, the SERNAC's Seal has never been applied. The reasons are unclear, but one possible explanation is that it needs to be better designed in the interests of providers since strict submission to this procedure does not guarantee the legality of their contracts and does not prevent the subsequent review by the judge of contracts already certified.[17]

Individual Complaints

The individual complaints procedure allows the consumer whose rights are affected to reach a separate agreement with the provider concerned. This procedure is currently not explicitly regulated in the CPA, as the 2018 reform abolished it.[18]

Proceedings are carried out entirely online, on the SERNAC website, particularly in the "consumer portal",[19] where the consumer enters the complaint and the supporting documents, and SERNAC sends them to the supplier. It is also possible to do it in person or by telephone. The procedure takes 18 days and ends with or without a response from the supplier. In other words, SERNAC does not seek an effective solution to the consumer's complaint. The agency does not issue any opinion in this procedure and only functions as a mailbox that sends and receives communications between the parties.

The main advantages of enforcing consumer rights before SERNAC are the time and cost involved in resolving the conflict.[20] The procedure is free of charge for the consumer, and the complaint can be submitted via the Internet. However, this administrative procedure also has some limitations. SERNAC's role here is merely that of a mediator between the parties. Moreover, the procedure is voluntary for the provider, who is not obliged to reply to the complaint or to appear before SERNAC. Failure to act does not entail any negative consequences for the provider. If the consumer and the provider come to an agreement, it has the force of an out-of-court settlement. The consumer is prevented from taking legal action for the exact cause of action, but the agreement does not give him the right of enforcement. Therefore, the consumer must take legal (declaratory) action to obtain redress if the trader fails to comply with the agreement. Nevertheless, this procedure has proven very effective as an alternative dispute resolution mechanism. For instance, in 2022, SERNAC received about 628,000 complaints, of which more than half were resolved in the consumer's favour.

17 María Elisa Morales, *Control Preventivo de Cláusulas Abusivas* (Der Ediciones 2018) 106

18 Law No. 21.081

19 See <https://www.sernac.cl/portal/617/w3-propertyvalue-518.html> accessed 21 June 2024

20 According to a SERNAC report of 2016, the average time for the resolution of a complaint was 15 days

Historical Perspective on the PVC Mechanism in Chile: Before and After Its Reform

Before the reform in 2018 (Law No. 21.081), the mediation process was not regulated by statute. Still, it was interpreted that SERNAC had the authority to begin this procedure based on its duty to protect the consumers' rights, including their collective and diffuse interests, based on Article 58(f) of the CPA.[21] This mediation was started by an official communication of SERNAC to the provider, in which SERNAC was meant to serve as the mediator to reach an agreement. The procedure was possible for both individual and collective claims. It was argued that the procedure was not correctly a mediation since SERNAC's role is arguably not an impartial mediator's role but rather an incumbent party for the protection of consumers' rights.[22]

The critical reform to the CPA enacted in 2018 changed this scenario, establishing a new mediation procedure called "*Procedimientos Voluntarios Colectivos*" (Collective Voluntary Procedures), commonly known as PVC. As the name suggests, this procedure is designed to regulate collective proceedings, leaving individual mediation procedures untouched. Even more, some have argued that SERNAC no longer has the prerogative to conduct mediation procedures for individual claims since its prerogative in Article 58(f) of the Consumer Protection Act was eliminated.[23] By contrast, others have argued that SERNAC will continue to conduct these procedures even without the express prerogative as it was established before the reform.[24]

The New Collective Mediation Procedures After the Reform

Law No. 21.081 was enacted in 2018, establishing several relevant changes to the CPA. One of the most significant changes was the introduction of a regulated mediation procedure conducted by SERNAC. As explained above, SERNAC was used to perform these procedures even without an express prerogative. However, the introduction of this new procedure was essential to institutionalise the process.[25]

21 Rodrigo Momberg, María Elisa Morales, and Alberto Pino-Emhart, 'Enforcement and Effectiveness of Consumer Law in Chile, a General Overview' in Hans Micklitz and Genevieve Saumier (eds) *Enforcement and Effectiveness of Consumer Law* (Springer 2018) 163

22 Claudio Fuentes Maureira, 'De la mediación colectiva al procedimiento voluntario colectivo' in Juan Ignacio Contardo, et al. (eds) *Litigación en materia de consumidores. Dogmática y práctica en la reforma de fortalecimiento al SERNAC* (Thomson Reuters 2019) 172–173

23 Macarena Vargas Pavez, 'Mecanismos alternativos y consumo. Análisis de la nueva Ley de protección a los derechos de los consumidores' in Juan Ignacio Contardo, et al. (eds) *Litigación en materia de consumidores. Dogmática y práctica en la reforma de fortalecimiento al SERNAC* (Thomson Reuters 2019) 157–158

24 Juan Enrique Vargas Viancos, 'El rol de las Asociaciones de Consumidores en la litigación de casos de consumo en Chile' in Juan Ignacio Contardo, et al. (eds) *Litigación en materia de consumidores. Dogmática y práctica en la reforma de fortalecimiento al SERNAC* (Thomson Reuters 2019) 362 n. 29

25 Rodrigo Momberg and María Elisa Morales, *Procedimientos Voluntarios Colectivos en el Derecho del Consumo Chile* (Tirant lo Blanch 2022) 22–23

According to Article 54 H of the CPA, the purpose of the PVC is to "obtain an expedited, complete and transparent solution, in the case of acts that might affect the collective or diffuse interest of consumers". The procedure is designed to be expedited since, initially, it is meant to last no longer than three months (Art. 54 J). This deadline can be extended for an additional three-month period, but only once, and if there are justified grounds to do so, such as an advanced negotiation or the need for more time to analyse the data or the offers formulated.

The PVC's purpose is to be 'complete', which means that the agreement reached with the providers includes all the aspects of the conflict. One question that can be raised is whether the agreement can consist of a solution to private aspects (damages and reimbursements to consumers) and administrative law aspects (such as fines and other sanctions for the infringement of the CPA). It has been argued that the PVC agreements could include these inflationary aspects.[26] SERNAC could not later persecute the providers for these fines and other administrative sanctions in this scenario. Others, however, claim that the agreement does not preclude SERNAC from later demanding these sanctions, given their administrative law nature.[27]

Finally, the purpose of 'transparency' requires these procedures to be made available to the general public. In this sense, SERNAC must advertise the procedure's beginning on its website within five days, and the law also requires it to advertise the decision in newspapers and on 'Diario Oficial' (Art. 54 Q). This is an important difference in relation to the previous mediation processes carried out by SERNAC, which were not made known to the public.

The PVC begins with a resolution by SERNAC. This decision can be made by SERNAC's own initiative, requested by the provider, or by virtue of a justified complaint of a consumer's association (Art. 54 H). The decision to begin the procedure is SERNAC's prerogative, and it is lawful to decide not to start the process.[28] The law also forbids SERNAC from beginning the procedure if a collective action claim has already been submitted regarding the same facts as long as these procedures remain active. The reason for this is to avoid having two parallel procedures dealing with the same conflict. It is worth noticing that the statute mentions that both claims should not have the same facts but does not mention the provider's identity. Therefore, SERNAC will not be able to begin a PVC if a collective action procedure is in progress regarding the same infraction despite different providers committing the same violation.[29] Relatedly, Article 54 H forbids initiating any collective action regarding the same facts once a PVC procedure has begun and is still pending.

26 Rodrigo Momberg and María Elisa Morales, *Procedimientos Voluntarios Colectivos en el Derecho del Consumo Chile* (Tirant lo Blanch 2022) 30

27 Juan Ignacio Contardo González, 'Naturaleza jurídica del acuerdo del procedimiento voluntario y su importancia para la extensión de los efectos' in Iñigo de la Maza and Juan Ignacio Contardo (eds) *Estudios de Derecho del Consumidor II* (Rubicon Editores 2021) 289–296

28 Maite Aguirrezabal Grünstein, *Defensa de los consumidores y acceso a la justicia. Un análisis del procedimiento colectivo en la legislación chilena* (2nd edn, Thomson Reuters 2019)

29 Momberg and Morales (n 26) 53

The content of the eventual agreement is regulated under Article 54 P. The agreement takes place between SERNAC and the provider. The consumer associations only have limited participation in the process and, therefore, cannot be parties to the agreement. Some authors, however, have argued that they could.[30] The agreement, in general, must specify the obligations and conditions that the parties assume. Article 54 P establishes that the agreement must contain at least the following elements:

1. The cease of the conduct that might have affected the collective or diffuse interest of consumers.
2. The determination of the reimbursements, compensations, or damages to be paid to each affected consumer, if proceeds.
3. A solution that is proportional to the damage caused reaches every affected consumer and is based on objective grounds.
4. The way in which the terms of the agreement will be enforced and the procedure by which the provider will reimburse, compensate, or pay the damages to the affected consumers.
5. The procedures by which the agreement will be enforced will be guaranteed at the provider's cost.

It is important to note that the agreement must include a determination of reimbursements, compensations, or damages to be paid to the affected consumers if this applies to the case. It follows that the PVC does not need to include this aspect since it must consist of this only if the infringement has harmed consumers. It might be the case that the infraction in question does not cause harm to consumers.[31]

Relatedly, it has been questioned whether the PVC must necessarily include an agreement on non-pecuniary damages, if applicable. According to SERNAC, the agreement may or may not include non-pecuniary damages to consumers.[32] However, it has been argued that the agreement must include non-pecuniary damages in case consumers have suffered this type of harm because the reparation of non-pecuniary damages is an essential consumers' right (Art. 3(e) of the CPA).[33]

The agreement must also indicate whether the *erga omnes* effect of Article 54 Q will be applied. This effect is described in this article in the following terms:

> The agreement will produce the effects of an extrajudicial transaction with respect to every consumer potentially affected, except those who have previously claimed their rights in court, have subscribed to agreements or

30 Contardo González (n 28) 290–292

31 In this sense, some agreements recently reached with SERNAC do not include damages, such as the agreements with Banco Santander (Resolución Exenta No. 772/2019 <https://www.sernac.cl/portal/609/articles-57116_archivo_02.pdf>) and the Cornershop company (Resolución Exenta No. 330/2022 <https://www.sernac.cl/portal/609/articles-63351_archivo_08.pdf> accessed 21 June 2024)

32 See <https://sernac.cl/portal/617/w3-article-57441.html> accessed 21 June 2024

33 Momberg and Morales (n 26) 69–70

transactions individually with the provider, or have reserved their rights to actions according to the penultimate paragraph.

It is important to note that the PVC procedure provides some incentives for suppliers to choose to participate. First, the supplier's participation is voluntary and can be withdrawn anytime. Secondly, the agreement does not imply a recognition of liability by the provider. This allows the provider to avoid fines and public disrepute resulting from a class action lawsuit.

The involvement of the public authority and the provider in a negotiation places this mixed enforcement mechanism on the list of ADRs. Ultimately, the courts will only intervene if the parties reach an agreement and decide to seek judicial approval. In this case, the PVC will have an *erga omnes* effect. This effect is a guarantee for the providers, as it excludes the possibility that the consumers, the public authority, or a consumer association will later take legal action against them on the same facts.

Some research shows that PVCs have been a genuinely effective ADR mechanism for obtaining redress and enforcing consumer protection rules. For example, nine new PVCs were opened in 2022, and ten PVCs opened in 2021 were closed, with favourable outcomes for 670,324 consumers who received compensation totalling more than USD 10,000,000. PVCs have also proved to be much more than a viable means of compensating for losses, as they have been particularly effective as a mechanism to control unfair terms (Momberg Uribe and Morales Ortiz, 2022: 115–131).[34]

Consumer Law Mechanisms of Enforcement Outside the CPA

As discussed in another paper,[35] private enforcement mechanisms exist outside consumer law but function as ADR mechanisms for consumers. In the Chilean context, these are found mainly in insurance and financial markets, as shown below. The Financial Market Commission (Comisión para el Mercado Financiero) plays a vital role in this aspect.

The "Ombudsman of the Insured" (Defensor Del Asegurado)

The Ombudsman of the Insured is a private, autonomous, and independent institution whose objective is to resolve any possible conflicts that may arise for the insured concerning insurance contracts in the insurance market. This entity provides this service completely free of charge.

The creation of the Ombudsman of the Insured corresponded to an initiative of the Insurance Companies' Private Regulation Board (Consejo de Autorregulación de las Compañías de Seguros), an entity in charge of ensuring the correct application of the rules of the Code of Good Corporate Practices, which aims to develop

34 Momberg and Morales (n 26) 115–131

35 Momberg, Morales, and Pino-Emhart (n 22) 164–165

the insurance market following the principles of free competition and good faith among companies and between them and their consumers.[36]

The Ombudsman of the Insured resolves each case based on a request. For the analysis of each case, it applies the contract signed by the parties, the legislation in force, and the general principles of equity, among others. Compliance with its rulings is mandatory for insurance companies, which have formally assumed this commitment in advance with the Chilean Insurers' Association. However, if the insured does not agree with the ombudsman's decision, she may submit her claim by any other means permitted by contract or law.

"Banking Ombudsman's Office" (Defensoría Del Cliente Bancario)

The Association of Banks and Financial Institutions (ABIF) established this private enforcement mechanism. It is a dispute resolution system through which customers of member banks have an independent body to resolve their complaints.[37] The function of this independent body is to answer the complaints and requirements, ensuring that the clients of the banks receive an independent resolution.[38]

The Banking Ombudsman's Office operates online as an alternative dispute resolution mechanism.[39] The procedure is regulated in the Consumer Ombudsman Regulation,[40] a private self-regulatory statute of the associated financial institutions.

The procedure can be initiated when the consumer and their bank have been unable to reach an agreement on a particular dispute when the bank has rejected a specific complaint by the consumer or when the bank has failed to respond to a consumer complaint within 30 working days.

Powers of the Financial Market Commission (*Comisión Para El Mercado Financiero*): Insurance Arbitration

Insurance arbitration is a mixed enforcement mechanism regulated in a particular insurance regulation outside the CPA.[41] It is mixed because it can be requested by the insured if the conditions specified by law are met. This is a particular judicial procedure that is processed and resolved in the form of a trial, in which the Financial Market Commission, in the cases it deems qualified and when the conditions established by law are met, acting as an arbitration judge can resolve a dispute between the insured or beneficiary and the insurance company in a way that is binding for the parties.

Whether or not this can be done will also depend on the general conditions of the insurance policy, such as whether there is a clause on conflict resolution under the denomination of 'Arbitration', 'Dispute Settlement', or another analogous clause.

36 See <https://www.ddachile.cl/Acerca-DdA.aspx> accessed 21 June 2024
37 See <https://www.defensoriadelclientedeabif.cl> accessed 21 June 2024
38 See <www.defensoriadelclientedeabif.cl/Sitio/QuienesSomos.aspx> accessed 21 June 2024
39 See <https://www.defensoriadelclientedeabif.cl/estatutos> accessed 21 June 2024
40 See <https://www.defensoriadelclientedeabif.cl/registrado> accessed 21 June 2024
41 Art. 3 letra i) D.F.L. No. 251

This procedure can be carried out online, in person or by mail.[42] Complaints and requests for a response on securities, insurance, and financial market issues before the Financial Market Commission (FMC)

Anyone can submit complaints to the Financial Market Commission (FMC) and request a response on aspects of the securities insurance and financial market. This enforcement mechanism is a mixed one, as it requires the initial action of the consumer. Any submission made to the Commission is dealt with per its legal powers, and its response time depends mainly on the complexity of the matter raised, the procedures to be carried out, the compilation of background information and/or the technical analysis of the case.

However, this mechanism does not resolve disputes concerning the interpretation, application and performance of the terms and conditions of the contracts, nor the determination and economic quantification of any damage or loss. The Commission's powers are, therefore, limited. The only result of this procedure is an official reply from the Commission with the information collected. This procedure can be carried out online, in person or by mail.[43]

Role of Technology in Consumer ADR: The Online Dispute Resolution for Consumer Disputes

In the Chilean legal system, the role of technology in alternative dispute resolution is very relevant in protecting individual consumer interests. In this field, the so-called "individual complaint" is processed entirely online via the SERNAC website. In addition, on the same website, there is the "I Want to Get Out" (*Me quiero salir*) platform, a tool for consumers to expressly request the termination of any contract with a telecommunications or insurance company. There is also the "Do Not Disturb" ("No Molester") tool, which is also an online ADR mechanism that consists of an anti-spam tool available on SERNAC's website so that consumers can express their wish to be removed from companies' lists in order not to receive promotions and advertising that they do not want.

Some statistics can demonstrate the relevance of such solutions. Thus, according to official data, SERNAC has received more than two million of these complaints by May 2024.[44] In addition, the "I Want to Get Out" ("*Me Quiero Salir*") platform was implemented on 11 June 2020 and received its first evaluation on 31 December of the same year. During those six months alone, SERNAC received more than 39,715 requests to terminate contracts in the telecommunications market. Of the total number of requests, 81.91% were answered favourably by the companies. Hence, more than 32,000 consumers could terminate their contracts expeditiously using this tool.[45] Most recently, in SERNAC's latest balance report, it was established that the service received more than 291,000 "Do Not Disturb"

42 See <https://www.cmfchile.cl/portal/principal/613/w3-article-1246.html> accessed 21 June 2024
43 See <https://www.cmfchile.cl/portal/principal/613/w3-article-666.html> accessed 21 June 2024
44 See <https://www.sernac.cl/portal/604/w3-propertyvalue-66192.html> accessed 21 June 2024
45 See <https://www.sernac.cl/portal/604/w3-article-62177.html> accessed 21 June 2024

and 47,000 "I Want to Get Out" requests, and 628,000 individual complaints, all processed entirely online.[46]

Moreover, it is worth noting that the online complaint procedure is available through SERNAC and the financial market through the CMF. Finally, the importance of technology and its role in ADR is also reflected in the possibility for any supplier to subscribe to the ADR system provided for in the law regarding the SERNAC Seal. The law establishes expressly that "this system may be carried out by electronic means".[47]

Challenges and Opportunities

To analyse the challenges and opportunities of ADR in Chilean consumer law, it is necessary to separate collective interests from individual interests. Regarding collective interests, the PVCs have proven to be an important ADR mechanism. Evidence shows that they operate in very diverse sectors of the economy, such as banks, insurance companies, airlines, the retail sector, etc. This mechanism makes it possible to resolve major consumer problems quickly and comprehensively, but it requires a very active role on the part of suppliers. However, the mechanism has a reactive nature since its design requires an infringement to be activated. The PVC mechanism also faces the challenge of assessing compliance. In fact, since its implementation in our system, no comprehensive analysis of compliance with the agreements has been made to determine their effectiveness.

Regarding the individual interests of consumers, there is much more to improve. There are no institutionalised ADR mechanisms except for the voluntary mediation procedure described previously and the "SERNAC Seal" system. The challenge here is to include a formal ADR mechanism into the CPA about individual consumer complaints and ideally integrate this regulation with the other mediation mechanisms that exist outside of consumer law in order to develop a more friendly and accessible system for the consumer, where settlement should be a real possibility. One step in this direction is the draft legislation that is being discussed in the Chilean Parliament regarding the 'SERNAC protects you' (*Sernac te protege)* bill, which seeks to give the state agency the power to impose administrative sanctions in case of infringement of individual consumer interests, including a number of incentives for the provider to reach an agreement with the consumer before and outside the court, in order to avoid monetary sanctions.

Conclusion

The Chilean legal system has a complex system for enforcing consumer rights. It is possible to identify public, private, and mixed mechanisms that offer different possibilities for protecting consumers' rights. Among these mechanisms, ADRs play a relevant role. The most important of these mechanisms is the voluntary collective

46 See <https://www.sernac.cl/portal/617/articles-52901_recurso_9.pdf> accessed 21 June 2024
47 According to Article 3 g of the Law No. 19.496

procedure (PVC), recently reformed in the CPA. In quantitative and qualitative terms, this mechanism is faster and less costly than the collective legal proceedings, and the results are very similar. However, there is still room for improvement, particularly with regard to the protection of individual interests.

In this sense, the mechanisms for protecting individual interests are not sufficiently developed in the current state of the legislation. For this reason, a reform of the CPA has been proposed in Congress in order to strengthen the enforcement mechanisms of the CPA, especially in the case of individual complaints. The proposal promotes enforcement through various ADR mechanisms, focusing on responsive regulation.[48] The draft also seeks to give SERNAC more powers. In particular, it is proposed that SERNAC should have the prerogative to impose administrative fines on providers. There are high hopes for this proposal in the coming years, as it is a renewed attempt to strengthen the protection of consumer rights. The 2018 reform did not achieve this goal, as the Constitutional Court, in a very controversial decision, ruled that part of the proposed statute was unconstitutional.[49]

References

Aguirrezabal Grünstein M, 'Algunas precisiones en torno a los intereses supraindividuales (colectivos y difusos)' (2006) 33 Revista Chilena de Derecho 69

Aguirrezabal Grünstein M, *Defensa de los consumidores y acceso a la justicia. Un análisis del procedimiento colectivo en la legislación chilena* (2nd edn, Thomson Reuters 2019)

Aguirrezabal Grünstein M, 'La extensión de los efectos de la sentencia dictada en procesos promovidos para la defensa de los intereses colectivos y difusos de consumidores y usuarios: Régimen en la ley chilena de protección al consumidor' (2010) 16 *Ius et Praxis* 99

Contardo González JI, 'Naturaleza jurídica del acuerdo del procedimiento voluntario y su importancia para la extensión de los efectos' in Iñigo de la Maza and JI Contardo (eds) *Estudios de Derecho del Consumidor II* (Rubicon Editores 2021)

Creutzfeldt N, 'An Introduction to Alternative Dispute Resolution (ADR) for Consumers in Europe' in C Cauffman and JM Smits (eds) *The Citizen in European Private Law: Norm-Setting, Enforcement and Choice* (Intersentia 2016)

Franck J, 'Private Enforcement Versus Public Enforcement' in Franz Hofmann and Franziska Kurz (eds) *Law of Remedies: A European Perspective* (Intersentia 2019)

Fuentes Maureira C, 'De la mediación colectiva al procedimiento voluntario colectivo' in Juan Ignacio Contardo, et al. (eds) *Litigación en materia de consumidores. Dogmática y práctica en la reforma de fortalecimiento al SERNAC* (Thomson Reuters 2019)

Momberg R and Morales ME, *Procedimientos Voluntarios Colectivos en el Derecho del Consumo Chile* (Tirant lo Blanch 2022)

Momberg R, Morales ME and Pino-Emhart A, 'Enforcement and Effectiveness of Consumer Law in Chile, A General Overview' in H Micklitzand and G Saumier (eds) *Enforcement and Effectiveness of Consumer Law* (Springer 2018)

48 Bill proposal available at <https://www.camara.cl/legislacion/ProyectosDeLey/tramitacion.aspx?prmID=16826&prmBOLETIN=16271-03>. For more details on the proposal, see <https://www.latercera.com/opinion/noticia/maria-elisa-morales-el-equilibrado-enfoque-responsivo-del-proyecto-sernac-te-protege/6DURFDCYDVEYLEQ3YXQKSBGK34/>

49 See more details in Pablo Soto Delgado, 'La potestad del Sernac para recibir reclamos y promover acuerdos individuales luego de ser eliminada por el Tribunal Constitucional' (2019) 87 *Revista de Derecho* (Concepción) 245

Momberg Uribe R, 'Leyes especiales y aplicación de la Ley Nº 19.496 sobre protección de los derechos de los consumidores. Análisis de casos' in María Elisa Morales and Pamela Mendoza (eds) *Derecho del consumo: Ley, doctrina y jurisprudencia* (Der Ediciones 2019)

Momberg Uribe R and Pino-Emhart A, 'Algunos aspectos relevantes para el ejercicio de acciones indemnizatorias en procedimientos colectivos' in Francisca Barrientos and Lucas del Villar (eds) *Interés general, las negociaciones extrajudiciales y juicios colectivos en el derecho del consumo* (Thomson Reuters 2021)

Morales ME, *Control Preventivo de Cláusulas Abusivas* (Der Ediciones 2018)

Soto Delgado P, 'La potestad del Sernac para recibir reclamos y promover acuerdos individuales luego de ser eliminada por el Tribunal Constitucional' (2019) 87 Revista de Derecho (Concepción) 245

Vargas Pavez M, 'Mecanismos alternativos y consumo. Análisis de la nueva Ley de protección a los derechos de los consumidores' in Juan Ignacio Contardo, et al. (eds) *Litigación en materia de consumidores. Dogmática y práctica en la reforma de fortalecimiento al SERNAC* (Thomson Reuters 2019)

Vargas Viancos JE, 'El rol de las Asociaciones de Consumidores en la litigación de casos de consumo en Chile' in Juan Ignacio Contardo, et al. (eds) *Litigación en materia de consumidores. Dogmática y práctica en la reforma de fortalecimiento al SERNAC* (Thomson Reuters 2019)

6 Consumer ADR in Georgia

Giorgi Amiranashvili

Introduction

Settling consumer disputes out of court holds considerable potential for consumers, retailers and the administration of justice. Access to easy, fair and cost-effective ADR strengthens consumer trust when buying from retailers, particularly online. The less formal and typically conciliatory nature of ADR procedures allows the parties to maintain customer relations even after a dispute.[1]

This chapter aims to explain the alternative mechanisms for resolving consumer disputes in Georgia and to give international readers a general insight into the subject. The chapter begins by presenting the legal framework for consumer protection and the general design of enforcement mechanisms. The second part of this chapter focuses on the Europeanization of consumer ADR. The third part of this chapter draws special attention to consumer arbitration. The fourth part of this chapter deals with the role of technology in consumer alternative dispute resolution. The chapter concludes by making some observations about the country's future development of consumer ADR.

Legal Framework for Consumer Protection

The obligation to protect consumer rights by law was first enshrined in the Constitution of Georgia[2] in 1995 and was reflected in the 1996 Law on Protection of Consumers' Rights. After 16 years, this Law was abolished as the result of the adoption of the Product Safety and Free Movement Code.[3,4] Therefore, to create guarantees

1 Baria Ahmed, *Remote ADR for Georgia: Covid-19 & Beyond* (Baria Ahmed Ltd. May 2020) 27 <https://www.undp.org/sites/g/files/zskgke326/files/migration/ge/UNDP_GE_DG_Remote-ADR-for-Georgia_COVID19-and-beyond---ENG.pdf> accessed 26 March 2024

2 Available in English at <https://matsne.gov.ge/document/view/30346?publication=36> accessed 26 March 2024

3 See in English <https://matsne.gov.ge/en/document/view/1659419?publication=34> accessed 26 March 2024

4 Kety Gujaraidze, Davit Maisuradze, Irakli Shakiashvili, Jaba Gvelebiani, Liana Akhobadze, Ana Khurtsidze, Nata Sturua and Gaioz Japaridze, *Regulatory Impact Assessment of the Draft Law of Georgia on Consumer Rights Protection* (Deutsche Gesellschaft für Internationale Zusammenarbeit (GIZ) December 2019) 7 <https://lawlibrary.info/ge/books/giz2020_ENG_RIA_CRP_LAw.pdf> accessed 26 March 2024

DOI: 10.4324/9781032689739-6

for consumer rights protection and the effective enjoyment of these rights, the necessity of elaborating and adopting an independent normative act emerged again in the sphere of consumer protection.

The necessity of adopting such an act was enhanced by signing the Association Agreement[5] between Georgia and the European Union on 27 June 2014. Under the Association Agreement, Georgia has committed to (gradually, by stipulated time frames) implementing reforms and ensuring progressive approximation of domestic legislation with nearly 300 EU legal acts, including in the sphere of consumer protection.[6] In 2013, the Committee on European Integration of the Parliament began to work on developing a legal framework for consumer protection. By the initiative of the Committee, the Parliament started deliberations on the Draft Law of Georgia on Consumer Rights Protection in July 2015.[7]

Parliamentary elections were held in Georgia in October 2016. In 2017, the new iteration of the Committee renewed work on the Draft Law. By this time, the issue of keeping up with deadlines for commitments set by the Association Agreement was on the agenda. Based on the requirements under the EU regulations and consultation with stakeholders, the committee started a significant revision of the Draft Law. The revised version of the Draft Law, dated July 2018, significantly differed from the previous one.[8] The proposed Draft Law of Georgia on Consumer Rights Protection can be considered an essential step towards establishing a new regulatory framework for consumer protection.[9] The Parliament considered the Draft Law on Protection of Consumer Rights in the third reading and passed it by 79 votes on 29 March 2022.[10]

5 Available in English at <https://eur-lex.europa.eu/legal-content/en/TXT/PDF/?uri=CELEX:22014A0830(02)> accessed 26 March 2024

6 Kety Gujaraidze, Davit Maisuradze, Irakli Shakiashvili, Jaba Gvelebiani, Liana Akhobadze, Ana Khurtsidze, Nata Sturua and Gaioz Japaridze, *Regulatory Impact Assessment of the Draft Law of Georgia on Consumer Rights Protection* (Deutsche Gesellschaft für Internationale Zusammenarbeit (GIZ) December 2019) 8

7 Kety Gujaraidze, Davit Maisuradze, Irakli Shakiashvili, Jaba Gvelebiani, Liana Akhobadze, Ana Khurtsidze, Nata Sturua and Gaioz Japaridze, *Regulatory Impact Assessment of the Draft Law of Georgia on Consumer Rights Protection* (Deutsche Gesellschaft für Internationale Zusammenarbeit (GIZ) December 2019) 8

8 Kety Gujaraidze, Davit Maisuradze, Irakli Shakiashvili, Jaba Gvelebiani, Liana Akhobadze, Ana Khurtsidze, Nata Sturua and Gaioz Japaridze, *Regulatory Impact Assessment of the Draft Law of Georgia on Consumer Rights Protection* (Deutsche Gesellschaft für Internationale Zusammenarbeit (GIZ) December 2019) 9

9 Giorgi Amiranashvili, 'Access to Justice for Consumers in Georgia' in Serkan Kaya (ed) *Access to Justice for Consumers in Emerging Economies (The Case of Georgia, Pakistan, Turkey and the United Arab Emirates)* (Ankara, Adalet Yayınevi 2021) 53 <https://www.academia.edu/64474346/Access_to_Justice_for_Consumers_in_Georgia> accessed 26 March 2024

10 See <https://parliament.ge/en/media/news/parlamentma-momkhmareblis-uflebebis-datsvis-shesakheb-akhali-kanoni-miigho> accessed 26 March 2024

The General Design of the Enforcement Mechanism

According to the law on Consumer Rights Protection, acting till 2012, the Anti-Monopoly Agency was authorised to control the enforcement of consumer protection legislation. Under the existing law, consumers' rights can be protected by being applied to the court. This means that the individual consumer has to go to court and garner the energy and money needed to enforce the rights. Outside the civil code, three ways exist to enforce consumer rights collectively. These rights are derived from the 2012 Law on Product Safety and Free Movement, the Administrative Violations Code and the Criminal Code of Georgia.[11]

The Civil Court examines consumer disputes by the Civil Procedure Code of Georgia. A special procedure for adjudication of consumer disputes does not exist.[12] Analysis of the norms prescribed by the Georgia legislation shows that the way to enforce consumer rights is to address the court. By the subject matter of the case, a consumer has the right to address civil, administrative or criminal courts. Alternative dispute resolution mechanisms could also be used to resolve consumer disputes. The Civil Procedure Code of Georgia envisages the possibility of dispute resolution through court mediation.[13]

Current Consumer Dispute Resolution Processes

On 27 June 2014, Georgia signed the Association Agreement (AA) with the European Union and European Atomic Energy Community and their Member States. The AA fully entered force on 1 July 2016 following the Agreement's ratification. After the agreement entered into force, the parties agreed to the Association's agenda to implement the objectives of the AA. The first Association agenda was adopted in November 2017 and covered 2017 through 2020. In August 2022, the Association's counsel adopted a new Association agenda, which sets new priorities from 2021 through 2027.[14]

One of the priority areas under the Association's agenda for 2021–2027 is "Democracy, Human Rights and Good Governance". In this area, in the justice

11 Kety Gujaraidze, Davit Maisuradze, Irakli Shakiashvili, Jaba Gvelebiani, Liana Akhobadze, Ana Khurtsidze, Nata Sturua and Gaioz Japaridze, *Regulatory Impact Assessment of the Draft Law of Georgia on Consumer Rights Protection* (Deutsche Gesellschaft für Internationale Zusammenarbeit (GIZ) December 2019) 114

12 Kety Gujaraidze, Davit Maisuradze, Irakli Shakiashvili, Jaba Gvelebiani, Liana Akhobadze, Ana Khurtsidze, Nata Sturua and Gaioz Japaridze, *Regulatory Impact Assessment of the Draft Law of Georgia on Consumer Rights Protection* (Deutsche Gesellschaft für Internationale Zusammenarbeit (GIZ) December 2019) 114

13 Kety Gujaraidze, Davit Maisuradze, Irakli Shakiashvili, Jaba Gvelebiani, Liana Akhobadze, Ana Khurtsidze, Nata Sturua and Gaioz Japaridze, *Regulatory Impact Assessment of the Draft Law of Georgia on Consumer Rights Protection* (Deutsche Gesellschaft für Internationale Zusammenarbeit (GIZ) December 2019) 119

14 Mariam Gotsiridze, Beka Injia and Lela Basilaia, *Qualitative Study in Arbitration in Georgia* (Georgian Association of Arbitrators, The USAID Economic Governance Program Grant: Diversifying Training Portfolio of Georgian Association of Arbitrators, USAID, GAA 2023) 28 <https://gaa.ge/wp-content/uploads/2024/03/Qualitative-Study-in-Arbitration-_ENG.pdf> accessed 26 March 2024

sector, one of the priorities set by the Association agenda concerns ADR and is defined as follows: "Enhance the use and quality of mediation; address deficiencies in consumer arbitration and create conditions for increasing the use of business-to-business arbitration".[15]

The Association's agenda does not provide any further details as to the deficiencies of consumer arbitration or the measures to address them. Notably, the previous Association agendas did not offer such a specific commitment concerning consumer or general arbitration. The Association agenda of 2017–2020 was more general in prioritising "Introduce fair and efficient, and more widely used, alternative means of dispute settlement".[16]

It should also be noted that consumer protection is a stand-alone priority in the economic and sectoral cooperation of the Association agenda for 2021–2027.[17] In light of this, consumer protection, including through the resolution of "deficiencies in consumer arbitration", is a priority under the current Association agenda. Georgia must implement the necessary measures to achieve this priority.[18]

Alternative Dispute Resolution for Consumer Disputes

Overview

On 29 March 2022, Georgia adopted law on the protection of consumer rights.[19] Consumer law clearly defines trader and consumer, and commercial relationships covered by the law. While providing detailed regulation of administrative mechanisms to protect consumer rights (the procedure before the Competition Agency), consumer law heavily overlooks the issue of formal dispute settlement, including consumer arbitration. Arbitration is mentioned only twice in consumer law.[20]

15 Mariam Gotsiridze, Beka Injia and Lela Basilaia, *Qualitative Study in Arbitration in Georgia* (Georgian Association of Arbitrators, The USAID Economic Governance Program Grant: Diversifying Training Portfolio of Georgian Association of Arbitrators, USAID, GAA 2023) 28 <https://gaa.ge/wp-content/uploads/2024/03/Qualitative-Study-in-Arbitration-_ENG.pdf> accessed 26 March 2024

16 Mariam Gotsiridze, Beka Injia and Lela Basilaia, *Qualitative Study in Arbitration in Georgia* (Georgian Association of Arbitrators, The USAID Economic Governance Program Grant: Diversifying Training Portfolio of Georgian Association of Arbitrators, USAID, GAA 2023) 28 <https://gaa.ge/wp-content/uploads/2024/03/Qualitative-Study-in-Arbitration-_ENG.pdf> accessed 26 March 2024

17 Mariam Gotsiridze, Beka Injia and Lela Basilaia, *Qualitative Study in Arbitration in Georgia* (Georgian Association of Arbitrators, The USAID Economic Governance Program Grant: Diversifying Training Portfolio of Georgian Association of Arbitrators, USAID, GAA 2023) 28 <https://gaa.ge/wp-content/uploads/2024/03/Qualitative-Study-in-Arbitration-_ENG.pdf> accessed 26 March 2024

18 Mariam Gotsiridze, Beka Injia and Lela Basilaia, *Qualitative Study in Arbitration in Georgia* (Georgian Association of Arbitrators, The USAID Economic Governance Program Grant: Diversifying Training Portfolio of Georgian Association of Arbitrators, USAID, GAA 2023) 28 <https://gaa.ge/wp-content/uploads/2024/03/Qualitative-Study-in-Arbitration-_ENG.pdf> accessed 26 March 2024

19 See in English <https://matsne.gov.ge/en/document/view/5420598?publication=0> accessed 26 March 2024

20 Mariam Gotsiridze, Beka Injia and Lela Basilaia, *Qualitative Study in Arbitration in Georgia* (Georgian Association of Arbitrators, The USAID Economic Governance Program Grant: Diversifying Training Portfolio of Georgian Association of Arbitrators, USAID, GAA 2023) 12–13

As per Article 28 (Mechanisms for the Protection of Consumer Rights), in the case of a violation of this law, a consumer shall have the right to apply to the legal entity under public law called the Georgian National Competition Agency or an authorised body governing the relevant field. The right provided for by the previous paragraph shall not deprive a consumer of the right to apply to a court or for arbitration and/or to resolve a dispute through mediation.

According to Article 37 (Participation of Non-Entrepreneurial (Non-Commercial) Legal Entities in the Protection of Consumer Rights) of the same law, non-entrepreneurial (non-commercial) legal entities shall be entitled to participate in the protection of consumer rights, in particular in the development and implementation of the policy of the protection of consumer rights, including to facilitate the resolution of a dispute through mediation.

The yardstick against which the Georgian Draft Law on Consumer Protection is measured is taken from a Model Law developed within the ZAP project. Later, the European Union adopted Directive 2013/11 on Alternative Dispute Resolution and Regulation 524/2013 on Online Dispute Resolution, establishing a new layer for dispute resolution outside courts. Correspondingly, these legislative measures are not respected in the Model Law.[21] Referring to the preamble of the AA and its objectives, where it is spelt out that new developments have to be taken into consideration, those directives and regulations not contained in the Annex of the AA, but some experts advising implementation include the Directive 2013/11 and the Regulation 524/2013.[22]

ADR for the Postal Service Customers

Draft Law on Post has been prepared and introduced to the government of Georgia in 2019. According to the Draft Law on Post, some functions will be granted and allocated to the Georgian National Communication Commission (GNCC). After adopting the law, postal operators should ensure the effectiveness of the dispute resolution mechanism. They can use and offer mediation as an alternative to customer dispute solution tools.[23]

21 Hans-W Micklitz, *Legal Opinion on the Draft Law of Georgia on the Protection of Consumer Rights (per March 2017)*, No. 6 (2018) (Deutsche Gesellschaft für Internationale Zusammenarbeit (GIZ) 2017) 9–11 <https://lawlibrary.info/ge/books/2018GIZ-GE-Comparative-Research-Consumer_Law.pdf.pdf> accessed 26 March 2024

22 Hans-W Micklitz, *Legal Opinion on the Draft Law of Georgia on the Protection of Consumer Rights (per March 2017)*, No. 6 (2018) (Deutsche Gesellschaft für Internationale Zusammenarbeit (GIZ) 2017) 43 <https://lawlibrary.info/ge/books/2018GIZ-GE-Comparative-Research-Consumer_Law.pdf.pdf> accessed 26 March 2024

23 *EU4Digital: Supporting Digital Economy and Society in the Eastern Partnership, eCommerce Report, Recommendations Proposed for eCommerce Environment Harmonisation in the EaP Countries: Georgia* (15 January 2021) 48–49 <https://eufordigital.eu/wp-content/uploads/2021/04/eCommerce-report-%E2%80%93-Recommendations-proposed-for-eCommerce-environment-harmonisation-in-the-EaP-countries-Georgia.pdf> accessed 26 March 2024

Consumer ADR for the Asylum Seekers and Refugees in Georgia

The law of Georgia on the activities of commercial banks gives commercial banks the right to refuse to open accounts or provide services without justification. Commercial banks invoke this article when they refuse to open accounts or offer asylum seekers and refugees other services.[24] The question is whether there is a need for amendments in the legislation to give access to the bank accounts to everyone lawfully resident in Georgia, including asylum seekers and refugees. That would interfere with contractual freedom, but such interference could be justified. For instance, the European Union adopted this approach by adopting the so-called Payment Accounts Directive (PAD).[25]

PAD requires that credit institutions immediately inform the consumer of the refusal and of the specific reason for that refusal, in writing and free of charge unless such disclosure would be contrary to objectives of national security, public policy or Anti-Money Laundering/Countering the Financing of Terrorism (AML/CFT) legislation. In the event of refusal, the credit institution must advise the consumer of the procedure to submit a complaint against the refusal and of the consumer's right to contact the relevant competent authority and designated alternative dispute resolution body and provide the appropriate contact details.[26]

Applying the approach that the European Union chose by adopting PAD could somewhat solve the problems of the unbanked population in Georgia. According to the Association Agreement, PAD is not on the list of the directives that Georgia has to implement. However, it is related to the approximation of Georgian legislation with Payment Services Directive 2 (PSD 2). Based on the information received from the National Bank of Georgia (NBG), Georgian legislation is planned to be harmonised with specific provisions of PAD voluntarily. Nevertheless, it has to be seen what particular articles will be implemented. Besides, a new alternative dispute resolution body is planned to be set up at the NBG to handle consumers' complaints about the violation of payment services legislation.[27]

24 Natia Gvazava, *Access to Financial Services for Asylum Seekers and Refugees in Georgia* (UNHCR Georgia 2023) 6 <https://help.unhcr.org/georgia/wp-content/uploads/sites/47/2023/07/Access-to-Financial-Services-for-Asylum-Seekers-and-Refugees-in-Georgia.pdf> accessed 26 March 2024

25 Natia Gvazava, *Access to Financial Services for Asylum Seekers and Refugees in Georgia* (UNHCR Georgia 2023) 6 <https://help.unhcr.org/georgia/wp-content/uploads/sites/47/2023/07/Access-to-Financial-Services-for-Asylum-Seekers-and-Refugees-in-Georgia.pdf> accessed 26 March 2024

26 Natia Gvazava, *Access to Financial Services for Asylum Seekers and Refugees in Georgia* (UNHCR Georgia 2023) 7 <https://help.unhcr.org/georgia/wp-content/uploads/sites/47/2023/07/Access-to-Financial-Services-for-Asylum-Seekers-and-Refugees-in-Georgia.pdf> accessed 26 March 2024

27 Natia Gvazava, *Access to Financial Services for Asylum Seekers and Refugees in Georgia* (UNHCR Georgia 2023) 8 <https://help.unhcr.org/georgia/wp-content/uploads/sites/47/2023/07/Access-to-Financial-Services-for-Asylum-Seekers-and-Refugees-in-Georgia.pdf> accessed 26 March 2024

By approximating Georgian legislation with PAD and PSD2 provisions, the legal situation of asylum seekers and refugees in Georgia will improve in several ways. If they are refused access to the payment account, the specific reasons for rejection (with the exception related to AML/CFT regulations and national security) will be explained, and they will be advised about the procedure for submitting complaints. A dispute resolution body will handle their complaints at the NBG. It will allow them to settle disputes more rapidly and inexpensively than by referring to courts.[28]

The Path Towards Harmonisation

The EU4Digital Facility prepared the recommendations for harmonising e-commerce among the Eastern partner countries and with the EU. The overall objective of the report is to provide recommendations to harmonise e-commerce among the Eastern partner countries (in particular, Georgia) and the European Union in three areas: ecosystem, legal framework and standards.[29] Recommendations regarding e-commerce legislation and standards frameworks are the following: i) Improve online alternative dispute resolution mechanism (out-of-court resolution for domestic and cross-border) and transparency in case of security incidents (communication of incidents, complaints handling principles). ii) Assure the maximum level of consumer support in disputes and security incidents.[30]

According to the analysis of legislation concerning ADR and ODR for consumer disputes, both laws (the Law of Georgia on Arbitration and the Law of Georgia on Mediation) require explicit agreement of the parties on the arbitration or the mediation as the dispute resolution mechanism. The legislation does not stipulate that consumers can voluntarily submit complaints against traders to entities offering alternative dispute resolution procedures. It does not establish harmonised quality requirements for ADR entities and ADR procedures. Besides, the law of Georgia on arbitration allows arbitration to hear private law disputes. Consumer disputes are not excluded from the scope of arbitration. As for online dispute resolution, Article 6(1) allows the arbitration to be held in any form as the parties agree. The legislation does not define rules for establishing online dispute resolution platform(s).[31]

28 Natia Gvazava, *Access to Financial Services for Asylum Seekers and Refugees in Georgia* (UNHCR Georgia 2023) 8 <https://help.unhcr.org/georgia/wp-content/uploads/sites/47/2023/07/Access-to-Financial-Services-for-Asylum-Seekers-and-Refugees-in-Georgia.pdf> accessed 26 March 2024

29 *EU4Digital: Supporting Digital Economy and Society in the Eastern Partnership, eCommerce Report, Recommendations Proposed for eCommerce Environment Harmonisation in the EaP Countries: Georgia* (15 January 2021) 3, 5

30 *EU4Digital: Supporting Digital Economy and Society in the Eastern Partnership, eCommerce Report, Recommendations Proposed for eCommerce Environment Harmonisation in the EaP Countries: Georgia* (15 January 2021) 6

31 *EU4Digital: Supporting Digital Economy and Society in the Eastern Partnership, eCommerce Report, Recommendations Proposed for eCommerce Environment Harmonisation in the EaP Countries: Georgia* (15 January 2021) 34

Thus, the availability of procedures for the out-of-court resolution of domestic and cross-border disputes concerning contractual obligations (ADR) is partially compatible as consumer's rights to complain and requirements for ADR aren't specified. Similarly, the availability of an online dispute resolution platform for consumer disputes (ADR) is partially compatible, as rules to establish ADR aren't specified.[32] To ensure the maximum level of consumer support in case of disputes and security incidents, it is recommended that the required conditions be set up to ensure e-commerce customer service by creating an online alternative dispute resolution mechanism and ensuring transparency in case of serious security incidents.[33]

Besides, in order to assure the availability of online procedures for the out-of-court resolution of domestic and cross-border disputes concerning e-commerce contractual obligations, the recommended actions are: i) To create a national legal framework of alternative dispute resolution (ADR) for consumer disputes supporting e-commerce by: Introducing alternative dispute resolution (ADR) means that allow settling a complaint out of court with the assistance of an impartial dispute resolution body; Establishing harmonised quality requirements for ADR entities and ADR procedures in order to ensure that consumers have access to high-quality, transparent, effective and fair out-of-court redress mechanisms to provide a higher level of consumer protection; introducing the type of ADR such as conciliation, ombudsmen, arbitration and complaints boards; laying down rules for online dispute resolution platform for consumer disputes facilitating the independent, impartial, transparent, adequate, fast and fair out-of-court resolution of disputes between consumers and traders online. ii) To create a mechanism for handling complaints by providers of e-commerce platforms and intermediation services by introducing a requirement for providers of online intermediation services to provide an internal system for handling complaints.[34]

Consumer Arbitration in Georgia

Consumer Arbitration According to the Law of Georgia on Arbitration

On 19 June 2009, Georgia adopted law on arbitration,[35] replacing the old, outdated law on private arbitration of 17 April 1997. The law on arbitration is based on

32 *EU4Digital: Supporting Digital Economy and Society in the Eastern Partnership, eCommerce Report, Recommendations Proposed for eCommerce Environment Harmonisation in the EaP Countries: Georgia* (15 January 2021) 60

33 *EU4Digital: Supporting Digital Economy and Society in the Eastern Partnership, eCommerce Report, Recommendations Proposed for eCommerce Environment Harmonisation in the EaP Countries: Georgia* (15 January 2021) 80

34 *EU4Digital: Supporting Digital Economy and Society in the Eastern Partnership, eCommerce Report, Recommendations Proposed for eCommerce Environment Harmonisation in the EaP Countries: Georgia* (15 January 2021) 81

35 See in English <https://matsne.gov.ge/en/document/view/89284?publication=8> accessed 26 March 2024

the Model Law on International Commercial Arbitration, designed by the United Nations Commission on International Trade Law (UNCITRAL).[36]

The law on arbitration does not differentiate between commercial and specialised arbitrations, including consumer arbitration. Thus, arbitration can resolve consumer disputes if they are arbitrable under the law. Consequently, all matters concerning consumer arbitration are to be dealt with in case of any commercial business-to-business arbitrations, including requirements to an arbitration clause, arbitration procedure, and recognition and enforcement of outcomes of such arbitration. One notable and important exception that would apply to the majority of consumer arbitration clauses concerns a specific form requirement for arbitration agreements. No other specific requirements in the law on arbitration could apply to consumer arbitration.[37]

The law of Georgia on arbitration makes pre-dispute and post-dispute arbitration agreements generally enforceable in all contracts, including contracts between businesses and consumers.[38] According to recent studies, the general legal framework in arbitration in Georgia is robust and does not require any significant reforms on a legislative basis.[39] However, this does not exclude the need for legislative reform and regulation about consumer arbitration expressly.[40]

The Peculiarities of Consumer Arbitration in Georgia

(i) Consumer Arbitration

Most cases resolved through arbitration in Georgia pertain to consumer relations. Most consumer-related cases arise primarily from financial transactions (loan disputes). A significant part of financial institutions' caseload is consumer-related. In almost all cases, the claimant is a trader; the consumer rarely or practically never initiates arbitration. There are several matters brought by consumers that yield essential decisions for protecting consumer rights, for example, in financial or insurance services.[41]

36 Mariam Gotsiridze, Beka Injia and Lela Basilaia, *Qualitative Study in Arbitration in Georgia* (Georgian Association of Arbitrators, The USAID Economic Governance Program Grant: Diversifying Training Portfolio of Georgian Association of Arbitrators, USAID, GAA 2023) 12

37 Mariam Gotsiridze, Beka Injia and Lela Basilaia, *Qualitative Study in Arbitration in Georgia* (Georgian Association of Arbitrators, The USAID Economic Governance Program Grant: Diversifying Training Portfolio of Georgian Association of Arbitrators, USAID, GAA 2023) 12

38 Christopher R Drahozal, *Models for Regulating Consumer Arbitration in Georgia* (EU, UNDP December 2021) 3

39 Mariam Gotsiridze, Beka Injia and Lela Basilaia, *Qualitative Study in Arbitration in Georgia* (Georgian Association of Arbitrators, The USAID Economic Governance Program Grant: Diversifying Training Portfolio of Georgian Association of Arbitrators, USAID, GAA 2023) 12

40 Mariam Gotsiridze, Beka Injia and Lela Basilaia, *Qualitative Study in Arbitration in Georgia* (Georgian Association of Arbitrators, The USAID Economic Governance Program Grant: Diversifying Training Portfolio of Georgian Association of Arbitrators, USAID, GAA 2023) 12

41 Mariam Gotsiridze, Beka Injia and Lela Basilaia, *Qualitative Study in Arbitration in Georgia* (Georgian Association of Arbitrators, The USAID Economic Governance Program Grant: Diversifying Training Portfolio of Georgian Association of Arbitrators, USAID, GAA 2023) 16

Some recent studies have revealed certain interesting circumstances reflecting current consumer arbitration trends. The practice of using arbitration as a dispute settlement mechanism varies among institutions. Two central banks changed their policy some seven to eight years ago and refused to put arbitration in their dispute settlement clauses. Other banks and microfinance organisations continue to use arbitration. Among other businesses providing consumer goods and services, none of the major online stores offer arbitration in their contracts.[42]

A sole arbitrator handles the majority of consumer arbitration cases. A three-member tribunal is rarely established on consumer disputes. It is also interesting that in the vast majority of matters, parties do not participate in the appointment of arbitrators. Most institutes administering consumer arbitrations recognise party agreement on the appointment of an arbitrator; however, in the absence of relevant agreement of the parties in the arbitration clause, institutional bodies will directly choose the sole arbitrator for the parties. In the majority of cases, the parties are not represented by counsel. Counsel would appear on behalf of the trader, while the consumer would not be represented by counsel or other representation in most cases.[43]

Arbitral institutes dealing predominantly with consumer arbitration cases are mostly profit-making legal entities. These institutes do not differentiate between consumer arbitration and business-to-business disputes and administer consumer arbitration matters under the same rules and procedure as for any other commercial case. However, it should be mentioned that some institutes have different regulations for small disputes, which encompass most consumer-related matters.[44]

Consumers have limited awareness and access to information about these institutes, procedures and practices. While most of these institutes run a website and display their arbitration rules therein, they do not provide separate rules of procedure or guidelines or other explanatory documents providing additional information on consumer arbitration in an easily understandable manner for consumers who are not trained lawyers.[45] In Georgia, an arbitration clause in a consumer agreement is a standard contract term prepared in advance by the trader, not negotiated with consumers. Consumers mostly do not have any information or knowledge about arbitration, and the trader does not provide any information or explanation about arbitration, the procedure or the consequences of consent to arbitration.[46]

42 Mariam Gotsiridze, Beka Injia and Lela Basilaia, *Qualitative Study in Arbitration in Georgia* (Georgian Association of Arbitrators, The USAID Economic Governance Program Grant: Diversifying Training Portfolio of Georgian Association of Arbitrators, USAID, GAA 2023) 16–17

43 Mariam Gotsiridze, Beka Injia and Lela Basilaia, *Qualitative Study in Arbitration in Georgia* (Georgian Association of Arbitrators, The USAID Economic Governance Program Grant: Diversifying Training Portfolio of Georgian Association of Arbitrators, USAID, GAA 2023) 18

44 Mariam Gotsiridze, Beka Injia and Lela Basilaia, *Qualitative Study in Arbitration in Georgia* (Georgian Association of Arbitrators, The USAID Economic Governance Program Grant: Diversifying Training Portfolio of Georgian Association of Arbitrators, USAID, GAA 2023) 18–19

45 Mariam Gotsiridze, Beka Injia and Lela Basilaia, *Qualitative Study in Arbitration in Georgia* (Georgian Association of Arbitrators, The USAID Economic Governance Program Grant: Diversifying Training Portfolio of Georgian Association of Arbitrators, USAID, GAA 2023) 19

46 Mariam Gotsiridze, Beka Injia and Lela Basilaia, *Qualitative Study in Arbitration in Georgia* (Georgian Association of Arbitrators, The USAID Economic Governance Program Grant: Diversifying Training Portfolio of Georgian Association of Arbitrators, USAID, GAA 2023) 20

The separate court statistics on consumer arbitration are not available. The decisions dealt with the award rendered on consumer arbitration matters arising out of loan and credit line agreements, loan guarantee agreements and, in one case, brokerage agreements.[47] In general, the court does not consider a challenge to the arbitration clause, arbitration procedure or the notice thereto from the consumer's perspective as a weaker party with low bargaining power and limited awareness of arbitration as a dispute settlement mechanism.[48]

The awareness and knowledge of arbitration are deficient among ordinary citizens, i.e., among potential or actual consumers. Consumers do not have a sufficient understanding of arbitration as a dispute settlement mechanism, its application and the consequences of its use, nor are they informed in any form or at any stage by traders or other relevant stakeholders or institutions to enable their active and informed participation in the process. The awareness of arbitration and its potential benefits is so low among consumers that there are only a handful of cases in hundreds of consumer matters resolved through arbitration, where consumers use the system to defend their rights. As mentioned above, most arbitration matters in Georgia are consumer-related. Thus, despite many challenges, arbitration plays a central role in consumer dispute settlement.[49]

Consumer arbitration can play an essential role in effectively resolving consumer disputes. In a highly overloaded court system, when the resolution of even the most straightforward legal matters might take months or even several years, arbitration can be a simple, faster and cheaper alternative. This could be achieved through the will, proper regulation and organisation of the process.[50]

The court delays in handling the simplest and the most straightforward procedure of recognising and enforcing arbitral awards are beyond unreasonable. This is a severe discouragement to users who want to use arbitration in consumer disputes. The arbitration system is highly underused by consumers as parties to the dispute. There are only a handful of known cases where consumers have launched arbitration against the trader. In all other cases initiated by a trader, the consumer either does not participate or is involved without proper representation against the experienced in-house counsel of the trader and, sometimes, even highly paid professional counsel engaged by the latter. The measures to reform the system should be directed at eliminating these

47 Mariam Gotsiridze, Beka Injia and Lela Basilaia, *Qualitative Study in Arbitration in Georgia* (Georgian Association of Arbitrators, The USAID Economic Governance Program Grant: Diversifying Training Portfolio of Georgian Association of Arbitrators, USAID, GAA 2023) 21–22

48 Mariam Gotsiridze, Beka Injia and Lela Basilaia, *Qualitative Study in Arbitration in Georgia* (Georgian Association of Arbitrators, The USAID Economic Governance Program Grant: Diversifying Training Portfolio of Georgian Association of Arbitrators, USAID, GAA 2023) 23

49 Mariam Gotsiridze, Beka Injia and Lela Basilaia, *Qualitative Study in Arbitration in Georgia* (Georgian Association of Arbitrators, The USAID Economic Governance Program Grant: Diversifying Training Portfolio of Georgian Association of Arbitrators, USAID, GAA 2023) 34

50 Mariam Gotsiridze, Beka Injia and Lela Basilaia, *Qualitative Study in Arbitration in Georgia* (Georgian Association of Arbitrators, The USAID Economic Governance Program Grant: Diversifying Training Portfolio of Georgian Association of Arbitrators, USAID, GAA 2023) 34–35

obstacles and creating an enabling environment for consumers to benefit from the system.[51]

(ii) Current Challenges and Future Prospects of Consumer Arbitration

The strong general legal framework is insufficient for developing consumer arbitration in Georgia. It faces serious challenges that cannot be resolved without intervention on multiple fronts, including legislative and regulatory reform in the field. The poor practices developed on consumer arbitration matters, which appear to be the vast majority of cases in the entire arbitration practice in Georgia, have a negative spillover effect on commercial arbitration that threatens the trust and reputation of this most favoured dispute resolution mechanism among businesses. Consumer arbitration should be distinguished from commercial arbitration and subjected to additional requirements.[52]

The reform of consumer arbitration should entail legislative and regulatory intervention as well as a concerted effort from various stakeholders and institutions to ensure higher awareness among consumers, access to relevant information and an enabling environment for the consumers to become users of the system themselves; the system of consumer dispute settlement/arbitration shall further guarantee the access to justice and protection of minimum requirements of fairness and due process for the consumers.[53]

The lack of bargaining power and capacity to make an informed decision disrupts the balance between the rights of the consumer and trader and makes consumer arbitration clauses unfair. The problem would be resolved if consumers were allowed to make informed decisions and certain fairness requirements were guaranteed in the arbitration clause. One way to ensure the consumer's informed consent is to provide arbitration clauses in a separate document. This way, the arbitration clause is no longer a mystical phrase in small letters in the standard provisions that no one pays attention to. This is a separate stand-alone document that catches the eye and invites separate revisions by the consumer.[54]

The level of awareness of arbitration among consumers is very low in Georgia; consumers are not provided with relevant information during contract negotiation or later in the arbitration process by all pertinent stakeholders. Access to

51 Mariam Gotsiridze, Beka Injia and Lela Basilaia, *Qualitative Study in Arbitration in Georgia* (Georgian Association of Arbitrators, The USAID Economic Governance Program Grant: Diversifying Training Portfolio of Georgian Association of Arbitrators, USAID, GAA 2023) 35

52 Mariam Gotsiridze, Beka Injia and Lela Basilaia, *Qualitative Study in Arbitration in Georgia* (Georgian Association of Arbitrators, The USAID Economic Governance Program Grant: Diversifying Training Portfolio of Georgian Association of Arbitrators, USAID, GAA 2023) 36

53 Mariam Gotsiridze, Beka Injia and Lela Basilaia, *Qualitative Study in Arbitration in Georgia* (Georgian Association of Arbitrators, The USAID Economic Governance Program Grant: Diversifying Training Portfolio of Georgian Association of Arbitrators, USAID, GAA 2023) 37

54 Mariam Gotsiridze, Beka Injia and Lela Basilaia, *Qualitative Study in Arbitration in Georgia* (Georgian Association of Arbitrators, The USAID Economic Governance Program Grant: Diversifying Training Portfolio of Georgian Association of Arbitrators, USAID, GAA 2023) 38

information is also problematic as traders, appropriate agencies, or arbitral institutes do not make sufficient information available to the consumer (through public, online means). In cases of limited available information, the access thereto is hindered by technical difficulties (the websites are not operational, there are no clear channels of communications for enquiries, information is not provided in a format and language that would be understandable for consumers, etc.).[55]

The availability of relevant information for consumers is key for the legitimate and effective use of arbitration in consumer relationships. Access to information shall be ensured at multiple levels; not only traders (businesses, financial institutions) but also other agencies and institutions, such as arbitral institutes, consumer protection agencies and other administrative structures dealing with consumer issues, could play an essential role in providing vital information and data to consumers.[56] It is a very positive trend that in Georgia, the majority of consumer arbitration cases are resolved by sole arbitrators, some institutions have separate procedures for small disputes, consumers are allowed to participate in proceedings without counsel, and arbitral institutes seem to generally understand the importance of assisting consumer as the uninformed and underrepresented party in the proceedings.[57]

However, these practices are spontaneous and inconsistent, lacking structure and sophistication. For example, while it is a good approach to encourage a sole arbitrator for small disputes such as the majority of consumer cases, some institutes directly appoint arbitrators and exclude the possibility of party agreement to choose a sole arbitrator; moreover, in some institutes, the same arbitrator or a small number of arbitrators deal with all disputes. In most matters, consumers do not participate or are not adequately represented in the proceedings.[58] The consumer arbitration system should be so well organised, with simplified and straightforward rules and procedures, that consumers should not require counsel. Unfortunately, this is not the case in Georgia at the moment, and the lack of proper representation in this situation is probably to the detriment of the consumer's case in the dispute.[59]

It can be observed that there is a generally positive trend of abandoning the malicious practice of using pocket arbitration and the affiliation of traders and arbitral

55 Mariam Gotsiridze, Beka Injia and Lela Basilaia, *Qualitative Study in Arbitration in Georgia* (Georgian Association of Arbitrators, The USAID Economic Governance Program Grant: Diversifying Training Portfolio of Georgian Association of Arbitrators, USAID, GAA 2023) 39

56 Mariam Gotsiridze, Beka Injia and Lela Basilaia, *Qualitative Study in Arbitration in Georgia* (Georgian Association of Arbitrators, The USAID Economic Governance Program Grant: Diversifying Training Portfolio of Georgian Association of Arbitrators, USAID, GAA 2023) 39

57 Mariam Gotsiridze, Beka Injia and Lela Basilaia, *Qualitative Study in Arbitration in Georgia* (Georgian Association of Arbitrators, The USAID Economic Governance Program Grant: Diversifying Training Portfolio of Georgian Association of Arbitrators, USAID, GAA 2023) 39

58 Mariam Gotsiridze, Beka Injia and Lela Basilaia, *Qualitative Study in Arbitration in Georgia* (Georgian Association of Arbitrators, The USAID Economic Governance Program Grant: Diversifying Training Portfolio of Georgian Association of Arbitrators, USAID, GAA 2023) 39

59 Mariam Gotsiridze, Beka Injia and Lela Basilaia, *Qualitative Study in Arbitration in Georgia* (Georgian Association of Arbitrators, The USAID Economic Governance Program Grant: Diversifying Training Portfolio of Georgian Association of Arbitrators, USAID, GAA 2023) 39–40

institutes in resolving consumer disputes. There are some concerns, however, that remain and continue to harm the reputation of arbitration. There are still some institutions that offer special arrangements to financial institutions or other traders; in the case of some arbitral institutes, the same individual or a small number of individuals decide all instances by the same trader or group of traders, thereby developing some sense of loyalty to them or perception thereto; there is still a considerable mistrust among consumers towards arbitration as institutions favouring traders' interests, etc.[60]

Georgia could consider developing additional ethical standards and requirements to exclude conflict of interest or any arbitrators or arbitral institutes affiliation with the trader. Arbitral institutes could be asked to establish relevant requirements, procedures and a proper list of arbitrators to ensure independent and impartial resolution of consumer matters. Furthermore, information campaigns could be conducted that would reassure consumers that old malignant practices of consumer arbitration have been abandoned and, thus, increase the legitimacy of and trust towards arbitration among consumers.[61]

Most arbitral institutes do not have special rules or procedures for resolving consumer arbitration matters. Arbitration rules and administrative procedures of these institutions, thus, do not differentiate between consumer arbitration and any other business-to-business disputes. Some institutes provide different procedures or approaches to small disputes based on monetary thresholds. Still, even in these cases, the rules for small disputes are not sophisticated enough and only provide some limited distinction from these institutes' general arbitration rules. Arbitral institutes do not provide sufficient information or assistance to a consumer in the arbitration process to ensure the effective use of arbitration and consumer participation in arbitral proceedings.[62]

Rules of procedure, policy and practice of arbitral institutes in the administration of disputes are vital to ensuring consumers' access to arbitration, providing minimum fair trial guarantees to consumers in arbitral proceedings, and making proceedings efficient and effective for consumer disputes in general. The procedure should be so straightforward that consumers should not require counsel or other representation in arbitration.[63] Georgia could establish a registry of arbitral institutes that would include institutions that comply with the requirements to

60 Mariam Gotsiridze, Beka Injia and Lela Basilaia, *Qualitative Study in Arbitration in Georgia* (Georgian Association of Arbitrators, The USAID Economic Governance Program Grant: Diversifying Training Portfolio of Georgian Association of Arbitrators, USAID, GAA 2023) 40

61 Mariam Gotsiridze, Beka Injia and Lela Basilaia, *Qualitative Study in Arbitration in Georgia* (Georgian Association of Arbitrators, The USAID Economic Governance Program Grant: Diversifying Training Portfolio of Georgian Association of Arbitrators, USAID, GAA 2023) 40

62 Mariam Gotsiridze, Beka Injia and Lela Basilaia, *Qualitative Study in Arbitration in Georgia* (Georgian Association of Arbitrators, The USAID Economic Governance Program Grant: Diversifying Training Portfolio of Georgian Association of Arbitrators, USAID, GAA 2023) 41

63 Mariam Gotsiridze, Beka Injia and Lela Basilaia, *Qualitative Study in Arbitration in Georgia* (Georgian Association of Arbitrators, The USAID Economic Governance Program Grant: Diversifying Training Portfolio of Georgian Association of Arbitrators, USAID, GAA 2023) 41

qualify for resolving consumer arbitration matters. These requirements and standards should be carefully considered to balance the protection of the rights of all parties to consumer relationships and ensure the independent development of arbitration practice and the operation of arbitral institutes in Georgia.[64]

Role of Technology in Consumer ADR: Online Dispute Resolution for Consumer Disputes

Utilising Information and Communications Technology (ICT) to Resolve Consumer Disputes in Georgia

Georgia has no special ODR tribunals for small claims and other minor disputes. There are provisions in the procedural rules for ODR. Georgia has a common court system with special chambers (civil, criminal and administrative) in the Supreme Court and Appellate Courts and special panels in District (City) Courts.[65] Georgian legislation allows for the application of the following ODR techniques in litigation: Online filing systems/platforms for filing statements (such as claims, counterclaims and responses) that are accessible online for the parties. According to the Civil Procedure Code of Georgia, examination of a party or interrogation of a witness may be conducted remotely from another court or administrative body using a telephone, video equipment or other technical means at a judge's discretion. According to the same code, a preliminary first hearing or a phone interview or videoconference with the parties and a phone interview or videoconference with a judge may also be conducted. Parties may choose whether to file claims, counterclaims and responses in electronic form or physical hardcopies. Other documents shall be submitted to the court as hard copies.[66]

Analysis of the norms prescribed by the Georgia legislation shows that the way to enforce consumer rights is to address the court. By the subject matter of the case, a consumer has the right to address civil, administrative or criminal courts. ADR mechanisms could also be used to resolve consumer disputes. The Civil Procedures Code of Georgia envisages the possibility of dispute resolution through court

64 Mariam Gotsiridze, Beka Injia and Lela Basilaia, *Qualitative Study in Arbitration in Georgia* (Georgian Association of Arbitrators, The USAID Economic Governance Program Grant: Diversifying Training Portfolio of Georgian Association of Arbitrators, USAID, GAA 2023) 41

65 Julia Hörnle, Matthew Hewitson and Illia Chernohorenko, *Online Dispute Resolution and Compliance With the Right to a Fair Trial and the Right to an Effective Remedy (Article 6 and 13 of the European Convention of Human Rights), Technical Study on Online Dispute Resolution Mechanisms* (European Committee on Legal Co-operation (CDCJ), CDCJ (2018) 5, Strasbourg 1 August 2018) 24 <https://rm.coe.int/cdcj-technical-study-on-online-dispute-resolution-mechanisms/16809f0079> accessed 26 March 2024

66 Julia Hörnle, Matthew Hewitson and Illia Chernohorenko, *Online Dispute Resolution and Compliance With the Right to a Fair Trial and the Right to an Effective Remedy (Article 6 and 13 of the European Convention of Human Rights), Technical Study on Online Dispute Resolution Mechanisms* (European Committee on Legal Co-operation (CDCJ), CDCJ (2018) 5, Strasbourg 1 August 2018) 24 <https://rm.coe.int/cdcj-technical-study-on-online-dispute-resolution-mechanisms/16809f0079> accessed 26 March 2024

mediation.[67] The National Enforcement Agency uses an electronic communication system with other state institutions and partner companies, but there is no online dispute resolution mechanism for private individuals concerning enforcement. There are no compulsory ADR procedures with *res judicata* effect.[68] Regarding utilising some forms of mediation in Georgia, relative to cost or ease of accessibility, the key will be in diagnosing the need and designing the services, with stakeholder ownership and buy-in to the systems. A pilot court-connected or court-annexed programme could be a good starting point for telephone mediation, which may be suited to low-value civil claims.[69]

Georgia's Readiness to Move to Online Dispute Resolution (ODR) for Consumer Disputes

The decision on the type and form of ODR will require detailed consideration for Georgia, particularly whether the service should form part of an online court service or be offered separately via professional bodies, such as ADR providers, for sector-specific (such as consumers) or low-value disputes.[70] For consumers, particularly in the spirit of the European Union Regulation on ODR, establishing an appropriate ADR service for the management of disputes around the provision of goods and services offers citizens the confidence to shop, facilitating trade and economic growth, with the knowledge that help is at hand should they experience a problem with a purchase.[71] Thus, piloting and trialling an ODR system, or several distinct ODR options and services, seems a timely step forward in light of the country's broader developments in the field of ADR and would keep in line with similar initiatives internationally.[72]

Challenges and Opportunities

Georgia can benefit from the use of ODR in numerous ways. First, the area of commercial activities will increase. More and more businesses or organisations are engaging in the process of ODR. Also, consumers would gain trust in the effective redress mechanism that ODR provides. Developing ODR in Georgia would

67 Kety Gujaraidze, Davit Maisuradze, Irakli Shakiashvili, Jaba Gvelebiani, Liana Akhobadze, Ana Khurtsidze, Nata Sturua and Gaioz Japaridze, *Regulatory Impact Assessment of the Draft Law of Georgia on Consumer Rights Protection* (Deutsche Gesellschaft für Internationale Zusammenarbeit (GIZ) December 2019) 119

68 Julia Hörnle, Matthew Hewitson and Illia Chernohorenko, *Online Dispute Resolution and Compliance with the Right to a Fair Trial and the Right to an Effective Remedy (Article 6 and 13 of the European Convention of Human Rights), Technical Study on Online Dispute Resolution Mechanisms* (European Committee on Legal Co-operation (CDCJ), CDCJ (2018) 5, Strasbourg 1 August 2018) 24

69 Baria Ahmed, *Remote ADR for Georgia: COVID-19 and Beyond* (Baria Ahmed Ltd. May 2020) 34

70 Baria Ahmed, *Remote ADR for Georgia: COVID-19 and Beyond* (Baria Ahmed Ltd. May 2020) 34

71 Baria Ahmed, *Remote ADR for Georgia: COVID-19 and Beyond* (Baria Ahmed Ltd. May 2020) 34

72 Baria Ahmed, *Remote ADR for Georgia: COVID-19 and Beyond* (Baria Ahmed Ltd. May 2020) 35

also increase the chances of attracting more neutral, third-party mediators. ODR obviously would encourage economic development because of the lower expenses compared to the traditional dispute resolution methods. ODR would also motivate developing countries to engage in cross-border international transactions and implement best practices of online dispute resolution. However, de facto use is not enough to fully develop the potential of ODR in Georgia. Virtual ADR continues to expand rather than disappear as the pandemic fades. Several challenges should be taken into consideration while implementing ODR.[73]

The Ministry of Economic Development encourages the communications service sector by simplifying the procedures when consumers bring disputes against operators and forbidding service suspensions in the event of a dispute. Furthermore, consumer's rights to confidentiality are protected. The regulation introduces a simple system of general authorisation instead of an individual license regime, which prevents abuse of powers and recognises principles of technological neutrality with the specific sanctions regime in case of violations.[74]

National regulatory authorities and/or the courts review disputes between end-users and service providers. Based on the Georgian Law on Arbitration, the Arbitration institution could review disputes between end-users and service providers. However, whenever any contractual term between both parties excludes the possibility of an end-user applying to the regulator or the court, such a term is doomed to be considered unlawful and against consumers' interests. Georgian National Regulatory Authority is the body which can provide free legal assistance to consumers via the Ombudsman institution. The balance between a service provider and a consumer at the arbitration institution would not be maintained to such an extent as at the NRA.[75]

Any disputes between communications providers are referred to the Georgian National Communications Commission within its powers. As it implies from the context of the Electronic Communications Law of Georgia, the powers of the regulator cover disputes raised by the failure of negotiations based on the mentioned law. Consumers' complaints, including individual applications, are also addressed by the national telecom regulator. Notably, they have a choice to apply to the communications service provider, the regulator or the court.[76] Besides, consumers have

73 Mariam Skhulukhia, 'Online Dispute Resolution in Georgia: The Benefits and Challenges' (2020) 13(1) *Caucasus Journal of Social Sciences* 98 <https://ug.edu.ge/storage/journals/May2022/I2RAjFfyTPiwt7BtboWd.pdf> accessed 26 March 2024

74 Mariam Skhulukhia, 'Online Dispute Resolution in Georgia: The Benefits and Challenges' (2020) 13(1) *Caucasus Journal of Social Sciences* 100 <https://ug.edu.ge/storage/journals/May2022/I2RAjFfyTPiwt7BtboWd.pdf> accessed 26 March 2024

75 Ekaterine Chakhrakia, *Dispute Resolution in Telecommunication Industry: The Role of National Regulatory Authorities in Settlement of Disputes* (Master Thesis, University of Oslo, Faculty of Law, 1 December 2010) 15–16 <https://www.duo.uio.no/bitstream/handle/10852/22912/EKATERINE_CHAKHRAKIA.pdf?sequence=1> accessed 26 March 2024

76 Ekaterine Chakhrakia, *Dispute Resolution in Telecommunication Industry: The Role of National Regulatory Authorities in Settlement of Disputes* (Master Thesis, University of Oslo, Faculty of

the option to submit applications to the Public Defender of Consumer Interests. The Public Defender investigates the complaint and represents the consumers before the Commission, which adopts the decision after a public hearing.[77] It is not available to settle disputes online. However, it is possible to submit an online complaint to the Public Defender of Consumers Interests, not the Commission.[78] According to a recent report, ensuring effective dispute resolution mechanisms in case of conflict between a consumer and an internet provider is a policy option to enhance consumer rights and choice, for example, by eliminating information asymmetries.[79] As per the study under the Central Asia Regional Economic Cooperation (CAREC), a partnership of 11 countries (including Georgia) and development partners, a potential long-term project is to design a system of online dispute resolution for consumers in the region.[80]

Conclusion

To sum up, this chapter shows that alternative dispute resolution mechanisms are available for resolving consumer disputes in Georgia, and the country has already taken some important steps to provide the possibility of consumer dispute resolution through arbitration or mediation. However, the previous discussion reveals that consumer ADR in Georgia still needs further improvement. The current legislation can be considered an essential step towards establishing the general regulatory framework for consumer ADR in Georgia. However, as already advised by some experts, it is desirable to implement Directive 2013/11 and Regulation 524/2013 as soon as possible to approximate it with EU standards fully. Besides, all recommendations and suggestions shown by recent studies should be considered when developing consumer ADR in the country.

Law, 1 December 2010) 24–25 <https://www.duo.uio.no/bitstream/handle/10852/22912/EKATERINE_CHAKHRAKIA.pdf?sequence=1> accessed 26 March 2024

77 *Complaint Handling and Dispute Settlement Procedures Available to Household Customers*, Status Review – December 2018, MedReg Working Group on Consumers Issues, ECRB Customers and Retail Markets Working Group, MED18–26GA-4.2.1, 17 <https://www.energy-community.org/dam/jcr:fd91de52-1691-4ae7-87a9-6a7ddb37fb68/ECRB-MEDREG_Complaint_Dispute_122018.pdf> accessed 26 March 2024. Thus, the Public Defender is not a decision-making body – it presents a claim to the Commission, and the latter adopts a decision: *Alternative Dispute Resolution in the Energy Community Contracting Parties, Italy and Georgia*, Status Review (The Energy Community Regulatory Board (ECRB) April 2016) 13 <https://energy-community.org/dam/jcr:9a364239-0866-4f2d-ac0d-29f0e22cd1ee/ECRB042016_Alternative.pdf> accessed 26 March 2024

78 *Alternative Dispute Resolution in the Energy Community Contracting Parties, Italy and Georgia*, Status Review (The Energy Community Regulatory Board (ECRB) April 2016) 21

79 *Fostering Business Development and Digitalisation in Georgia* (OECD Publishing, Paris 2022) 81–82 <https://www.oecd.org/eurasia/competitiveness-programme/FosteringBusinessDevelopmentand%20DigitalisationinGeorgia_220513_1025.PDFO.pdf> accessed 26 March 2024

80 *E-Commerce in CAREC Countries: Laws and Policies* (Asian Development Bank August 2021) 55 <https://www.adb.org/sites/default/files/publication/725671/e-commerce-carec-laws-policies.pdf> accessed 26 March 2024

References

Ahmed B, *Remote ADR for Georgia: COVID-19 and Beyond* (Baria Ahmed Ltd. May 2020) <https://www.undp.org/sites/g/files/zskgke326/files/migration/ge/UNDP_GE_DG_Remote-ADR-for-Georgia_COVID19-and-beyond – ENG.pdf> accessed 26 March 2024

Alternative Dispute Resolution in the Energy Community Contracting Parties, Italy and Georgia, Status Review, April 2016, The Energy Community Regulatory Board (ECRB) <https://energy-community.org/dam/jcr:9a364239–0866–4f2d-ac0d-29f0e22cd1ee/ECRB042016_Alternative.pdf> accessed 26 March 2024

Amiranashvili G, 'Access to Justice for Consumers in Georgia' in Serkan Kaya (ed) *Access to Justice for Consumers in Emerging Economies (The Case of Georgia, Pakistan, Turkey and the United Arab Emirates)* (Ankara, Adalet Yayınevi 2021) <https://www.academia.edu/64474346/Access_to_Justice_for_Consumers_in_Georgi> accessed 26 March 2024

Chakhrakia E, *Dispute Resolution in Telecommunication Industry: The Role of National Regulatory Authorities in Settlement of Disputes* (Master Thesis, University of Oslo, Faculty of Law, 1 December 2010) <https://www.duo.uio.no/bitstream/handle/10852/22912/EKATERINE_CHAKHRAKIA.pdf?sequence=1> accessed 26 March 2024

Christopher RD, *Models for Regulating Consumer Arbitration in Georgia* (EU, UNDP December 2021)

Complaint Handling and Dispute Settlement Procedures Available to Household Customers, Status Review – December 2018, MedReg Working Group on Consumers Issues, ECRB Customers and Retail Markets Working Group, MED18–26GA-4.2.1 <https://www.energy-community.org/dam/jcr:fd91de52–1691–4ae7–87a9–6a7ddb37fb68/ECRB-MEDREG_Complaint_Dispute_122018.pdf> accessed 26 March 2024

E-Commerce in CAREC Countries: Laws and Policies (Asian Development Bank August 2021) <https://www.adb.org/sites/default/files/publication/725671/e-commerce-carec-laws-policies.pdf> accessed 26 March 2024

EU4Digital: Supporting Digital Economy and Society in the Eastern Partnership, eCommerce Report, Recommendations Proposed for eCommerce Environment Harmonisation in the EaP Countries: Georgia, 15 January 2021 <https://eufordigital.eu/wp-content/uploads/2021/04/eCommerce-report-%E2%80%93-Recommendations-proposed-for-e Commerce-environment-harmonisation-in-the-EaP-countries-Georgia.pdf> accessed 26 March 2024

Fostering Business Development and Digitalisation in Georgia (OECD Publishing, Paris 2022) <https://www.oecd.org/eurasia/competitiveness-programme/FosteringBusiness-Developmentand%20DigitalisationinGeorgia_220513_1025.PDFO.pdf> accessed 26 March 2024

Gotsiridze M, Injia B and Basilaia L, *Qualitative Study in Arbitration in Georgia*, Georgian Association of Arbitrators, The USAID Economic Governance Program Grant: Diversifying Training Portfolio of Georgian Association of Arbitrators, USAID, GAA, 2023 <https://gaa.ge/wp-content/uploads/2024/03/Qualitative-Study-in-Arbitration-_ENG.pdf> accessed 26 March 2024

Gujaraidze K, Maisuradze D, Shakiashvili I, Gvelebiani J, Akhobadze L, Khurtsidze A, Sturua N and Japaridze G, 'Regulatory Impact Assessment of the Draft Law of Georgia on Consumer Rights Protection, December 2019, Deutsche Gesellschaft für Internationale Zusammenarbeit (GIZ)' <https://lawlibrary.info/ge/books/giz2020_ENG_RIA_CRP_LAw.pdf> accessed 26 March 2024

Gvazava N, *Access to Financial Services for Asylum Seekers and Refugees in Georgia* (UNHCR Georgia 2023) <https://help.unhcr.org/georgia/wp-content/uploads/sites/47/2023/07/Access-to-Financial-Services-for-Asylum-Seekers-and-Refugees-in-Georgia.pdf> accessed 26 March 2024

Hörnle J, Hewitson M and Chernohorenko I, *Online Dispute Resolution and Compliance With the Right to a Fair Trial and the Right to an Effective Remedy (Article 6 and 13 of the European Convention of Human Rights), Technical Study on Online Dispute Resolution Mechanisms*, European Committee on Legal Co-operation (CDCJ), CDCJ (2018) 5, Strasbourg, 1 August 2018 <https://rm.coe.int/cdcj-technical-study-on-online-dispute-resolution-mechanisms/16809f0079> accessed 26 March 2024

Micklitz H-W, *Legal Opinion on the Draft Law of Georgia on the Protection of Consumer Rights (Per March 2017)*, № 6 (2018) (Deutsche Gesellschaft für Internationale Zusammenarbeit (GIZ) 2017) <https://lawlibrary.info/ge/books/2018GIZ-GE-Comparative-Research-Consumer_Law.pdf.pdf> accessed 26 March 2024

Skhulukhia M, 'Online Dispute Resolution in Georgia: The Benefits and Challenges' (2020) 13(1) Caucasus Journal of Social Sciences <https://ug.edu.ge/storage/journals/May2022/I2RAjFfyTPiwt7BtboWd.pdf> accessed 26 March 2024

7 Consumer ADR in China

Yi Lu

Introduction

As one of the largest consumer markets in the world, China has a complex consumer protection system. The Consumer Rights Protection Law (CRPL)[1] of 1994 established the fundamental principles of China's consumer policy. The primary objectives of China's consumer policy are to protect the legitimate rights and interests of consumers, maintain social and economic stability, and facilitate the healthy development of the socialist market economy.[2] On the other hand, given the constraints of the conventional dispute resolution system and the substantial number of disputes, China has endeavoured to enhance the efficacy of alternative dispute resolution (ADR) mechanisms. The development of China's ADR mechanisms has been facilitated by the *Social Co-Governance Strategy*. This strategy is guided by Xi Jinping Thought on Socialism with Chinese Characteristics for a New Era, the rule of law, and the spirit of the 18th and 19th National Congress of the Communist Party of China (CPC/Party). The system is distinguished by the leadership of the Party and implementation by governments based on democratic consultation, social coordination, and public participation, guaranteed by the rule of law and supported by various technologies.[3] The primary objective of ADR is to facilitate amicable consumer dispute resolution.

In commemoration of the 30th anniversary of the CRPL, China issued the Implementation Regulation of the CRPL (IRCRPL) in 2024. The IRCRPL extends the *Social Co-Governance Strategy* to the consumer markets by initiating the *Consumer Protection Co-Governance Strategy*.[4] This represents a novel approach to consumer rights protection in China, which differs from previous strategies insofar as it requires the involvement of all members of society, including both public and

1 Consumer Rights and Interests Protection Law of the People's Republic of China (Amended) (中华人民共和国消费者权益保护法) 2013
2 CRPL, Art. 1
3 'The Reform of Diversified Dispute Resolution Mechanism of China's Courts (2015–2020)' SPC (20 February 2021) <https://www.court.gov.cn/upload/file/2021/02/20/16/19/20210220161916_60128.pdf> accessed 31 October 2024
4 Implementing Regulation for the Law of the People's Republic of China on the Protection of Consumer Rights and Interests (中华人民共和国消费者权益保护法实施条例) 2024 (IRCRPL), Art. 3

DOI: 10.4324/9781032689739-7

private actors. This marks a new precedent in the country's legal history on consumer protection.

In light of the convergence of the *Social Co-Governance System* and the *Consumer Protection Co-Governance Strategy*, as well as the rapid development of ADR mechanisms, there has never been a more opportune moment to conduct a thorough review of consumer ADR in China. As the *Consumer Protection Co-Governance Strategy* is distinguished by the preponderance of public powers, with the CPC leadership preceding government enforcement, consumer ADR under the guidance of this strategy also presents unique Chinese characteristics.

This chapter aims to provide a comprehensive examination featuring Chinese characteristics. The initial step is to analyse the legal framework for consumer protection in China and evaluate its effectiveness. The subsequent section is devoted to an examination of the efficacy of ADR mechanisms in addressing consumer disputes.

The General Design of the Legal Framework

The legal system of China pertaining to consumer protection comprises legal documents, standards, and policy papers. Legal documents are legally binding, while standards provide technical benchmarks for evaluating the conformity of consumer products or services with the law. Policy papers formulated by the CPC or the administration are soft laws that provide guidance to ensure consumer protection. Representative examples of the three categories are provided in Figure 7.1.

Legal Documents

China has established a legal system with the CRPL as its primary authority, relying on other legal documents, including fundamental laws, statutes, administrative

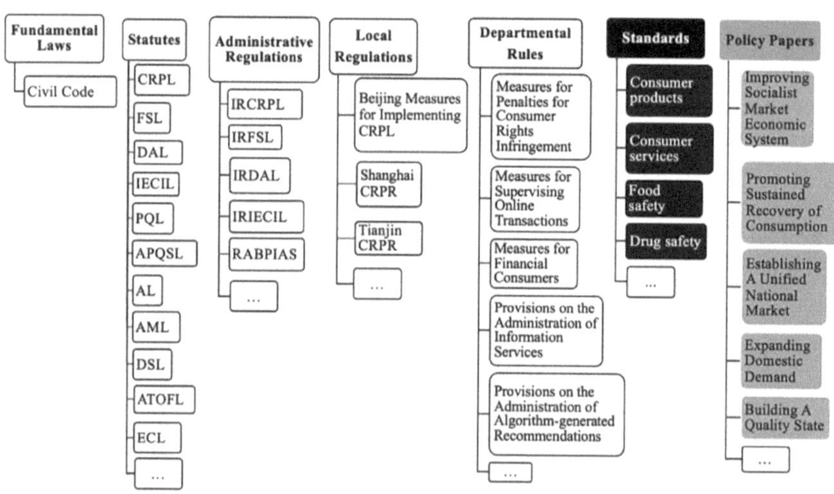

Figure 7.1 China's Legal System on Consumer Protection

regulations, and local regulations. These legal documents are classified in accordance with the general hierarchy prescribed by the Constitution[5] and the Legislation Law.[6] The initial five branches of Figure 7.1 present the pertinent legal documents.

Fundamental Laws

The National People's Congress (NPC), the legislative body, is responsible for enacting and amending the fundamental laws that govern criminal offences, civil affairs, state organs, and other pertinent matters.[7]

- The Civil Code.[8] It establishes the basic legal frameworks governing civil affairs, to safeguard the legitimate rights and interests of civil subjects, regulate civil relations, and maintain the social and economic order. The Civil Code affords protection to consumers, including the rights to life and health, the right to know, the right to choose, the right to fair trade, and the right to information security, among others. In addition, it recognises consumers as a distinct group of people who are also entitled to protection under certain statutes with special provisions.[9]

Statutes

The Standing Committee of the NPC is responsible for enacting and amending laws that fall outside the purview of the NPC itself.[10] The CRPL is included in this category. A list of other pertinent statutes which address specific elements of consumer protection is provided.

- CRPL. The CRPL serves to establish the basic framework of China's consumer protection system and to define the fundamental principles and rules governing the protection of consumer rights and interests.
- Food Safety Law (FSL).[11]
- Drug Administration Law (DAL).[12]
- Import and Export Commodity Inspection Law (IECIL).[13]
- Product Quality Law (PQL).[14]

5 Constitution of the People's Republic of China (Amended in 2018) (中华人民共和国宪法（2018修正）)
6 Legislation Law of the People's Republic of China (Amended in 2023) (中华人民共和国立法法（2023修正）)
7 Constitution, Art. 62; Legislation Law, Art. 10
8 Civil Code of the People's Republic of China (中华人民共和国民法典) 2021
9 Civil Code, Art. 128
10 Constitution, Art. 67; Legislation Law, Art.10
11 Food Safety Law of the People's Republic of China (中华人民共和国食品安全法) 2021
12 Drug Administration Law of the People's Republic of China (中华人民共和国药品管理法) 2019
13 Import and Export Commodity Inspection Law of the People's Republic of China (中华人民共和国进出口商品检验法) 2021
14 Product Quality Law of the People's Republic of China (中华人民共和国产品质量法) 2018

- Agricultural Products Quality and Safety Law (APQSL).[15]
- Advertising Law (AL).[16]
- Anti-Monopoly Law (AML)[17]
- Data Security Law (DSL)[18]
- Anti-Telecom and Online Fraud Law (ATOFL)[19]
- E-commerce Law (ECL)[20]

Administrative Regulations

The State Council, the administrative body, is responsible for enacting administrative regulations to implement laws within the scope of its administrative functions and authority as defined by the Constitution.[21] Selected examples of administrative regulations pertaining to consumer protection are as follows:

- IRCRPL. The IRCRPL, scheduled for implementation on 1 July 2024, is designed to address genuine concerns regarding safeguarding consumer rights and interests. It aims to reinforce the obligations of operators, enrich the duties of consumer organisations, and initially establish the *Consumer Protection Co-Governance System*.
- Implementing Regulation for the FSL (IRFSL).[22]
- Implementing Regulation for the DAL (IRDAL).[23]
- Implementing Regulation for the Import and Export Commodity Inspection Law (IRIECIL).[24]
- Regulations on the Administration of Business Premises of Internet Access Service (RABPIAS).[25]

Local Regulations

In light of their specific conditions and actual needs, local people's congresses or standing committees at the provincial level may formulate local regulations,

15 Agricultural Products Quality and Safety of the People's Republic of China (中华人民共和国农产品质量安全法) 2023
16 Advertising Law of the People's Republic of China (中华人民共和国广告法) 2021
17 Anti-Monopoly Law of the People's Republic of China (中华人民共和国反垄断法) 2022
18 Data Security Law of the People's Republic of China (中华人民共和国数据安全法) 2021
19 Anti-Telecom and Online Fraud Law of the People's Republic of China (中华人民共和国反电信网络诈骗法) 2022
20 E-Commerce Law of the People's Republic of China (中华人民共和国电子商务法) 2019
21 Constitution, Art. 89; Legislation Law, Art. 72
22 Implementing Regulation for the Food Safety Law of the People's Republic of China (中华人民共和国食品安全法实施条例) 2019
23 Implementing Regulation for the Drug Administration Law of the People's Republic of China (中华人民共和国药品管理法实施条例) 2019
24 Implementing Regulation for the Law of the People's Republic of China on Import and Export Commodity Inspection (中华人民共和国进出口商品检验法实施条例) 2022
25 Regulations on the Administration of Business Premises of Internet Access Service (互联网上网服务营业场所管理条例) 2022

provided such regulations do not contradict the Constitution, the laws, or the administrative regulations.[26] For instance, the following cities have formulated local regulations to strengthen consumer protection in their jurisdictions.

- Measures of Beijing Municipality for the Implementation of the CRPL.[27]
- Regulations of Shanghai Municipality on Consumers' Rights and Interests Protection (Shanghai CRPR).[28]
- Tianjin Consumer Rights and Interests Protection Regulation (Tianjin CRPR).[29]

Departmental Rules

Departments within the State Council are permitted to draft departmental regulations implementing laws, administrative regulations, resolutions, and decrees.[30] The following are the representative departmental rules:

- Measures for Penalties for Infringement upon Rights and Interests of Consumers.[31]
- Measures for the Supervision and Administration of Online Transactions.[32]
- Administrative Measures for the Protection of Consumers' Rights and Interests by Banking and Insurance Institutions.[33]
- Provisions on the Administration of Information Services of Mobile Internet Applications (PAISMIA).[34]
- Provisions on the Administration of Algorithm-generated Recommendations for Internet Information Services (PAARIIS).[35]

The Standard System

National standards in consumption-related fields serve as an essential supplement to the detailed implementation of the legal system. They provide operators

26 Constitution, Art. 90; Legislation Law, Art. 80

27 Measures of Beijing Municipality for the Implementation of the CRPL (北京市实施《中华人民共和国消费者权益保护法》办法) 1998

28 Regulations of Shanghai Municipality on Consumers' Rights and Interests Protection (上海市消费者权益保护条例) 2022

29 Tianjin Consumer Rights and Interests Protection Regulation (天津市消费者权益保护条例) 2019

30 Constitution, Art. 100; Legislation Law, Art. 91

31 Measures for Penalties for Infringement upon Rights and Interests of Consumer (侵害消费者权益行为处罚办法) 2020

32 Measures for the Supervision and Administration of Online Transactions (网络交易监督管理办法) 2021

33 Administrative Measures for the Protection of Consumers' Rights and Interests by banking and Insurance Institutions (银行保险机构消费者权益保护管理办法) 2023

34 Provisions on the Administration of Information Services of Mobile Internet Applications (移动互联网应用程序信息服务管理规定) 2022

35 Provisions on the Administration of Algorithm-generated Recommendations for Internet Information Services (互联网信息服务算法推荐管理规定) 2022

with operational specifications and technical standards for the quality of goods and services. Furthermore, they possess the capacity to guide and standardise the high-quality development of the industry and the level of consumer rights protection. China has a comprehensive standard system that can be classified into five categories: national standards, industry standards, local standards, industrial standards, and enterprise standards. National standards may be further divided into two categories: mandatory standards and recommended standards. Industry standards and local standards are recommended standards.[36] Figure 7.2 presents a categorisation of the 262 national consumer protection standards approved by the State Administration for Market Regulation (SAMR) in 2023.

Post-Pandemic National Consumer Policies

The Covid-19 has severely disrupted the consumer market. To mitigate these challenges and reinforce consumer protection, the CPC and state authorities have released a series of policies to advance consumer rights. Although these policy papers are not legally binding, they have identified the direction, path, and principal measures for the protection of consumer rights and interests in the form of soft law.

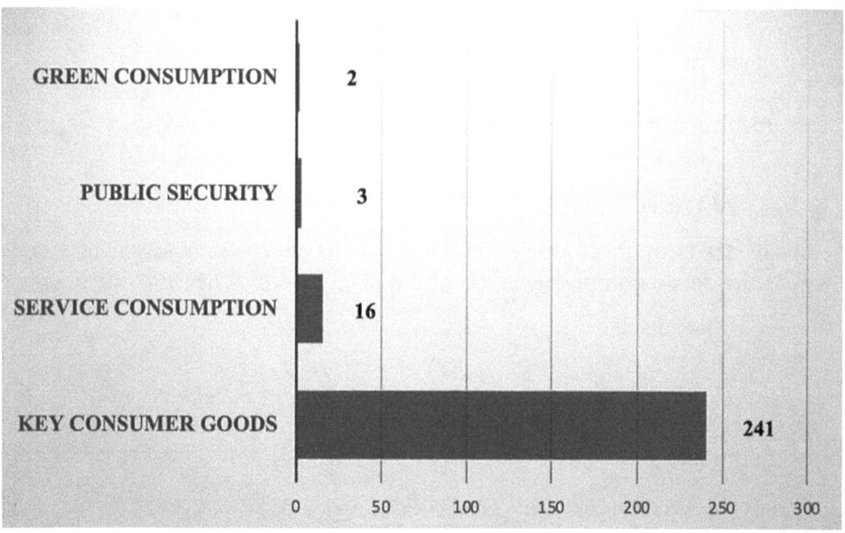

Figure 7.2 SAMR Approved National Standards in 2023[37]

36 Standardisation Law of the People's Republic of China (2017 Revision) (中华人民共和国标准化法(2017修订）) 2018

37 The chart is based on the data presented in the China Consumers Association (CCA) 2023 Annual Report. 'Annual Report on the Protection of Consumer Rights and Interests in China (中国消费者权益保护状况年度报告 (2023))' (27 May 2023) <https://www.cca.org.cn/Detail?catalogId=492862039744581&contentType=article&contentId=551488720109637> accessed 31 October 2024

To Enhance the Socialist Market Economic System

In 2020, the CPC and the State Council sought to enhance the quality and efficiency of commodity and service markets with a particular focus on strengthening consumer rights and interests and exploring the establishment of a class-action lawsuit system.[38]

To Promote the Sustained Recovery of Consumption

In 2022, the State Council issued an opinion that sought to reinforce the protection of consumer rights and interests in the context of the platform economy.[39] First, it will persist in optimising the national 12315 platform and the local 12345 government service hotline and further expand avenues for consumer complaints and reports. Second, the consumer dispute resolution mechanism, including ODR mechanisms and the public interest litigation (PIL) system, will be optimised. Third, it will fully implement the 'compensation before dispute resolution' and guide offline stores on the return of goods without cause.

To Construct a Unified National Market

The CPC and the State Council have resolved to establish a Unified National Market in 2022.[40] This resolution underscores the significance of establishing efficacious consumer complaint and reporting channels, optimising the process of consumer dispute resolution and feedback mechanisms, and establishing linkage mechanisms to protect consumer rights and interests.

To Build a Quality State

In 2023, the CPC and the State Council prioritised the quality and utility of consumer products.[41] They proposed three transformations: from China's manufacturing to China's creation, from China's speed to China's quality, and from China's products to China's brands. Moreover, the outline called for all pertinent departments to enhance product and service quality guarantee and dispute handling procedures and facilitate third-party quality dispute arbitration.

To Expand Domestic Demand

In order to mitigate the impact of the pandemic on the consumer market, the State Council has underscored the importance of strategic planning for expanding

38 Opinions of the Central Committee of the Communist Party of China and the State Council on Accelerating the Improvement of the Socialist Market Economic System in the New Era (中共中央和国务院关于新时代加快完善社会主义市场经济体制的意见) 2020

39 Opinions of the General Office of the State Council on Further Releasing Consumption Potential and Promoting Sustained Recovery of Consumption (国务院办公厅关于进一步释放消费潜力促进消费持续恢复的意见) 2022

40 Opinions of the Central Committee of the Communist Party of China and the State Council on Accelerating the Construction of a Nationally Unified Big Market (中共中央和国务院关于加快建设全国统一大市场的意见) 2022

41 Outline of Building a Quality State (质量强国建设纲要) 2023

domestic demand from 2022 to 2035.[42] In alignment with this directive, the National Development and Reform Commission (NDRC) has delineated specific measures for the recovery and expansion of consumption. These measures emphasise the following aspects:

1) Stabilise Bulk Consumption;
2) Expand Service Consumption;
3) Expand Service Consumption;
4) Promote Consumption in Rural Areas;
5) Expand New Types of Consumption; and
6) Improve Consumption Facilities.

Current Consumer Dispute Resolution Processes

In response to the emergence of new consumption models, the China Consumers Association (CCA) has identified the maintenance of market order, the protection of consumer fairness, and the addressing of the following new consumption issues of societal concern as key elements of consumer protection in the digital economy era.[43]

1) Telecommunications fraud. The ATOFL delineates the obligations of corporations regarding the prevention of telecommunications network fraud.
2) Platform economy. The AML has enhanced the anti-monopoly rules and is conducive to protecting the overall rights and interests of consumers.
3) Protection of the rights and interests of the elderly. The State Council has proposed a five-year plan to enhance consumer rights and protection in relation to older people.[44] This will entail a comprehensive investigation of infringements in the field of consumption of products and services for the elderly, as well as the implementation of measures to prevent and combat pension fund-raising fraud in elderly care Institutions.[45]
4) Online markets. The PAISMIA stipulates that application providers and distribution platforms must guarantee network security and maintain a favourable network ecology. The PAARIIS offers guidance for constructing an algorithmic security governance system, protecting consumers' right to know, and safeguarding vulnerable groups among network users.

42 Outline of Strategic Planning for Expanding Domestic Demand (2022–2035) (扩大内需战略规划纲要（2022－2035年) 2022

43 CCA 2022 Annual Report. 'Annual Report on the Protection of Consumer Rights and Interests in China (中国消费者权益保护状况年度报告 (2022))' (16 May 2022) <https://www.cca.org.cn/Detail?catalogId=492862039744581&contentType=article&contentId=535616349122629> accessed 31 October 2024

44 The '14th Five-Year Plan' for the Modernization of Market Regulation ('十四五'市场监管现代化规划) 2021

45 Opinions on Strengthening the Prevention and Reduction of Illegal Fund-raising in Elderly Care Institutions (关于加强养老机构非法集资防范化解工作的意见) 2022

5) Other areas. The SAMR elucidates the regulations pertaining to pricing violations,[46] as well as the compliance guidelines,[47] which serve to guide the healthy development of the blind box economy. These guidelines are designed to protect consumers' rights to information and fair trade.

China's regulatory model has been shaped by its distinctive legal tradition and social and economic development.[48] Moreover, it has been subject to international influence on specific aspects of consumer protection.

The Recall System

The system synthesises the advantages of various models. For example, its development was influenced by the U.S. model in several key respects: its rigorous regulations, streamlined implementation, extensive coverage, scientific methods, and technical means in the identification of product defects, risk assessment, and evaluation of recall effects. In addition, China has adopted the EU's product precautionary principle, which emphasises the prevention of product defects at the design and production stages. This has included the establishment of a robust information-sharing and cooperation mechanism to promote coordination and cooperation, the strengthening of ex-ante prevention and ex-post supervision, and the promotion of the establishment of a multi-sectoral coordinated and information-sharing supervision mechanism.

The Public Interest Litigation System

The system bears a resemblance to EU representative actions, which stipulate that only a duly qualified entity, such as a consumer organisation or a public body, may act as a claimant party on behalf of these consumers.[49] This is because China shares the EU's concerns that class actions can be abused as a form of extortion, with the possibility of frivolous, repetitive, and unmeritorious claims.[50]

Alternative Dispute Resolution for Consumer Disputes

China is working to establish a robust ADR mechanism for consumer dispute settlement. This part examines China's consumer ADR system's evolution and status.

46 Provisions on Clearly Marking Prices and Prohibiting Price Frauds (明码标价和禁止价格欺诈规定) 2022

47 Compliance Guidelines for Blind Box Business Activities (for Trial Implementation) (盲盒经营行为规范指引（试行）) 2023

48 SPC (n 3)

49 Directive (EU) 2020/1828 of the European Parliament and of the Council of 25 November 2020 on representative actions for the protection of the collective interests of consumers and repealing Directive 2009/22/EC, *Official Journal of the European Union*, L 409/1, 4 December 2020, Art. 4

50 Tiana Leia Russell, 'Exporting Class Actions to the European Union' (2010) 28 *Boston University International Law Journal* 141, 150

Historical Development of Consumer ADR

The practice of dispute resolution via mediation has been employed in China for a period spanning thousands of years. In traditional Chinese culture, the concept of 'harmony makes money' and 'fighting is a lose-lose situation, and cooperation is a win-win situation' is generally accepted when faced with disputes.[51] The concept of ADR emerged in China at the beginning of the 21st century. In the 1980s to the 1990s, courts and litigation were regarded as symbols of the authority of the rule of law. The state actively used litigation to integrate and replace traditional dispute resolution methods such as mediation and administrative adjudication. However, the tendency to seek immediate results and the neglect of traditional dispute resolution mechanisms have caused chaos in the social order. In July 2002, the focus of national policies shifted to the reform of trial methods, including mediation, settlement, and strengthening the connection with private ADR procedures.[52] In 2014, the CPC officially recognised the development of a diversified dispute resolution mechanism as one of its key objectives.[53] This concept represents neither a simple continuation of the traditional approach to dispute resolution nor an imitation of the Western ADR trend. Instead, it is based on the actual needs of China's social and legal development, integrating China's tradition of advocating harmony with the culture of negotiation and win-win pursued by the contemporary world.

Arbitration

China's arbitration system has undergone a transformation from a preliminary procedure for court trials to administrative arbitration and, subsequently, to a dispute resolution mechanism that is parallel and independent of the aforementioned two proceedings. The arbitration law distinguished arbitration institutions from the system of national administrative agencies and affirmed their independence.[54]

Mediation

Mediation can be categorised into two distinct types. The first is the court mediation system, which has undergone three distinct phases: the pre-litigation era, the litigation era, and the post-litigation era.[55] Since 2002, there has been a resurgence of

51 SPC (n 3)

52 Fan Yu (范愉), 'Guaranteeing the Sustainable Development of Society With Diversified Dispute Resolution Mechanisms (当代世界多元化纠纷解决机制的发展与启示)' (2017) 3 China Applied Law (中国应用法学) 48

53 Decision of the Central Committee of the Communist Party of China on Several Major Issues Concerning Comprehensively Advancing the Rule of Law (中共中央关于全面推进依法治国若干重大问题的决定), 23 October 2014

54 Arbitration Law of the People's Republic of China (Revision 2017) (中华人民共和国仲裁法(2017修正)) 2018, Art. 8

55 Hong Dongying (洪冬英), 'Research on the Changes of Mediation System in Contemporary China (当代中国调解制度的变迁研究)' (2007) *East China University of Political Science and Law* (华东政法大学) 26

interest in reviving and reconstructing court mediation. The second type is people's mediation, which is conducted by private third parties such as consumer associations and other private entities. Recently, these parties have become increasingly active in resolving consumer disputes.

China's Consumer ADR

The CRPL offers four avenues for consumers to resolve disputes: (1) Negotiate with the operator; (2) request a mediation presided over by the consumer association; (3) complain to relevant administrative agencies; and (4) apply for arbitration based on the arbitration agreement with the operator.[56] In addition, courts also provide ADR services in different formats, which are referred to as judicial ADR. Figure 7.3 illustrates the various avenues for consumers to pursue alternative dispute resolution, including both non-judicial and judicial ADR options.

The process of direct negotiation and reaching settlement agreements with operators is a popular choice for consumers. The low cost and flexibility associated with this approach make it an attractive option for dispute resolution. However, concerns have been raised due to the voluntary, equal, and fair nature of the proposed approach.[57] Consumers may not benefit fully from the process due to information asymmetry and unequal economic status. Furthermore, the agreements lack legal enforceability, increasing the risk of non-compliance from operators. Finally, the CPRL does not set a timeframe within which operators must respond to consumer settlement requests.

It is the responsibility of consumer associations to resolve disputes. In 2022, the CCA handled 1.152 million consumer complaints, representing a 5.7% increase from the previous year. A total of 915,752 complaints were successfully resolved, representing a 79.5% complaint resolution rate. Additionally, the CCA assisted

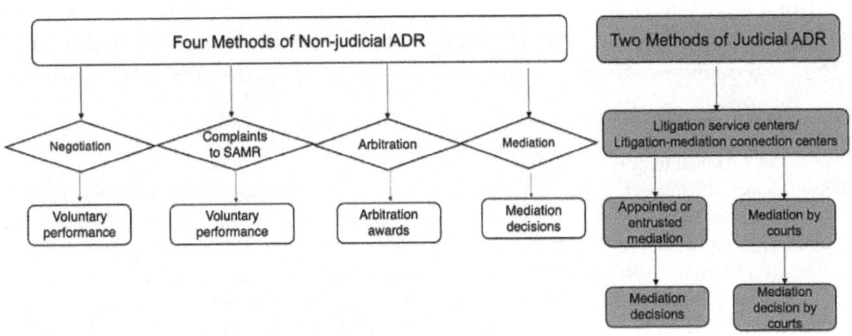

Figure 7.3 Consumer ADR Channels in China

56 CRPL, Art. 39
57 Cao Jie (曹洁), 'On Consumer Dispute Resolution Mechanisms (论消费者纠纷解决机制)' (2012) *Shanghai Jiaotong University* (上海交通大学) 33

consumers in recovering economic losses amounting to 1.38 billion yuan.[58] Local consumer councils are also engaged in the organisation of mediation.[59]

Consumer associations are quasi-official organisations that are supported and guided by SAMR. Their mediators are experts in consumer disputes and are more likely to propose reasonable mediation agreements. It is important to note, however, that even if a mediation agreement is finally reached through the efforts of a third party, it is not legally enforceable.

Consumers may report their rights infringements to local branches of SAMR by the 12315 hotline or via the 1235.com platform. Relevant administrative agencies have the duty to respond by investigating the businesses involved, punishing any violations, and presiding over mediation in order to resolve the dispute. However, it is worth noting that administrative mediation is not legally enforceable. Consequently, agencies frequently find themselves in a challenging position where fines have been imposed but the compensation agreement has not yet been performed.[60]

An arbitration institution can arbitrate on the facts and make an award concerning the rights and obligations of disputes between consumers and operators according to the agreement between the parties. The arbitration award is legally binding on both parties. Arbitrations are more flexible and time-efficient than litigation. Arbitration awards are legally binding compared to negotiations and mediations. However, arbitration also has limitations. First, it is based on an arbitration agreement that may not be easily concluded between the two parties. Secondly, the arbitration award is final, and no other dispute resolution methods will be available thereafter. Third, arbitrations are not convenient for geographical reasons. The fact that arbitration committees are only in large cities makes it difficult for consumers in smaller towns, which comprise a large portion of the Chinese market. Finally, arbitration is not economically efficient due to the high fees and lack of arbitration mechanisms for small-amount consumer losses.[61]

Efforts have been made to connect the methods mentioned above. For example, the Ningbo Municipal Arbitration Commission has established an arbitration office in the local consumer council to facilitate the docking of arbitration and mediation.

58 CCA 2022 Annual Report (n 43)

59 See 'Launch of Guangzhou-Macau Consumer Dispute Online Mediation Platform, Allowing Consumers to Mediate Remotely 'Face-to-Face' with the Merchants Being Sued (广州市消委会：启用穗·澳消费纠纷网络调解平台 消费者可与被诉商家远程'面对面'调解)' (Guangzhou Consumer Council, 14 March 2019) <https://www.gd.gov.cn/hdjl/hygq/content/post_2223534.html> accessed 31 October 2024; 'Shenzhen Consumer Council Provides Consumers with 'Full-Chain, One-Stop' Professional Mediation Services (深圳市消委会为消费者提供'全链条、一站式'专业调解服务)' (*China Quality Newspaper*, 16 February 2022) <http://www.ce.cn/cysc/zljd/zlxx/202202/16/t20220216_37333250.shtml> accessed 31 October 2024

60 Cao (n 57)

61 Xu Yan (徐燕), 'The Dilemma and Way Out of Small Consumption Arbitration (小额消费仲裁的困境与出路)' (2021) *Southwest University of Political Science and Law* (西南政法大学) 21

Judges are invited by consumer councils to attend mediations to benchmark mediations with litigation.[62]

Role of Technology in Consumer ADR – Online Dispute Resolution for Consumer

The Online Dispute Resolution (ODR) system has been designed as a method to achieve ADR. The United Nations Conference on Trade and Development (UNCTAD) reports that ODR has been highly successful in China. China has been particularly proactive in promoting the use of ODR systems for the resolution of consumer disputes.[63] China's ODR platforms can be classified into three categories:

- The first category comprises dispute resolution platforms established by e-commerce enterprises themselves, such as Taobao.com. These platforms publish a range of dispute-handling rules, provide buyers and sellers with a variety of methods for resolving disputes, and ensure the enforcement of dispute-resolution outcomes using deposits and intra-platform restrictions.[64]
- The second category comprises ODR platforms created by third parties. The earliest ODR platforms include the China E-Commerce Law Network, the 'China Online Dispute Resolution Centre,' the CIETAC Domain Name Dispute Resolution Centre, and the China Consumers' Association Complaint Settlement Platform. Following the proposal by the central government[65] to actively develop internet arbitration, local arbitration commissions have established their own internet arbitration courts.
- The third category comprises online dispute resolution platforms constructed by official organisations and based on the people's court system. This category of platform encompasses both litigation and mediation as two principal avenues for dispute resolution. In 2016, the Supreme People's Court proposed the 'Internet +' strategy,[66] which aimed to enhance the utilisation of contemporary information technology in the development of diversified dispute resolution

62 'Ningbo, Zhejiang: Establishment of the 'Docking + ODR' Mechanism to Promote Consumer Dispute Resolution (浙江宁波：建立'诉调对接+ODR'机制　助推消费纠纷化解)' (*China News*, 17 July 2020) <https://www.chinanews.com.cn/sh/2020/07–17/9240653.shtml> accessed 31 October 2024

63 'Consumer Trust in the Digital Economy: The Case for Online Dispute Resolution' (2021) UNCTAD Research Paper No. 72 UNCTAD/SER.RP/2021/15 <https://unctad.org/system/files/official-document/ser-rp-2021d15_en.pdf> accessed 31 October 2024

64 Taobao Platform Dispute Resolution Rules (淘宝平台争议处理规则) 2023

65 Promulgation of Several Opinions on Improving the Arbitration System and Enhancing the Credibility of Arbitration (关于完善仲裁制度提高仲裁公信力的若干意见), 2018

66 Article 2(15), Opinions of the SPC on People's Courts Further Deepening the Reform of Diversified Dispute Resolution Mechanism (最高人民法院关于人民法院进一步深化多元化纠纷解决机制改革的意见), 2016

mechanisms. As of July 2024, 3,504 courts across the country had established online mediation platforms.[67]

Challenges and Opportunities

While there are advantages inherent to ADR as a means of resolving consumer disputes, the field of Consumer ADR is confronted with several obstacles. First, it is challenging to promote the use of small claims arbitration. Therefore, there is a need to increase consumer awareness of arbitration procedures for minor disputes. Second, parties have low trust in ODR platforms, which has been an important factor constraining the development of ODR. Third, it is challenging to enforce non-judicial ADR awards. Except for awards reached through judicial ADR mechanisms, all other ADR mechanisms provide non-legally binding outcomes.

Nevertheless, the current global and domestic economic and technological development has provided many opportunities for consumer ADR. First, cross-border e-commerce paves the road for the development of consumer ODR. For example, the UNCTAD and the China Silk Road Group entered into an agreement to facilitate ODR for consumers in Southeast Asia in 2019.[68] Second, the accelerated advancement of artificial intelligence (AI) has created a surge in potential avenues for the application of ODR. AI can facilitate the description of disputes using structured data, thereby enabling the matching of disputes with appropriate ODR methods based on the type of dispute.[69]

Conclusion

In conjunction with the rapid growth of the Chinese economy and society, the consumer ADR in China has undergone considerable development. This chapter presents a comprehensive analysis of the Chinese consumer ADR system. To begin, the legal system for consumer protection in China is comprised of various legal documents, with the CRPL serving as the primary law. The CPC and the state continue to refine and enhance the systems for the protection of consumer rights and interests. Regarding the judicial branch, there are no specialised courts in China. Nevertheless, specific procedures are in place to safeguard consumers' rights and interests.

Regarding consumer ADR, China has established a comprehensive system comprising non-judicial ADR and judicial ADR channels. The non-judicial ADR

67 People's Court Mediation Platform (人民法院调解平台) <https://tiaojie.court.gov.cn/> accessed 31 October 2024

68 'Partnership to Deliver Online Dispute Resolution to Consumers' (*UNCTAD*, 11 July 2019) <https://unctad.org/news/partnership-deliver-online-dispute-resolution-consumers> accessed 31 October 2024

69 'Technology and Future: Intelligent Development of ODR and Establishment of Digital Ecosystem – Review of the 19th World ODR Conference (科技与未来：ODR智能化发展与数字生态系统建立 – 第19届世界ODR大会综述)' (*Sohu.com*, 16 December 2019) <https://www.sohu.com/a/360785099_455313> accessed 31 October 2024

channels have been utilised with the greatest frequency, offering a variety of options for consumers, including negotiation, mediation, administrative appeals, and arbitration. In response to this, ODR has been developed rapidly in order to facilitate ADR. In accordance with the principles outlined in the *Consumer Protection Co-Governance Strategy*, consumer ADR in China is characterised by a distinct set of characteristics which are primarily shaped by public powers. In conclusion, China has been striving to mobilise the collective efforts of society to develop consumer ADR, with the objective of safeguarding consumers from domestic and cross-border transactions.

References

Official Documents

Administrative Measures for the Protection of Consumers' Rights and Interests by Banking and Insurance Institutions (银行保险机构消费者权益保护管理办法) 2023
Advertising Law of the People's Republic of China (中华人民共和国广告法) 2021
Agricultural Products Quality and Safety of the People's Republic of China (中华人民共和国农产品质量安全法) 2023
Anti-Monopoly Law of the People's Republic of China (中华人民共和国反垄断法) 2022
Anti-Telecom and Online Fraud Law of the People's Republic of China (中华人民共和国反电信网络诈骗法) 2022
Arbitration Law of the People's Republic of China (Revision 2017) (中华人民共和国仲裁法(2017修正)) 2018
Civil Code of the People's Republic of China (中华人民共和国民法典) 2021
Compliance Guidelines for Blind Box Business Activities (for Trial Implementation) (盲盒经营行为规范指引（试行）) 2023
Constitution of the People's Republic of China (Amended in 2018) (中华人民共和国宪法（2018修正）)
Consumer Rights and Interests Protection Law of the People's Republic of China (Amended) (中华人民共和国消费者权益保护法) 2014
Data Security Law of the People's Republic of China (中华人民共和国数据安全法) 2021
Decision of the Central Committee of the Communist Party of China on Several Major Issues Concerning Comprehensively Advancing the Rule of Law (中共中央关于全面推进依法治国若干重大问题的决定), 23 October 2014
Directive (EU) 2020/1828 of the European Parliament and of the Council of 25 November 2020 on representative actions for the protection of the collective interests of consumers and repealing Directive 2009/22/EC, Official Journal of the European Union, L 409/1, 4 December 2020
Drug Administration Law of the People's Republic of China (中华人民共和国药品管理法) 2019
E-commerce Law of the People's Republic of China (中华人民共和国电子商务法) 2019
Food Safety Law of the People's Republic of China (中华人民共和国食品安全法) 2021
Implementing Regulation for the Drug Administration Law of the People's Republic of China (中华人民共和国药品管理法实施条例) 2019
Implementing Regulation for the Food Safety Law of the People's Republic of China (中华人民共和国食品安全法实施条例) 2019
Implementing Regulation for the Law of the People's Republic of China on Import and Export Commodity Inspection (中华人民共和国进出口商品检验法实施条例) 2022
Implementing Regulation for the Law of the People's Republic of China on the Protection of Consumer Rights and Interests (中华人民共和国消费者权益保护法实施条例) 2024

Import and Export Commodity Inspection Law of the People's Republic of China (中华人民共和国进出口商品检验法) 2021
Legislation Law of the People's Republic of China (Amended in 2023) (中华人民共和国立法法（2023修正)
Measures for Penalties for Infringement upon Rights and Interests of Consumer (侵害消费者权益行为处罚办法) 2020
Measures for the Supervision and Administration of Online Transactions (网络交易监督管理办法) 2021
Measures of Beijing Municipality for the Implementation of the CRPL (北京市实施《中华人民共和国消费者权益保护法》办法) 1998
Opinions of the Central Committee of the Communist Party of China and the State Council on Accelerating the Improvement of the Socialist Market Economic System in the New Era (中共中央和国务院关于新时代加快完善社会主义市场经济体制的意见) 2020
Opinions of the Central Committee of the Communist Party of China and the State Council on Accelerating the Construction of a Nationally Unified Big Market (中共中央和国务院关于加快建设全国统一大市场的意见) 2022
Opinions of the General Office of the State Council on Further Releasing Consumption Potential and Promoting Sustained Recovery of Consumption (国务院办公厅关于进一步释放消费潜力促进消费持续恢复的意见) 2022
Opinions on Strengthening the Prevention and Reduction of Illegal Fund-raising in Elderly Care Institutions (关于加强养老机构非法集资防范化解工作的意见) 2022
Opinions of the SPC on People's Courts Further Deepening the Reform of Diversified Dispute Resolution Mechanism (最高人民法院关于人民法院进一步深化多元化纠纷解决机制改革的意见) 2016
Outline of Building a Quality State (质量强国建设纲要) 2023
Outline of Strategic Planning for Expanding Domestic Demand (2022–2035) (扩大内需战略规划纲要（2022－2035年) 2022
Product Quality Law of the People's Republic of China (中华人民共和国产品质量法) 2018
Promulgation of Several Opinions on Improving the Arbitration System and Enhancing the Credibility of Arbitration (关于完善仲裁制度提高仲裁公信力的若干意见) 2018
Provisions on the Administration of Algorithm-generated Recommendations for Internet Information Services (互联网信息服务算法推荐管理规定) 2022
Regulations of Shanghai Municipality on Consumers' Rights and Interests Protection (上海市消费者权益保护条例) 2022
Regulations on the Administration of Business Premises of Internet Access Service (互联网上网服务营业场所管理条例) 2022
Specification for E-commerce mode (电子商务模式规范) 2018
Standardisation Law of the People's Republic of China (2017 Revision) (中华人民共和国标准化法（2017修订) 2018
The '14th Five-Year Plan' for the Modernization of Market Regulation ('十四五'市场监管现代化规划) 2021
Tianjin Consumer Rights and Interests Protection Regulation (天津市消费者权益保护条例) 2019

Books and Articles

Dongying H (洪冬英), 'Research on the Changes of Mediation System in Contemporary China (当代中国调解制度的变迁研究)' (2007) East China University of Political Science and Law (华东政法大学)
Jie C (曹洁), 'On Consumer Dispute Resolution Mechanisms (论消费者纠纷解决机制)' (2012) Shanghai Jiaotong University (上海交通大学)
Jinping X, *The Governance of China IV* (Foreign Languages Press 2022)

Russell TL, 'Exporting Class Actions to the European Union' (2010) 28 Boston University International Law Journal 141

Yan X (徐燕), 'Dilemmas and Solutions for Small-Claim Arbitration (小额消费仲裁的困境与出路)' (2021) Southwest University of Political Science and Law (西南政法大学)

Yu F (范愉), 'Guaranteeing the Sustainable Development of Society with Diversified Dispute Resolution Mechanisms (当代世界多元化纠纷解决机制的发展与启示)' (2017) 3 China Applied Law (中国应用法学) 48

Online Resources

'Annual Report on the Protection of Consumer Rights and Interests in China (中国消费者权益保护状况年度报告 (2023))' (27 May 2023) <https://www.cca.org.cn/Detail?catalogId=492862039744581&contentType=article&contentId=551488720109637> accessed 31 October 2024

'Annual Report on the Protection of Consumer Rights and Interests in China (中国消费者权益保护状况年度报告 (2022))' (16 May 2022) <https://www.cca.org.cn/Detail?catalogId=492862039744581&contentType=article&contentId=535616349122629> accessed 31 October 2024

'Launch of Guangzhou-Macau Consumer Dispute Online Mediation Platform, Allowing Consumers to Mediate Remotely 'Face-to-Face' with the Merchants Being Sued (广州市消委会：启用穗•澳消费纠纷网络调解平台　消费者可与被诉商家远程'面对面'调解)' Guangzhou Consumer Council (14 March 2019) <https://www.gd.gov.cn/hdjl/hygq/content/post_2223534.html> accessed 31 October 2024

'Ningbo, Zhejiang: Establishment of the 'Docking + ODR' Mechanism to Promote Consumer Dispute Resolution (浙江宁波：建立'诉调对接+ODR'机制　助推消费纠纷化解)' (*China News*, 17 July 2020) <https://www.chinanews.com.cn/sh/2020/07–17/9240653.shtml> accessed 31 October 2024

'Shenzhen Consumer Council Provides Consumers with 'Full-Chain, One-Stop' Professional Mediation Services (深圳市消委会为消费者提供'全链条、一站式'专业调解服务)' (*China Quality Newspaper*, 16 February 2022) <http://www.ce.cn/cysc/zljd/zlxx/202202/16/t20220216_37333250.shtml> accessed 31 October 2024

Taobao Platform Dispute Resolution Rules (淘宝平台争议处理规则) 2023

'The Reform of Diversified Dispute Resolution Mechanism of China's Courts (2015–2020)' SPC (20 February 2021) <https://www.court.gov.cn/upload/file/2021/02/20/16/19/20210220161916_60128.pdf> accessed 31 October 2024

8 Consumer ADR in Romania

Cătălin Gabriel Stănescu

Introduction

Consumer protection in Romania underwent gradual transformations after the fall of communism in 1989. Like other formerly communist countries in Central and Eastern Europe, Romania underwent a challenging transition from a communist to a capitalist political, economic, and legal system. As the government worked towards joining the European Union (EU) and eventually became a member in 2007, one significant change was made to Romanian law to comply with EU regulations.

In the context of time, Romanian consumer legislation has undergone significant changes since the early 2000s, categorised into two phases: pre-accession (1999–2006) and post-accession (2007-present). Each phase has brought about substantial changes in both substance and institutions. In terms of substance, the alignment of national law with EU regulations and the introduction of local legislative initiatives have expanded the scope of consumer law and improved consumer rights and remedies. In terms of institutions, the role of national courts and organisations, including alternative dispute resolution (ADR) bodies, has expanded.

Legislative changes and the growing awareness and advocacy of civil society in support of consumer rights have shaped the evolution of Romanian consumer law. This is evident in the increasing volume of consumer complaints filed with the National Authority for Consumer Protection (NACP), as well as with courts and ADR entities, particularly in matters related to finance. Following the fall of communism, consumer protection laws swiftly came into effect with the introduction of Government Ordinance (GO) 21/1992 on Consumer Protection Act.[1] This ordinance set the legal framework for ensuring the welfare of consumers in their transactions with businesses that market goods and services for consumption.[2] The 2004 Consumer Code was another significant law with widespread applicability.[3]

1 GO 21/1992 on consumer protection, published in the Official Gazette No. 212/1992 (RO) and republished in the Official Gazette No. 208/2007 (RO)

2 GO 21/1992, Statement of Reasons 6 (personal archive); Rodica Diana Apan, *Protectia juridica a consumatorilor. Creditul destinat consumului si domeniile conexe* (Sfera juridica 2007) 25

3 Law 296/2004 concerning the Consumer Code (2004 Consumer Code), republished in the Official Gazette No. 224/24.03.2008 (RO)

DOI: 10.4324/9781032689739-8

In 1993, Romania began aligning its legislation with the EU acquis as a requirement for EU accession.[4] The negotiation chapter on consumer protection was tentatively closed in 2001, and the government signed the Accession Treaty on 25 April 2005, committing to further harmonisation efforts.[5] Since the country's accession to the European Union in 2007, Romanian consumers enjoy similar legal protections to those afforded to any consumers within the union. At least on paper, Romanian consumer protection law balanced the relationship between consumers and traders.[6] However, enforcement remains a significant issue.[7]

Legal Framework for Consumer Protection

The regulatory framework is rather complex, and consumer protection legislation can be split into general and specific categories. The general legislation includes the 2004 Consumer Code[8] and the 1992 Consumer Protection Act.[9] The Consumer Code defines the legal relationship between economic operators and consumers when acquiring products and services, including financial services. It establishes the legislative foundation for access to products and services and the right to receive accurate and comprehensive information regarding product characteristics. Additionally, the Code safeguards against abusive practices. As per its provisions, the Romanian Government was expected to establish and uphold a firm consumer protection policy while considering pertinent international agreements (particularly those of the EU).[10] However, that did not happen. Other general provisions can be found in the New Civil Code,[11] the Civil Procedure Code,[12] and the legal act governing judicial fees.[13]

The specific legislation is more developed – mainly transposing EU law – and covers particular areas of consumer protection, such as the protection of consumers against unfair contract terms[14]; consumer protection in distance contracts and contracts negotiated away from business premises[15]; guarantees for the conformity of

4 Law 20/1993 on ratification of the European Agreement of Association between Romania and the European Community and its Member States, published in the Official Gazette No. 73/1993, Title V, Arts. 69–71 and Title VI, Art. 93

5 Apan (n 3) 17–18

6 Camelia Toader, 'Enforcement and Effectiveness of Consumer Law in Romania' in H-W Micklitz and G Saumier (eds) *Enforcement and Effectiveness of Consumer Law* (Springer 2018)

7 Cătălin Gabriel Stănescu, 'The Enforcement of Consumer Financial Protection in Romania' (2023) 12 *EuCML* 102

8 2004 Consumer Code (n 4)

9 GO 21/1992 (n 2)

10 Toader (n 7) 514

11 Art. 1177 of the 2011 Civil Code (Law No. 287/2009 concerning the Civil Code), republished in the Official Gazette No. 505/2011 (RO)

12 Art. 121 and 125 of Civil Procedure Code, republished in the Official Gazette No. 247/2015 (RO)

13 Art. 29 (1)(f) of GO 80/2013 on judicial fees, published in the Official Gazette No. 80/2013 (RO)

14 Law No. 193/2000 on abusive terms in contracts concluded between professionals and consumers, published in the Official Gazette No. 543/2012 (RO)

15 Government Emergency Ordinance (GEO) 34/2014 on consumer rights in contracts concluded with professionals, published in the Official Gazette No. 427/2014 (RO)

products[16]; protection against unfair commercial practices[17]; and protection against misleading and comparative advertising.[18] While no comprehensive policy has been developed, Romania has witnessed an increased focus on consumer protection *vis-à-vis* financial services, especially following the 2008 financial crisis. This has led to the adoption of a very contentious piece of legislation[19] and the implementation of rules against abusive debt collection practices in the transposition of the Consumer Mortgage Directive[20] into national law.[21] To date, disputes arising from financial agreements remain the most litigated matter in Romanian consumer protection. This might also explain why a specific ADR body was implemented by law to cover consumer finance-related disputes.

The General Design of the Enforcement Mechanism

The National Authority for Consumer Protection

The Romanian Government established the first body responsible for consumer protection in August 1992 through the Consumer Protection Act.[22] Originally named the Office for Consumer Protection, it has been known as the National Authority for Consumer Protection (NACP) since 2003. By law, the NACP is a specialised body of central public administration under the government's control and fully funded by the state.[23] However, the agency's legal status presents two

16 Law No. 449/2003 on the sale of goods and associated guarantees, republished in the Official Gazette No. 347/2008, abrogated by GEO 140/2021 on certain aspects concerning sales contracts, published in the Official Gazette No. 1245/2021 (RO)

17 Law No. 363/2007 on combating unfair practices of traders in relation to consumers and harmonising legislation with European law on consumer protection legislation, published in the Official Gazette No. 58/2007 (RO)

18 Law No. 158/2008 on misleading and comparative advertising, republished in the Official Gazette No. 454/2013 (RO)

19 Law 77/2016 on commissioning real estate property payment on redemption of obligations through loans, published in the Official Gazette no 33/2016 (RO). Several banks challenged the law before the Constitutional Court, and it suffered numerous amendments and subsequent constitutional challenges until it lost its consumer protection mechanism. See Cătălin Gabriel Stănescu 'How the Romanian Constitutional Court Highjacked Consumer Financial Protection' in Hans-W Micklitz and Christian Twigg-Flesner (eds), *The Transformation of Consumer Law and Policy in Europe* (Hart Publishing 2023)

20 Directive 2014/17/EU of the European Parliament and of the Council of 4 February 2014 on credit agreements for consumers relating to residential immovable property and amending Directives 2008/48/EC and 2013/36/EU and Regulation (EU) No. 1093/2010, [2014] *OJ L* 60, 28.2.2014/34

21 GEO 52/2016 on credit agreements offered to consumers for immovable property and amending and supplementing Government Emergency Ordinance 50/2010 on credit agreements for consumers, published in the Official Gazette No. 727/2016 (RO). See Cătălin Gabriel Stănescu and Albert Albanezi, 'Romania's Struggle to Regulate Abusive Debt Collection Practices' in Cătălin Gabriel Stănescu (ed) *Regulation of Debt Collection in Europe: Understanding Informal Debt Collection* (Routledge 2023)

22 GO 21/1992 on consumer protection, republished in the Official Gazette No. 208/2007 (RO)

23 id at Art. 27 corroborated with Art. 1(1) and (3) of Government Decision (GD) 700/2012 on the organisation and functioning of the National Authority for Consumer Protection, published in the Official Gazette No. 491/2012 (RO)

significant areas for improvement. Its resources depend on budgetary allocations and governmental priorities, as it receives state financing. Secondly, the agency can be politically controlled or subordinated, impacting its ability to function independently.[24]

A president leads the organisation.[25] Its headquarters are in Bucharest,[26] with one office in each county seat.[27] Its employees have public servant status and are appointed through the procedures established by Law No. 188/1999 on the legal status of public servants.[28] After receiving a new designation, the organisation adopted a new structure based on special directorates and services. These included the General Directorate for Control, Market Supervision and European Harmonization, the Directorate for Banking and Non-Banking Financial Products and Services, the Directorate for Alternative Dispute Resolution, the Directorate for Personal Insolvency, and the Directorate for Precious Metals.[29] The NACP has several relevant functions. These include supervising compliance with consumer protection laws, investigating violations, taking measures to limit negative consequences, and receiving, resolving, or forwarding consumer complaints for resolution.[30]

The National Authority for Energy Regulation

Romania's energy sector is overseen by the National Authority for Energy Regulation (NAER),[31] an independent regulatory body. NAER's primary objective is to safeguard users' and consumers' interests, promote healthy competition, and ensure nationwide services are efficient, cost-effective, and of satisfactory quality standards.[32] NAER maintains a reliable and transparent tariff system, balances operators' economic goals with general social objectives, and advocates for environmental protection and efficient energy use.[33] NAER also provides advisory and reporting services to the government and parliament and offers observations and recommendations on issues in the regulated electricity and gas sectors.[34] Furthermore, it maintains bilateral relations with all European regulators, particularly those of

24 Stănescu (n 8) 102
25 Art. 5(1) of GD 700/2012
26 Art. 1(2) of GD 700/2012
27 Art. 7(5) of GD 700/2012
28 Law No. 188/1999 on the status of public servants, republished in the Official Gazette No. 365/2007, abrogated and replaced by the 2019 Administrative Code (GEO 57/2019), published in the Official Gazette No. 555/2019
29 Annex 1 of GEO 57/2019
30 Art. 3(i), (j), and (u) of GD 700/2012
31 NAER functions on the basis of Law No. 123/2012 on electricity and natural gas, published in the Official Gazette No. 485/2012 and GEO 33/2007 on organisation and functioning of the National Authority for Energy Regulation, published in the Official Gazette No. 337/2007 (RO)
32 Art. 1(1) and 8 of GEO 33/2007
33 Art. 9(4)(g) of GEO 33/2007
34 Informatii generale <https://anre.ro/despre/statutul-si-rolul/> accessed 30 April 2024

countries sharing a border with Romania. It collaborates with many non-EU regulators to share best practices and experiences.[35]

Consumers who have complaints regarding electric services can lodge them according to NAER Order No. 16/2015.[36] Complaints may concern billing, difficulty in contacting the company, dissatisfaction with the service, or other issues. The most recent statistics indicate that in 2022, approximately 39,000 complaints were filed by users in the energy and natural gas sectors, both natural and legal persons. Differentiated statistics are not available. These figures indicate a 64% increase in complaints compared to 2021. The most common issues signalled by users concerned difficulty in contracting and billing errors.[37]

The National Authority for Management and Regulation in Communications

In Romania's telecommunication sector, the National Authority for Management and Regulation in Communications (NAMRC)[38] is responsible for ensuring the fair treatment of communication users. This is achieved by promoting competition within the communications market, managing scarce resources, and encouraging innovation and efficient investments in infrastructure.[39] The agency's primary focus is protecting the interests of communication users in Romania by promoting competition in the communications market.[40] It receives complaints from electronic communications users regarding mobile telephony services and the Internet.[41] According to stats available for 2023, the number of complaints continues to increase, with 3825 requests filed. Of these, 70% of the complaints regarded electronic communications, with issues such as the unilateral modification of contracts by service providers (12%), performance of contracts (11%), or billing of services (11%).[42]

Current Consumer Dispute Resolution Processes

Romania's judicial system operates under a pyramid structure, with the High Court of Cassation and Justice holding the top position.[43] The system is composed of 15 courts of appeal, 41 tribunals, four specialised tribunals, and 177 courts of first

35 Art. 11(3) of GEO 33/2007

36 Order 16/2015 approving the Framework Procedure on the obligation of electricity and gas suppliers to resolve end-customer complaints, published in the Official Gazette No. 193/2015 (RO)

37 NAER, 'Annual Report' (2022) <https://anre.ro/wp-content/uploads/2023/07/Raport-anual-2022.pdf> accessed 30 April 2024

38 GEO 22/2009 on the establishment of the National Authority for Administration and Regulation in Communications, published in the Official Gazette No. 174/2009

39 Art. 5 of GEO 22/2009

40 Art. 6(2) of GEO 22/2009

41 Art. 10(1) point 12 of GEO 22/2009

42 NAMRC, 'Press Release' (January 2024) <https://www.ancom.ro/bilant-202358-peste-3800-de-reclamatii-primite-de-ancom-din-partea-utilizatorilor-de-servicii-de-comunicatii-electronice-si-de-servicii-postale_7036> accessed 30 April 2024

43 Toader (n 7) 520

instance.[44] The judges are independent, obey only the law, and decide on their own competence to solve cases.[45] Only superior courts may review court decisions.

Currently, Romania lacks a dedicated tribunal specifically for consumer disputes and typically assigns such cases to civil courts with jurisdiction according to the law. If the matter involves a penalty imposed by the NACP, it will be referred to the administrative chamber of the appropriate court. Despite a notable uptick in cases in recent years, primarily attributed to the financial crisis, courts or chambers specialised in consumer matters have yet to be established.

Depending on their value, consumer disputes may be referred to either the court of first instance or the tribunal. If the amount is below RON 200,000 or EUR 45,000, the Court of First Instance is the appropriate authority, while the Tribunal handles disputes above this threshold.46 Decisions made by the Court in the First Instance can be appealed at the next court level. Regarding territorial jurisdiction, it is essential to note that professionals may only make requests within the jurisdiction where the consumer has established their habitual residence.47 However, once compensation has been requested, the consumer and professional may agree on the appropriate jurisdiction.48 Consumers can bring legal action against the professional in either the jurisdiction of their residence or where the professional is based (known as an alternative jurisdiction).49

To file a claim with the court as a consumer, one must follow the standard requirements for initiating legal proceedings. There is no specific procedure for consumer protection cases, and legal representation is not mandatory. Additionally, consumers are not required to go through an administrative procedure before taking legal action, simplifying the process, and avoiding extra formalities. However, it has been suggested that a particular procedure be explicitly created for consumer litigation.[50] This would make it easier for consumers to access the courts and receive a timelier resolution to their issues. The current procedure can be lengthy

44 Romania's Judicial System's structure and figures are available at <https://e-justice.europa.eu/content_judicial_systems_in_member_states-16-ro-maximizeMS-ro.do?member=1> accessed 30 April 2024

45 Art. 124(3) of the Romanian Constitution and Art. 2(3) of Law 303/2022

46 According to the Romanian Civil Procedure Code, Art. 94 pt. 1(k) the court of first instance is competent on: "any other claims assessable in money up to and including 200,000 lei, regardless of the status of the parties, professional or non-professional"

47 Art. 113(1) pt. 8, apart from the courts referred to in Articles 107 to 112 of the Romanian Civil Procedure Code, the following courts have jurisdiction:

> the court for the place where the consumer is domiciled, in actions for enforcement, for a declaration of absolute nullity, for the annulment, cancellation, termination or unilateral rescission of a contract concluded with a trader or in actions for damages for harm caused to consumers;

Art. 121 – "Claims brought by a professional against a consumer can only be brought before the court of the consumer's domicile"

48 Art. 126(1) of the Romanian Civil Procedure Code

49 Art. 113 of the Romanian Civil Procedure Code

50 Toader (n 7) 521–522

due to the regularisation period, during which judges examine the case to ensure that all procedural requirements have been met. This can cause significant harm to consumers. Despite this, such a procedure has yet to be established.

Regarding the burden of proof, according to the regulations on unfair terms, if an economic operator asserts that a standard pre-written clause was directly negotiated with the consumer, they are responsible for providing evidence to support their claim.[51] Similarly, the regulations regarding the distance marketing of consumer financial services state that any contract term or condition responsible for proving the supplier's compliance with their obligations to the consumer is considered an unfair term in consumer contracts.[52]

It is worth noting that claims made for consumer protection are exempt from judicial fees if the applicant is a natural person or a consumer protection association.[53] This exemption is designed to encourage litigation and to empower consumers to rely on the rights granted through consumer protection legislation. While the claims are exempt from fees, consumers may still request legal financial aid[54] to cover costs such as legal assistance, expert, or bailiff fees.[55] Legal aid is granted to persons whose average net monthly income per family member in the two months preceding the application is less than the equivalent of 25% of the basic gross minimum wage in the country. In this case, the amounts constituting legal aid shall be advanced in full by the State. Should the average net monthly income per family member be below the equivalent of 50% of the minimum gross basic wage in the country, legal aid is reduced to 50%. The amount of public legal assistance granted, separately or cumulatively, maybe, at most, over one year, the maximum amount equivalent to ten gross national minimum basic salaries at the level of the year in which the aid application was made.[56]

Alternative Dispute Resolution for Consumer Disputes

Historical Development of ADR Mechanisms

Government Ordinance 38/2015 concerning the alternative resolution of disputes between consumers and traders (GO 38/2015) transposed the ADR Directive into national legislation.[57] Yet, at the time of the transposition, Romania already had a legal framework for mediation and conciliation, which also applied to consumer disputes. For instance, Law 192/2006[58] regarding mediation procedures and the

51 Art. 4(3) of Law No. 193/2000

52 GO 85/2004 on the protection of consumers in the conclusion and performance of distance contracts for financial services, republished in the Official Gazette No. 365/2008 (RO)

53 Art. 29(1)(f) of the GEO 80/2013 on judicial fees, published in the Official Gazette No. 392/2013 (RO)

54 GO 51/2008, on legal aid in civil matters, published in the Official Gazette No. 327/2008 (RO)

55 Arts. 6 and 7

56 Art. 8 of GO 51/2008

57 GO 38/2015 concerning the alternative resolution of disputes between consumers and traders, published in the Official Gazette No. 654/2015 (RO)

58 Law No. 192/2006 concerning mediation procedures and the professional organisation of mediators, published in the Official Gazette No. 441/2006 (RO)

professional organisation of mediators provided an alternative dispute resolution mechanism with a third party specialised in mediation, ensuring a procedure based on neutrality, impartiality, and confidentiality.

As highlighted in the Explanatory Memorandum of GO 38/2015, based on GO 27/2002[59] provisions, several public institutions could already resolve individual consumer claims, with the NACP covering a broad spectrum of sectors. As shown in the document, in 2013, as many as 72% of the total claims were resolved amicably. If such an outcome were not possible, the territorial structures of the NACP would launch investigations, possibly applying administrative fines if necessary. In a relatively confident manner, it is stated that "this system already boasts a tradition of 20 years in Romania, tackling all fields of interests for consumers."[60] The initially designated competent authority was the Minister of Economy, Energy, and Business Environment through its ADR department, which was set up within the Legal and Institutional Relations Directorate.[61] Currently, the competent authority is the Minister of Energy, SMEs and Business Environment.[62]

Among the reasons for adopting ADR mechanisms was the slowness of classical dispute procedures. This was deemed one of the main obstacles for consumers, especially in online concluded contracts, whether cross-border or not.[63] Additional difficulties stemmed from the hurdle of identifying the correct type of action, the complexity of procedural rules, or the esotericism of legal language.[64] The purpose of ADR was to provide a solution independently and fairly by avoiding the complexity of court proceedings.[65]

ADR Entities

GO 38/2015 defines ADR entities as "entities that provide for the resolution of a dispute through an ADR procedure and which may operate exclusively within the NACP, a central public authority, or an autonomous administrative authority with responsibilities in the field of consumer protection."[66] By design, Romania does not have a single ADR entity for consumer disputes, but several. Public, private, or mixed funds finance ADR entities.[67] As such, ADR entities are publicly operated and limited in number.

59 GO 27/2002 on the regulation of petition resolution, published in the Official Gazette No. 84/2002

60 GO 38/2015, 'Explanatory Memorandum' <https://www.cdep.ro/proiecte/2015/700/80/1/em991.pdf> accessed 30 April 2024

61 In 2020, the Minister of Economy was still the competent authority

62 Art. 30 of GO 38/2015

63 Juanita Goicovici, 'Noile proceduri de solutionare alternativa a litigiilor dintre comercianti si consumatori' [2015] *SUBB Jurisprudentia* 53

64 Juanita Goicovici, 'Noile proceduri de solutionare alternativa a litigiilor dintre comercianti si consumatori' [2015] *SUBB Jurisprudentia* 57

65 Juanita Goicovici, 'Noile proceduri de solutionare alternativa a litigiilor dintre comercianti si consumatori' [2015] *SUBB Jurisprudentia* 57

66 Art. 3(1)(h) of GO 38/2015

67 Art. 17 of GO 38/2015

The main one, the ADR Directorate, functions within NACP and is competent to "alternatively resolve" national and cross-border disputes arising from sales contracts or service contracts concluded with a trader carrying out activities in Romania in the sectors of activity in which ANPC is competent. Alternative mechanisms include mediation, conciliation, negotiation, or arbitration, which are believed to offer mutually beneficial solutions.[68]

Another ADR entity set up by law is the Alternative Banking Dispute Resolution Centre (ABDRC), which is competent solely in banking disputes between consumers and traders whose activity is regulated, authorised, and supervised by the Romanian National Bank, as well as branches of foreign traders who undertake banking operations in Romania.[69] It is strange, for no other industry has a dedicated ADR entity by law. According to GO 38/2015's Explanatory Memorandum, the decision was motivated by the complexity of the banking sector and the impact of banking services on consumers.[70] The ABDRC enjoys a unique character under the law. This character is revealed by three distinguishing features concerning its legal status, financing, and responsibilities. *First,* the ABDRC is defined as an autonomous, non-governmental, apolitical legal entity of public interest without lucrative scope.[71] *Second,* ABDRC's financing stems primarily from private sources. *Third*, it functions independently of any public body with consumer protection responsibilities.

The Authority for Financial Supervision has also set up an ADR entity – nationally known as ADR-Fin, which is competent *vis-à-vis* financial products and services stemming from three non-banking markets: insurance, capital markets, and private pensions.[72]

The European Consumer Centre – Romania

For cross-border transactions, the European Consumer Centre in Romania, part of the European Consumer Centres Network, was competent to settle disputes amicably, respectively, those arising from purchases by consumers resident in Romania of defective products or services from an economic operator situated in another EU Member State, or purchases by consumers resident in another EU Members State of faulty products or services from an economic operator located in Romania.

The piecemeal approach could undermine the effectiveness of ADR mechanisms, especially since ADR entities are allowed to elaborate their own rules of procedure.[73] These will also determine what type of solution the ADR body will render: a *proposed* one (not binding on the parties unless both accept it),[74] an

68 ANPC, <https://reclamatiisal.anpc.ro/> accessed 4 April 2024
69 Art. 21 of GO 38/2015
70 GO 38/2015, Explanatory Memorandum (n 61) 6
71 Art. 21(1) of GO 38/2015
72 ASF, <https://asfromania.ro/ro/a/1551/sal-fin> accessed 4 April 2024
73 Art. 15 of GEO 38/2015
74 Art. 11 of GEO 38/2015

imposed one (binding on the parties)[75] or both. In the latter case, the consumer will ultimately choose between the two types.[76] Given the implications, the parties should familiarise themselves with the specific procedure of the ADR entity they have designated before engaging in this process.[77] From this perspective, it would have been better to have the competent authority establish the procedural rules for all entities, which would have eased the task of consumers.[78]

The set-up of ADR entities may also negatively contribute to their effectiveness, for they appear biased in design. For instance, trade associations and scholars heavily criticised the NACP as an ADR entity for consumer-related disputes, given that the NACP's primary role is supervising and enforcing consumer law.[79] Similar worries surround the law-appointed ABDRC, given that its financing comes mainly from banking institutions, donations or sponsorships,[80] and some of its members, if not all, of its honorary members have a long-standing reputation for defending banking institutions and their interests.

Advantages of ADR Mechanisms

Freedom is the main principle when it comes to ADR, under a double aspect: a) the *consumer's* freedom to resort to an ADR entity and b) the *consumer's* freedom to accept or not the solution proposed by the ADR entity.[81] The non-binding nature of ADR derives from the idea that the trader cannot compel the consumer to turn to an ADR entity outside the courts to settle the dispute and cannot be deprived of his constitutional right of access to justice and the guarantees of impartiality offered by the judge.[82]

All the ADR entities highlight similar advantages brought to consumers: *accessibility, affordability,* and *swiftness*. Although not explicitly stated, *professionalism* and *equity* are also often present among ADR's principles (and advantages), although they benefit all stakeholders, not only consumers. *Accessibility* generally refers to the ease with which a consumer can *voluntarily* resort to ADR mechanisms and the fact that they *do not need* legal representation. However, since consumers are not required to pay judicial fees, the ADR procedures cannot be regarded as more *affordable* than regular judicial procedures. On the contrary, if the consumers require technical expert reports, legalised translations, or any other cost-requiring

75 Art. 12 of GEO 38/2015

76 Art. 10 of GEO 38/2015

77 Ionela-Diana Patrasc-Balan, 'Online Dispute Resolution Stemming from Sales or Service Contracts in European Union' (2019) 65 *Analele Stiintifice ale Universitatii Alexandru Ioan Cuza din Iasi, Stiinte Juridice* 107

78 Octavia Maria Cilibiu, 'Issues Concerning Alternative Dispute Resolution Between Consumers and Traders' (2015) *Annals Constantin Brancusi U. Targu Jiu Juridical Sci.* Series 79

79 Octavia Maria Cilibiu, 'Issues Concerning Alternative Dispute Resolution Between Consumers and Traders' (2015) *Annals Constantin Brancusi U. Targu Jiu Juridical Sci.* Series 84

80 Art. 21(3) of GO 38/2015

81 Goicovici (n 64) 54–55

82 Goicovici (n 64) 55

evidence or choose to be assisted by an attorney, they will bear the expenses notwithstanding the result of the ADR procedure. This state of affairs leaves consumers at a disadvantage in comparison to traditional judicial procedures. This is because, in a court of law, consumers can request and obtain legal aid, exemptions, or reductions of legal costs. Furthermore, if the court's ruling is in their favour, they can recover their legal expenses. Nonetheless, since the law establishes clear and relatively short deadlines – a maximum of 90 days to issue an imposed solution on the parties – it is much *swifter* than a regular judicial procedure.[83]

Legal Framework for ADR Mechanisms

The framework for ADR mechanisms is done by law – GO 38/2015 – which establishes and details the a) scope of application,[84] b) access to ADR entities and procedures,[85] c) requirements for ADR entities (such as expertise, independence and impartiality, but also transparency)[86], d) efficacy requirements (such as availability and accessibility, gratuity)[87] and fairness of ADR procedures,[88] e) types ADR solutions (proposed (conciliation) or imposed (arbitration)),[89] set up conditions for ADR entities,[90] and disclosure obligations of ADR entities towards the competent authority.[91]

Role of Technology in Consumer ADR – Online Dispute Resolution for Consumer Disputes

The online dispute resolution (ODR) platform[92] provided for by Regulation (EU) 524/2013 on consumer online dispute resolution and developed by the Commission has been accessible to consumers and traders across the European Union since 15 February 2016.[93] Its objective was to help consumers and traders resolve their domestic and cross-border disputes over online purchases of goods and services with the help of alternative dispute resolution bodies, in line with the ADR Directive.

Although Romania does not explicitly utilise ICT to resolve consumer disputes, such options do exist and appear to be favoured by consumers with the required technical skills. From the data available from the official reports of ABDRC, once the electronic submission of the ADR request via online form was made available,

83 ASF Romania, <https://asfromania.ro/ro/a/1551/sal-fin> accessed 4 April 2024
84 Art. 2 of GO 38/2015
85 Art. 5 of GO 38/2015
86 Arts. 6–7 of GO 38/2015
87 Art. 8 of GO 38/2015
88 Art. 9 of GO 38/2015
89 Arts. 10,13 of GO 38/2015
90 Art. 17 of GO 38/2015
91 Art. 18 of GO 38/2015
92 EU-ODR, <https://webgate.ec.europa.eu/odr/main/?event=main.home.show> accessed 30 April 2024
93 Commission, 'Report of the Consumer Law Fitness Check' SWD (2017) 209 Final

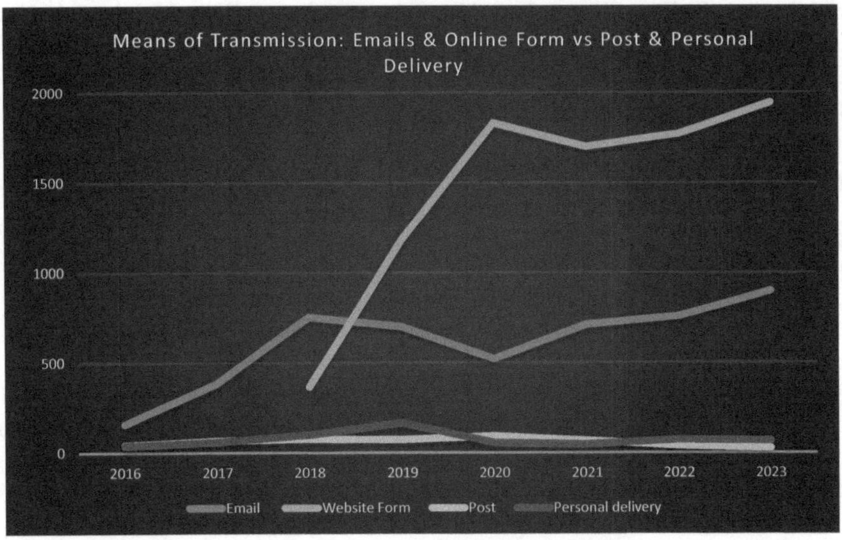

Figure 8.1 Means of Transmission: Email and Online Form versus Post and Personal Delivery

Source: ABDRC Yearly Reports 2016–2023. Compiled by the author. The data indicates the consumer preference for using ITC in applying for an ABDRC ADR solution.

it became the preferred option (See Figure 8.1). Around the same period, the email delivery option also took off, while traditional means, such as post and personal delivery, maintained a relatively steady but low number.

According to an EC Report on the application of ADR and ODR,[94] the ODR platform was one of the most visited sites of the EC, with 2.5 million visits in 2022. Yet less than 2% of visitors lodged a complaint form. The report also revealed that many consumers arriving on the platform did not understand its purpose and needed orientation.[95] Even more problematic was that 80 to 85% of complaints go unanswered on the platform, and only about 1% of the complaints (i.e. less than 200 cases) result in an ADR outcome.

The low engagement rate impacted consumers' satisfaction and trust in the tool's usefulness, with 56% reporting they would not use the platform again.[96] The lack of a realistic solution led the EC to the conclusion that the ODR mechanism is non-functional. Moreover, the rapid development of online complaint-handling systems in digital marketplaces has become one of the primary dispute-resolution

94 Commission, 'Report on the application of Directive 2013/11/EU of the European Parliament and of the Council on alternative dispute resolution for consumer disputes and Regulation (EU) No. 524/2013 of the European Parliament and of the Council on online dispute resolution for consumer disputes' COM (2023) 648 final

95 Report 2023, 8

96 Report 2023, 9

channels for SMEs selling online. All of these made the ODR platform redundant and led to the conclusion that it should be repealed.[97] A proposal in this regard was already launched at the end of 2023.[98] Once adopted, this will immediately and directly impact the relevant Romanian law.

Challenges and Opportunities

At the EU level, a 2019 report on implementing the ADR/ODR framework[99] revealed that consumer ADR was under-used due to the lack of awareness,[100] the complexity and diversity of the ADR landscape and the general reluctance of traders to participate.[101] A recent fitness check of EU consumer law on digital fairness[102] noted that most consumers (87.7%) did not take any action to solve encountered problems. Of those respondents, 12.3% sought to hold economic operators accountable, and only 3.1% mentioned they had brought a dispute to an ADR mechanism, mainly a consumer ombudsman.[103] This suggests that the role of ADR in enforcing consumer law remains marginal at best. Similar conclusions can be drawn from the Romanian experience.

As a challenge, NACP's example is telling. Until 1 July 2018, the ADR Directorate did not handle any cases because it did not obtain the necessary legal status.[104] The eight requests received, until authorisation, were redirected.[105] After authorisation, only nine more requests were registered in 2018.[106] In 2019, there were 11 requests, none of which were solved: three consumers renounced their complaints, two were rejected, and six were closed.[107] In 2020, the number of requests increased to 12. Yet again, none of them led to a conclusion. Eight were closed due to economic operators' refusal to participate in the procedure, two ended up

97 Report 2023, 10

98 Commission, 'Proposal for repealing Regulation (EU) No. 524/2013 and Amending Regulations (EU) 2017/2394 and (EU) 2018/1724 with regards to the discontinuation of the European ODR Platform (Text with EEA relevance)' COM (2023) 647 Final 2023/0375 (COD)

99 Commission, 'Report on the Application of Directive 2013/11/EU of the European Parliament and of the Council on Alternative Dispute Resolution for Consumer Disputes and Regulation (EU) No. 524/2013 of the European Parliament and of the Council on Online Dispute Resolution for Consumer Disputes' COM (2019) 425 Final

100 Report 2019, 5. According to the Report, only 6% of consumers who experienced a problem with a trader had reported it to an ADR body

101 Report 2019, 1

102 Commission, 'Factual Summary – Public Consultation on the Fitness Check of EU Consumer Law on Digital Fairness' Ref. Ares (2023)2578495

103 Factual Summary 2023, 4

104 NACP, 'Activity Report' (2018) <https://anpc.ro/wp-content/uploads/2022/06/RAPORT_ANPC_2018.pdf> accessed 29 April 2024

105 NACP, 'Activity Report' (2018) <https://anpc.ro/wp-content/uploads/2022/06/RAPORT_ANPC_2018.pdf> accessed 29 April 2024

106 NACP, 'Activity Report' (2018) <https://anpc.ro/wp-content/uploads/2022/06/RAPORT_ANPC_2018.pdf> accessed 29 April 2024 19

107 NACP, 'Activity Report' (2019) <https://anpc.ro/wp-content/uploads/2022/06/Raport_ANPC_2019.pdf> accessed 29 April 2024

with a proposed solution that the economic operators did not accept, and two were rejected due to lack of merit or legal standing.[108]

In 2021, there were 11 requests. Two were closed because the economic operators did not consent to the procedure, one was amicably settled before the finalisation of the ADR procedure, and eight were rejected due to procedural issues.[109] The latest activity report, dating from 2022, notes a 500% increase in the number of requests – 359 – however, there is no data as to if and how many of these resulted in an amicable settlement.[110] The only indication concerning results is that all ODR cases received through the European platform were solved.[111] Despite the high percentage, the outcome remains underwhelming.

The ABDRC's does not fare much better. While the number of compliant complaints increases steadily, it still does not exceed 3000 per year. Of these, a little more than 600 result in a decision accepted by the parties (see Figure 8.2). While the yearly percentage of accepted solutions relative to the number of files appears to be high (over 88% in 2023), the figure is much lower when calculated against the number of compliant complaints (22.7%) (see Figure 8.3).

The most significant challenges ADR procedures face in Romania are the lack of *attractiveness, trust,* or *awareness*. NACP also suffered from a lack of qualified staff, reflected in the few cases handled each year by the relevant institutions. Moreover, NACP utilises the mechanism by which it only proposes a solution to involved parties, enabling either party to reject it.[112] Concomitantly, companies rarely offer detailed information about ADR entities. A 2020 market study revealed that most traders did not adequately inform consumers of ADR procedures[113] and were reluctant to participate. NACP and ABDRC have attempted to solve these issues in recent years.

One of the opportunities would be to address the need *for more awareness*; as of 2022, NACP requires traders to display the information plate concerning ADR. The leaflet shall be made by the trader according to the model and displayed in a visible place near the cash register or next to the opening hours, in the sales area or, where appropriate, the service area, including the sale of tourist services, tourist packages, or air tickets. Traders operating sales websites, online order-taking and advertising of products and services, tourist services, the marketing of tourist packages

108 NACP, 'Activity Report' (2020) <https://anpc.ro/wp-content/uploads/2022/06/RAPORT_ANPC_2020.pdf> accessed 29 April 2024

109 NACP, 'Activity Report' (2021) <https://anpc.ro/wp-content/uploads/2022/06/RAPORT_ANPC_2021.pdf> accessed 29 April 2024

110 NACP, 'Activity Report' (2022) <https://anpc.ro/wp-content/uploads/2023/03/RAPORT-ANPC-ANUL-2022.pdf> accessed 29 April 2024

111 NACP, 'Activity Report' (2022) <https://anpc.ro/wp-content/uploads/2023/03/RAPORT-ANPC-ANUL-2022.pdf> accessed 29 April 2024

112 Aura-Elena Amironesei, 'Case C-380/19: A Renewal of the Standards of the Information Obligation Which is Imposed to Traders in Relation to Alternative Dispute Resolution (ADR)' (2020) 66 *Analele Stiintifice Ale Universitatii Alexandru Ioan Cuza Din Iasi Stiinte Juridice* 11

113 Lavinia Elena Smarandache, 'Extrajudicial Disputes Settlement Mechanisms Between the Credit Institutions and Consumers' (2016) *R.R.D.A.* 75

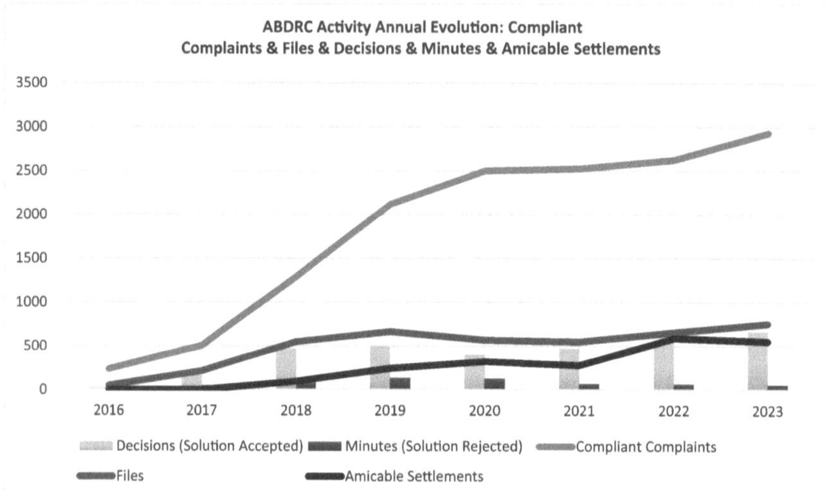

Figure 8.2 ABDRC Activity's Annual Evolution

Source: ABDRC Annual Reports 2016–2023. Compiled by the author. The chart reveals an increasing number of compliant complaints and amicable settlements, but a steady (low) number of files and solutions.

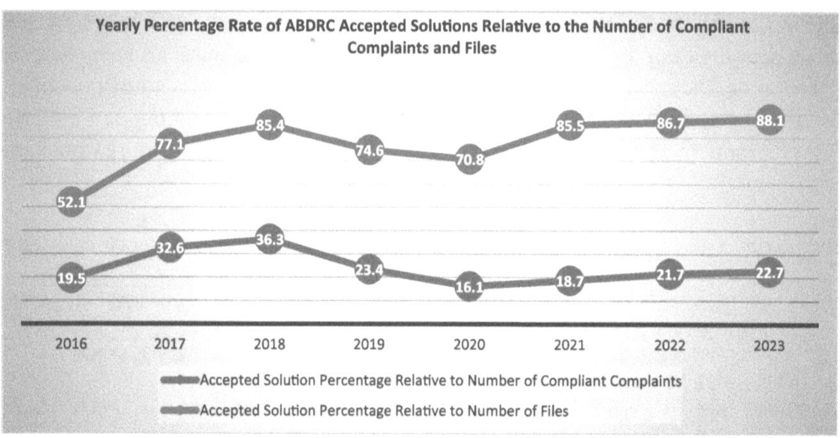

Figure 8.3 Yearly Percentage of ABDRC Accepted Solutions Relative to the Number of Compliant Complaints and Files

Source: ABDRC Yearly Reports 2016–2022. Compiled by the author. The data shows a high and steady percentage of accepted solutions.

services or airline tickets, including e-commerce, are obliged to display an icon on the first page of their website. The leaflet and icons can be found and downloaded at NACP's website.[114] During 2020 and 2021, the work of the ADR Directorate was carried out by a single person with the function of the Head of Service, although the authority advertised 12 positions in 2017,[115] and 25 in 2019.[116] These numbers remained only on paper. Only in 2022 did the Directorate get the minimum staff necessary to operate regarding *qualified personnel*.[117]

Finally, to make the procedure more *attractive*, NACP signed commitment protocols with four operators with the highest number of petitions received by the Directorate.[118] The ABDRC focused mainly on raising awareness via various information and lobbying campaigns as well as mass and social media appearances.[119] In addition, it sought to make the procedure more attractive through consumer testimonials,[120] attempted to lower the rate of banks' refusal to participate in it[121] and urged national judges to recommend ADR procedures in consumer financial disputes.[122]

Conclusion

As a result, there is uncertainty surrounding the effectiveness of ADR legislative measures in Romania and their ability to increase consumer trust in cross-border commerce. Although the percentage of out-of-court settlements of consumer disputes is growing, it remains low. This indicates that the success of the procedure cannot be determined conclusively.

In 2018, the European Commission identified several challenges hindering the effectiveness of consumer ADR procedures, such as awareness and perceptions of ADR. These challenges are still relevant and must be addressed. Improving the legislative package, particularly at the national level, is necessary to increase consumer and professional engagement in ADR procedures. Providing a stable, impartial, and transparent framework for resolving consumer disputes is also essential. The legal and institutional framework must convince consumers and professionals of ADR's effectiveness, usefulness, predictability, and advantages.

114 Lavinia Elena Smarandache, 'Extrajudicial Disputes Settlement Mechanisms Between the Credit Institutions and Consumers' (2016) *R.R.D.A.* 38

115 Lavinia Elena Smarandache, 'Extrajudicial Disputes Settlement Mechanisms Between the Credit Institutions and Consumers' (2016) *R.R.D.A.* 24

116 NACP (n 109) 40

117 NACP (n 112) 38–39

118 NACP (n 112) 38

119 ABDRC, 'Activity Report' (2023) <https://csalb.ro/wp-content/uploads/2024/02/ENG_Raport-anual-CSALB_2023_final.pdf> accessed 30 April 2024

120 ABDRC, 'Testimonials' <https://csalb.ro/en/testimonials/> accessed 30 April 2024

121 ABDRC, 'Testimonials' <https://csalb.ro/en/testimonials/> accessed 30 April 2024

122 R.S., 'CSALB: Judecătorii sunt sfătuiţi să recomande concilierea dintre consumatori şi bănci la începutul proceselor din instanţe' (22 May 2024) *Judirice* <https://www.bursa.ro/csalb-judecatorii-sunt-sfatuiti-sa-recomande-concilierea-dintre-consumatori-si-banci-la-inceputul-proceselor-din-instante-02556255> accessed 22 May 2024

References

Amironesei AE, 'Case C-380/19: A Renewal of the Standards of the Information Obligation Which Is Imposed to Traders in Relation to Alternative Dispute Resolution (ADR)' [2020] 66 Analele Stiintifice Ale Universitatii Alexandru Ioan Cuza Din Iasi Stiinte Juridice

Apan RD, *Protectia juridica a consumatorilor. Creditul destinat consumului si domeniile conexe* (Sfera juridica 2007)

Cilibiu OM, 'Issues Concerning Alternative Dispute Resolution Between Consumers and Traders' [2015] Annals Constantin Brancusi U. Targu Jiu Juridical Sci. Series 79

Goicovici J, 'Noile proceduri de solutionare alternativa a litigiilor dintre comercianti si consumatori' [2015] SUBB Jurisprudentia no 4

Patrasc-Balan I-D, 'Online Dispute Resolution Stemming From Sales or Service Contracts in European Union' [2019] 65 Analele Stiintifice ale Universitatii Alexandru Ioan Cuza Din Iasi, Stiinte Juridice

Smarandache LE, 'Extrajudicial Disputes Settlement Mechanisms Between the Credit Institutions and Consumers' [2016] (7) Revista Romana de Drept al Afacerilor 75

SR, 'Judecătorii sunt sfătuiţi să recomande concilierea dintre consumatori şi bănci la începutul proceselor din instanţe' (22 May 2024) Judirice

Stănescu C-G, 'How the Romanian Constitutional Court Highjacked Consumer Financial Protection' in H-W Micklitz and C Twigg-Flesner (eds) *The Transformation of Consumer Law and Policy in Europe* (Hart Publishing 2023)

Stănescu C-G, 'The Enforcement of Consumer Financial Protection in Romania' (2023) 12(3) Journal of European Consumer and Market Law

Stănescu C-G and Albanezi A, 'Romania's Struggle to Regulate Abusive Debt Collection Practices' in C-G Stănescu (ed) *Regulation of Debt Collection in Europe* (Routledge 2023)

Toader C, 'Enforcement and Effectiveness of Consumer Law in Romania' in H-W Micklitz and G Saumier (eds) *Enforcement and Effectiveness of Consumer Law* (Springer 2018)

9 Consumer ADR in the Kingdom of Saudi Arabia

Hani Abdulghani Alharbi

Introduction

In Saudi Arabia, ADR mechanisms have evolved significantly over time, marked by a transition from reliance on traditional judicial systems to embracing arbitration and mediation. Despite the longstanding presence of ADR, a pervasive lack of trust among the public previously hindered its widespread adoption, prompting continued dependence on the judiciary. However, legislative amendments in 2012, followed by substantial legal reforms in 2016, catalysed a paradigm shift, fostering increased utilisation and acceptance of ADR for conflict resolution. These reforms provided consumers with clear regulations and operational standards, thereby instilling confidence in the efficacy of ADR.

Notably, Saudi Arabia leverages the SCCA for arbitration services while adopting the ratified Greece international convention, which delineates the framework for mediation. This structured approach ensures accountability among involved parties and arbitrators, fostering smoother dispute resolution processes and setting clear expectations for consumers. Furthermore, the onset of the COVID-19 pandemic prompted the establishment of an ODR system, enabling remote conflict resolution via the Internet. ODR not only addresses the challenges posed by the pandemic but also promises to revolutionise dispute resolution by expediting proceedings and incentivising more significant consideration of ADR over traditional court litigation.

Legal Framework for Consumer Protection

ADR provides disputing parties with different channels to resolve a complaint out of court with the help of an impartial party. ADR was introduced to solve customer disputes because it provides them with a faster, easier, and less costly process than going to court. ADR is relevant in the business realm because solving issues requires the active participation of the conflicting parties. Accordingly, ADR provides more effective and long-lasting solutions to the challenges being raised among the conflicting parties.[1]

1 Ilijana Todorovic and Bobby Harges, 'Alternative Dispute Resolution in the World of Commercial Disputes' (2022) 5 *Journal of Strategic Contracting and Negotiation* 224

DOI: 10.4324/9781032689739-9

The process has an educational element because the expressive nature of the involved parties allows them to learn where they exceeded the limits. Reduced dispute resolution costs are also crucial for businesses. Saudi consumers should prioritise using ADR in their day-to-day operations. The government requires consumers to adhere to the Ministry of Finance guidelines when using ADR to settle disputes. For instance, the Saudi government requires that ADR will only be involved in settling disputes arising from an assessment provided by the General Authority of Zakat and Tax (GAZT) based on tax or zakat regulations.[2] In addition, Saudi law requires the taxpayers to request GAZT to the ADR committee for consideration. Notably, GAZT can accept or reject the request and settle the matter instead.

The General Design of the Enforcement Mechanism

Traditional ADR Methods

ADR has increasingly become a popular dispute-resolution method in Saudi Arabia. Mediation is among the traditional ADR methods recognised because people perceive it as more adversarial and efficient. Mediation is a prominent ADR approach since Article 8 of Saudi's Royal Decree encourages parties involved in a commercial dispute to mediate before filing a case in a court of law.[3] The Saudi government also established mediation offices in labour courts, demonstrating its commitment to ensuring that citizens and the business community can quickly solve their challenges. Munduate et al. define mediation as a process whereby a neutral third party helps the conflicting parties resolve disputes by incorporating specialised negotiation and communication approaches such as integration, pressing, compensation, and inaction.[4]

In addition, arbitration is another traditional ADR approach common in Saudi Arabia, especially after the 2012 arbitration law and the establishment of an office in Riyadh to handle arbitration complaints.[5] Initially, arbitration was unpopular in Saudi based on the distrust between the conflicting parties to have the best interests to achieve a common goal.[6] Arbitration refers to a process where the conflicting

2 Ernst & Young LLP, 'Saudi Arabia Establishes Alternative Dispute Resolution Committee' (*globaltaxnews.ey.com*, 2018) <https://globaltaxnews.ey.com/news/2018-5972-saudi-arabia-establishes-alternative-dispute-resolution-committee#:~:text=The%20ADR%20rules%20provide%3A> accessed 9 October 2023

3 Faisal Daudpota, 'Saudi Arabia: An Overview of Its Commercial Franchise Law' [2019] *SSRN Electronic Journal* <http://dx.doi.org/10.2139/ssrn.3492577> accessed 9 October 2023

4 Lourdes Munduate, Francisco J Medina, and Martin C Euwema, 'Mediation: Understanding a Constructive Conflict Management Tool in the Workplace' (2022) 38 *Journal of Work and Organizational Psychology* 165

5 Khalid Alnowaiser, 'The New Arbitration Law and Its Impact on Investment in Saudi Arabia' (2012) 29(6) *Journal of International Arbitration* 723

6 Zeyad Khoshaim, Abdullah Alajlan and Noura Alabdul Jabbar, 'Arbitration Procedures and Practice in Saudi Arabia: Overview' (*Practical Law*, 2023) <https://uk.practicallaw.thomsonreuters.com/w-040-2432?transitionType=Default&contextData=(sc.Default)&firstPage=true> accessed 11 October 2023

parties identify third parties to resolve a stand-off. Bedaiwi further identifies reconciliation as another ADR approach that gives comparable results to mediation and arbitration, thus increasing its popularity in Saudi Arabia.[7]

The Evolution and Development of Contemporary ADR Methods

ADR methods have a prolonged history in Saudi Arabia, beginning in the ancient days when the elderly in the community helped in dispute resolution. However, the evolution and development of ADR methods in Saudi Arabia can be discussed by identifying the main events in which they were applied. In 1940, an ADR approach helped to solve the diplomatic conflict between the Saudi and British governments due to the ownership of the Buraimi oases.[8] Different Gulf states, including Abu Dhabi and the Sultanate of Muscat, claimed ownership of the oases and further enjoyed protection from the British government. An agreement to solve the conflict using arbitration was signed in 1954 at Nice, and arbitrators began their work in 1955.[9] arbitration was also involved in solving the dispute between KSA and Aramco; a company contracted to export oil over the exclusive rights of transportation. The tribunal ruled in favour of Aramco, which had a longstanding negative implication on ADR approaches within the country, for instance, following the issuance of Council of Ministers Resolution No. (58), dated 06/10/1963, government agencies were banned from using arbitration as a method of dispute resolution without seeking approval from the Council of Ministers.[10]

The negative perception of using ADR as a method of dispute resolution took a turn in 2012 when a new arbitration law issued by Royal Decree No. (M/34) was introduced. The 2012 arbitration law provides guidelines that disputing parties must comply with when using arbitration. Since then, ADR approaches are increasingly gaining popularity. It is essential to note that the Saudi government acknowledged ADR as a potential dispute resolution mechanism after recognising its potential to derive satisfactory solutions for all parties involved. In addition, the Saudi government advocates for increased reform in legislation to enhance the efficiency of ADR mechanisms in dispute resolution.

7 Ahmad Bedaiwi, 'Penn State Law Alternative Dispute Resolution: Toward a Clear, Reliable and Effective Dispute Resolution System in Saudi Arabia' (2019) <https://elibrary.law.psu.edu/cgi/viewcontent.cgi?article=1013&context=sjd> accessed 9 October 2023

8 Abdulaziz Aldomaiji, 'How Has Arbitration Emerged in Saudi Arabia?' (*Lawyer Monthly|Legal News Magazine*, 28 July 2022) <https://www.lawyer-monthly.com/2022/07/how-has-arbitration-emerged-in-saudi-arabia/> accessed 9 October 2023

9 Loretta Malintoppi and Alvin Yap, 'Part II Guide to Key Preliminary and Procedural Issues, 8 Challenges of Arbitrators in Investment Arbitration: Still Work in Progress?' in Katia Yannaca-Small (ed) *From: Arbitration Under International Investment Agreements: A Guide to the Key Issues* (2nd edn, Oxford 2018)

10 Loretta Malintoppi and Alvin Yap, 'Part II Guide to Key Preliminary and Procedural Issues, 8 Challenges of Arbitrators in Investment Arbitration: Still Work in Progress?' in Katia Yannaca-Small (ed) *From: Arbitration Under International Investment Agreements: A Guide to the Key Issues* (2nd edn, Oxford 2018) 45

An Overview of the Bodies and Institutions Involved in Consumer ADR

The regulations introduced by the Saudi government demonstrate that ADR is highly regulated. Accordingly, the government established some bodies and institutions to regulate the use of ADR mechanisms as protective measures following the negative repercussions experienced after Saudi lost cases against the British over Buraini oases and Aramco.[11] One of the bodies involved in Saudi's ADR approach is the Council of Ministers Resolution, which came up with the regulations to guide arbitration in the country's jurisdiction.[12]

The regulations provided by this body determine how consumers in the country can initiate dispute resolution using ADR approaches, witness calling, experts, and ways to deal with failure to abide by the summons. The 2012 new arbitration law added new bodies dealing with the arbitration process among the ADR approaches allowed in the country. Another institution introduced by the 2012 law is the General Authority of Zakat and Tax (GAZT), which is responsible for assessing tax compliance and the validity of a complaint to be successful. Accordingly, Saudi consumers intending to use ADR must seek approval from GAZT. In addition, the Council of Ministers is relevant in using ADR effectively because government agencies must seek its approval.

Public Versus Privately Operated Bodies

Both public and privately owned bodies can operate ADR mechanisms in Saudi Arabia. Despite the differences, ADR bodies, whether public or private, intend to provide consumers with much faster, easier, and cost-efficient dispute resolution mechanisms. Public ADR focuses on addressing challenges associated with matters of concern to a majority of the people, such as city or nationwide policies. An example of a public ADR in Saudi involves the Buraimi oases because matters of boundaries create public interest.[13] Explorers had shown that Buraimi oases were rich in oil, which led the Saudi King, Abdulaziz Al Saud, to claim territory ownership. However, these claims were vehemently opposed by Oman and Trucial States (today's United Arab Emirates), who enjoyed support from the British government. The contention between these states led to an arbitration between the aggrieved parties. Attempts to own the territory were stopped until a solution was found. The Saudi government lost this case in the arbitration based on boundary reforms in the region.

On the other hand, private ADR focuses on addressing conflicts that do not trigger public interest. Examples of such conflicts include a case between a state and a private company over tax compliance, a conflict between two individual

11 Marianne Routh, "UNCITRAL Model Law on International Commercial Arbitration' in Frank-Bernd Weigand and Antje Baumann (eds) *Practioner's Handbook on International Commercial Arbitration* (3rd edn, Oxford 2019)

12 Nancy Turck, 'Dispute Resolution in Saudi Arabia' (1988) <https://core.ac.uk/download/pdf/216910929.pdf> accessed 9 October 2023

13 Omar S Abdellatif and Abdulaziz Al Meajel, 'The Buraimi Crisis: The Anglo-American Rivalry in the Arabian Peninsula, 1949–1955' (2021) 11 *Armstrong Undergraduate Journal of History* 102

entrepreneurs, or a complaint involving a seller and a buyer. According to Fine et al., the advocates for the private ADR argue that it is not realistic to have the judicial system address all complaints despite its ability to do so because it is overloaded, which causes delays in solving disputes.[14] Therefore, the Saudi Republic needs to consider using other alternatives that can help resolve disputes.

Current Consumer Dispute Resolution Processes

An Overview and Discussion of Different ADR Mechanisms

The Saudi government developed the SCCA model clauses as its ADR mechanism, especially on arbitration. The first edition of the SCCA Arbitration Rules was adopted in May 2016. The second edition of the SCCA Rules was adopted in May 2023 following a rigorous process involving the Advisory Committee, local and international practitioners, public consultation, and compliance with international arbitration regulations.[15] According to Article 4 of the SCCA Arbitration Rules, the complainant issues an arbitration request to other parties of interest accompanying relevant documents and submits the same request to the SCCA.[16]

In addition, the request for arbitration requires the parties to complete some requirements such as the presence of a statement referring the dispute to SCCA, names and contact details of parties of interest, a copy of the legal instruments leading to the emergence of the dispute, a description of the claim, and statement of the amount claimed. In addition, there should be a proposal for where arbitration should occur, and the language used. The complainant is required to pay a fee that will be incurred in the arbitration process. Further, the interested parties are legally responsible for answering the arbitration request within 30 days.[17] The SCCA court appoints one arbitrator if the parties have not agreed on the number of arbitrators that should be involved in the case. However, the SCCA court can appoint three arbitrators depending on the complexity and size of the case and any other unique factors characterising the complaint. The Arbitral Tribunal takes charge of information exchange between the parties of interest to eliminate delays.

Mediation in Saudi supports international grievances among consumers following the ratification of the UN Convention on Global Settlements in 2020. Article 1 of the convention agreement determines the scope of the mediation mechanism's

14 Erika S Fine and Elizabeth S Plapinger, 'Introduction to Overview of Private ADR' in Erika S Fine and Elizabeth S Plapinger (eds) *ADR and the Courts* (Butterworth-Heinemann 1987) 9

15 SCCA, 'Arbitration Rules – Saudi Center for Commercial Arbitration' (*sadr.org*, 2023) <https://sadr.org/ADRServices-arbitration-arbitration-rules?lang=en#:~:text=SCCA%20Model%20Clauses&text=Parties%20are%20encouraged%20to%20consider> accessed 9 October 2023

16 SCCA, 'Arbitration Rules – Saudi Center for Commercial Arbitration' (*sadr.org*, 2023) <https://sadr.org/ADRServices-arbitration-arbitration-rules?lang=en#:~:text=SCCA%20Model%20Clauses&text=Parties%20are%20encouraged%20to%20consider> accessed 9 October 2023

17 SCCA, 'Arbitration Rules – Saudi Center for Commercial Arbitration' (*sadr.org*, 2023) <https://sadr.org/ADRServices-arbitration-arbitration-rules?lang=en#:~:text=SCCA%20Model%20Clauses&text=Parties%20are%20encouraged%20to%20consider> accessed 9 October 2023

application. The convention includes a provision of adequate evidence concerning the dispute before applying the law in any member country. In addition, the mediation provides a ground through which the parties can refuse to grant relief. The Saudi mechanisms used in arbitration and mediation create some policies that users must abide by during the dispute resolution process.

The Role and Functionality of Mechanisms

According to Sturner et al., the role of consumer ADR is to provide them with user-friendly, swift, and cheap strategies to solve disputes among traders.[18] Consumers often opt for ADR mechanisms when confronted with relatively small financial value conflicts or those deemed unworthy of extensive time and resources typically demanded by the judicial system.

The ombudsman selected for the ADR processes is an intermediary, which minimises complainants' effort, especially when the consumers are unaware of legal provisions associated with the conflict. In addition, the ADR plays an essential role in enhancing access to justice by applying the law to individuals whose rights are infringed. To emphasise this, the Sharia law in Saudi Arabia requires the ADR to comply with the country's laws and legislation. As a result, Consumers seek access to justice by employing Alternative Dispute Resolution (ADR) methods to address and resolve their complaints lodged against other traders or entities.

Legal Requirements and Underpinnings During the Formation and Functionality of the Mechanisms

The formation and functioning of the Saudi ADR mechanisms demands strict adherence to the rules and regulations associated with the country's rule of law. Saudi ADR laws have a long and controversial history, given the government lost in the case against Aramco using arbitration. *Saudi Arabia v Aramco* arbitration followed a conflict in the interpretation of the concession agreement 1933 that had given the latter exclusive rights to transport oil extracted in the country. The Saudi government has developed numerous decrees and laws providing a standard to ensure that the ADR approaches will be efficient in addressing any emerging disputes. The ADR decrees include the Cabinet Decree 103 and the Royal Decree No. 28004. Royal Decree No. 28004 was issued in 2016 and established an independent professional ADR Centre within the Saudi Ministry of Justice, setting forth standards for ADR practitioners, training requirements, and standards upon which disputes will be settled and resolved, while Cabinet Decree 103 provides a comprehensive framework for ADR. The laws include the Singapore Convention on Mediation 2019, Commercial Courts Law, and the Arbitration Law 2012.[19]

18 Michael Stürner, Fernando Gascón Inchausti, and Remo Caponi, *The Role of Consumer ADR in the Administration of Justice* (National and International Perspectives 2014) 130

19 Hamed Hassan Merah and James MacPherson, 'Global Arbitration Review – The Middle Eastern and African Arbitration Review 2021' (*globalarbitrationreview.com*, 2021) <https://

In addition, the legal requirements of the ADR mechanisms, like reciprocity and enforcement of arbitral awards, determine the scope of validity for each approach.[20] This ensures that consumers use the proper ADR mechanism in addressing varying challenges experienced in day-to-day activities. This also helps provide the consumers with the proper mechanism to ensure the challenges they encounter are solved through ADR. Finally, to enhance the functionality of the ADR mechanisms, the Saudi legal framework outlines that consumers raising complaints must comply with specific attributes for the approaches to be practical. For example, the law specifies which party is responsible for communication, legal fees, and the particular qualities or standards they are required to adhere to.

These measures are essential in ensuring no delays or disagreements between the parties on how the procedure should be undertaken. Article 14 of the SCCA rules requires that arbitrators have full legal potential and a university degree in Sharia law. In addition, all awards given following the completion of the ADR process must be within the parameters of the Sharia Law.

Benefits of the Mechanisms in Consumer Conflict Resolution

ADR mechanisms are cost-efficient because of the minimum litigation costs incurred. However, consumers must be aware that when using arbitration, they are responsible for compensating the arbitrator. Another advantage of ADR mechanisms is their ability to save time because the ombudsman requires a very short time to help conflicting parties establish a permanent solution to their problem. In addition, ADR involves a flexible process, mainly because the parties involved can choose their arbitrator or mediator individually. Finally, ADR gives consumers privacy when addressing challenges because the cases are resolved privately, unlike public court proceedings.

Alternative Dispute Resolution for Consumer Disputes

Overview

It is essential to understand the impact of ADR on Saudi's consumer rights protection, satisfaction, and overall well-being. According to Cooley, ADR and consumer rights protection have been considered an 'odd-couple for prolonged periods.'[21]

globalarbitrationreview.com/review/the-middle-eastern-and-african-arbitration-review/2021/article/saudi-arabia> accessed 9 October 2023

20 Zeyad Khoshaim, Abdullah Alajlan, and Noura Alabdul Jabbar, 'Arbitration Procedures and Practice in Saudi Arabia: Overview' (*Practical Law*, 2023) <https://uk.practicallaw.thomsonreuters.com/w-040-2432?transitionType=Default&contextData=(sc.Default)&firstPage=true> accessed 11 October 2023

21 John Cooley, 'Loyola Consumer Law Review Alternative Dispute Resolution and Consumer Protection: An "Odd-Couple" Thriving in the Offices of State Attorneys General Recommended Citation' (1988) 1 *Loy. Consumer L. Rev* <https://core.ac.uk/download/pdf/268430447.pdf> accessed 9 October 2023

The relationship between ADR and the protection of consumer rights is essential to clarify and understand an odd couple due to the significant variation in their approach. ADR focuses on peace-making between the parties involved in a dispute, while consumer protection involves aggressive laws to protect consumers. Nusantara et al., define the protection of consumer rights as a scenario whereby the sellers have equal rights with the buyers.[22] It gives consumers the right to know the products they buy in detail, including exposure to the manufacturing process. Similarly, consumer protection rights allow consumers to know the ingredients used to make food products. Accordingly, consumer protection demands that sellers defraud or engage in acts of omission concerning their interests, face the law and compensate buyers. Cooley further argues that ADR effectively protects consumer rights because it helps the conflicting parties easily agree.[23] In addition, the parties are able to communicate better, which enhances the other party's understanding of their concerns, making it easy to reach a concession.

Using ADR as a dispute resolution mechanism positively impacts consumers' satisfaction. The advantages of using ADR include the easy application process, the speed of solving a conflict, and cost-effectiveness. The conflicting parties consider ADR approaches as an alternative to the legal court process.[24] In addition; the parties also have an opportunity to consider pursuing the conflict in the legal system if unsatisfied with the settlement. The ADR mechanisms are essential in enhancing the overall well-being of the consumers. One of the advantages of using ADR is its ability to provide long-lasting solutions when addressing consumer disputes.[25] The primary benefit of ADR is protecting involved parties from other disputes that might escalate the current issues or limit the conflict resolution process. Accordingly, the parties involved in dispute resolution are confident and satisfied with the process, which enhances their confidence in the solution acquired from the process. Therefore, the ADR mechanism helps maintain order in the entire process by ensuring each party understands what is required from them. In addition, the ADR conflict resolution mechanism provides consumers with a standard or expected code of behaviour when solving problems. For instance, the parties involved in the conflict understand what is required from them, such as their time before a response to the arbitration is given.

22 Redi Nusantara, Augusty Tae Ferdinand, and I Made Sukresna, 'Consumerism and Consumer Protection' (2023) 16 *Baltic Journal of Law and Politics* 843 <https://versita.com/menuscript/index.php/Versita/article/view/1364> accessed 9 October 2023

23 John Cooley, 'Loyola Consumer Law Review Alternative Dispute Resolution and Consumer Protection: An "Odd-Couple" Thriving in the Offices of State Attorneys General Recommended Citation' (1988) 1 *Loy. Consumer L. Rev, 11* <https://core.ac.uk/download/pdf/268430447.pdf> accessed 9 October 2023

24 Kristen Blankley et al., 'Nebraska Law Review Nebraska Law Review Recommended Citation Recommended Citation' (2021) <https://digitalcommons.unl.edu/cgi/viewcontent.cgi?article=3298&context=nlr> accessed 9 October 2023

25 Kevin Gibson, 'Promises and Problems in Alternative Dispute Resolution for the Elderly' (2001) <https://scholarship.law.marquette.edu/cgi/viewcontent.cgi?article=1252&context=elders> accessed 9 October 2023

Practical ADR Cases in Saudi Arabia: A Critique of Both Successful and Unsuccessful Cases

There have been successful and unsuccessful ADR cases in Saudi Arabia. An example of a successful case was between *Samsung v the Saudi government.*[26] The two parties agreed to engage in arbitration to solve the issue under contention. The parties had signed an investment contract, and Samsung was supposed to construct the Seawater Desalination and Yanbu 3 electric power plant in Saudi Arabia. However, the Saudi government violated the investment agreement when terminating the contract. The contract violated in this case is the International Centre for Settlement of Investment dispute.[27] Given the complexity of the issue, three arbitrators listened to the case and provided suitable solutions. The arbitral tribunal ruled in favour of Samsung since it was confirmed that the state had applied for an investor-state dispute settlement. This case emphasises the need for investment teams to comply with all the terms outlined in the agreement to ensure they do not attract any legal implications.

The Buraimi Oases dispute is an example of an unsuccessful ADR case in Saudi Arabia. The Buraimi dispute was a territorial conflict between the Saudi government, Oman, and the UAE. The arbitration was unsuccessful because the British arbitrator withdrew from the process, arguing that the Saudi government wanted to influence the outcome. The withdrawal of the British arbitrator meant that the dispute resolution process was halted, and other mechanisms were being considered to derive the most viable solution. Eventually, the British government decided to rescind unilaterally and took over the Oasis in 1955. In this case, the collapse of the arbitration process is one reason why the Saudi government was strict in its ADR approaches until the 2012 amendments.

Role of Technology in Consumer ADR – Online Dispute Resolution for Consumer Disputes

Challenges Experienced in the Different ADR Processes

Several challenges are experienced in the different ADR processes. One shared challenge across these processes is the potential to delay court proceedings if the parties resort to the judicial system. Regarding arbitration, parties generally cannot abandon the process and resort to court if the arbitration is binding, unlike mediation, which doesn't require reaching an agreement for resolution.[28] On the other hand, there are challenges specific to arbitration and mediation. Arbitration

26 Janeba E, 'Investor State Dispute Settlement and Host Country Regulation: Insights From Economic Theory' [2021] *Handbook of International Investment Law and Policy* 665

27 Investment Policy Hub, '*Samsung v Saudi Arabia*, Investment Dispute Settlement Navigator, UNCTAD Investment Policy Hub' (*investmentpolicy.unctad.org*, 2022) <https://investmentpolicy.unctad.org/investment-dispute-settlement/cases/856/samsung-v-saudi-arabia> accessed 9 October 2023

28 Valbon Mulaj, 'The Advantages and Disadvantages of Arbitration in Relation to the Regular Courts in Kosovo' (2018) 59 *Hungarian Journal of Legal Studies* 118

creates a probability whereby the conflicting parties will doubt and disregard the ruling if the arbitrator's independence is questionable. In addition, the finality of arbitration does not create room for appeals.[29] If parties are unsatisfied, there are limited opportunities to correct the issue. Finally, arbitration can exhibit unpredictability, leading to uncertainty for the parties involved regarding the outcome. Regarding the arbitrability of consumer disputes in the country, some jurisdictions may not allow certain consumer disputes to be resolved through arbitration. If parties in Saudi Arabia agree to arbitration before a dispute emerges, such an arbitration agreement might be considered invalid.

Mediation also has limitations, creating an opportunity to dissatisfy the conflicting parties. Foremost, mediation can lead the parties to engage in endless negotiations when they cannot agree on the same solution. Lengthy proceedings tend to be tedious and can easily influence the parties to lose focus on addressing the present challenge. In addition, interpersonal traits such as language barriers, cultural obstacles, and emotional barriers cannot derive a binding solution.[30] This means that a lot of time can be spent trying to find a suitable solution, yet the parties consider pursuing the matter further in court because the process did not satisfy their interests.

Anticipated Changes in ADR Processes

The advancement in technology has the potential to have a significant impact on Saudi's arbitration process. Advancements in computing present new opportunities for the parties of interest and arbitrators to share information, prepare, organise, and make decisions in cases.[31] The speed of sharing the evidence documents will reduce the waiting time the parties require before acquiring a solution. In addition, virtual communication is another facilitating factor in arbitration in Saudi. The general public is familiar with videoconferencing tools, which personalise communication for parties located long distances. In addition, technology makes it easy to collect information related to past cases, which can help to inform current decisions. As technology continuously advances, one can expect it will have a more in-depth impact on the ADR processes.

The Effectiveness of the Anticipated Changes in Addressing the Challenges

The only problem that the anticipated change will help address is minimising the time taken to resolve a conflict in court if ADR failed in the first place. Technology

29 Md Manjur Hossain Patoari et al., 'Legal and Administrative Challenges of Alternative Dispute Resolution (ADR) as a Peaceful Means of Resolving the Land Dispute in the Rural Areas of Bangladesh' (2020) 11 *Beijing Law Review* 415

30 Dale Bagshaw, 'Mediation in the World Today: Opportunities and Challenges' (2015) 2 *Journal of Mediation and Applied Conflict Analysis* <https://core.ac.uk/download/pdf/297018241.pdf> accessed 9 October 2023

31 Vianney Sebayiga, 'Evaluating the Role of Technology-Powered Alternative Dispute Resolution (ADR) in a Post-Pandemic Africa' [2023] *SSRN Electronic Journal* <https://papers.ssrn.com/sol3/papers.cfm?abstract_id=4136496> accessed 9 October 2023

integration speeds up the process since information sharing is quickly completed.[32] The anticipated changes will also help further reduce the cost of ADR processes. For instance, while it was vital for the arbitrators to meet and negotiate in the past, this can be conducted virtually, removing the transportation costs. In addition, using technology enables translators to be used in the arbitration process, which eliminates language barriers. This measure can ensure the parties can communicate efficiently without hiring a professional translator. As a result, the anticipated changes can significantly help address most of the challenges associated with the ADR processes.

Challenges and Opportunities

ADR mechanisms such as arbitration and mediation have a longstanding history in Saudi Arabia dispute resolution. The evolution of the ADR processes in the country has been marked by changes in legislation to provide more guidelines and increase people's trust in the process. Saudi Arabia has experienced successful and unsuccessful applications of the ADR mechanism, such as in the case of *Samsung v Saudi Arabia* and the *Buraimi* dispute. In addition, the Saudi government has adopted the SCCA law, which provides a mechanism to guide the use of arbitration while also ratifying an international convention law concerning the use of mediation. There is also a positive connection between the ADR and the protection of consumer rights, satisfaction, and the overall well-being of consumers. However, it is crucial to tackle the significant challenges linked to ADR, including potential delays in court proceedings if parties opt for litigation and the possibility of not fully satisfying all conflicting parties. By addressing these issues, these mechanisms can significantly alleviate the burden of relying solely on the judicial system and encourage the utilisation of alternative methods for resolving disputes.

The advancement of ADR mechanisms helps to improve consumer protection because conflicting parties can settle on a lasting solution for the issues under contention. In addition, ADR mechanisms allow open discussions between conflicting parties, which creates an opportunity for them to better understand the expectations they have of each other.[33] Finally, ADR enhances the protection of consumers by ensuring that the conflicting parties identify the most viable solution to the challenges encountered, which increases the level of satisfaction between the conflicting parties.

Advancements in technology are among the anticipated changes that will facilitate the ADR processes in Saudi Arabia. During the COVID-19 pandemic, most dispute resolution systems moved online, creating systems for online dispute

32 Colin Rule, 'Technology and the Future of Dispute Resolution' (2015) <https://law.scu.edu/wp-content/uploads/Rule-Technology-and-the-Future-of-Dispute-Resolution-copy.pdf> accessed 9 October 2023

33 Marco Loos, 'Consumer ADR After Implementation of the ADR Directive: Enforcing European Consumer Rights at the Detriment of European Consumer Law' [2015] *SSRN Electronic Journal* <https://papers.ssrn.com/sol3/papers.cfm?abstract_id=2685651> accessed 9 October 2023

resolution. ODR is effective in addressing both local and international consumer disputes. However, Alharbi argues that the Sharia laws, which greatly define Saudi culture, make it challenging to integrate online platforms into the system, and this ultimately threatens the usage of ODR.[34] Nonetheless, there are numerous advantages associated with ODR, including accessibility, ease of ease, cost-effectiveness, and flexibility.[35] More research should be conducted in this area to identify ways to enhance the effectiveness of ODR in dispute resolution.

Conclusion

The evolution of ADR mechanisms in Saudi Arabia signifies a critical shift towards more efficient, cost-effective, and user-friendly methods for resolving consumer disputes. Historically marked by distrust and limited application, ADR mechanisms such as arbitration and mediation have gradually gained acceptance, particularly following legislative reforms in 2012 and 2016. The SCCA and the ratified Greece international convention have established robust frameworks that enhance the credibility and efficacy of these mechanisms. Additionally, the introduction of ODR during the COVID-19 pandemic has further streamlined the process, allowing for faster and more accessible conflict resolution. These advancements underscore the Saudi government's commitment to protecting consumer rights and ensuring equitable and satisfactory outcomes for all parties involved.

However, the integration and effectiveness of ADR mechanisms in Saudi Arabia are not without challenges. Issues such as potential delays in court proceedings, the finality of arbitration decisions, and cultural barriers in mediation must be addressed to enhance ADR processes' overall efficiency and acceptance. The anticipated technological advancements, particularly in facilitating ODR, promise to overcome some of these challenges by reducing costs, eliminating language barriers, and expediting the resolution process. As Saudi Arabia continues to refine its ADR frameworks, it is imperative to ensure that these mechanisms align with Sharia law and cultural norms to maintain their legitimacy and acceptance. In conclusion, while ADR mechanisms have made significant strides in Saudi Arabia, ongoing efforts to address existing challenges and leverage technological advancements will further enhance their effectiveness and foster a more robust consumer protection landscape.

References

Abdellatif OS and Al Meajel A, 'The Buraimi Crisis: The Anglo-American Rivalry in the Arabian Peninsula, 1949–1955' (2021) 11 Armstrong Undergraduate Journal of History

34 Dr Mohammad Alharbi, 'Key Challenges Facing Online Dispute Resolution in Saudi Arabia' (2019) 88 *Journal of Law, Policy and Globalization* 76

35 Karolina Mania, 'Online Dispute Resolution: The Future of Justice' (2015) 1 *International Comparative Jurisprudence* 76 <https://www.sciencedirect.com/science/article/pii/S2351667415000074> accessed 9 October 2023

Aldomaiji A, 'How Has Arbitration Emerged in Saudi Arabia?' (*Lawyer Monthly|Legal News Magazine*, 28 July 2022) <https://www.lawyer-monthly.com/2022/07/how-has-arbitration-emerged-in-saudi-arabia/> accessed 9 October 2023

Alharbi M, 'Key Challenges Facing Online Dispute Resolution in Saudi Arabia' (2019) 88 Journal of Law, Policy and Globalization 76

Alnowaiser K, 'The New Arbitration Law and Its Impact on Investment in Saudi Arabia' (2012) 29 Journal of International Arbitration 723

Bagshaw D, 'Mediation in the World Today: Opportunities and Challenges' (2015) 2 Journal of Mediation and Applied Conflict Analysis <https://core.ac.uk/download/pdf/297018241.pdf> accessed 9 October 2023

Bedaiwi A, 'Penn State Law Alternative Dispute Resolution: Toward a Clear, Reliable and Effective Dispute Resolution System in Saudi Arabia' (2019) <https://elibrary.law.psu.edu/cgi/viewcontent.cgi?article=1013&context=sjd> accessed 9 October 2023

Blankley K, et al., 'Nebraska Law Review Nebraska Law Review Recommended Citation Recommended Citation' (2021) <https://digitalcommons.unl.edu/cgi/viewcontent.cgi?article=3298&context=nlr> accessed 9 October 2023

Cooley J, 'Loyola Consumer Law Review Alternative Dispute Resolution and Consumer Protection: An "Odd-Couple" Thriving in the Offices of State Attorneys General Recommended Citation' (1988) 1 Loy. Consumer L. Rev <https://core.ac.uk/download/pdf/268430447.pdf> accessed 9 October 2023

Daudpota F, 'Saudi Arabia: An Overview of Its Commercial Franchise Law' [2019] SSRN Electronic Journal <https://papers.ssrn.com/sol3/papers.cfm?abstract_id=3492577> accessed 9 October 2023

Ernst & Young LLP, 'Saudi Arabia Establishes Alternative Dispute Resolution Committee' (*globaltaxnews.ey.com*, 2018) <https://globaltaxnews.ey.com/news/2018–5972-saudi-arabia-establishes-alternative-dispute-resolution-committee#:~:text=The%20ADR%20rules%20provide%3A> accessed 9 October 2023

Fine ES and Plapinger ES, 'Introduction to Overview of Private ADR' (1987) ADR and the Courts 9

Gibson K, 'Promises and Problems in Alternative Dispute Resolution for the Elderly' (2001) <https://scholarship.law.marquette.edu/cgi/viewcontent.cgi?article=1252&context=elders> accessed 9 October 2023

Investment Policy Hub, 'Samsung v. Saudi Arabia|Investment Dispute Settlement Navigator|UNCTAD Investment Policy Hub' (*investmentpolicy.unctad.org*, 2022) <https://investmentpolicy.unctad.org/investment-dispute-settlement/cases/856/samsung-v-saudi-arabia> accessed 9 October 2023

Khoshaim Z, Alajlan A and Jabbar NA, 'Arbitration Procedures and Practice in Saudi Arabia: Overview' (*Practical Law*, 2023) <https://uk.practicallaw.thomsonreuters.com/w-040–2432?transitionType=Default&contextData=(sc.Default)&firstPage=true> accessed 11 October 2023

Lominack R, 'Examining Alternative Dispute Resolution in the International Business Domain' (2003) 1 South Carolina Journal of International Law and Business South Carolina Journal of International Law and Business <https://scholarcommons.sc.edu/cgi/viewcontent.cgi?article=1127&context=scjilb> accessed 9 October 2023

Loos M, 'Consumer ADR after Implementation of the ADR Directive: Enforcing European Consumer Rights at the Detriment of European Consumer Law' (2015) SSRN Electronic Journal <https://papers.ssrn.com/sol3/papers.cfm?abstract_id=2685651> accessed 9 October 2023

Loretta M and Alvin Y, 'Part II Guide to Key Preliminary and Procedural Issues, 8 Challenges of Arbitrators in Investment Arbitration: Still Work in Progress?' (2018) Arbitration Under International Investment Agreements

Mania K, 'Online Dispute Resolution: The Future of Justice' (2015) 1 International Comparative Jurisprudence 76 https://www.sciencedirect.com/science/article/pii/S2351667415000074

Marianne R, 'Part IV International Treaties, 20 UNCITRAL Model Law on International Commercial Arbitration' [2019] Practitioner's Handbook on International Commercial Arbitration

Merah HH and MacPherson J, 'Global Arbitration Review – The Middle Eastern and African Arbitration Review 2021' (*globalarbitrationreview.com*, 2021) <https://globalarbitrationreview.com/review/the-middle-eastern-and-african-arbitration-review/2021/article/saudi-arabia> accessed 9 October 2023

Mulaj V, 'The Advantages and Disadvantages of Arbitration in Relation to the Regular Courts in Kosovo' (2018) 59 Hungarian Journal of Legal Studies 118

Munduate L, Medina FJ and Euwema MC, 'Mediation: Understanding a Constructive Conflict Management Tool in the Workplace' (2022) 38 Journal of Work and Organizational Psychology 165

Nusantara R, Ferdinand AT and Sukresna IM, 'Consumerism and Consumer Protection' (2023) 16 Baltic Journal of Law & Politics 843 <https://versita.com/menuscript/index.php/Versita/article/view/1364> accessed 9 October 2023

Patoari MdMH, et al., 'Legal and Administrative Challenges of Alternative Dispute Resolution (ADR) as a Peaceful Means of Resolving the Land Dispute in the Rural Areas of Bangladesh' (2020) 11 Beijing Law Review 415

Quinlan H, et al., 'Arbitration Procedures and Practice in Saudi Arabia: Overview' (*signon.thomsonreuters.com*, 2017) <https://uk.practicallaw.thomsonreuters.com/5-632-8065?transitionType=Default&contextData=(sc.Default)&firstPage=true> accessed 9 October 2023

Rabinovich-Einy O, 'The Past, Present, and Future of Online Dispute Resolution' (2021) 74 Current Legal Problems 125

Rule C, 'Technology and the Future of Dispute Resolution' (2015) <https://law.scu.edu/wp-content/uploads/Rule-Technology-and-the-Future-of-Dispute-Resolution-copy.pdf> accessed 9 October 2023

SCCA, 'Arbitration Rules – Saudi Center for Commercial Arbitration' (*sadr.org*, 2023) <https://sadr.org/ADRServices-arbitration-arbitration-rules?lang=en#:~:text=SCCA%20Model%20Clauses&text=Parties%20are%20encouraged%20to%20consider> accessed 9 October 2023

Sebayiga V, 'Evaluating the Role of Technology-Powered Alternative Dispute Resolution (ADR) in a Post-Pandemic Africa' [2023] SSRN Electronic Journal <https://papers.ssrn.com/sol3/papers.cfm?abstract_id=4136496> accessed 9 October 2023

Stürner M, Inchausti FG and Caponi R, *The Role of Consumer ADR in the Administration of Justice* (New Trends in Access to Justice Under EU Directive 2014)

Sulistianingsih D, et al., 'Online Dispute Resolution: Does the System Actually Enhance the Mediation Framework?' (2023) 9 Cogent Social Sciences

Todorovic I and Harges B, 'Alternative Dispute Resolution in the World of Commercial Disputes' (2022) 5 Journal of Strategic Contracting and Negotiation 214

Turck N, 'Dispute Resolution in Saudi Arabia' (1988) <https://core.ac.uk/download/pdf/216910929.pdf> accessed 9 October 2023

Turrini M, 'Mediation in Saudi Arabia: Ratification of the Singapore Convention on Mediation and the SCCA Emergency Mediation Program|White & Case LLP' (www.whitecase.com, 15 June 2020) <https://www.whitecase.com/insight-alert/mediation-saudi-arabia-ratification-singapore-convention-mediation-and-scca-emergency> accessed 9 October 2023

10 Consumer ADR in South Africa

Tjakie Naude

Introduction

Substantive consumer rights have little value if consumers have no accessible means of enforcing them. The South African Consumer Protection Act No. 68 of 2008 ('CPA'), the consumer legislation with the broadest reach, explicitly recognises consumers' right to redress in its preamble and headings of two parts dealing with enforcement.[1]

National regulators like the National Credit Regulator ('NCR'), National Consumer Commission ('NCC') and Financial Sector Conduct Authority ('FSCA') do not have sufficient resources to deal with all complaints by consumers falling under their broad jurisdiction.[2] In addition, the ordinary courts (except for the Small Claims Courts) are out of reach of ordinary consumers, most of whom are hyper-vulnerable.[3] It is, therefore, good that consumer legislation in South Africa promotes alternative dispute resolution ('ADR'). In South Africa, ADR agents comprise industry ombuds[4] enforcing accredited industry codes of conduct (so co-regulation), ombuds created by statute, provincial consumer protection authorities who mediate disputes before referring them to provincial consumer tribunals, and other ADR agents, including dispute resolution systems developed by industry self-regulation.[5]

1 Chapter 3 Part A and Part C of the CPA

2 Tanya Woker, 'Consumer Protection and Alternative Dispute Resolution' (2016) 28 *SA Merc LJ* 21 22 ('Woker 2016'). For a full discussion of enforcement bodies recognised under the CPA, see Corlia Van Heerden, 'Chapter 3' in Tjakie Naude and Sieg Eiselen (eds) *Commentary on the Consumer Protection Act* (Revision Service 9, Juta 2023)

3 This will be explained more. 49.1% of South Africans lived below the poverty line as defined by the government in 2019 (the latest figures; Stats SA, Five facts about poverty in South Africa (2019) <https://www.statssa.gov.za/?p=12075> accessed 19 April 2024. The unemployment rate was 41.1% at the end of 2023 (Stats SA, Quarterly Labour Force Survey (QLFS)-Q4: 2023 Q4, <https://www.statssa.gov.za/publications/P0211/Media%20release%20QLFS%20Q4%202023.pdf> accessed 19 April 2024)

4 The original Nordic spelling of ombudsman is often abbreviated to ombud to remove perceived gender bias, even though 'ombudsman' is gender-neutral in the original language

5 Section 134A of the National Credit Act requires registration of everyone offering ADR to credit consumers with the National Credit Regulator; for criticism see Woker 2016 (n 2) 30–31. Alternative

DOI: 10.4324/9781032689739-10

The next part will examine the legal framework for consumer protection in South Africa, after which the general design of the enforcement mechanism will be discussed in the third part. The fourth part will consider redress via tribunals and courts, and in the fifth part ADR in consumer matters will be considered. The sixth part will analyse online dispute resolution ('ODR'), after which challenges and opportunities will be considered in Part VII before Part VIII concludes the chapter.

Legal Framework for Consumer Protection

Consumer Protection Policy

There is no single all-encompassing policy for consumer protection. Instead, the national government has created regulatory systems which cover different aspects of consumer protection and are overseen by the Department of Trade and Industry, with the main goals of 'competitive and socially responsible business and consumer regulations, for easy access to redress and efficient markets'.[6]

Since national and provincial governments have concurrent jurisdiction over consumer protection, provincial governments typically promulgate legislation that empowers the provincial consumer protection authorities to enforce national and provincial consumer laws and mandates provincial consumer tribunals to decide consumer cases.[7]

The Principal Legal Framework Governing Consumer Rights and Remedies

South Africa has an uncodified mixed legal system based on Roman-Dutch law and English law developed by the courts. The uncodified common law is supplemented by legislation. No single piece of legislation governs all aspects of consumer protection. The National Credit Act No. 34 of 2005 ('NCA') regulates consumer credit agreements. The Conduct of Financial Institutions Bill will likely be enacted this year (2024) and be supplemented by, *inter alia*, conduct standards issued by the sectoral regulator, the FSCA. The CPA is the broadest legislation and governs the supply of goods and services in the ordinary course of business to natural persons and small juristic persons for counter-performance (but not for credit). It has a savings provision for the common law rights of consumers.[8] Other legislation on consumer legislation includes the Rental Housing Act No. 50 of 1999 and the Protection of Personal Information Act No. 4 of 2013.

---

dispute resolution means methods of dispute resolution beyond the courts. In this paper, dispute resolution via tribunals will be discussed in a separate part from alternative dispute resolution more generally

6 Department of Trade and Industry, 'Legislation and Business Regulation' <https://www.thedtic.gov.za/legislation/legislation-and-business-regulation/> accessed 22 March 2024

7 See, for example, the Eastern Cape Consumer Protection Act No. 3 of 2018

8 ibid s 2(10)

The Regulatory Model That Inspired the National Regime of Consumer Protection

The UN guidelines on consumer protection inspired the South African CPA, which recognises a number of 'fundamental consumer rights'. A few aspects of the CPA are based on English legislation[9] or EU Consumer law, although modified (for example, the orange list of terms which are presumed to be unfair, based largely on the indicative list of the EC Directive on Unfair Terms in Consumer Contracts,[10] and amplified with reference to, *inter alia*, the German Civil Code).[11] Currently, financial services are regulated by a 'Treating Customers Fairly' model inspired by a similar approach in English law.[12]

The General Design of the Enforcement Mechanisms

The main mechanisms for enforcing consumer law include administrative regulators and provincial consumer authorities, who are authorised under national legislation to issue compliance notices to suppliers contravening the legislation and also to consider consumer complaints.[13] Suppliers may appeal against the issuing of compliance notices by regulators to specialised tribunals (the National Consumer Tribunal ('NCT'), which enforces the NCA and the CPA, as well as provincial consumer tribunals).[14] The NCT may impose hefty fines for non-compliance with compliance notices.[15]

Other enforcement mechanisms and authorities for specific sectors are created by national legislation (some are mentioned below).[16] The ordinary courts also retain some jurisdiction regarding the enforcement of consumers' CPA rights, as consumers may approach the courts after having exhausted all other avenues of redress available under national legislation, including the ombuds, the NCC and the National Consumer Tribunal (s 69). The next part will discuss enforcement via courts and tribunals (fourth part), after which ADR will be discussed in the fifth part.

Current Consumer Dispute Resolution Processes in Courts and Tribunals

National Consumer Tribunal

As noted above, the National Consumer Tribunal ('NCT') may hear consumer disputes based on the CPA and the NCA. However, the NCT does not award damages.

9 For example, s 44 CPA regarding the supplier's right to sell the goods
10 Council Directive (EC) 93/13 on unfair terms in consumer contracts [1993] *OJ L* 95
11 See Reg 44 of the Consumer Protection Act Regulations of 1 April 2011
12 FSCA, 'Treating Customers Fairly' <https://www.fsca.co.za/Regulatory%20Frameworks/Pages/Treating-customers-fairly.aspx> accessed 19 April 2024
13 For example, under s 84, 99, 100 CPA
14 For example, under s 101 CPA
15 For example, under s 112 CPA
16 See also Tjakie Naude and Jacolien Barnard, 'Enforcement and Effectiveness of Consumer Law in South Africa' in Hans-W Micklitz and Genevieve Saumier (eds) *Enforcement and Effectiveness of Consumer Law* (Springer 2018) 565–568, 574

The NCT has issued thousands of consent orders for debt rearrangement regarding the NCA, as the process is more cost-effective than the equivalent in the Magistrates Court.[17] The NCT follows an informal procedure.[18] This makes the NCT more accessible than the ordinary courts, which have a complex, accusatorial process. However, even in the NCT, most consumers are represented in practice, as most consumers do not know what proof is required and which parts of the legislation are applicable.[19] Redrafting the Consumer Protection Act in plain language might alleviate the problem.

The National Consumer Commission sometimes asks the NCT to order relief for a particular consumer against a recalcitrant supplier and/or asks for the imposition of a fine for prohibited conduct, particularly where the supplier did not comply with the recommendation of an industry ombud.[20] Judgements of the NCT are treated as judgments of the High Court for enforcement and appeals.[21] As will be discussed below, s 52 of the CPA suggests that only the ordinary courts have jurisdiction to hear disputes regarding unfair contract terms (governed by ss 48–52 CPA), unconscionable conduct (s 40) and misrepresentations (s 41). The NCT has also held that it does not have jurisdiction over unfair contract terms.[22] However, more recently, the NCT was prepared to hear a matter involving s 48 CPA.[23]

Provincial Consumer Tribunals (or 'Consumer Courts')

National and provincial governments have concurrent jurisdiction over consumer protection. Therefore, most provinces have consumer protection legislation and set up consumer tribunals.[24] These tribunals follow an informal procedure. In some provinces, an official called the Consumer Protector brings cases on behalf of consumers to the tribunal after mediation was unsuccessful. Consumers, therefore, do not need legal representation.

The enforcement of judgments of provincial tribunals has been problematic, even though the CPA provides that their judgments have the same status as judgments of the NCT.[25] The provincial legislation should spell out their status. The legislation should also provide specifically for the certification of judgments,

17 Tanya Woker, 'Consumer Protection: An Overview Since 1994' [2019] *Stellenbosch LR* 97, 102 ('Woker 2019')

18 Rule 21(1) of the National Consumer Tribunal Rules

19 Woker 2019 (n 17) 112

20 For example, *NCC v Western Car Sales CC t/a Western Car Sales* (NCT/81554/2017/73(2)(b)) [2017] ZANCT 102 (14 September 2017)

21 Sections 59, 152 NCA

22 *NCC v Western Car Sales* (n 19)

23 *NCC v Ismacube (Pty) Ltd t/a Ismega* (NCT/138658/2020/73(2)(b)) [2021] ZANCT 46 (22 August 2021)

24 MA Du Plessis, 'Enforcement and Execution Shortcomings of Consumer Courts' [2010] *SA Merc LJ* 519; Stephen Newman and Mark Tait, 'Resolving Provincial Cross-Border Disputes Under the Consumer Protection Act' [2018] Obiter 684, 689; Van Heerden, 'Section 69' in *Commentary on the CPA* 69–14

25 Du Plessis (n 24)

so that sheriffs may easily accept them as equivalent to High Court judgements for enforcement.[26] The Eastern Cape legislation provides that judgements of its tribunal have the same status as that of a Magistrates Court.[27] Not all provincial consumer legislation provides for administrative fines for prohibited conduct.[28] This is because some provinces' legislation predated the CPA and was based on now-repealed national legislation on consumer affairs.[29]

It is also unclear whether provincial consumer tribunals have jurisdiction over suppliers operating in more than one province or over cross-border suppliers.[30] The CPA suggests that provincial consumer tribunals only have jurisdiction over suppliers operating exclusively within that province.[31] However, the national government may not remove provinces' concurrent power to make legislation protecting consumers residing within their province, especially if the transaction was concluded there. Research has shown that the NCC often refers cross-border matters referred to it by a provincial authority back to that same provincial authority.[32] Access to the provincial consumer protection authorities is essential for consumers' right to redress. The CPA and provincial legislation should be amended to clarify provincial authorities' jurisdiction.[33]

Rental Housing Tribunals

Under the Rental Housing Act 50 of 1999, provinces must set up rental housing tribunals. This has been done in all provinces. These tribunals have jurisdiction over 'unfair practices' as defined.

Ordinary Courts

According to s 69 CPA, the consumer may approach an ordinary court regarding a dispute under the Act after all other avenues of redress available under national legislation have been exhausted. The other avenues mentioned in s 69 are ombuds, provincial consumer courts, the NCC and the NCT. The motivation for generally making the courts the last resort may lie in the other bodies' specialised knowledge of consumer law.

This is problematic because the Small Claims Courts are 'ordinary courts', and there are 415 of them, including in remote areas, making them easily accessible to consumers. They follow a simple procedure, and legal representation is not

26 Du Plessis (n 24)
27 Section 41, Eastern Cape Consumer Protection Act 3 of 2018
28 Woker 2019 (n 17) 111
29 See also Woker 2019 (n 17) 111
30 Newman and Tait (n 25) 685
31 Section 84(b)
32 Newman and Tait (n 25) 686
33 Newman and Tait (n 25) 689–700; MA Du Plessis, 'Redress for Consumers in Terms of the Consumer Protection Act 68 of 2008: The Watchdog's Failure to Support an Accredited Industry Ombud – Alternative Suggestions' (2022) 33 *Stell LR* 230, 235

allowed.[34] Low-income consumers in rural areas can more easily access their local small claims court than their provincial consumer protection authority, ombuds or the NCC, which only operate from large cities, with resultant costs of calls or data. Section 69 is unconstitutional for unjustifiably depriving such consumers of their right to access court where the alternative system created by the legislation is not equivalently accessible.[35]

Section 52 CPA, on the other hand, is headed 'Powers of court to ensure fair, just and reasonable terms and conditions' and only refers to courts in its body, whereas 'court' is defined in s 1 only to include the ordinary courts. It appears that the intention was to give the ordinary courts sole jurisdiction to hear matters relating to unfair terms (s 48), unconscionable conduct (s 40), and misrepresentations (s 41), to which s 52 applies. This is how the National Consumer Tribunal interpreted s 52 in some matters.[36] However, the NCT was subsequently willing to make orders based on the supplier contravening s 48 (together with other sections).[37] It appears sensible that the specialist tribunals should have jurisdiction to rule on the unfairness of contract terms, unconscionable conduct and misrepresentations, as these specialist tribunals work with the CPA more regularly than the ordinary courts.[38] Moreover, apart from the Small Claims Courts, the ordinary courts are out of reach of most consumers.[39] Even with legal representation, the court process is intimidating, time-consuming, complicated and too expensive for most consumers. By contrast, the NCT has a simplified procedure.

There is no reduced tariff for consumers bringing matters to the ordinary courts, namely the Magistrates Courts, High Courts, Supreme Court of Appeal and Constitutional Court. Legal Aid South Africa assists low-income citizens with legal fees, including for consumer cases, according to a means test.[40] Only the ordinary courts may award damages. If the claim before the court concerns conduct prohibited by the CPA, the claimant must file a certificate from the NCT that the conduct was prohibited.[41] Consumers may bring class actions, which the courts have fashioned requirements and rules.[42] The Rules Board is currently considering a draft rule on the certification of class actions for the Rules of Court.[43]

The main shortcomings of the judicial enforcement of consumer rights include the high costs and delays, except in the Small Claims Courts. There are no dedicated active consumer organisations who bring cases on behalf of consumers,

34 Small Claims Court Act 61 of 1984
35 Section 34 of the Constitution of the Republic of South Africa, 1996; Naude and Barnard (n 16) 581
36 For example, *National Consumer Commission v Western Car Sales* (n 21) para 42
37 *National Consumer Commission v Ismacube (Pty) Ltd* (n 24)
38 See also Mupanvaganhu, 'An Analysis of the Dispute Settlement Mechanism under the *Consumer Protection Act* 68 of 2008' (2017) 15 *Potchefstroom Electronic Law Journal* 319; 334–337
39 See also Woker 2016 (n 2) 23–24
40 See Legal Aid South Africa's website <https://legal-aid.co.za/> accessed 21 April 2024. The bar for being disqualified is relatively low
41 Section 115 CPA
42 Van Heerden 'Section 69' in Naude and Eiselen (n 2) para 4
43 Rule of Court, Rule 11A

although some organisations with a more general focus have taken action on consumer protection.[44]

Alternative Dispute Resolution for Consumer Disputes

There are various ADR mechanisms in South Africa, in particular, ombuds and mediation by provincial consumer protection authorities. Various industry bodies set up voluntary dispute resolution systems. This includes one for the advertising industry set up about fifty years ago, the long-term insurance ombudsman in 1985 and other ombuds in the financial sector in the 1990s.[45] Statute created the pension funds adjudicator in 1956, which still operates.

One of the reasons why dispute resolution via ombuds and ADR is generally widespread in South Africa is the high monetary and time costs of court action for most consumers, apart from in the Small Claims Courts. Therefore, ADR is crucial to providing relief to consumers, as it does not require legal representation and is faster if properly set up. Businesses also benefit from this cheaper form of dispute resolution. The industry as a whole benefits when consumers know they may contract with confidence that issues with suppliers will be effectively addressed. Ombuds and regulators also have expertise that courts do not readily have.[46] An additional advantage is that ombuds are mandated to consider both the law and fairness and can recommend novel, suitable solutions, whereas courts must apply the law.[47] The national regulators, funded by the government, do not have sufficient resources to deal with all complaints in the sector.[48] In contrast, ombuds are funded by levies payable by suppliers in the sector. In addition, an attempt to repair the supplier-customer relationship by a relatively speedy negotiated agreement is in everyone's interest. Suppliers who do not cooperate in ADR procedures (co-)created by their industry run the risk of reputational harm, for example, if the consumer posts a negative review on a website like hellopeter.com. Customers who know about ADR procedures are more likely to refrain from posting negative reviews until ADR is attempted. If the parties to ADR reach a negotiated settlement, it can be made a consent order by a court or the NCT, where the latter has jurisdiction.[49]

After the democratic government came to power in 1994, there was a surge in consumer legislation providing for dispute resolution.[50] The Financial Services Ombud Schemes Act 27 of 2004, provided that financial services sector schemes

44 For example, *Afriforum v Minister of Trade and Industry and Others* 2013 (4) SA 63 (GNP)
45 Woker 2016 (n 2) 32, 38
46 Woker 2016 (n 2) 32
47 Woker 2016 (n 2) 32
48 National Consumer Commission *Annual Report 2013/2014* 12; National Consumer Commission *Annual Report 2015/2016* 11
49 Section 70(3) CPA
50 For example, Long-Term Insurance Act 52 of 1998; National Credit Act 34 of 2005; Consumer Protection Act 68 of 2008

must be subject to recognition and supervision by the Ombud Council created by the Act.[51]

Ombuds

Ombuds[52] are widely used in South Africa. Some large companies and institutions created internal 'ombuds', sometimes called 'internal arbitrators', for consumers to complain to after they attempted to resolve a dispute with the suppliers' employees. These ombuds or arbitrators must show independence regarding complaints. Examples of organisations with internal ombuds are large insurance companies (e.g. Old Mutual, Sanlam), universities (e.g. University of Cape Town; Stellenbosch University) and city councils (e.g. Cape Town). These ombuds or internal arbitrators investigate complaints and either mediate towards a solution or make recommendations for the company or institution to follow. If the consumer is not satisfied, the internal ombud/arbitrator refers them to the industry ombud.

Some ombud schemes not connected to an individual supplier are created by statute. The Pension Funds Adjudicator was previously mentioned.[53] Some other ombuds in the financial services sector were initially voluntary schemes but later regulated by statute.[54] The National Financial Ombud Scheme was recognised by the Ombud Council, operating in terms of the Financial Sector Regulation Act 9 of 2017, as an industry ombud scheme in 2024 to amalgamate four previously existing ombuds, which now constitute the new ombud's four divisions. These divisions are the banking, credit, long-term insurance and short-term insurance sectors. The Ombud Council regulates the ombuds in the financial services sector by imposing standards of good practice and hearing complaints against ombuds.[55] Another statutory ombud in the financial services sector is the FAIS Ombud (Office of the Ombud for Financial Services Providers), which deals with financial advisory and intermediary services.[56] The FAIS Ombud must make a final determination in certain instances and act akin to a court (or rather like an arbitrator).[57] Similarly, the National Financial Ombud Scheme may issue a ruling.

Other statutory ombuds are the Community Schemes Ombud Service,[58] which deals with sectional property schemes and home associations; the Legal Services Ombud 58; and the Health Ombudsman of South Africa.[59] Most ombuds are funded

51 Section 18 CPA
52 On the terminology change from ombudsman see n 4
53 Pension Funds Act 24 of 1956
54 For example, the Banking Ombudsman and the Long-Term Insurance and Short-Term Insurance Ombudsmen
55 Chapter 14 of the Financial Sector Regulation Act, 9 of 2017
56 Financial Advisory and Intermediary Services Act, 37 of 2002
57 Section 28 of the Financial Advisory and Intermediary Services Act, 37 of 2002 (confirmed in *Ombud for Financial Services Providers v CS Brokers CC* (Case no 781/2020) [2021] ZASCA 117 para 10)
58 Community Schemes Ombud Services Act 9 of 2011
59 National Health Amendment Act 12 of 2013

by levies imposed by law on suppliers in the relevant industry. The Public Protector considers complaints against the government, including by consumers of government services, and is also an ombud (funded by the government).[60] Again, these ombuds may typically make rulings subject to an appeal. They, therefore, act as arbitrators in a sense.

Other ombud schemes are created by industry associations but accredited by government departments in terms of legislation to hear complaints against any supplier in the sector based on an industry code of conduct that went through a rigorous and public adoption process. The CPA provides for such co-regulation in the form of accredited industry ombuds,[61] currently the Motor Industry Ombudsman of South Africa and the Consumer Goods and Service Ombud. Levies payable by businesses in the sector fund the scheme.[62] Co-regulation in this form harnesses the advantages of self-regulation but minimises the disadvantages thereof.[63] Even though only the courts may award damages, these ombuds should be willing to mediate damages claims.[64] Where the CGSO or MIOSA cannot get the parties to settle a dispute but gives a 'decision' in favour of the consumer, this decision is not enforceable against the supplier per se. However, the supplier risks a hefty administrative fine if it refuses to give effect to the consumer's rights under the CPA.[65]

The previously mentioned ombuds allow online complaints as well as telephonic and walk-in complaints. They only have offices in one or two major cities, however. Ombuds in South Africa are industry experts and have the other advantages of ADR, which were set out previously. Accountability, impartiality, fairness and efficiency are promoted by the submission of annual reports to their boards and relevant government departments (in case of co-regulation).[66] Their boards include consumer journalists or representatives from consumer bodies and industry. Publication online of some of their anonymised decisions, as well as their opinions on contentious issues, also advance the goals of accountability, impartiality and fairness.

Legal requirements for co-regulated industry ombuds are laid down in the industry codes of conduct, which are promulgated under the legislation involved after public consultation and scrutiny by the national regulator. These codes of conduct would, for example, state that the ombud must act 'honestly, independently and objectively', with 'regard to fairness, justice, equity and the provisions

60 Public Protector Act 23 of 1994
61 ibid s 82
62 *Consumer Goods and Services Ombud NPC v Voltex (Pty) Ltd* (18096/2017) 2021 ZAGPPHC 309 (26 March 2021)
63 Woker 2016 (n 2) 34
64 Van Heerden 'Section 69' in Naude and Eiselen (n 2) 69–31
65 Cf *Stemmet v Motus Corporation (Pty) Ltd t/a Milnerton Multifranchise* (NCT/83884/2017/75(1)(b)) [2018] ZANCT 21 (25 March 2018) para 22
66 The annual reports are published on their websites (for example, see <https://www.miosa.co.za/annual-report.php> accessed 21 April 2024)

of the Act and the Code' and must balance the rights of consumers and industry.[67] The Consumer Goods and Services Ombud deals with so many types of goods and services that it has correctly called for the creation of more industry-specific accredited ombuds and suggested that its own mandate be limited to retail industry complaints.[68] Ombuds are regarded as the most effective consumer ADR mechanism in South Africa.[69]

Mediation Used by Provincial Consumer Protection Authorities, Including Rental Housing Tribunals

It was noted previously that most provinces have set up provincial consumer tribunals (also recognised under the National Consumer Protection Act). There are also rental housing tribunals in all provinces. Where complaints are received by provincial consumer protection bodies or rental housing tribunals, mediation will first be considered and attempted, if appropriate, before the tribunal itself will hear the matter.[70]

National Regulators Dealing With Consumer Complaints

The NCR, *inter alia*, enforces compliance with the National Credit Act. It, therefore, can act against credit providers, credit bureaux and debt counsellors. It attempts to resolve complaints by consumers but refers others to ombuds.[71] The NCC does not have the capacity to deal with all consumer complaints in the many sectors falling under its jurisdiction.[72] The CPA contains conflicting provisions regarding the NCC's obligation to deal with individual complaints. Section 99 provides that one of the NCC's roles is to promote the 'informal resolution of any dispute arising in terms of this Act between a consumer and a supplier but is not responsible for intervening in or directly adjudicating any such dispute'.

67 See for example, Preamble to the Consumer Goods and Services Industry Code of Conduct, <https://www.cgso.org.za/dl/code%20of%20the%20consumer%20goods%20and%20services%20ombud%20-%2028%20feb%202013.pdf> accessed 12 April 2024

68 CGSO Annual Report 2016/17, as noted by Woker 2019 (n 17) 113

69 Woker 2019 (n 17) 113

70 National Government has published draft Regulations under the Rental Housing Act to deal with unfair practices and with procedure, previously dealt with in provincial legislation (Regulations under the Rental Housing Act 1999, published for comment in General Notice 1913 in Government Gazette 46063 of 18 March 2022). These draft regulations also provide that the case manager must consider whether mediation is appropriate (it will not be appropriate if the matter is urgent) and refer the matter to mediation (see regs 6, 38–41)

71 See for example the statistics in its Annual Report 2022/2023 p. 43 (<https://www.ncr.org.za/documents/pages/Annual%20Reports/29%20September%202023%20-%20NCR%20Annual%20Reports.pdf> accessed 21 April 2024)

72 Already in the first four months after the NCC started operating in 2011, it reported large numbers of complaints and requests for advice, which it could not cope with (National Consumer Commission, *National Consumer Commission Progress Report on the Work Done Since Inception in April 2011* (6 September 2011) <https://pmg.org.za/committeemeeting/13371/> accessed 29 March 2024)

However, s 69 provides that the consumer must first approach the NCC to resolve a complaint before they may approach a court regarding the complaint. The NCC has said in the past that it takes on systemic complaints, for example, which may result in recommendations regarding a whole industry. Its current website has a prominent link to 'Complaints', so perhaps the NCC takes on more complaints now. However, its 2022/2023 Annual Report states that it only conducted 357 investigations that year, suggesting that it probably referred most others to ombuds and provincial authorities.[73]

Other regulators created by statute which may mediate and, if necessary, decide consumer complaints in the relevant sectors include the Information Regulator,[74] the Independent Communications Authority of South Africa,[75] the National Home Builders Registration Council,[76] Estate Agency Affairs Board,[77] Health Professions Council of South Africa[78] and the Council for Medical Schemes.[79]

Debt Counsellors

Debt counsellors are private parties whose main function under the NCA is to help over-indebted consumers pay off their debts, including negotiating and proposing debt-rearrangement plans.[80] Debt counsellors must be registered with the National Credit Regulator, and special training is required.[81]

Voluntarily Formed Private ADR Agents

The Consumer Protection Act mentions other alternative dispute resolution agents in its list of possible avenues of redress in s 69. The NCA also allows such agents to be registered.[82] These would be private bodies offering mediation and arbitration.[83] Note that contract terms of suppliers, which force consumers to agree in advance to subject future disputes to private arbitration not covered by legislation, are presumed to be unfair under the Consumer Protection Act Regulations.[84]

73 Annual Report <https://thencc.org.za/wp-content/uploads/2023/10/2022–23-Annual-Report.pdf> accessed 12 April 2024
74 Created by the Protection of Personal Information Act 4 of 2013
75 Created by the Independent Communications Authority of South Africa Act 13 of 2000. It enforces, *inter alia*, the End-User and Subscriber Service Charter Regulations (Fourth Amendment, 2023) and the Mobile Broadband Services Regulations, 2021
76 Under the Housing Consumers Protection Measures Act 95 of 1998
77 Created by the Estate Agency Affairs Act 112 of 1976
78 Established by the Health Professions Act 56 of 1974
79 Established by the Medical Schemes Act 131 of 1998
80 Section 86 NCA. For more detail see Woker 2016 (n 2) 45–46
81 Section 44 NCA
82 Section 134A NCA
83 See, for example, SA Consumer Complaints, <https://www.saconsumercomplaints.co.za/about-us/> accessed 21 April 2024
84 Regulation 44(3)(x) of the Consumer Protection Act Regulations of 1 April 2011

Industry associations may also set up complaints mechanisms not accredited under consumer legislation, which amount to private ADR. Benefits include that voluntary codes of practice can quickly be set up and amended and do not need to be approved by a government body. Again, industry experts are involved. Speedy redress is likely as members of the association are likely to accept the ruling of the expert appointed. Examples are the Advertising Regulatory Board and complaints procedures of the Wireless Application Services Providers Association (WASPA) and the South African Institute of Timber Builders. These bodies make use of mediation and arbitration. Such systems will not disqualify consumers from rather laying a complaint with the Consumer Goods and Services Ombud, accredited under the CPA, for example, if they fear bias against them.

Role of Technology in Consumer ADR – Online Dispute Resolution for Consumer Disputes

The ombuds typically utilise information and communications technology to resolve consumer disputes, e.g. via online complaint forms and communication with the parties by e-mails and SMS text messages.[85] Cupido concluded that ODR is feasible in South Africa but in a different form than in countries in the global north.[86] She found the legal and technical infrastructure for a framework for ODR to be in place, although there is still a digital divide.[87] Although mobile phone penetration in South Africa is high, many consumers, especially low-income consumers outside the major cities, still do not have access to affordable data to conduct online dispute resolution via ombuds.[88] However, increasing internet access is a priority for the South African government.[89] In the meantime, parties with a lower income will often not have enough data for synchronous online meetings, but at most for ODR via emails. ODR has the benefit of making dispute resolution processes of ombuds and other agencies with no offices outside major cities accessible to more consumers.

85 See for example the complaints handling processes detailed on various ombuds' websites, for example, <https://www.faisombud.co.za/how-to-complain/complaints-handling-process/, https://nfosa.co.za/complaints-process-flowchart/ and https://www.cgso.org.za/cgso/the-process/> accessed 8 April 2024

86 Robin Cupido, *The Feasibility of Implementing Online Dispute Resolution as a Distinct Method of Dispute Resolution on the African Continent* (Unpublished PhD Thesis, University of Cape Town 2024) 195–196

87 Robin Cupido, *The Feasibility of Implementing Online Dispute Resolution as a Distinct Method of Dispute Resolution on the African Continent* (Unpublished PhD Thesis, University of Cape Town 2024) 196

88 See also Robin Cupido, *The Feasibility of Implementing Online Dispute Resolution as a Distinct Method of Dispute Resolution on the African Continent* (Unpublished PhD Thesis, University of Cape Town 2024) 188ff

89 South African Official News, 'Government Accelerates Programme to Connect Citizens to Internet' (*msn.com*, 5 April 2024) <https://www.msn.com/en-xl/news/other/government-accelerates-programme-to-connect-citizens-to-internet/ar-BB1last3> accessed 8 April 2024

Cupido identified 'a basic set of underlying principles' that should apply to ODR.[90] The enforceability of ODR rulings is a challenge.[91] Another challenge might be that several South African consumers have a low level of literacy, and others may not be fluent in English or other languages read by the person conducting the ODR process.[92]

Challenges and Opportunities

Statistics in ombuds' annual reports generally show efficiency in dealing with complaints received.[93] However, they also suggest that consumers in more rural provinces where many low-income consumers live contact the ombuds far less than consumers in the 'richer' provinces of Gauteng and the Western Cape.[94] This may reflect the digital divide persisting there, which may also affect awareness of the ombuds. As noted above, even though the ombuds and provincial consumer protection authorities are currently the most effective in solving disputes through mediation and persuasive recommendations, they often are hampered regarding enforcement against recalcitrant suppliers because of their legislative frameworks. At least provincial legislation could be fixed to enable effective enforcement, including clarifying jurisdiction over cross-border disputes and bringing pre-CPA legislation into line with the CPA.[95]

The Consumer Protection Act should be amended to address problems with enforcement. The role of the NCC should be clearer and adequately considered. If the industry ombuds in this sector should remain unable to make enforceable rulings against suppliers, the NCC should be obliged to intervene in individual complaints against suppliers against whom an ombud made a ruling or recommendation.[96] Since the NCC is unable to deal with all individual complaints, the CPA should no longer suggest that provincial authorities do not have jurisdiction over cross-provincial disputes.[97]

The CGSO does sterling work, but more specialised industries within its purview should instead set up accredited industry ombuds to increase consumer trust. As noted, no active, dedicated consumer organisations bring court cases on behalf of consumers, but not-for-profit organisations with a broader focus sometimes get involved. The important ADR principle of accessibility viewed against multilingualism in South Africa (12 official languages) means that cultural and linguistic diversity must be considered.

90 Cupido (n 85) 194
91 Cupido (n 85) 194
92 11.6% of adult males and 12.5% of adult females were functionally illiterate in 2019 (Department of Higher Education and Training *Fact Sheet – Adult illiteracy in South Africa* (2022))
93 See for example CGSO Annual Report 2022–2023
94 See for example CGSO Annual Report 2022–2023
95 See text at n 30
96 Tanya Woker, 'Evaluating the Role of the National Consumer Commission in Ensuring That Consumers Have Access to Redress' (2017) 29 *SA Merc LJ* 1
97 See (n 30)

Conclusion

South Africa has a complex consumer protection enforcement system. One single body cannot be tasked with consumer redress and dispute resolution, given the inequality of South African society. Complexity is created in that some consumers have a low income, live far away from major cities, and do not have ready access to Wi-Fi or data to access ODR systems. Walking into their local small claims court might be the only affordable option for them to get redress. Other middle-class consumers and some low-income consumers in large cities have access to Wi-Fi and can access the ombuds, who conduct ODR, faster than courts decide cases. Some consumers with a low income live in large cities and can access provincial and national enforcement bodies that are only situated in one or two large cities. In addition, there is a view that only the ordinary courts should have jurisdiction to deal with certain complex matters (such as unfair contract terms) and not the National Consumer Tribunal. Some believe that consumers who can afford it should be allowed to go directly to court, at least on damages and unfair contract terms.

It is a challenge to write legislative provisions on consumer redress that adequately address these complexities, plus the problem of forum shopping or bringing cases simultaneously in more than one forum,[98] and to draft the provisions in plain language. A call for the National Consumer Commission to take charge of redress[99] would assist consumers with resources to access that body online but would not assist those with the lowest income on its own. Information campaigns are needed to inform all consumers of the various options. There is a dire need for consumer organisations to assist with information campaigns and take on cases on behalf of consumers. However, as South Africa is a global south country with other pressing needs, funding consumer organisations is not currently a priority for the government and individual consumers.

References

Cupido R, *The Feasibility of Implementing Online Dispute Resolution as a Distinct Method of Dispute Resolution on the African Continent* (Unpublished PhD Thesis, University of Cape Town, 2024)

Department of Higher Education and Training, *Fact Sheet – Adult Illiteracy in South Africa* (2022)

Department of Trade and Industry, ‘Legislation and Business Regulation’ <https://www.thedtic.gov.za/legislation/legislation-and-business-regulation> accessed 22 March 2024

Du Plessis MA, ‘Enforcement and Execution Shortcomings of Consumer Courts’ (2010) SA Mercantile LJ 519

Du Plessis MA, ‘Redress for Consumers in Terms of the Consumer Protection Act 68 of 2008: The Watchdog’s Failure to Support an Accredited Industry Ombud – Alternative Suggestions’ (2022) 33 Stellenbosch LR 230

98 See for example Mupanvaganhu (n 38) 332

99 See for example by Woker (n 94)

Financial Sector Conduct Authority, 'Treating Customers Fairly' <https://www.fsca.co.za/Regulatory%20Frameworks/Pages/Treating-customers-fairly.aspx> accessed 19 April 2024

Mupanvaganhu Y, 'An Analysis of the Dispute Settlement Mechanism Under the *Consumer Protection Act* 68 of 2008' (2017) 15 Potchefstroom Electronic LJ 319

Naude T and Barnard J, 'Enforcement and Effectiveness of Consumer Law in South Africa' in Hans-W Micklitz and Genevieve Saumier (eds) *Enforcement and Effectiveness of Consumer Law* (Springer 2018) 565

Newman S and Tait M, 'Resolving Provincial Cross-Border Disputes Under the Consumer Protection Act' [2018] Obiter 684

South African Official News, 'Government Accelerates Programme to Connect Citizens to Internet' (*msn.com*, 5 April 2024) <https://www.msn.com/en-xl/news/other/government-accelerates-programme-to-connect-citizens-to-internet/ar-BB1last3> accessed 8 April 2024

Stats SA, 'Five Facts About Poverty in South Africa, 2019' <https://www.statssa.gov.za/?p=12075> accessed 19 April 2024

Stats SA, 'Quarterly Labour Force Survey (QLFS)-Q4: 2023 Q4' <https://www.statssa.gov.za/publications/P0211/Media%20release%20QLFS%20Q4%202023.pdf> accessed 19 April 2024

Van Heerden C, 'Chapter 3' in Tjakie Naude and Sieg Eiselen (eds) *Commentary on the Consumer Protection Act* (Revision Service 9, Juta 2023)

Woker T, 'Consumer Protection and Alternative Dispute Resolution' (2016) 28 SA Mercantile LJ 21, 22

Woker T, 'Consumer Protection: An Overview Since 1994' (2019) Stellenbosch LR 97

Woker T, 'Evaluating the Role of the National Consumer Commission in Ensuring That Consumers Have Access to Redress' (2017) 29 SA Mercantile LJ 1

11 Consumer ADR in India

Akash Gupta, Arushi Bajpai, and Janani Sivaraman

Introduction

The consumer protection landscape in India has undergone significant transformation since the introduction of the Consumer Protection Act in 1986. This pioneering legislation was a response to the burgeoning need to shield consumers from exploitation by large sellers and conglomerates, marking a pivotal moment in enhancing consumers' social and economic welfare. With the advent of the Consumer Protection Act of 2019, India took a substantial step forward, reinforcing the safeguards provided by its predecessor and emphasising the importance of expeditious and effective dispute resolution. This evolution in consumer protection law reflects the dynamic nature of the market and consumer rights, necessitating the integration of ADR and ODR mechanisms to manage the increasing volume and complexity of consumer grievances.

This chapter delves into the legal framework that underpins consumer protection in India, tracing its development from historical laws to the contemporary landscape defined by the 2019 Act. It highlights the pivotal role of specialised consumer courts and the establishment of the Central Consumer Protection Authority (CCPA), underscoring their contributions to safeguarding consumer rights. However, the chapter also recognises the challenges posed by the growing backlog of cases and the limitations of the current judicial system. Through a detailed examination of ADR and ODR mechanisms, the authors propose innovative solutions to streamline and enhance the adjudication of consumer disputes, advocating for a more efficient, accessible, and consumer-friendly approach. This exploration offers insights into the future of consumer justice in India, emphasising the need for continuous adaptation and the potential benefits of privatising justice in the consumer sector.

Legal Framework for Consumer Protection

Laws surrounding consumer protection were always prevalent in India. They were seen in the form of preventative or punitive laws in the Indian Penal Code 1860,[1]

1 Indian Penal Code 1860, s 264–267 and s 272–276

DOI: 10.4324/9781032689739-11

Drugs and Cosmetics Act 1940, and the Sale of Goods Act 1930. While such laws contained provisions for consumer protection, India had not yet enacted a law about consumer rights protection. A United Nations Resolution[2] was passed that prescribed guidelines for states to enact laws for consumer protection, a compensatory law.[3] Subsequently, consumer protection laws in India were first introduced in 1986, when a need to enhance the safeguards for consumer rights was seen across the country.[4] Before the Consumer Protection Act 1986 was enacted, consumers had to file civil suits for damages under the Law of Torts if they suffered grievances arising from faulty products or services. Before the 1986 Act, India followed the principle of *caveat emptor*, meaning buyers were responsible for identifying defects in the goods they purchased.

While drafting the Consumer Protection Act of 1986 (1986 Act), there was a rising need for protecting the interests of consumers, and the Act made a shift and was based on the principle of *'caveat vendor'*, which translates to 'let the seller beware'. The enactment of the new statute brought about significant changes, such as the setting up of specialised consumer courts at the district, state, and national levels. The main objective of the 1986 Act was to uphold the interests of the consumers and provide an adequate grievance redressal mechanism and compensation to consumers in the appropriate cases. The 1986 Act underwent three amendments to keep up with the changing demands of the markets and society. Subsequently, with a substantial rise in consumerism, drastic changes in purchase trends and increased use of technology, the 1986 Act was replaced by the Consumer Protection Act of 2019.[5] This new law addresses issues by introducing 'product liability',[6] making manufacturers and service providers responsible for compensating consumers for injuries caused by defects. The new Act of 2019 also aims to use information, communication, and technology to make the grievance redressal mechanism efficient and straightforward for all consumers.

This chapter aims to provide a general idea of the consumer protection laws and their enforcement mechanism in India. Additionally, it highlights the steps taken by the country to bolster the practice of alternative dispute resolution methods, specifically in adjudicating consumer disputes. Finally, this chapter aims to provide insight into the challenges faced by the Indian legal system and the solutions and opportunities that lie ahead.

The General Design of the Enforcement Mechanism

The passing of the Consumer Protection Act in 1986 was considered a milestone to improve the social and economic well-being of consumers in India. The 1986 Act

2 United Nations General Assembly Resolution 39/248 of 1985

3 RNP Dhary, *Consumer Protection Law: Provisions and Procedure* (Deep and Deep Publishers 2005) 182

4 Chawla N and Kumar B, 'E-Commerce and Consumer Protection in India: The Emerging Trend' (2022) 180 *J Bus Ethics* 581, 604

5 The Consumer Protection Act 2019 (35 of 2019)

6 ibid s 2(34)

and the 2019 Act guarantee the rights of safety, information, choice, redressal, and education to all consumers in India. As for enforcement, the 2019 Act established a special authority called the CCPA,[7] which is focused on protecting consumers. It is presided over by the Department of Consumer Affairs and the Ministry of Consumer Affairs, Food and Public Distribution. The Central Consumers Protection Authority has been set up to promote, protect and enforce the rights of consumers as a class in India. The CCPA is the apex investigative body for all consumer issues and has the rights to order recalls of unsafe goods, discontinue unfair trade practices, monitor the markets, direct retraction of misleading advertisements or marketing campaigns, and impose penalties on sellers, manufacturers, or endorsers for engaging in unfair practices.[8]

Further, the 2019 Act has also retained the Consumer Protection Councils set up in the 1986 Act. These entities have been set up at the district, state, and national levels and are presided over by ministers in charge. The roles undertaken by these councils are mainly advisory in nature, and they play a crucial role in making region-specific policies. Further, the Act also has adjudicatory commissions in place at the district, state, and national levels. Unlike the commissions or the council, the CCPA is the primary body for investigating, implementing, and enforcing consumer protection laws in India. The CCPA undertakes such investigations or hears complaints when a specific unfair trade practice or other illegal activity affects consumers as a class of persons. The bifurcation of these functions into different bodies provides a checks and balances system for the proper functioning and protection of consumer rights.

The 2019 Act has revolutionised the grievance redressal mechanism by making the filing of complaints and the entire adjudication process consumer-centric. Under this Act, an individual purchasing goods/services, consumer associations, governments, one or more consumers when with similar interests, legal heirs, guardians, and central authorities have been authorised to file complaints before the designated authorities. The new Act encourages the use of ICT and has introduced the feature of online filing for all complaints. Parties must provide a notice to the other party before filing a complaint to provide a chance to settle the dispute before it reaches the commission. Depending on the claim's monetary value, parties can file their complaint with the district, state, or national commission. The parties or their representatives can then submit an online complaint. The main advantage provided by consumer courts is that these courts are specialised forums for addressing consumer grievances and protecting consumer rights. Therefore, such courts have a nuanced understanding of consumer mindsets and laws. These courts have also been designed in a consumer-friendly manner to reduce the requirement of legal counsel and thereby reduce the financial burden on consumers seeking justice.

7 ibid s 3

8 'Central Consumer Protection Authority Established to Promote, Protect and Enforce the Rights of Consumers; Will Function from Indian Institute of Public Administration Premises' (*Press Information Bureau*, 30 July 202) <https://pib.gov.in/PressReleasePage.aspx?PRID=1642422> accessed 14 November 2023

Consumer courts operate with a simplified procedural framework, avoiding the hyper-technical interpretations often associated with civil courts. The streamlined procedures in consumer courts contribute to timely adjudication, addressing the concerns of delays and protracted legal battles commonly experienced in civil courts. Further, consumer courts are inclined to provide relief to consumers who may have entered into contracts with unfavourable terms, recognising the power imbalance in most business-to-consumer transactions.

Current Consumer Dispute Resolution Processes

The Judicial System

The Constitution of India provides for a hierarchical system of courts headed by the Supreme Court in New Delhi, which enjoys jurisdiction within the whole territory of India. Article 124 of the Constitution provides for the creation of the Supreme Court and appointing judges.[9] In the realm of judicial authority, all Supreme Court judges possess equal status. Yet, the Chief Justice of India holds a distinct position as the foremost among equals, serving as the Master of the Roster and the Administrative Head of the Supreme Court. The twenty-five high courts across India stand at the middle of the pyramid. The Constitution provides for a high court in each state under Article 214.[10] Both the Supreme Court of India and the various high courts are constitutional courts and have the powers to deal with original cases appeals and hold writ jurisdiction in their respective territories.[11]

At the base of the hierarchy lies the subordinate judiciary, organised at the district level and includes the district and sessions court, usually covering one revenue district.[12] Every judicial body under a particular state is supervised and regulated by the High Court of that State.[13] By virtue of Article 141, all legal pronouncements made by the Supreme Court of India are absolutely authoritative in nature and are binding over all courts and tribunals situated within the territory of India.[14]

The Constitution of India was framed in a manner that incorporated a singular and integrated judicial structure encompassing the entire country, with the Supreme Court assuming the responsibility of supervising and directing the complete judicial administration across the nation. The drafters of the Constitution provided some essential safeguards in order to protect certain values that are upheld to this date, one of which is the independence of the judiciary. Non-interference from the legislature and executive has aided Indian Courts in exercising their functions systematically and transparently. The Supreme Court, on various occasions, has been the champion of fundamental rights, as it has been endowed with the authority of

9 The Constitution of India 1950, Art. 124

10 The Constitution of India 1950, Art. 214

11 The Constitution of India 1950, Art. 32 and Art. 226

12 Pawan Chaudhary 'Manmauji', 'Indian Judicial System: Its Nature and Structure and Distinction between Law and Justice' (1999) 45(3) *Indian Journal of Public Administration* 303, 305

13 The Constitution of India 1950, Art. 235

14 The Constitution of India 1950, Art. 141

judicial review in order to examine the constitutionality and validity of laws passed by the legislature. The Supreme Court also enjoys final authority on understanding and interpreting provisions of the Constitution and other laws.

Consumer Disputes

The objective of the Consumer Protection Act is to protect consumers at large from exploitation at the hands of large and established sellers. To this end, the 2019 Act established various bodies to provide consumers with speedy and inexpensive redressal mechanisms. The Act established a special authority called the Central Consumers Protection Authority (CCPA),[15] which focused on protecting consumers. A Mediation Cell 16 was also set up in every consumer court to help resolve disputes. Furthermore, the pecuniary jurisdiction of consumer courts at all levels was increased.[16] The 2019 Act also includes provisions regulating the three-tier quasi-judicial entities: the District Consumer Disputes Redressal Commission, the State Consumer Disputes Redressal Commission, and the National Consumer Disputes Redressal Commission. Each of these bodies possesses original jurisdiction based on the monetary value of the claim. If the claim does not exceed Rs. 1 Crore, it lies before the District Commission.[17] If the claim ranges from Rs. 1 Crore to Rs. 10 Crore, the complaint directly goes to the State Commission.[18] Similarly, if the claim ranges above Rs. 10 Crore, it will be directly entertained by the National Commission.[19] The National Commission is also vested with the authority to consider appeals from the State Commission. While all plaintiffs are encouraged to file their objections at the specialised consumer commissions, aggrieved parties also have the alternative to approach district courts or high courts with original jurisdiction.[20]

According to the Consumer Protection Act of 2019, each filed complaint must be accompanied by a prescribed fee, which can be in the form of a demand draft from a bank or an Indian postal order, payable to the President or Registrar of the relevant commission. The fees range from USD 30 to USD 72 for cases brought before the State Commission. In contrast, for National Commission cases, the fee is USD 90.[21,22] In the case of an appeal before the State Commission or the National

15 The Consumer Protection Act, 2019 (35 of 2019) s 3

16 Ankur Saha and Sri Ram Khanna, 'Evolution of Consumer Courts in India: The Consumers Protection Act 2019 and Emerging Themes of Consumer Jurisprudence' (2021) 9(1) *International Journal on Consumer Law and Practice* 115, 125

17 The Consumer Protection Act, 2019 (35 of 2019) s 34

18 The Consumer Protection Act, 2019 (35 of 2019) s 47

19 The Consumer Protection Act, 2019 (35 of 2019) s 58

20 The High Courts at Delhi, Bombay, Calcutta, and Madras are the only high courts with original jurisdiction in addition to the power of issuing writs

21 Priyanka Ajjannavar, 'India: Procedure To File Complaint Under Consumer Protection (Amendment) Act, 2019' (*Mondaq*, 6 August 2020) <https://www.mondaq.com/india/dodd-frank-consumer-protection-act/973520/procedure-to-file-complaint-under-consumer-protection-amendment-act-2019> accessed 16 December 2023

22 Exchange Rate: USD 1 = INR 83.05

Commission, a deposit equivalent to 50% of the total award amount issued by the lower commission is mandatory. However, if the value of the goods or services, as consideration, is up to rupees five lakh, the consumer is exempted from paying the fee. Further, while the Consumer Protection Act 2019 does not contain any specific provisions on legal aid, the National Legal Services Authority provides free legal aid for eligible persons.[23]

Judicial Enforcement of Consumer Rights

Since the introduction of consumer protection laws in India, the legal system has seen many advantages, ensuring that aggrieved consumers are the recipients of justice. The institution of specialised courts that only focus on consumer disputes makes the process of adjudication speedy, and the best interests of the consumers are upheld; further, the low costs for filing and easy processes ensure that consumers are not burdened with heavy expenses for court procedures and legal counsels.

Over the years, the only downfalls of this mechanism have been that consumer courts can handle cases only up to a certain monetary value, and higher-value cases must go to regular Courts. Further, with consumer courts in India having a backlog of over 500,000 cases as of 2023,[24] the need of the hour has become the privatisation of justice for faster adjudication and to reduce the burden on consumer courts. Additionally, the lack of expertise in this subject matter and for allied complex cases like medical malpractice or patent disputes have made adjudication of disputes more tedious in nature.

Alternative Dispute Resolution for Consumer Disputes

Overview

ADR refers to various techniques intended to settle a disagreement out of court. These methods help people resolve their disputes faster and more affordably rather than going through a regular court process. ADR mechanism allows parties to work out their disagreements in a way that suits them best, thereby upholding party autonomy.[25]

Before formal courts in India, people used to settle disputes through an informal mediation process known as 'Panchayat'. A well-liked member of the local community, frequently referred to as the Sarpanch oversaw the Panchayat. He was assisted by others from various castes in the community. The proceedings

23 The Legal Services Authorities Act 1987 (39 of 1987) s 12(h)

24 'The Pendency in the Consumer Commissions Shows a Declining Trend. Number of Cases Pending in Consumer Commission Come Down From 5.55 Lakhs in December 2022 to 5.45 Lakhs in September 2023' (*Press Information Bureau*, 20 September 2023) <https://pib.gov.in/PressReleasePage.aspx?PRID=1962143#:~:text=The%20pendency%20in%20the%20consumer,5.45%20lakhs%20in%20September%202023> accessed 21 December 2023

25 Tan JA, 'WIPO Guide on Alternative Dispute Resolution (ADR) Options for . . .' <https://www.wipo.int/edocs/pubdocs/en/wipo_pub_guide_adr.pdf> accessed 5 January 2024

were oral, and there were no written records. Panchayat's decisions were widely accepted and considered binding despite lacking legal authority.[26] Traders used mediation extensively in pre-British India and were invited to settle conflicts using an informal procedure that blended arbitration and mediation.[27] However, during the British period, various legislations were introduced, and in 1772, courts were authorised to refer to mediation at the party's request or their own discretion. Until 1996, arbitration in independent India was controlled by the Arbitration Act of 1940, superseding the Indian Arbitration Act of 1899.

In the 1980s, this concept of settling disputes outside the traditional courtroom setups gained momentum with the introduction of Lok Adalats, based on the ancient method used by tribal people for dispute resolution.[28] Subsequently, the Committee for Implementing Legal Aid Schemes (CILAS), chaired by former Chief Justice PN Bhagwati, recommended the setting up of the Legal Services Authorities, which was brought into existence in 1987. This Act promoted the resurgence of Lok Adalats to provide an early and affordable means of resolving disputes.[29] The official recognition of mediation and conciliation in the legal system came in 1996 with the enactment of the Arbitration and Conciliation Act 1996. Additionally, the Civil Procedure Code (CPC) was amended in 1999, introducing Section 89, which further emphasises the importance of mediation and alternative dispute resolution methods.[30]

ADR Mechanisms for Consumer Disputes in India

ADR mechanisms allow parties to resolve their disputes privately without going to regular courts and paying hefty costs, thereby providing greater autonomy to parties in disputes. The Supreme Court of India first introduced ADR mechanisms in resolving consumer disputes in the case of *M/s Afcons Infra Ltd v M/s Cherian Varkey Construction Company Ltd*,[31] which held that ADR could be used for all consumer disputes. This means people could use arbitration or mediation to settle their issues. But later, in another case in 2016, Justice DY Chandrachud held that some specific disputes could not be resolved through arbitration if a special forum already had the power to handle such disputes. So, if the legislature gave a special commission the authority to deal with consumer disputes, those disputes could not be resolved through arbitration.[32] The same reasoning was followed in

26 Shivaraj S Huchhanavar, 'In Search of True "Alternative" to Existing Justice Dispensing System in India' (2013) 7(1) *NALSAR Law Review* 1, 3

27 Anil Xavier, 'Mediation: Its Origin and Growth in India' (2006) 27(2) *Hamline Journal of Public Law and Policy* 275, 275

28 Anamika Yadav, 'The Evolution and Development of ADR in India and Its Different Kinds' (2020) 3(5) *International Journal of Law Management & Humanities* 578, 579

29 Krishna Agrawal, 'Justice Dispensation Through the Alternative Dispute Resolution System in India' (2014) 2(2) *Russian Law Journal* 63, 64

30 Xavier (n 28) 275

31 *M/s Afcons Infra Ltd v M/s Cherian Varkey Construction Company Ltd* [(2010) 8 SCC 24]

32 *A Ayyasamy v A Paramasivam* [(2016) 10 SCC 386]

the case of *M/s Emaar MGF Land Ltd v Aftab Singh*[33] where the Court held that an alternate mechanism may conclude consumer disputes. The Court further held that an arbitration agreement would not bar the jurisdiction of the Consumer forum to entertain a complaint. This is also evident in the recently passed Consumer Protection Act of 2019, which included mediation as a dispute resolution mechanism.[34]

While India has a robust law governing arbitration based on the UNCITRAL Model Law on International Commercial Arbitration, there existed a dilemma regarding what type of disputes could be resolved through ADR mechanisms. The Supreme Court resolved this dilemma in the case of *Vidya Drolia and Others v Durga Trading Corporation*, where a four-fold test was laid down to determine the arbitrability of claims.[35] Applying these tests to matters of consumer disputes, it can be deduced that certain disputes cannot be brought under the gist of non-arbitrability as, firstly, it may include matters involving *rights in personam* between consumers and sellers. Secondly, these matters do not relate to the sovereign functions of the State. Thirdly, none of the laws specifically state that arbitration cannot be used for consumer disputes. Hence, it is evident that blocking all consumer matters from arbitration would not be a prudent choice for consumers. Yet, the Supreme Court, in the case of *Smt. M. Hemalatha Devi and Others v B. Udayasri*[36] denied the appointment of an arbitrator on a request put by the consumer, holding that consumer disputes are non-arbitrable. The Court held that a consumer dispute may be subjected to arbitration only if the consumer opts for arbitration once the dispute has arisen. This judgement is not in line with the four-fold test laid down in *Vidya Drolia*[37] and hence, the issue of arbitrability of consumer disputes is not settled law in India.

In order to encourage parties to address complaints through mediation following the admission of a complaint or at any later point, the Consumer Protection Act, 2019[38] introduced mediation in Chapter V. As per the act, the matter may be referred to mediation if the Central Authority believes that there is a possibility of a settlement.[39] Mediation as a dispute resolution process is incredibly encouraged for all consumer disputes as it leads parties to a solution agreeable by both parties rather than a decision forced by a court. Unlike arbitration or conciliation, where a third party makes a final decision binding, mediation allows consumers more autonomy and helps level the playing field between the seller and consumer. Settlement agreements entered into by parties post the mediation proceeding are binding on the parties and are enforceable due to Section 27 of the Mediation Act 2023. The mediation settlement agreements can be enforced like court judgments, enhancing the enforceability of mediated settlements by the provisions of the Code of Civil

33 *M/s Emaar MGF Land Ltd v Aftab Singh [(2018) SCC Online SC 2945]*
34 The Consumer Protection Act, 2019 (35 of 2019) s 37
35 *Vidya Drolia and Others v Durga Trading Corporation* [AIR 2019 SC 3498]
36 *Smt. M. Hemalatha Devi and Others v B. Udayasri [Civil Appeal Nos. 6500–6501/2023]*
37 *Vidya Drolia and Others v Durga Trading Corporation [AIR 2019 SC 3498]*
38 The Consumer Protection Act 2019 (35 of 2019)
39 ibid Ch V

Procedure 1908, in the same manner as if it were a judgement or decree passed by a court.[40] The corresponding State will cover All costs associated with the mediation process, including the mediator's fee, administrative support fees, and other related expenditures.[41]

Integration of ADR Mechanisms into the Legal System

The integration of ADR mechanisms into the legal system was motivated by various factors, but the overcrowding of litigants, massive backlog of cases and heavy expenditure fast-tracked ADR into becoming the most favoured form of dispute resolution. The inefficiencies in the legal system, including escalating litigation costs, have prompted a search for more accessible and cost-effective avenues for justice. While ADR may alleviate some of these concerns, addressing the root causes, such as archaic laws and procedural complexities, is equally important. Efforts to reform laws and streamline legal processes should run parallel to promoting ADR.[42] While ADR has many advantages, it is essential to recognise that not all disputes are fit for ADR,[43] especially those involving questions of law, constitutional issues, or public interest. In some instances, the argument favouring ADR must be carefully weighed against the potential consequences of bypassing judicial scrutiny.

ADR Institutions in India

The new Mediation Act of 2023[44] in India introduces rules for mediation in Chapter III.[45] It sets up the Mediation Council[46] to oversee and regulate mediation institutions and mediators. The Council also promotes mediation, offers training, and keeps records of settlement agreements. The Mediation Act of 2023 contemplates the creation of a 'Mediation Service Provider' in India.[47] This provider will manage and oversee mediation institutions and mediators in the country. The Mediation Council, formed under this act, will promote international and domestic mediation. It will also handle training, education, and certifications in mediation and keep a record of mediation settlement agreements made in India. The Government of India has provided for an INR 4 crore allocation in the financial budget of

40 The Mediation Act 2023, s 27

41 Latha Shanmugam, 'India: The Consumer Protection Act, 2019' (*Mondaq*, 28 August 2019) <https://www.mondaq.com/india/dodd-frank-consumer-protection-act/840626/the-consumer-protection-act-2019> accessed 17 December 2023

42 Jasmine Joseph, 'Alternate to Alternatives: Critical Review of the Claims of ADR' [2011] *SSRN Electronic Journal* <https://papers.ssrn.com/sol3/papers.cfm?abstract_id=1969935> accessed 17 December 2023

43 Simon Roberts, 'Alternative Dispute Resolution and Civil Justice: An Unresolved Relationship' (1993) 56(3) *The Modern Law Review* 452, 455

44 The Mediation Act 2023 (32 of 2023)

45 ibid Ch III

46 ibid s 31

47 ibid s 40

2024 to the New Delhi International Arbitration Centre and INR 5 million each to all the Mediation and Arbitration Councils in India with the aim of improving the ADR facilities in India.

There are two kinds of arbitral proceedings in India: institutional arbitration and ad hoc arbitration. In cases with no arbitration agreement, the parties may choose to have the arbitral tribunal set the procedure or decide it themselves. Ad-hoc arbitrations make up the majority of arbitrations in India. In institutional arbitration, the involved parties consent to have their disagreements heard by a certain organisation like the India International Arbitration Centre (IIAC – body set up by an Act of Parliament), Delhi International Arbitration Centre (DIAC – a centre set up by the High Court of Delhi), Indian Council of Arbitration (ICA), Mumbai Centre for International Arbitration (MCIA), International Arbitration and Mediation Centre Hyderabad, Construction Industry Arbitration Council (CIAC), LCIA India, International Centre for Alternative Dispute Resolution (ICDAR), etc. The Government of Telangana has made ardent efforts to privatise justice by including a mandatory arbitration clause in contracts between private vendors and the Government of Telangana undertakings that mandate arbitration under the aegis of IAMC, Hyderabad.[48] This model can be implemented in India to facilitate the more efficient adjudication of consumer disputes and promote the use of the ADR mechanism.

Role of Technology in Consumer ADR – Online Dispute Resolution for Consumer Disputes

Information and Communications Technology (ICT) in dispute resolution is the use of digital tools to facilitate the resolution of issues faced by consumers by leveraging electronic platforms to increase the efficiency of the process. Various government bodies have attempted to utilise the potential of ICT through various programmes to help resolve issues within their sector. The Department of Consumer Affairs also has initiatives like the National Consumer Helpline,[49] which makes registering complaints easier, and the Integrated Consumer Grievance Redressal Mechanism,[50] a portal which has enabled various stakeholders onto a single platform where grievances can be registered, facilitating awareness, and creation and protection of consumer rights.[51]

48 'Telangana Becomes the 1st State to Designate IAMC, Hyderabad as the Arbitral/Mediation Institution in All Contracts Above 3 Crores' (*Live Law*, 7 April 2022) <https://www.livelaw.in/law-firms/deals/iamc-arbitralmediation-institution-adr-196014?msclkid=0b14d6f8b64411ecb0d1ccdc4c1874d9> accessed 14 January 2024

49 Department of Consumer Affairs, 'National Consumer Helpline' <https://consumerhelpline.gov.in/> accessed 6 December 2023

50 Department of Consumer Affairs, 'Annual Report 2019–20' <https://consumeraffairs.nic.in/sites/default/files/file-uploads/annualreports/1596167686_Annual%20Report%202019–20.pdf> accessed 7 December 2023

51 Department of Consumer Affairs, 'INGRAM' <https://consumerhelpline.gov.in/about-portal.php#:~:text=The%20Department%20of%20Consumer%20Affairs%20has%20launched%20this%20portal%20as,Ombudsmen%20and%20call%20centres%20etc.> accessed 7 December 2023

The Consumer App took this a step further to bring together features like complaint registration, grievance tracking, submission of documents, and providing suggestions.[52] The Online Conciliation and Mediation Centre (OCMC), established under the Ministry of Consumer Affairs, provides the infrastructure to resolve consumer disputes through online mediation. It aims to make resolution quicker, more accessible, and safer.[53]

The High Level Committee on Deepening Digital Payments has recommended using an ODR system to handle complaints arising from UPI or other payment system usage. It was suggested that there be an automated and human level to resolve disputes.[54] The Reserve Bank of India has also advised Payment System Operators and their participators to establish ODRs to resolve disputes and grievances.[55] Further, legislation has also been amended to accommodate the growth in the use of technology, such as the admission of electronic evidence under the Code of Criminal Procedure.[56] In *Grid Corporation of Orissa Ltd. v Aes Corporation And Others*, the Supreme Court held that

> When an effective consultation can be achieved by resort to electronic media and remote conferencing, it is not necessary that the two persons required to act in consultation with each other must necessarily sit together at one place unless it is the requirement of law or the ruling contract between the parties.[57]

This shows that courts welcome the idea of settling disputes online instead of pursuing traditional methods. The need for more efficient dispute-resolution methods was mainly seen during the COVID-19 pandemic, which ultimately propelled the use of ODR.[58] Although in a nascent stage, India has begun to utilise ICT to resolve disputes.

Various dispute resolution centres, like the Indian Institute for Arbitration and Mediation[59] and Bangalore International Mediation, Arbitration and Conciliation Centre have started offering online resolution services. In a stakeholder meeting by NITI Aayog, various judges have identified the potential of ODR, with Justice

52 Department of Consumer Affairs, 'Consumer App' <https://consumerhelpline.gov.in/apps/consumerapp/> accessed 7 December 2023

53 National Law School of India University, Bengaluru, 'Online Consumer Mediation Centre' <https://www.nls.ac.in/centres/online-consumer-mediation-centre/> accessed 7 December 2023

54 RBI, 'Report of the High Level Committee on Deepening of Digital Payments' (May 2019) <https://rbidocs.rbi.org.in/rdocs/PublicationReport/Pdfs/CDDP03062019634B0EEF3F7144C3B65360B280E420AC.pdf> accessed 9 December 2023

55 Online Dispute Resolution (ODR) System for Digital Payments 2020, RBI/2020–21/21 <https://m.rbi.org.in/Scripts/BS_CircularIndexDisplay.aspx?Id=11946> accessed 8 December 2023

56 Code of Criminal Procedure 1973, s 65

57 *Grid Corporation of Orissa Ltd. v Aes Corporation and Others* [2002 (7) SCC 736]

58 NITI Aayog, 'Designing the Future of Dispute Resolution the ODR Policy Plan or India' (2021) <https://www.niti.gov.in/sites/default/files/2023–03/Designing-The-Future-of-Dispute-Resolution-The-ODR-Policy-Plan-for-India.pdf> accessed 10 December 2023

59 Indian Institute of Arbitration and Mediation, 'Peacegate App' <https://www.arbitrationindia.com/peacegate.html> accessed 10 December 2023

DY Chandrachud noting that dispute resolution should be considered a service that is available and not just related to a court.[60] Justice Indu Malhotra also suggested that these services be mandatory for specific categories to change attitudes towards these processes.

While India has undergone a major digital transformation in the past decade, this technology integration has faced its own challenges. Access to devices and an internet connection is still lacking in many country areas.[61] Another obstacle is the low digital literacy rate, which stands at 38% of households in the country, with 31% in rural areas and 67% in urban areas.[62] Additionally, there is a lack of awareness regarding technology-integrated services since they deviate significantly from the conventional approach, resulting in low confidence in ODR.[63] Doubts regarding its enforceability have impacted the use of these services. Further, India is where people trust courts for dispute resolution, making it difficult for ADR to gain a strong foothold.[64]

There are still major apprehensions with respect to data privacy and whether documents will remain encrypted and confidential, for which legislations which focus on regulating technology-integrated dispute resolution processes have not yet been introduced, leading to questions as to whether these mechanisms are safe.[65] Investing in improving digital access in rural areas and introducing digital literacy programs will make these mechanisms more accessible. Further, implementing legislation to regulate the use of technology for ADR, with a specific emphasis on confidentiality and enforceability, will improve the faith in the employability of ADR mechanisms. Targeted measures that deal with significant obstacles are essential to developing technology-integrated ADR as an alternative to traditional dispute resolution methods. To this end, many private organisations like SAMA, Presolve 360, and CORD in India have been using ODR methods to resolve disputes, especially consumer disputes, as the value of the claims is on the lower end.[66]

60 PIB Delhi, 'NITI Aayog – Catalysing Online Dispute Resolution (ODR) in India' (7 June 2020) <https://pib.gov.in/PressReleasePage.aspx?PRID=1630080> accessed 11 December 2023

61 IDR, 'The Pitfalls of Technology in India' (21 April 2023) <https://idronline.org/article/inequality/the-pitfalls-of-technology-in-india/> accessed 12 December 2023

62 IDR, 'India's Digital Divide: From Bad to Worse?' (16 February 2023) <https://idronline.org/article/inequality/indias-digital-divide-from-bad-to-worse/> accessed 12 December 2023

63 NITI Aayog, 'Designing the Future of Dispute Resolution the ODR Policy Plan or India' (2021) <https://www.niti.gov.in/sites/default/files/2023–03/Designing-The-Future-of-Dispute-Resolution-The-ODR-Policy-Plan-for-India.pdf> accessed 10 December 2023

64 NITI Aayog, 'Designing the Future of Dispute Resolution the ODR Policy Plan or India' (2021) <https://www.niti.gov.in/sites/default/files/2023–03/Designing-The-Future-of-Dispute-Resolution-The-ODR-Policy-Plan-for-India.pdf> accessed 10 December 2023

65 Ministry of Business, Innovation and Employment, 'Online Dispute Resolution' (February 2017) <https://www.mbie.govt.nz/assets/00ddebf604/online-dispute-resolution-report-2018.pdf> accessed 14 December 2023

66 Gupta A and Bajpai A, 'Online Dispute Resolution in India: A Distant Reality or Dream?' in *Contemporary Perspectives on International Arbitration Practice* (1st edn, Thomson Reuters 2023) 217

Challenges and Opportunities

Consumer ADR in India faces several challenges, hindering its effectiveness and progress as a viable alternative to traditional dispute resolution. There is a lack of awareness among consumers and a limited understanding of ADR, the process, and its benefits. The accessibility of ADR, a crucial factor in its widespread adoption, exhibits disparities, particularly in non-urban areas, which might lack the infrastructure and trained personnel necessary for effective implementation. This imbalance raises concerns that such regions might be disadvantaged due to a lack of alternatives to traditional methods. Even in areas that have the necessary infrastructure, there is a need for experienced and reliable centres that provide these services.[67] Although ADR outcomes are legally binding, India lacks strong legislative support towards ADR processes.[68] This leaves such processes susceptible to inconsistencies in the interpretation and enforcement of awards. This has eroded consumer trust towards such alternative methods, further amplified by the fact that these awards do not have any precedent value.[69]

Another challenge is the concern that ADR methods, like mediation, involve bias that may not be controlled as they can be in litigation.[70] Disputes generally vary due to intricate cultural and linguistic differences. When differing values and beliefs come into play, ADR professionals must assist the parties in reaching an outcome, keeping these values and beliefs in mind.[71] In order to be able to communicate with other parties effectively, these cultural and linguistic diversities must be considered. These can act as communication barriers and impede the ability of parties to express their issue completely and of professionals to reach a fair conclusion. Further, since accessibility has already been a concern for ADR mechanisms, addressing diversity can promote an inclusive and welcoming environment for parties from all cultural and linguistic backgrounds.

Given the growth in technology and commerce, ADR needs to be developed as a reliable alternative, even mandatory in some cases, to reduce the burden on courts in dealing with all issues. Measures can be taken to actively increase all parties' awareness of ADR methods actively, encouraging such recourse. The government

67 Chourasia A, *Challenges in Implementation of the Alternative Dispute Resolution in . . .* <https://jlrjs.com/wp-content/uploads/2023/07/233.-Aaryavart-Chourasia.pdf> accessed 24 December 2023

68 Chourasia A, *Challenges in Implementation of the Alternative Dispute Resolution in . . .* <https://jlrjs.com/wp-content/uploads/2023/07/233.-Aaryavart-Chourasia.pdf> accessed 24 December 2023

69 Dr. Anil Kumar Singh, 'ADR Mechanism in India: Achievements and Challenges' (2016) 5 IJR 8 <https://www.worldwidejournals.com/paripex/recent_issues_pdf/2016/August/adr-mechanism-in-india-achievements-and-challenges_August_2016_1909046205_6404265.pdf> accessed 24 December 2023

70 David A Hoffman and Katherine Triantafillou, 'Cultural and Diversity Issues in Mediation and Negotiation' in David A Hoffman (ed) *Mediation: A Practice Guide for Mediators, Lawyers and Other Professionals* (2013) <https://blc.law/wp-content/uploads/2016/12/The-Massachusetts-General-Hospital-Textbook-on-Diversity-and-Cultural-Sensitivity-in-Mental-Health-Chapter-10.pdf> accessed 24 December 2023

71 Wolters Kluwer, 'How Do Cultural Differences Influence Mediation?' (21 February 2022) <https://www.lexology.com/library/detail.aspx?g=5780dd00–80f3–4ae1-addc-ec8374434fed> accessed 26 December 2023

and consumer organisations can work together to campaign or organise educational programs to help eradicate misinformation. There can also be initiatives to invest in developing the required infrastructure, particularly in non-urban areas.[72]

In order to develop trust and faith in alternatives for dispute resolution, there is a need for procedures to monitor these systems. They must be regularly evaluated to ensure conformation with regulations and fairness. This can also lead to discovering new weaknesses and scope for improvement. By effectively utilising the strengths of stakeholders, the government, industry, and consumer organisations can contribute collectively to the improvement of ADR methods and encourage a fair and efficient alternative.

Conclusion

With the intent of protecting the rights and welfare of consumers, the Consumer Protection Act of 2019 is on track to transform how consumer disputes are managed in India. While the Act has enabled India to take many steps forward, the current dispute resolution process within the judiciary and the specialised courts is struggling with pending cases and a massive backlog, resulting in an unnecessary financial burden and loss of time for consumers. The way forward is seemingly privatising justice to reduce the burden on the courts and provide consumers with the justice they seek. Utilising other avenues that provide justice, like arbitration, mediation, and conciliation, will provide a much-needed breather for the judiciary and make the adjudication process efficient for the consumers. Online dispute resolution is the future, but it may already be the present.

The law is at its strongest when it provides clarity and predictability to the people. The Supreme Court must endeavour to provide clarity on the arbitrability issue of consumer disputes. In cases where the consumers give clear and unequivocal consent for arbitration, arbitration clauses in consumer contracts must be enforceable, like in the United States of America.

Further, the Government of India has been taking initiatives to make India a five trillion USD economy, which can only be achieved if India can provide a conducive environment for commercial dispute resolution. To realise the dream of Viksit Bharat 2047 and move from developing to developed, India must start improving the enforcement of contracts, providing the best dispute resolution forums for ease of enforcement of contracts.

References

A Ayyasamy v A Paramasivam [(2016) 10 SCC 386]

Agrawal K, 'Justice Dispensation Through the Alternative Dispute Resolution System in India' (2014) 2(2) Russian Law Journal 63, 64

72 Indian National Bar Association, 'Suggestive Measure to Strengthen ADR in India' <https://www.indianbarassociation.org/suggestive-measure-to-strengthen-adr-in-india/> accessed 25 December 2023

Ajjannavar P, 'India: Procedure to File Complaint Under Consumer Protection (Amendment) Act, 2019' (*Mondaq*, 6 August 2020) accessed 16 December 2023

'Central Consumer Protection Authority Established to Promote, Protect and Enforce the Rights of Consumers; Will Function From Indian Institute of Public Administration Premises' (Press Information Bureau) accessed 14 November 2023

Chaudhary P, ' "Manmauji", Indian Judicial System: Its Nature & Structure and Distinction between Law and Justice' (1999) 45(3) Indian Journal of Public Administration 303, 305

Chaudhary RNP, *Consumer Protection Law: Provisions and Procedure* (Deep and Deep Publishers 2005)

Chawla N and Kumar B, 'E-Commerce and Consumer Protection in India: The Emerging Trend' (2022) J Bus Ethics 180

Chourasia A, 'Challenges in Implementation of the Alternative Dispute Resolution in India' (2022) Journal of Legal Research and Juridical Sciences. accessed 24 December 2023

Code of Criminal Procedure 1973

Department of Consumer Affairs, 'Annual Report 2019–20' accessed 7 December 2023

Department of Consumer Affairs, 'Consumer App' accessed 7 December 2023

Department of Consumer Affairs, 'INGRAM' accessed 7 December 2023

Department of Consumer Affairs, 'National Consumer Helpline' accessed 6 December 2023

Grid Corporation of Orissa Ltd. v. Aes Corporation and Ors. 2002 (7) SCC 736

Gupta A and Bajpai A, 'Online Dispute Resolution in India: A Distant Reality or Dream?' in *Contemporary Perspectives on International Arbitration Practice* (1st edn, Thomson Reuters 2023) 217, 232

Hoffman D and Triantafillou K, 'Cultural and Diversity Issues in Mediation and Negotiation' in David A. Hoffman (ed) *Mediation: A Practice Guide for Mediators, Lawyers, and Other Professionals* (2013) accessed 24 December 2023

Huchhanavar SS, 'In Search of True "Alternative" to Existing Justice Dispensing System in India' (2013) 7(1) NALSAR Law Review 1, 3

IDR, 'India's Digital Divide: From Bad to Worse?' (16 February 2023) accessed 12 December 2023

IDR, 'The Pitfalls of Technology in India' (21 April 2023) accessed 12 December 2023

Indian Institute of Arbitration and Mediation, 'Peacegate App' accessed 10 December 2023

Indian National Bar Association, 'Suggestive Measure to Strengthen ADR in India' accessed 25 December 2023

Indian Penal Code 1860

Joseph J, 'Alternate to Alternatives: Critical Review of the Claims of ADR' (2011) SSRN Electronic Journal, accessed 17 December 2023

Ministry of Business, Innovation and Employment, 'Online Dispute Resolution' (February 2017) accessed 14 December 2023

M/s Afcons Infra Ltd v M/s Cherian Varkey Construction Company Ltd [(2010) 8 SCC 24]

M/s Emaar MGF Land Ltd v Aftab Singh [(2018) SCC OnLine SC 2945]

National Law School of India University, Bengaluru, 'Online Consumer Mediation Centre' accessed 7 December 2023

NITI Aayog, 'Designing the Future of Dispute Resolution the ODR Policy Plan or India' (2021) accessed 10 December 2023

Online Dispute Resolution (ODR) System for Digital Payments 2020, RBI/2020–21/21, accessed 8 December 2023

PIB Delhi, 'NITI Aayog – Catalysing Online Dispute Resolution (ODR) in India' (7 June 2020) accessed 11 December 2023

RBI, 'Report of the High Level Committee on Deepening of Digital Payments' (May 2019) accessed 9 December 2023

Roberts S, 'Alternative Dispute Resolution and Civil Justice: An Unresolved Relationship' (1993) 56(3) The Modern Law Review 452, 455

Saha A and Khanna SR, 'Evolution of Consumer Courts in India: The Consumers Protection Act 2019 and Emerging Themes of Consumer Jurisprudence' (2021) 9(1) International Journal on Consumer Law and Practice 115, 125

Shanmugam L, 'India: The Consumer Protection Act, 2019' (*Mondaq*, 2019) accessed 17 December 2023

Singh AK, 'ADR Mechanism in India: Achievements and Challenges' (2016) 5 IJR 8 accessed 24 December 2023

Smt. M. Hemalatha Devi and Ors. v. B. Udayasri [Civil Appeal Nos. 6500–6501/2023]

Tan JA, 'WIPO Guide on Alternative Dispute Resolution (ADR) Options for Intellectual Property Offices and Courts' (2018) accessed 5 January 2024

'Telangana Becomes the 1st State to Designate IAMC, Hyderabad as the Arbitral/Mediation Institution in All Contracts Above 3 Crores' (*Live Law*, 7 April 2022) accessed 14 January 2024

The Consumer Protection Act, 2019 (35 of 2019)

The Constitution of India 1950

The Legal Services Authorities Act, 1987 (39 of 1987)

The Mediation Act 2023

'The Pendency in the Consumer Commissions Shows a Declining Trend. Number of Cases Pending in Consumer Commission Come Down From 5.55 Lakhs in December 2022 to 5.45 Lakhs in September 2023' (Press Information Bureau) accessed 21 December 2023

United Nations General Assembly Resolution 39/248 of 1985

Vidya Drolia & Ors. v Durga Trading Corporation [AIR 2019 SC 3498]

Wolters Kluwer, 'How Do Cultural Differences Influence Mediation?' (21 February 2022) accessed 26 December 2023

Xavier A, 'Mediation: Its Origin and Growth in India' (2006) 27(2) Hamline Journal of Public Law & Policy 275

Yadav A, 'The Evolution and Development of ADR in India and Its Different Kinds' (2020) 3(5) International Journal of Law Management & Humanities 578, 579

12 Consumer ADR in Brazil

Luca Dal Pubel and Andrea Marighetto

Introduction

Contracts have evolved into streamlined legal documents, often requiring minimal prior discussion or negotiation. Companies are trending towards standardising their contract templates to the extent that they present them in pre-printed forms to consumers. Paradoxically, this massifies legal certainty for contracts as they become more uniform and standardised. However, it also poses a risk for consumers who may accept the contract without engaging in any negotiation and, in some cases, without fully understanding all its clauses. The rise of the consumer society has transformed contracts into widely used tools, diluting their original essence and the equilibrium between parties. The prevalent shift towards a 'uniform and standardised' nature has deprived consumers of the opportunity to negotiate specific clauses and individual interests. Simultaneously, this trend has undermined the framework of traditional contractual remedies, which have, over time, demonstrated inadequacies or incompleteness.[1]

In Brazil, the widespread use of contracts has often reduced the exercise of private autonomy to a mere choice in purchasing a product or service, stripping the contract of its personal touch. The contract's content is no longer the outcome of a negotiation between parties, as the company typically dictates the text and clauses unilaterally. Customers are then obligated (if they wish to purchase the product or service) to accept the content without the ability to modify it.[2] This trend is also evident in contracts resulting from free economic negotiations between equally strong parties (such as between companies), where numerous conditions and legal constraints are imposed. The concept of pure economic negotiation, which aligns with contractual autonomy and personal fulfilment principles, is becoming

1 Robert Scott, 'The Paradox of Contracting in Markets' (2020) 83(2) *Law and Contemporary Problems* 76; Claudia Lima Marques, *Contratos no Código de Defesa do Consumidor* (RT 2019) 200

2 Miguel Reale, *Nova fase do Direito* (Saraiva 1990) 90; Francisco Amaral, *Direito Civil. Introdução* (Renovar 2003) 124; Zygmunt Bauman, *Capitalismo Parasitário* (Eliana Aguiar tr, Zahar 2010) 90; Beyla Esther Fellous, *Proteção do consumidor no Mercosul e na União Europeia* (Editora Revista dos Tribunais 2003) 336; Jean Calais-Auloy and Frank Steinmetz, *Droit de la Consommation* (4th edn, Dalloz 1996) 86; Maria Antonieta Zanardo Donato, *Proteção ao consumidor: conceito e extensão* (Revista dos Tribunais 1993) 19

DOI: 10.4324/9781032689739-12

increasingly rare.[3] In most cases, parties have limited freedom to negotiate privately. The debate surrounding the traditional notion of private autonomy and the contract has led to a notable enhancement of policies to protect consumers. In response, the state has intervened by implementing public and private economic measures to harmonise the diverse and conflicting interests of over 115 million consumers with Brazil's industrial and commercial sectors. This sector has propelled Brazil to become one of the world's leading economies (currently ranking ninth), a founding member of the Brics, and a member of the G20 (currently holding the presidency).[4] The state is focused on implementing economic policies using specific instruments to address the significant growth of an increasingly important market economy. This includes establishing public law rules to integrate consumer protection measures, such as those in the CDC.

Legal Framework for Consumer Protection

Brazil boasts a robust legal framework dedicated to consumer protection, where such protection holds constitutional significance. The 1988 Federal Constitution acknowledges consumer rights as fundamental to individuals, with provisions enshrined in two pivotal sections. Article 5 delineates fundamental freedoms for every citizen, affirming equality before the law and guaranteeing the inviolability of life, liberty, equality, security, and property. It also mandates state promotion of consumer defence in accordance with the law. Moreover, Article 170 establishes consumer protection as a cornerstone principle within the 'Economic and Financial Order'.[5] These constitutional tenets underpin the CDC, enacted in 1990 through Law 8078, which delineates various consumer rights and establishes the National Consumer Defence System (SNDC).[6] This system comprises federal, state, municipal, and federal district agencies alongside private consumer defence entities.

3 Andrea Marighetto, *Acesso ao Contrato* (Quartier Latin 2012) 87; Carlos Roberto Gonçalves, *Direito Civil Brasileiro. Parte Geral* (Saraiva 2016) 35; Luiz Ottavio Rodrigues Junior, 'Autonomia da vontade, autonomia privada e autodeterminação: Notas sobre a evolução de um conceito na Modernidade e na Pós-modernidade' (2004) 163 *Revista de Informação Legislativa* 115; Clóvis Beviláqua, *Teoria geral do direito civil* (Servanda 2015) 203; Kleber Luiz Zanchim, *Contratos Empresariais: Categoria – Interface com contratos de consumo e Paritários – Revisão Judicia* (Quartier Latin 2012) 69

4 International Monetary Fund, 'Brazil' (*International Monetary Fund*, 2024) <https://www.imf.org/en/Countries/BRA> accessed 24 February 2024

5 Gilmar Ferreira Mendes, Inocêncio Mártires Coelho and Paulo Gustavo Gonet Branco, *Curso de Direito Constitucional* (Saraiva 2009) 1297; Kildare Gonçalves Carvalho, *Direito Constitucional* (Del Rey 2009) 198; José Afonso da Silva, *Curso de direito constitucional positivo* (Malheiros 2006) 288; Ingo W Sarlet, *A eficácia dos direitos fundamentais* (Livraria do Advogado 2006) 242

6 Antônio Carlos Morato and Paulo de Tarso Neri (eds), *20 anos do Código de Defesa do Consumidor: Estudos em homenagem ao Prof. José Geraldo Brito Filomeno* (Editora Atlas 2010) 199–200; Claudia Lima Marques, Antônio Herman V Benjamin, and Bruno Miragem, *Comentários ao Código de Defesa do Consumidor* (RT 2021) 1177; Amanda Flávio de Oliveira, 'O Sistema Nacional de Defesa do Consumidor: histórico' (2002) 44 *Revista de Direito do Consumidor* 95–105

The system has led to a significant rise in institutions aimed at resolving issues and preventing consumer disputes. These include special civil and criminal judicial courts (*Juizados Especiais Cíveis and Criminais*), the specific public prosecutor's office for consumer protection (*Promotorias de Proteção ao Consumidor*),[7] police stations specialised in investigating crimes against consumer relations (*Delegacias Especializadas na investigação de crimes contra as relações de consumo*), legal aid (*Assistência Judiciária*), and consumer associations.[8] Consumer protection is necessary to prevent abuses in unfair competition practices, enhance public services, and align with the evolving dynamics of consumer relations by harmonising the interests of all parties involved. Consumer practice and defence have primarily relied on special civil and criminal judicial courts (*Juizados Especiais Cíveis and Criminais*), which provide a specialised channel for accessing protection in consumer relations.

In addition to these judicial structures, specific consumer support systems have been established, such as SACs (*Serviços de Atendimento ao Consumidor*) and PROCONs (*Programa de Proteção e Defesa do Consumidor*). These structures play a vital role in ensuring consumer rights are upheld and provide avenues for resolving consumer disputes. The SACs focus on assisting consumers, initially through telephone support and now, as per the legislative change in Decree No. 11.034/2022, also via instant messaging, while adhering to rules on compliance and LGPD (*Lei Geral de Proteção de Dados*/General Data Protection Law) for personal data protection. In contrast, PROCONs are public bodies that function extrajudicially, serving as significant alternative dispute resolution mechanisms. All these tools are, therefore, envisaged for the implementation of a rebalancing policy in consumer relations. The guidelines of Brazilian consumer policy can be found mainly summarised in Articles 4 and 5 of the Consumer Code.[9] They identify the consumer's primary needs, respect for his dignity, protection of his economic interests, and improvement of their quality of life. The Consumer Code is based on and integrated with other important principles that govern legal relationships, such as the principle of objective good faith, which is also provided for and regulated by Brazilian legislation in Article 422 of the Civil Code.[10]

7 Ministerio Publico Distrito Federal e Territorios, 'Procuradoria-Geral de Justiça' (*Ministério Público do Distrito Federal e Territórios*, 2020) <https://www.lawteacher.net/oscola-referencing/website.php> accessed 20 January 2024

8 Marques, Benjamin and Miragem (n 6) 1198–1208

9 *Código de Defesa do Consumidor*|Law No. 8.078, de 11 September 1990

10 Adalberto Pasqualotto, 'O Código de Defesa do Consumidor em face do Código Civil de 2002' in Roberto Pfeiffer and Adalberto Pasqualotto (eds) *Código de Defesa do Consumidor e o Código Civil de 2002: convergências e assimetrias* (Revista dos Tribunais 2005) 99–129; Judith Martins-Costa, *A boa-fé no Direito Privado – Sistema e tópica no processo obrigacional* (RT 2000) 437–472; Antônio Manoel da Rocha e Menezes Cordeiro, *Da boa-fé no direito civil* (Almedina 2007) 1197–1208; Paulo Nalin, 'Ética e boa-fé no adimplemento contratual' in Luiz Edson Fachin (ed) *Repensando fundamentos do direito civil brasileiro contemporâneo* (Renovar 1998) 253; Clovis V do Couto e Silva, *A obrigação como processo* (FGV 2007) 157–162; Álvaro Villaça Azevedo, *Teoria Geral dos Contratos Típicos e Atípicos* (Editora Atlas 2002) 39

The General Design of the Enforcement Mechanism

Numerous principles incorporated into the CDC trace back to the 1988 Constitutional Charter.[11] These principles stand as noteworthy innovations within the Brazilian legal system, providing a concrete assurance of balance, trust, and the protection of legitimate expectations in consumer relationships. With the enactment of the 1988 Constitution, consumer protection gained recognition as a constitutional guarantee, aligning with Article 5, XXXII, of the Constitutional Charter, which stipulates that 'the State shall promote, through legislation, the defence of the consumer.' Simultaneously, this principle evolved into a guiding tenet of the economic order in accordance with Article 170, IV, of the Constitutional Charter.[12]

In adherence to the Transitional Constitutional Provisions (letter ADCT), Article 48 mandated the commencement of drafting the CDC within 120 days of the Constitutional Charter's formulation. Consequently, on 11 September 1990, Law No. 8.078 was promulgated, giving birth to the Consumer Defence Code. This legislation, effective 180 days after its publication on March 11, 1991, lays down regulations for the protection and defence of consumers, with a focus on public order and social interest. The constitutional perspective and provision underscore the acknowledgement of the significance of consumer relations as a manifestation of a state policy and interest. The state is tasked with safeguarding the nature and legitimacy of these relations and ensuring that behaviours contrary to them face appropriate civil and administrative sanctions. This is crucial in specific consumer, supplier, or service provider interactions. Marques emphasises that the CDC operates within a post-modern social framework, distinct from the modern era where the concept of 'modern codifications' prevailed.[13] This distinction arises from the CDC's origins in a societal context different from the 19th century, during which the Civil Code of 1916 was conceived and embraced. The latter exemplifies a liberal approach, focusing on balancing the interests of contractual parties autonomously without requiring state intervention to address contractual imbalances.[14]

Consumer protection policies, including the CDC, fundamentally aim to ensure consumer welfare, primarily focusing on two dimensions: safeguarding both physical and psychological well-being and economic security, particularly during the critical stages deemed most susceptible within the consumer-supplier dynamic – namely, before, during, and after negotiations. Consequently, consumers

11 Constituição da República Federativa do Brasil de 1988; Luís Roberto Barroso, *Interpretação e aplicação da Constituição: fundamentos de uma dogmática constitucional transformadora* (Saraiva 2003) 147; Ingo W Sarlet (ed) *Dignidade da pessoa humana e direitos fundamentais na constituição federal de 1988* (Livraria do Advogado 2007) 63–70

12 Paulo Bonavides, *Curso de Direito Constitucional* (Malheiros 2006) 255–257; Eros Roberto Grau, *A Ordem Econômica na Constituição de 1988* (Malheiros 2010) 122–127; Sérgio Campinho, *O Direito de Empresa à Luz do Novo Código Civil* (Renovar 2008) 448–449

13 Marques (n 1) 254–267; Newton De Lucca, *Direito do consumidor: teoria geral da relação jurídica de consumo* (Quartier Latin 2008) 68

14 Marques (n 1) 647

are regarded as vulnerable in relation to suppliers, owing to numerous exploitative practices commonly observed in the consumer market (Article 4, I, CDC).[15]

It is noteworthy to mention Marques's observation that the introductory clause of Article 4 of the CDC emphasises transparency and the essential need for harmonious consumer relations. This harmony is to be achieved through the requirement of objective good faith in interactions between consumers and suppliers. As articulated in Article 4, Section III, the CDC concentrates the state's efforts on regulating consumer contracts to align the interests of all parties involved in consumer relations and ensure the compatibility of consumer protection with the imperatives of economic and technological progress. Hence, the guiding principles of the Economic Order, as delineated in Article 170 of the Constitution, must be enforced, consistently prioritising the safeguarding of good faith and equilibrium in consumer-supplier relations. Once more, Grinover underscores the consumer's position as vulnerable within the contractual dynamic. This assertion stems from the recognition that suppliers and service providers hold sway and dominance over the market, placing consumers at a disadvantage. Consequently, the state must assume responsibility for safeguarding and advocating for consumer rights. This entails ensuring consumers are well-informed about essential product and service attributes and, most importantly, avenues for legal redress in contractual matters.[16]

The CDC embodies several principles reflecting national policies to safeguard individuals and consumers. Notably, the protection principle stands out, designed to shield consumers from all forms of harm – physical, emotional, or psychological – placing them on equal footing with suppliers or service providers, thus fostering an environment of fairness and equality. This principle is delineated in Article 6, Clause I, of the CDC, asserting that the consumer's primary entitlement is to life, health, and safety protection against risks stemming from flawed practices in products and services deemed hazardous or detrimental. Furthermore, (ii) the principle of vulnerability operates under the premise that, within socio-economic and legal frameworks, consumers are inherently deemed legally inadequate entities; (iii) the principle of the right to information, sourced from Article 4, Clause IV, Article 6, Clause III, and Article 8, Section 1 of the CDC, mandates that suppliers or service providers convey pertinent product or service data to consumers in a clear, objective, comprehensive, and suitable manner; (iv) the right to receive information, established by Decree No. 4.680 of 2003, compels suppliers to furnish information on products designated for human or animal consumption, particularly concerning transgenic products, and by Law No. 10.962 of 2004, requires traders to present prices in an understandable format accessible to all. Article 6, the sole paragraph of the CDC, explicitly addresses the imperative to safeguard the right of access to information for individuals with disabilities.

Additionally, (v) the principle of transparency, aligned with the principle of the right to receive information, mandates that suppliers consistently operate transparently to prevent deceiving or misleading consumers, as outlined in Article 4 and

15 Marques, Benjamin and Miragem (n 6) 144–145

16 Ada Pellegrini Grinover, *Código Brasileiro de Defesa do Consumidor* (Forense 2022) 337

Article 6, Clause IV, of the CDC; (vi) the principle of facilitating defence simplifies the burden of proof, requiring the plaintiff to substantiate claims per Article 373 of the Code of Civil Procedure, thereby enabling consumers to present their defence effectively, under Article 6, Clause VIII, of the CDC. Consequently, this allows the reversal of the burden of proof, wherein the judge may rule against the supplier or service provider if they fail to counter the consumer's claims. (vii) The principle of solidarity, governed by Articles 3 and 7, paragraph a(25), Sections 1 and 34 of the CDC, holds suppliers accountable for compensating consumers for damages resulting from consumption operations, encompassing all parties involved in the creation, construction, assembly, or operation of the consumer transaction. (viii) The principle of contract maintenance/revision grants consumers the right to request contract preservation or modification if contractual services become inequitable or burdensome due to subsequent factors, in line with the principle of proportionality; (ix) the principle of objective good faith, explicitly referenced in Article 4 Clause III and Article 51 Clause IV of the CDC, is paramount.[17] In essence, fairness must prevail in consumer relations, ensuring that no abusive or unjust practices are imposed upon the parties involved. (x) The principle of the unavailability of rights stipulates that suppliers are barred from waiving consumer rights, as only legal authority can sanction revisions to these rights in accordance with contract regulations, whether they pertain to public order or societal interest. This principle, articulated and mandated by Article 51 of the CDC, empowers the nullification of unfair clauses.[18]

Furthermore, Title II of the CDC (comprising provisions from Article 61 to Article 80) is pivotal in upholding public policies and interests to delineate forms of criminal liability. Article 61 specifies that conduct outlined in subsequent articles constitutes offences against consumer relations as per this Code, save for exceptions specified in the Penal Code and other pertinent statutes. Among the array of criminal offences, particular attention is warranted for the stipulations of Article 175, addressing the offence of 'commercial fraud,' as well as Articles 267 and 285, delineating crimes against public health, alongside other provisions targeting behaviours detrimental to consumers. These offences are primarily classified as crimes of danger, wherein, for consumer protection, the mere exposure of legal interests and the risk of harm suffices, obviating the necessity for an actual event. Therefore, it is posited that the consumer, both in theory and in practice, stands as the singular economic actor directly enshrined within the Fundamental Directives of the Constitution, embodying a legal entity inherently susceptible to its contractual counterpart, the supplier.[19] This delineates the rationale for the distinctive treatment requisite to the consumer, encapsulating the principle and entitlement to equality among contractual parties and the imperative to combat the differential treatment of disparate entities.

17 Marques, Benjamin and Miragem (n 6) 701–704

18 Gustavo Tepedino (ed), *Temas de Direito Civil* (Renovar 1999) 244–246

19 Marques, Benjamin and Miragem (n 6) 893–890

In response to the constitutional framework governing consumer law, a consumer protection system has been established, prioritising preserving and acknowledging societal realities and safeguarding human dignity. Indeed, the integration of consumer law within constitutional provisions underscores its profound societal significance, as actions aimed at fostering equilibrium within consumer relations inherently benefit society at large. Article 81, single paragraph, Section III of the CDC addresses the defence of homogeneous individual interests in cases of collective protection. The Consumer Code provides various ways to defend consumer rights, individually or collectively. Collective protection involves legal action by specific or determinable parties united by interests or rights with the same origin, allowing them to seek collective protection. Thus, homogeneous individual interests are considered a form of collective right, although they may also be seen as simple individual rights.

To initiate a collective action, certain conditions must be met, including (i) pursuing different objectives and characteristics that can be combined due to the indivisibility of the law, (ii) enabling a better assessment of the case through collective action, and (iii) using the process in a manner beneficial to all interested parties without compromising the underlying right. Regarding the procedure, Article 94 of the Consumer Code states that after the action is filed, a notice will be published by the competent authority. Interested parties can then join the process as joint litigants unless the authorities responsible for consumer protection have already disseminated the information widely through social media. Article 82 of the Consumer Code also specifies who is authorised to collaborate to defend consumer interests and rights.[20] The legal framework for collective protection is provided by Law No. 7.347 of 1995, also known as the Public Civil Action Law. Article 91 of the Consumer Code allows for the connection with the mechanism for collective applications under Law No. 7.347 of 1995. This enables those authorised under Article 82 of the Consumer Code to bring a collective civil liability action for individually suffered damages.[21]

It is noteworthy that while the law on public civil action is designed to protect all widespread and collective interests in a strict sense, the collective action outlined in the Consumer Code aims explicitly to safeguard consumer interests and rights. Regarding the judicial route, the criterion for determining the most appropriate route is outlined in Article 81 of the Consumer Code, which focuses on using the legal process in a manner beneficial to various interested parties without compromising the underlying right. Another interesting aspect is that in collective action concerning homogeneous individual rights, the settlement and enforcement of damages can be carried out individually, as outlined in Articles 97 and 101 of the Consumer Code.[22] Additionally, Article 104 of the Consumer Code specifies that any collective actions initiated will not benefit the authors of individual actions unless a suspension is requested within 30 days of the initiation.[23]

20 Marques, Benjamin and Miragem (n 6) 987–1012
21 Marques, Benjamin and Miragem (n 6) 987–1012
22 Marques, Benjamin and Miragem (n 6) 1086–1087
23 Marques, Benjamin and Miragem (n 6) 1086–1087

In summary, the CDC protects homogeneous individual rights as a form of collective protection, which can be enforced if they have a common origin and are pursued by specific or determinable parties. Therefore, these rights can be protected through a collective application, with the possibility of also being the subject of an individual application.

Current Consumer Dispute Resolution Processes

At the heart of the consumer protection system are the PROCONs.[24] PROCONs are federal and municipal consumer protection and defence agencies that help consumers enforce their rights and mediate disputes. These agencies are located throughout Brazil and operate adjunctly to the judicial system by resolving disputes between consumers and businesses over goods or services outside the courtroom. The complaint is referred to the appropriate civil court if the PROCON cannot resolve or mediate a dispute. It is important to note that PROCONs were established by the National Consumer Defence System (SNDC) (Presidential Decree No. 2181/1997) at both federal and state levels to advance consumer protection. Specifically, their various extrajudicial functions include consumer guidance, support, and complaints verification; oversight of commercial establishments; promotion of studies, research, and projects; enforcement through administrative sanctions for violations of consumer laws; and promotion of alternative dispute resolution.[25]

The last function, in particular, is considered highly relevant. Through PROCONs, it is possible to avoid initiating judicial processes and obtain quicker solutions that align with win-win principles. The work of PROCONs is invaluable as it accurately gauges the current state of consumer relations.[26] They also seem to be the most qualified entities to assess the extent to which suppliers and consumers are aware of and comply with the law regarding the resolution of extrajudicial cases.[27] Unlike PROCONs, the Special Civil Courts (established by Law No. 9099 of 1995) engage in full-fledged jurisdictional activities. However, they also offer the possibility of conciliation between parties at the first hearing. These courts handle simplified procedures aimed at facilitating conflict resolution in everyday life. They deal with cases of limited complexity and value (not exceeding 40 minimum monthly wages)[28] and do not require the assistance of a lawyer if the case's value

24 There are 27 state PROCONs and many municipalities have PROCONS that offer consumer protection services to local consumers

25 Joel Figueira Junior, *Manual dos Juizados Especiais Civeis Estatuais e Federais* (RT 2006) 108, 109; Maria Eugenia Reis Finkelstein and Fernando Sacco Neto, *Manual de Direito do Consumidor* (Elsevier 2010) 110–111

26 Maria Stella Gregori and Mariangela Sarrubbo fragata, 'Mediação e arbitragem nas relações de consumo' [2021] Consultor Jurídico <https://www.conjur.com.br/2021-jan-20/garantias-consumo-mediacao-arbitragem-relacoes-consumo/> accessed 1 March 2024

27 Maria Stella Gregori and Mariangela Sarrubbo fragata, 'Mediação e arbitragem nas relações de consumo' [2021] Consultor Jurídico <https://www.conjur.com.br/2021-jan-20/garantias-consumo-mediacao-arbitragem-relacoes-consumo/> accessed 1 March 2024

28 As of 2024, the minimum wage in Brazil is $1.412 Brazilian reals (BRL) per month

does not exceed 20 minimum monthly wages. The proceedings are quick and free of charge.

The amendments to the Civil Procedure Code in 2015 also significantly changed the initial hearings of the Special Courts. These changes transformed the conciliation hearing into a genuine session for self-settlement disputes or mediation. If mediation fails to resolve the dispute, the process will proceed with a judgement from the judge. This represents a significant advancement in citizens' access to justice, particularly for those considered most vulnerable, such as consumers. The process is characterised by its speed, informality, limited appeals, and its focus on achieving a peaceful and mediated resolution to conflicts. The advantage of this approach is that it aims to reach a negotiated resolution to the dispute. If this is not possible, the party disputed by the consumer must comply with the judgment, which is enforceable in all respects. This means that the consumer has the chance to win the case and a greater likelihood of receiving compensation.

Alternative Dispute Resolution for Consumer Disputes

Arbitration

Arbitration has been a longstanding method for resolving civil and commercial disputes outside of Brazilian courts throughout its history.[29] However, its significance notably expanded following the enactment of Law No. 9.307 on 23 September 1996, commonly known as the Arbitration Act, which formalised and regulated the arbitration process.[30] This evolution accelerated remarkably with Brazil's ratification of the 1958 New York Convention[31] and the Brazilian Supreme Court's declaration of arbitration's constitutionality in 2001.

The 1996 Arbitration Act draws upon principles from the UNCITRAL Model Law and applies universally to both international and domestic arbitration. Subsequent amendments, such as Law No. 13.129 of 26 May 2015, have broadened the scope of arbitration, including cases involving state entities.[32] Arbitration applies to a wide array of civil and commercial disputes, as articulated in Article 1, which affirms the right of contractually capable parties to use arbitration for resolving conflicts concerning freely transferable property rights. Parties involved in a

29 Gevaerd J, 'Consumer Protection and Arbitration in Mass Consumption Adhesion Contracts: A Comparative Look Between Brazil and US' (2019) 1(1) *Revista Brasileira de Alternative Dispute Resolution* 133

30 The 1996 Arbitration Act was recently amended through the Law No. 13,129 of 26 May 2015 (the 2015 Arbitration Act). Some important contributions that the 2015 Arbitration Act makes are that it brings some clarity as far as the subject matter that can be arbitrated in Brazil and further restricts the participation of national courts in arbitral proceedings. See Erica Franzetti in Arbitration in Brazil, Lexology, 2019, accessed 1 March 2024. <https://www.lexology.com/library/detail.aspx?g=ad2085a8–020b-49d4-bd4e-5b5d2ada12e1> accessed 1 March 2024

31 The New York Convention was ratified with Decree No. 4311 on 23 July 2002 by the President of the Republic Fernando Henrique Cardoso

32 Brazilian Arbitration Act (Law No. 9.307), Art. 1(1) (Braz.)

dispute can initiate arbitration through an arbitration agreement, whether in the form of a clause within a contract or a separate agreement.[33] The Act grants parties autonomy to stipulate the venue for arbitration proceedings[34] and adopt the rules of any arbitral institution or specialised entity, domestic or international.[35] Presently, arbitration in Brazil is widely utilised, particularly in sectors such as construction, infrastructure (including oil, gas, and electricity), corporate contracts, insurance agreements, and commercial and financial transactions.[36]

Arbitration can represent a potential option for resolving consumer disputes while still preserving the consumer's right to pursue legal action in the courts of their residence. Utilising arbitration to resolve consumer conflicts in Brazil is feasible and potentially advantageous. However, it is important to note a significant legal decision by the Supreme Court of Justice (STJ) invalidated a clause in an adhesion contract that mandated arbitration for dispute resolution.[37] This ruling is considered crucial because it illustrates the limitations of adhesion contracts, which cannot unilaterally impose an arbitration clause on consumers. However, the decision also specifies that accepting the arbitration clause can be deemed valid if a consumer is fully aware of and consents to arbitration. Justice Nancy Andrighi[38] of the STJ emphasised that the Consumer Code only prohibits the compulsory or unilateral use of arbitration clauses, leaving open the possibility of their use when a consumer is aware of and consents to them.[39] The ruling is significant, especially considering the continuous and substantial growth of arbitration in Brazil, particularly in recent years. Following the update of the CDC in 2015, arbitration has also been modernised to enhance its legal certainty in conflict resolution. It increasingly represents a constitutional guarantee of access to justice and due legal process, emphasising the principles of equality between parties, impartiality, and the arbitrator's freedom of conviction. It is worth noting that even in arbitration, the requirement to justify judicial decisions is a constitutional norm.

Mediation

Mediation is increasingly gaining traction as an indispensable dispute resolution mechanism.[40] Nowadays, it is commonplace to find mediation clauses in many major contracts, and many professionals are receiving training in mediation

33 ibid Art. 3 (Braz.)

34 ibid Art. 11 (Braz.)

35 ibid Art. 5 (Braz.)

36 International Bar Association, 'Brazil Country Guide: Arbitration' (*IBA*, March 2024) <https://www.ibanet.org/document?id=Brazil-country-guide-arbitration> accessed 10 March 2024

37 Supremo Tribunal de Justiça (STJ), *Gomes v JJ Empreendimentos*, Case No. 1.785.783-GO, Decision on Special Appeal, 5 Nov. 2019, para 9 (Braz.)

38 Minister of the Superior Tribunal de Justiça (STJ)

39 In this scenario, parties must also adhere to the regulations outlined in Article 4(2) of the Brazilian Arbitration Act (Law No. 9.307 of 1996)

40 Giusti and Dalmaso Marques, 'Brazil' in Jonathan Cotto (ed) *The Dispute Resolution Review* (Law Business Research 2016) 74–92

techniques. Mediation is already practised within the judicial bodies, as it is founded on the voluntary agreement of the parties and the selection of a more comprehensive conflict resolution approach.[41] However, the formal regulation of mediation as a legal institution is a relatively recent development,[42] marked by the enactment of Federal Law No. 13.140/15, commonly known as the Brazilian Mediation Act and the new Civil Procedure Code (CPC) of 2015.

The Mediation Act formally acknowledges mediation as a viable avenue for settling conflicts between private entities and facilitating the self-resolution of disputes within public administration.[43] The growing significance of mediation is evident in the CPC, which mandates that cases brought before the judiciary must undergo mediation or conciliation before the defendant presents their defence and the lawsuit proceeds.[44] The judge schedules a mediation or conciliation hearing, and the parties are required to participate unless both parties expressly request that the hearing not be scheduled.[45] If a party fails or refuses to participate in the hearing without a justified cause, the court may impose a fine of up to 2% of the claim amount.[46] Typically, parties submit their disputes for mediation before initiating court proceedings if a prior agreement exists, although mediation clauses are not standard in private contracts. In the absence of such an agreement, courts often encourage parties to participate in mediation or conciliation. Section III of the Mediation Act provides general provisions concerning procedural rules for both extrajudicial and judicial mediations. In case of extrajudicial mediation, the party interested in mediating must send a formal invitation to the other party, stating the mediation's scope, date, and place of the first meeting. The counterparty has thirty (30) days to respond; otherwise, the mediation will be considered rejected.[47]

Mediation shows excellent potential for growth in consumer disputes, providing consumers with a more efficient and cost-effective alternative to traditional legal procedures. It is in line with the objectives and principles of the CDC. Article 3 of the Mediation Act states that conflicts concerning available or unavailable rights that allow transactions may be subject to mediation. Article 4 of the CDC also includes 'alternative mechanisms for resolving consumer conflicts' as one of its objectives under Section V. Mediation differs from the conciliation process employed by PROCONs to resolve consumer disputes, where the third side proposes solutions and intervenes directly to obtain agreement. Mediation is a voluntary process where the mediator empowers the parties to reach their agreement. Mediation has been utilised in significant consumer incidents, such as the 2017

41 Guilherme M Martins, 'A mediação e os conflitos de consumo' (2017) 63 *Revista do Ministério Público do Rio de Janeiro* 71–83

42 Interest in mediation began to grow in Brazil in the early nineties, largely influenced by Argentine legislation, specifically Law No. 24,573/95, which addresses extrajudicial mediation

43 Brazilian Mediation Act (Law No. 13,140 of 2015), Art. 1

44 Civil Procedure Code, Law No. 13.105/15, Art. 334

45 Civil Procedure Code, Law No. 13.105/15, Art. 334 s 4º

46 Civil Procedure Code, Law No. 13.105/15, art. 334 s 8º

47 Brazilian Mediation Act (Law No. 13,140, of 26 June 26 2015), Art. 21

TAM Linhas Aéreas plane crash, which caused the deaths of all 187 passengers and crew on board, as well as 12 individuals on the ground.[48]

The impact of the accident and the significant number of individuals affected led the Economic Law Secretariat of the Ministry of Justice, through the Department of Consumer Protection and Defence (DPDC), to develop the first Brazilian mediation programme in consumer disputes involving diffuse interests and homogeneous collective rights. The programme provided fifteen thousand services, leading to agreements in 92% of cases.[49] In 2009, another mediation programme was established for a different plane disaster involving an Air France aircraft. However, as Martins points out, these cases remain isolated, though concerning homogeneous rights resolved extrajudicially with public government institutions' assistance.[50] Consumer law can progress through mediation as it aligns with the principles and goals of the Consumer Code, as stated in Article 3 of the Mediation Act, Law No. 13.140/2015. When we examine the connection between Article 3 of the Mediation Act and Article 6 of the CDC, which recognises education as a fundamental right to shift away from adversarial dispute resolution methods, we understand that mediation can be vital for resolving conflicts in consumer relationships. Consumers and suppliers should acknowledge that pursuing dispute resolution through mediation can safeguard consumers and help uphold and foster trust between them and suppliers.

Role of Technology in Consumer ADR – Online Dispute Resolution for Consumer Disputes

The technology significantly enhances global consumer ADR by improving accessibility and efficiency. The widespread use of smartphones and the internet has made ODR platforms popular. These platforms enable users to resolve disputes entirely online, increasing accessibility for remote consumers and reducing the judicial system's burden.

In Brazil, Consumidor.gov.br, or simply 'Consumidor,' managed by the National Consumer Secretariat (SENACON) of the Ministry of Justice, is a key platform for consumer rights. This free service facilitates direct dialogue between consumers and traders, offering quick and efficient online dispute resolution, bypassing PROCONs' intermediation.[51] The platform was institutionalised by Decree No. 8.573 of 19 November 2015, at the SENACON initiative within the National Consumption and Citizenship Plan (PLANDEC) of 2013 to encourage the self-settlement of consumer demands between consumers and traders.[52] From its implementation and for

48 Flight Safety Foundation, 'Aviation Safety Network' (*Aviation Safety Net*, 17 July 2007) <https://aviation-safety.net/database/record.php?id=20070717–0> accessed 1 March 2024

49 Guilherme M Martins, 'A mediação e os conflitos de consumo' (2017) 63 *Revista do Ministério Público do Rio de Janeiro* 71–83

50 Guilherme M Martins, 'A mediação e os conflitos de consumo' (2017) 63 *Revista do Ministério Público do Rio de Janeiro* 71–83

51 See 'Sobre o Serviço' <https://consumidor.gov.br/pages/conteudo/sobre-servico> accessed 1 March 2024

52 Presidência da República, Secretaria-Geral, Decreto No. 8.573, de 19 de novembro de 2015, Art. 1

the first three years, Banco do Brasil developed the platform under the supervision of the Ministry of Justice[53] and monitored by PROCONs, Public Defenders, Public Prosecutors, regulatory agencies, and other bodies with the objective and purpose of improving consumer protection policies. The direct collaboration between Banco do Brasil and SENACON ended on 10 June 2017. From that date, the Ministry of Justice, through the SENACON, has managed the entire platform, including its data system.

Officially launched on 27 June 2014, the platform has registered almost eight million complaints and has a base of over five million registered users and more than 1406 accredited companies.[54] The Southeast, which is composed of the states of Espírito Santo, Minas Gerais, Rio de Janeiro, and São Paulo, is the region with the most significant proportion of complaints, followed by the South, which includes the states of Paraná, the Rio Grande do Sul, and Santa Catarina. Currently, 77% of complaints registered with Consumidor.gov.br are resolved by participating companies, which respond to consumer demands within an average of seven days.[55] Such a fast and free-of-charge service represents a big incentive for consumers to use the platform. In 2019, the number of complaints completed was 780,189, and 131 were accredited companies. As of March 2024, the number of complaints completed through the platform is 7,957,696, the registered users are 5,576,582, and 1406 are registered companies.[56] The most complained-about sectors were banking and financial services, telecommunications, air transport, and e-commerce. A 2019 survey reported a high degree of overall satisfaction among the platform users.[57] However, more data are needed to assess the consumers' satisfaction with the ODR process. Consumers' satisfaction could be measured by incorporating a satisfaction survey in the platform[58] to evaluate the efficiency and quality of the platform and the process. The number of complaints completed, albeit high (compared to those of the EU ODR platform as shown by the data provided by the European Commission), is nevertheless considered low for a population of about 215 million.

Such a number suggests that there is still a low degree of awareness among consumers and could represent a limit to the platform's success. According to a 2019 survey, consumers believe the platform should be promoted through several

53 See the technical cooperation agreement signed between the Ministry of Justice (MJ), through the National Consumer Secretariat, and Banco do Brasil on 10 June 2014

54 As of March 2024, the number of complaints completed through the platform is 7,957,679, the registered users are 5,576,559, and 1,406 are the registered companies. See Consumidor.gov.br, 'Indicador Infográfico: Paraná' <https://www.consumidor.gov.br/pages/indicador/infografico/abrir#parana> accessed 14 March 2024

55 'Consumidor.br.gov Boletim' (2022) <https://www.consumidor.gov.br/pages/publicacao/externo/> accessed 14 March 2024

56 'Consumidor.br.gov Boletim' (2022) <https://www.consumidor.gov.br/pages/publicacao/externo/> accessed 14 March 2024

57 The survey showed that 79.4% of consumers had their problems solved, 73.3% had a great experience, and 96.4% would recommend the platform. For more information about the survey, see 'Consumidor.br.gov Pesquisa' (2019)

58 Maria José Schmidt-Kessen et al., 'Success or Failure? – Effectiveness of Consumer ODR Platforms in Brazil and in the EU' (2020) 43(3) *Journal of Consumer Policy* 659–686

channels, such as social media, television, radio, newspapers, and public institutions.[59] More marketing surveys and questionnaires aimed at consumers or even ordinary citizens could help identify promotion strategies to increase consumer awareness about the platform.

Consumidor offers an alternative for consumers to resolve their problems with registered companies. The company registration on the Consumidor platform is regulated by Ordinance No. 15 of 27 March 2020, of SENACON within the scope of powers conferred by Article 3, Letters II and X, and Article 9 of Decree No. 2.181 of 20 March 1997. The object of registering companies on the platform is to facilitate the online mediation of consumer disputes notified electronically. A great merit of the Ordinance, promoted by the then secretary of SENACOM, is having imposed a duty of registration for specific categories of companies within 30 days of the publication, which took place on 1 April 2020. The companies that must proceed with the registration are the following: *(a)* Companies acting nationally or regionally in sectors involving public services and essential activities (per Decree No. 10.282 of 20 March 2020); *(b)* digital internet service platforms dedicated to the individual or collective transport of passengers or the delivery of food, or that carry out promotions, offer, sales or intermediation of owned or third-party products, commercialisation of advertisements, publicity, as well as connection, application, content providers, and other social networks for-profit purposes; *(c)* economic agents listed among the two hundred companies with most complaints annually registered in the National Consumer Protection Information System ('SINDEC'), according to a survey from the General Coordination of the SINDEC of the National Consumer Secretariat of the Ministry of Justice and Public Security. In addition, the Ordinance specifies that the obligation to register applies to companies indicated by letters *(a)* and *(c)* only when: (i) they had gross sales of at least 100,000,000 Brazilian Reais in the last fiscal year; (ii) reached a monthly average equal to or greater than 1000 (one thousand) complaints in their customer service channels in the last fiscal year; (iii) are claimed in more than five hundred lawsuits that involve consumer relations.[60] With this Ordinance, the Ministry of Justice, via SENACON, aimed to promote the platform as an alternative conflict resolution system and enhance access to justice during COVID-19 isolation. On 8 April 2021, SENACON issued Ordinance No. 12/2021, revoking Ordinance No. 15/2020, allowing companies to skip registration if demands were low or registration did not aid online dispute resolution with consumers.

To file a complaint on Consumidor, consumers register and check if the company is listed. After submitting a complaint, the company has ten days to respond and may request more information. This initiates a negotiation phase. Once the

59 See Consumidor.gov.br, 'Pesquisa' (2019) (survey results indicating that 85.9% of respondents prefer social media, 67.5% TV, 40.1% radio, 39.3% newspapers and magazines, and 37.2% institutional bodies as channels for wider disclosure of Consumidor)

60 Impresa nacional, 'Portaria No. 15, De 27 De Março DE 2020' (*Govbr*, 27 March 2020) <https://www.in.gov.br/web/dou/-/portaria-n-15-de-27-de-marco-de-2020–250710160> accessed 24 January 2024

company responds, the consumer has 20 days to assess the resolution and assign a satisfaction score from one to five, with one being the lowest level of satisfaction and five the highest.

Lastly, the consumer can enter a final comment. After the evaluation, the complaint is finalised and closed, and interacting with or changing the registered review is no longer possible.[61] Suppose the complaint is not resolved through the platform. In that case, the consumer can take the complaint directly to the PROCON or resort to other National Consumer Defense System bodies like the Public Defender's Office, the Public Prosecutor's Office, and the Special Civil Court.[62] The Consumidor platform offers a simple, cost-free ODR scheme based on direct dialogue between consumers and suppliers for quick dispute resolution. Consumers can evaluate suppliers' performance, with ratings visible to the public, allowing consumers to monitor company performance. Companies can showcase their commitment through rankings based on dispute resolution rate, consumer satisfaction, response time, and complaint response rate.[63] While agreements reached through Consumidor are not binding, its ranking system deters companies. It encourages them to resolve disputes and show commitment to consumer satisfaction. Consumidor provides an online alternative to PROCONS ADR services. According to the data, consumers decidedly prefer the online platform to resolve their disputes with the dispute resolution offered by government agencies.

The Consumidor.gov.br platform presents many positive features: user-friendly, easy to navigate, free of charge for users, easy access to the process, direct negotiation between traders and consumers, and a time-effective response mechanism. These features make it an effective alternative to the traditional court system for consumers. However, to determine if the Consumidor ODR mechanism truly enhances consumer protection and access to justice, it should be evaluated on its ability to reduce court cases and match the consumer protection level of the traditional court system, as suggested by Schmidt-Kessen, Nogueira, and Gamito.[64] More data and data analysis are needed to make this assessment and establish a correlation between the decrease in court cases and the enhancement of consumer access to justice through ODR.

Challenges and Opportunities

Brazil recently followed the European example by enacting Law No. 13,709 of 2018, known as the General Data Protection Law (Lei Geral de Proteção de Dados or LGPD). This law governs the rights, duties, and transparency regarding public and private companies' processing and use of personal data and consumer

61 'Consumidor', Consumidor, <https://www.consumidor.gov.br/pages/conteudo/publico/1> accessed 7 April 2024

62 'Consumidor', Consumidor, <https://www.consumidor.gov.br/pages/conteudo/publico/1> accessed 7 April 2024

63 'Consumidor', Consumidor, <https://www.consumidor.gov.br/pages/indicador/geral/abrir> accessed 8 April 2024

64 Schmidt-Kessen et al. (n 57)

information. In line with Article 43 of the Consumer Code, which grants consumers the right to access information about their data stored in archives and registers, these companies are required to make such information available. Under the LGPD, specifically Articles 9, 18, and 19, consumers have the right to request all information regarding their data with a simple request. Companies are directly responsible for managing and processing data use, ensuring transparency and confidentiality. The Autoridade Nacional de Proteção de Dados (ANPD) is the official public body responsible for regulating, enforcing, and sanctioning violations of the law, with penalties of up to 2% of the company's turnover, limited to 50 million reals. Some exceptions to the law exist, particularly concerning data used for credit protection, emergencies, health, and state security purposes.

Conclusion

In conclusion, consumer rights protection in Brazil is governed by a robust legal framework that recognises the fundamental importance of safeguarding consumer interests. ADR mechanisms, including arbitration and mediation, have the potential to resolve consumer disputes efficiently and amicably. Furthermore, the emergence of ODR platforms offers a promising avenue for enhancing accessibility and convenience in resolving consumer grievances. However, despite these advancements, challenges persist. One challenge is ensuring widespread awareness and utilisation of ADR and ODR mechanisms among consumers and businesses.

Additionally, the effectiveness of ODR platforms in addressing the diverse nature of consumer disputes and ensuring procedural fairness requires continuous refinement. Nonetheless, these challenges present opportunities for improvement. Strengthening public education initiatives to promote awareness of ADR and ODR options can empower consumers to assert their rights effectively. Brazil's consumer protection framework demonstrates a proactive approach to safeguarding consumer rights, emphasising transparency, fairness, and access to justice. By providing robust legal mechanisms and institutions, Brazil ensures that consumers are empowered to assert their rights and seek redress in disputes, ultimately fostering trust and confidence in the marketplace.

References

Amaral F, *Direito Civil. Introdução* (Renovar 2003)
Azevedo ÁV, *Teoria Geral dos Contratos Típicos e Atípicos* (Editora Atlas 2002)
Barroso LR, *Interpretação e Aplicação da Constituição: Fundamentos de uma Dogmática Constitucional Transformadora* (Saraiva 2003)
Bauman Z, *Capitalismo Parasitário* (Eliana Aguiar tr, Zahar 2010)
Beviláqua C, *Teoria Geral do Direito Civil* (Servanda 2015)
Bonavides P, *Curso de Direito Constitucional* (Malheiros 2006)
Brazilian Arbitration Act (1996)
Brazilian Mediation Act (2015)
Calais-Auloy J and Steinmetz F, *Droit de la Consommation* (4th edn, Dalloz 1996)
Campinho S, *O Direito de Empresa à Luz do Novo Código Civil* (Renovar 2008)
Carvalho KG, *Direito Constitucional* (Del Rey 2009)

Civil Procedure Code (2015)
Constitution of the Federative Republic of Brazil (1988)
Consumer Protection Code (1990)
Couto e Silva CV, *A Obrigação como Processo* (FGV 2007)
De Lucca N, *Direito do Consumidor: Teoria Geral da Relação Jurídica de Consumo* (Quartier Latin 2008)
Donato MAZ, *Proteção ao Consumidor: Conceito e Extensão* (Revista dos Tribunais 1993)
Fellous BE, *Proteção do Consumidor no Mercosul e na União Europeia* (Editora Revista dos Tribunais 2003)
Figueira Junior J, *Manual dos Juizados Especiais Cíveis Estaduais e Federais* (RT 2006)
Finkelstein MER and Sacco Neto F, *Manual de Direito do Consumidor* (Elsevier 2010)
Flávio de Oliveira A, 'O Sistema Nacional de Defesa do Consumidor: Histórico' (2002) 44 Revista de Direito do Consumidor
Flight Safety Foundation, 'Aviation Safety Network' (*Aviation Safety Net*, 17 July 2007) <https://aviation-safety.net/database/record.php?id=20070717-0> accessed 1 March 2024
Gevaerd J, 'Consumer Protection and Arbitration in Mass Consumption Adhesion Contracts: A Comparative Look Between Brazil and US' (2019) 1(1) Revista Brasileira de Alternative Dispute Resolution 133
Gonçalves CR, *Direito Civil Brasileiro. Parte Geral* (Saraiva 2016)
Grau ER, *A Ordem Econômica na Constituição de 1988* (Malheiros 2010)
Gregori MS and Fragata MS, 'Mediação e Arbitragem nas Relações de Consumo' (2021)
Grinover AP, *Código Brasileiro de Defesa do Consumidor* (Forense 2022)
Gustavo G and Dalmaso Marques R, 'Brazil' in Jonathan Cotto (ed) *The Dispute Resolution Review* (Law Business Research 2016)
Impresa Nacional, 'Portaria Nº 15, De 27 De Março De 2020' (*Govbr*, 27 March 2020) <https://www.in.gov.br/web/dou/-/portaria-n-15-de-27-de-marco-de-2020-250710160> accessed 24 January 2024
International Monetary Fund, *Brazil* (International Monetary Fund 2024) <https://www.imf.org/en/Countries/BRA> accessed 24 January 2024
Marighetto A, *Acesso ao Contrato* (Quartier Latin 2012)
Marques CL, *Contratos no Código de Defesa do Consumidor* (RT 2019)
Marques CL, Benjamin AHV and Miragem B, *Comentários ao Código de Defesa do Consumidor* (RT 2021)
Martins GM, 'A Mediação e os Conflitos de Consumo' (2017) 63 Revista do Ministério Público do Rio de Janeiro 71, 83
Martins-Costa J, *A Boa-fé no Direito Privado – Sistema e Tópica no Processo Obrigacional* (RT 2000)
Mendes GF, Coelho IM and Branco PGG, *Curso de Direito Constitucional* (Saraiva 2009)
Ministerio Publico Distrito Federal e Territorios, 'Procuradoria-Geral de Justiça' (*Ministério Público do Distrito Federal e Territórios*, 2020) <https://www.lawteacher.net/oscolareferencing/website.php> accessed 20 January 2024
Morato AC and de Neri TP (eds), *20 Anos do Código de Defesa do Consumidor: Estudos em Homenagem ao Prof. José Geraldo Brito Filomeno* (Editora Atlas 2010)
Nalin P, 'Ética e Boa-fé no Adimplemento Contratual' in Luiz Edson Fachin (ed) *Repensando Fundamentos do Direito Civil Brasileiro Contemporâneo* (Renovar 1998)
Pasqualotto A, 'O Código de Defesa do Consumidor em Face do Código Civil de 2002' in Roberto Pfeiffer and Adalberto Pasqualotto (eds) *Código de Defesa do Consumidor e o Código Civil de 2002: Convergências e Assimetrias* (Revista dos Tribunais 2005)
Reale M, *Nova Fase do Direito* (Saraiva 1990)
Rocha e Menezes Cordeiro AM, *Da Boa-fé no Direito Civil* (Almedina 2007)
Rodrigues Junior LO, 'Autonomia da Vontade, Autonomia Privada e Autodeterminação: Notas sobre a Evolução de um Conceito na Modernidade e na Pós-modernidade' (2004) 163 Revista de Informação Legislativa

Sarlet IW, *A Eficácia dos Direitos Fundamentais* (Livraria do Advogado 2006)
Sarlet IW (ed), *Dignidade da Pessoa Humana e Direitos Fundamentais na Constituição Federal de 1988* (Libraria do Advogado 2007)
Schmidt-Kessen MJ, et al., 'Success or Failure? – Effectiveness of Consumer ODR Platforms in Brazil and in the EU' (2020) 43(3) Journal of Consumer Policy
Silva JA, *Curso de Direito Constitucional Positivo* (Malheiros 2006)
Supremo Tribunal de Justiça (STJ), *Gomes v JJ Empreendimentos*, Case No. 1.785.783-GO, Decision on Special Appeal, 5 November 2019, para 9 (Braz)
Tepedino G (ed), *Temas de Direito Civil* (Renovar 1999)
Zanchim KL, *Contratos Empresariais: Categoria – Interface com Contratos de Consumo e Paritários – Revisão Judicial* (Quartier Latin 2012)

13 Consumer ADR in Malaysia

Maizatul Farisah Mohd Mokhtar

Introduction

There is no specific concept of consumer, but this concept is regards to any matter related to buyer and seller that involves many aspects from the legal framework to the consumer protection institution.[1] In Malaysia, the idea of the consumer began in the 1960s when there were unstable prices in Malaysia, especially during the festive season whereby Malaysian citizens demanded the Malaysian government play a role in stabilising prices as well as the establishment of consumer movement in Malaysia.[2] Furthermore, generally, the awareness of the consumer begins because of several factors; escalating inflation, rapid industrialisation, high-pressure selling techniques and the sophistication in goods and services have, *inter alia*, forced consumers to re-evaluate their position vis-à-vis their economic wealth, the shrinking dollar, their bargaining power, redress for grievances, and their health.[3] Consumer protection is designed to promote and protect consumer interests. The purposes of consumer protection are to promote industry responsiveness to consumer requirements, consumer confidence in quality of service, widespread access to services, and affordability of services to Malaysians.[4]

According to the Consumer Protection Act 1999 (Act 599) under Section 3 'consumer' means a person who acquires or uses goods or services of a kind ordinarily acquired for personal, domestic or household purpose, use or consumption and does not acquire or use the goods or services, or hold himself out as acquiring or using the goods or services, primarily for the purpose of resupplying them in trade; consuming them in the course of a manufacturing process; or in the case

1 Christie Ding Yean Joon and Sakina Shaik Ahmad Yusoff, 'Development of Consumer Protection: Challenges and the Way Forward for Consumer Protection Institution in Malaysia' (2016) 20 *JUUM Journal of Law and Society* 71

2 Christie Ding Yean Joon and Sakina Shaik Ahmad Yusoff, 'Development of Consumer Protection: Challenges and the Way Forward for Consumer Protection Institution in Malaysia' (2016) 20 *JUUM Journal of Law and Society* 71

3 Christie Ding Yean Joon and Sakina Shaik Ahmad Yusoff, 'Development of Consumer Protection: Challenges and the Way Forward for Consumer Protection Institution in Malaysia' (2016) 20 *JUUM Journal of Law and Society* 71

4 Mohamad Fazli Sabri, 'The Development of Consumer Protection Policies in Malaysia' (2014) 4(6) *International Journal of Business and Social Research* 98

DOI: 10.4324/9781032689739-13

of goods, repairing or treating, in trade, other goods or fixtures on land. In addition, the Ministry of Domestic Trade, Co-operatives, and Consumerisms (currently changed to The Ministry of Domestic Trade and Costs of Living) defines consumer as 'a person who buys goods and services for his personal use or for domestic or household purpose'.[5]

All people have a right to access safe goods and quality services, to be treated fairly and offered effective solutions if things go wrong. Consumer rights are generally a reference to a body of law that pertains to things the producers of goods must do to protect customers from harm. If one of these 'rights' has been violated and you have been harmed as a result, you may wish to speak to an attorney. You might have a cause of action for harm caused by a violation of your consumer rights, and if you have suffered harm, there is also a chance others have.

Legal Framework for Consumer Protection

Overview

There are a number of specific statutes dealing with some elements of consumer protection and are administered by various Ministries in Malaysia. These laws govern consumers, especially as a safeguard and protection against lemon products and services, such as a product that repeatedly fails to meet the standards of quality and performance and provide a mechanism to redress consumers by providing remedies such as monetary compensation and non-compensation due to damages and loss suffered by consumers. Among these statutes, which are under the purview of the Ministry of Domestic Trade, Co-operatives, and Consumerism, are the Price Control Act 1946, the Trade Descriptions Act 1972, the Hire Purchase Act 1967, the Weight and Measures Act 1972, the Consumer Protection Act 1999, etc.

Furthermore, in Malaysia, the application of lemon law as a means of consumer protection can be found in the Sale of Goods Act 1957 (Act 382) and the Consumer Protection 1999 (Act 599) that govern remedies for defective goods. SOGA provides the implied condition to fulfil the purpose, merchantability, and conformity with description, a consumer who ends up with a lemon can obtain redress or remedy in court and the burden upon the consumer who purchases the goods to prove that the goods are lemon or were defective. Meanwhile, in CPA, Parts V and VI (Sections 30 to 49) contain provisions that confer certain implied guarantees in respect of consumer goods and set out the remedies available to a consumer where such goods fail to comply with any of the implied guarantees. Besides that, the CPA also apply a criminal sanction as stated under Section 25; any contravention of Part II (Misleading and Deceptive Conduct, False Representation and Unfair Practice) or Part III (Safety of Goods and Services) of the CPA can result in criminal sanctions for defective product.

5 *Background of Tribunal: Who is Consumer* (Official Portal Ministry of Domestic Trade and Cost of Living) <https://www.kpdn.gov.my/en/consumerism/consumer-rights/tribunal-for-consumer-claim/background-of-the-tribunal> accessed 23 March 2024

Consumer Rights and Protection in Malaysia

There are several situations where the consumer in Malaysia has the right and is entitled to protection under the Consumer Protection Act (Act 599). Under Part II of CPA refers to misleading and deceptive conduct, false representation and unfair practice by sellers or business owners whereby business owners who mislead consumers can be fined up to RM 250,000. Furthermore, goods and services must comply with safety standards set by the ministry. Part III, Section 19 of the CPA states that the minister sets the standards based on recommendations and consultations with relevant and competent agencies. It is unacceptable to sell goods or services that have failed to pass the safety standards set. An official complaint for claims can be sent to TTPM. Vendors that are caught selling products that do not comply with set safety standards can be fined up to RM 250,000.

Additionally, Part V of the CPA stated that all goods and services supplied must be guaranteed with respect to satisfactory quality, purpose, description, price, repair, and spare parts. As a consumer, you have the right to receive fair judgement which includes compensation for your purchase of goods or services received that had a misleading trade description, was of poor quality or if you received unsatisfactory services. You can submit a claim for compensation to the Tribunal for Consumer Claims Malaysia. In addition, consumers in Malaysia also have the right relating to guarantees against suppliers and manufacturers which are Part VI Rights Against Suppliers in Respect of Guarantees in The Supply of Goods, Part VII Rights Against Manufacturers in Respect of Guarantees in The Supply of Goods, and Part IX Rights Against Suppliers in Respect of Guarantees in The Supply of Service.

Besides CPA, the rights of consumers in Malaysia also can be found in The National Consumer Policy (NDP).[6] The National Consumer Policy (NCP) was launched on 26 July 2002. NDP was established to protect consumer rights by promoting self-protection among consumers and self-regulation among traders.[7] Emphasising consumer awareness and proactive market engagement, the policy encourages informed and responsible consumer behaviour.[8] It ensures access to accurate information, facilitates redress for disputes, and promotes fair trading practices. The NDP calls for ethical business conduct and voluntary compliance with standards to enhance consumer welfare. NDP aims to instil self-protection for consumers, self-regulation for traders and manufacturers, and to achieve an effective level of consumer protection level, thus providing an environment conducive to establishing a fair market and sustainable development in keeping abreast with local and global economic developments (Ministry of Domestic Trade and Costs of Living).

The strategies[9] of the policy are to raise the standard of living, laws to protect consumers, fair and ethical trade, consumer education, sustainable consumption,

6 'National Consumer Policy' (Official Portal Ministry of Domestic Trade and Cost of Living) <https://kpdnkk-gov-my.page.tl/NATIONAL-CONSUMER-POLICY.htm> accessed 10 April 2024

7 s 4.1.2 Improving self-regulation among traders of National Consumer Policy (NDP)

8 s 5.1 Enhance the quality, quantity, and accessibility of information of the National Consumer Policy (NDP)

9 There are 13 strategies under the National Consume Policy (NDP)

redress mechanisms, consumer forums between government, manufacturers and consumers, and international cooperation in consumer matters. Strategies include strengthening legal frameworks, improving enforcement, and establishing user-friendly systems for resolving complaints, with coordinated efforts among government agencies, NGOs, and the private sector. The policy also supports initiatives to educate consumers and businesses alike about their rights and responsibilities in the marketplace, fostering a fair and transparent trading environment.

The General Design of the Enforcement Mechanism

Complaint

The Consumer Profile Research conducted by the Domestic Trade, Cooperative and Consumerism Ministry (KPDNKK) (now replaced by the current ministry – The Ministry of Domestic Trade and Costs of Living) in 2015 revealed that only 58% of Malaysian consumers were properly aware of their rights.[10] If a consumer is not satisfied with the price or even the quality of goods and services you have received, they can lodge a complaint with The Ministry of Domestic Trade and Costs of Living. A consumer in Malaysia is protected under the Consumer Protection Act 1999 (CPA). The Consumer Complaint Management Centre (CCMC) receives complaints from complainants via telephone, website, letters, and walk-ins.[11] There are many situations in our daily lives where consumers have the right to make legal claims through this ministry. In addition, consumers are frequently misled in these circumstances, which include fraudulent services, fraudulent pricing, internet transaction fraud, sales of petroleum substances, absence of price tags, motor vehicle workshop scams, scratch-and-win fraud, fraudulent hire purchase agreements, and malpractice in direct selling.[12]

Tribunal for Consumer Claims Malaysia (TCCM)

The Tribunal for Consumer Claim Malaysia is established under the Consumer Protection Act 1999 (Act 599) which serves to hear and pass judgement on claims filed by consumers under Act 599 and subject to the provisions of the Act. Generally, the purpose of the establishment of this tribunal under CPA as highlighted by Mohammad Ariff JC in the case of *Sheila a/p Sangar v Proton Edar Sdn Bhd and Anor*[13] is to achieve fair and speedy justice for the aggrieved consumer. The

10 Jariah Masud and Sharifah Azizah Haron, 'Consumer Understanding of Year 2009 Consumer Month Celebration Theme: Consumer Power: I Consumer I Power' (2013) 16(1) *Malaysian Journal of Consumer and Family Economics* 20–28

11 *Consumer Claim* (Official Portal Ministry of Domestic Trade and Cost of Living) <https://www.kpdn.gov.my/en/consumerism/hak-pengguna/consumer-complaints> accessed 10 March 2024

12 *Consumer Claim* (Official Portal Ministry of Domestic Trade and Cost of Living) <https://www.kpdn.gov.my/en/consumerism/hak-pengguna/consumer-complaints> accessed 10 March 2024

13 *(2009) 4 MLJ 285 (HC) para 292*

branches of TTCM are available in every state in Malaysia.[14] Hence, the TCCM plays a crucial role in the Malaysian consumer protection landscape by offering a dedicated venue for consumers to seek legal recourse in a manner that is both efficient and cost-effective.[15]

Before the establishment of the Tribunal, all disputes between consumers and traders, suppliers or manufacturers of goods or a service provider had to be brought to a civil court, which involved complicated procedures, high costs, and time-consuming.[16] These are some of the reasons why consumers are reluctant to file their claims against irresponsible and unethical traders,[17] suppliers or manufacturers or service providers in civil courts, especially if the amount claimed is small, even though now there is a small claims court in each state to hear a claim not exceeding RM 5,000.00.[18]

Understanding this situation, the Tribunal for Consumer Claims Malaysian was established to provide an alternative channel[19] other than a civil court for consumers to claim compensation on the purchase of goods or services supplied by merchants or service providers in a simple, inexpensive, and speedy manner. Under section 90 of the CPA, the Tribunal has jurisdiction to hear claims for redress for the purchase of goods and services allowed under the jurisdiction of the Tribunal with the total amount claimed not exceeding RM 50,000.00 and accrued claims within three years of the claim. Meanwhile, there are claims that the tribunal has no jurisdiction to hear which are claims arising out of personal injury or death, claims for the recovery of land or any estate or interest relating to land, disputes over title to any land or any estate or any interest relating to land, disputes over the rights of any person under a will or intestate of death, disputes relating to matters of the franchise, goodwill, trade secrets or other intellectual property any right of action; and when any tribunal has been established under any other written law to hear and decide on the claim in respect of the subject matter of the claim. Meanwhile, as illustrated in Table 13.1, there has been a notable increase in both the number of cases filed and the total amount claimed at the Tribunal for Consumer Claims Malaysia from 2021 to 2023. While the volume of cases rose from 4,845 in 2021 to 8,455 by 2023, the awarded amounts also grew significantly, with the peak award reaching MYR 26,777,781.37 in 2023. Although data for 2024 only covers the first quarter, it already reflects a substantial amount of claims (MYR 22,092,478.69) and awards (MYR 3,493,066.78), underscoring the Tribunal's ongoing role in consumer dispute resolution in Malaysia.

14 *Tribunal for Consumer Claims* (Official Portal of Tribunal for Consumer Claims) <https://ttpm.kpdn.gov.my/portal/home> accessed 14 May 2024

15 Sabri (n 5)

16 Naemah Amin and Elistina Abu Bakar, 'ADR for Consumers: An Appraisal of the Tribunal for Consumer Claims Malaysia' in Mohammad Naqib Ishan Jan and Ashgar Ali Ali Mohammad (eds) *Mediation in Malaysia: The Law and Practice* (Lexis Nexis 2010) 171–182

17 Sabri (n 4) 99

18 Order 93 of Rule 2 of Rules of Court 2012

19 Naemah (n 16) 172

Table 13.1 Number of cases, amount claims and amount awarded at Tribunal for Consumer Claims.

Year	*Case filed*	*Amount Claims (MYR)*	*Amount Awarded (MYR)*
2021	4,845	32,150,429.99	4,491,149.11
2022	7,109	61,253,961.82	9,173,232.11
2023	8,455	80,028,798.28	26,777,781.37
2024	2,172	22,092,478.69	3,493,066.78

Source: Tribunal for Consumer Claims Malaysia[20] Data updated until 31 March 2024.

Role of Civil Courts

As discussed in the previous part, a consumer involved in a dispute may submit a complaint and claim at the Tribunal for Consumer Claims Malaysia (TCCM). However, only consumers who fall under the definition provided in Section 3 of the Consumer Protection Act 1999 (Act 599) (CPA) are eligible to submit claims at TCCM. This definition is limited to individuals using movable property for personal, household, or domestic purposes. What about consumers who use goods or services for business purposes or those dealing with immovable property, which do not fall under the 'consumer' categories defined by the CPA? Consumers facing disputes in these situations can lodge complaints and claims at the Civil Court, governed by the Rules of Court 2012 (ROC).

Consumer disputes can be resolved through civil court claims under small claims under Order 93 of ROC. However, before the consumer files the case to court, the consumer or the party must ensure that the law's requirement is fulfilled as stated in the Rules of Court. The party bringing the action in court, known as the plaintiff, must be a person.[21] Additionally, the subject matter of the claim must be below RM 5,000, as specified in Order 93, Rule 2 of the ROC 2012. The defendant, who is defending the claim, is not limited to just an individual; any legal entity, such as a company or agent, can be sued, as per Order 93 Rule 1 of the ROC. Furthermore, no legal representation is allowed for either party except where the defendant is legally required to be represented by an authorised person.[22]

20 *Statistic of Ministry of Domestic Trade and Cost of Living for Year 2021* (Ministry of Domestic Trade and Cost of Living) <https://www.kpdn.gov.my/en/media-kpdnhep/arkib/statistik-utama-kpdn/2021> accessed 25 May 2024

Statistic of Ministry of Domestic Trade and Cost of Living for Year 2022 (Ministry of Domestic Trade and Cost of Living 2022) <https://www.kpdn.gov.my/en/media-kpdnhep/arkib/statistik-utama-kpdn/2022> accessed 25 May 2024; *Statistic of Ministry of Domestic Trade and Cost of Living for Year 2023* (Ministry of Domestic Trade and Cost of Living 2023) accessed 25 May 2024 <https://www.kpdn.gov.my/en/media-kpdnhep/arkib/statistik-utama-kpdn/2023-arkib-statistik> accessed 25 May 2024; 'Statistic of Ministry of Domestic Trade and Cost of Living for year 2024' (until 31 March 2024) (Ministry of Domestic Trade and Cost of Living) 2024 <https://www.kpdn.gov.my/ms/media-kpdnhep/penerbitan/statistik-utama-kpdn/statistiks-utama-kpdn-20232> accessed 25 May 2024

21 Order 93 Rule 1 of the Rules of Court (ROC) 2012

22 ibid Order 93 Rule 7

Current Consumer Dispute Resolution Processes

Generally, the Tribunal for Consumer Claims (TCC) established under the Consumer Protection Act 1999 (Act 599) contains some noteworthy features, which are that the procedures are more straightforward than those governing court proceedings, counsel may not represent the parties, an award made, or a settlement recorded by the Tribunal is deemed to be an order of the Magistrate's court and enforceable accordingly. The Tribunal must make its award without delay and, where practicable, within 60 days from the first day of the hearing.

Filing and Registration Procedures

The procedure relating to the filing, registration, and hearing of claims before the Tribunal are provided in Part XII of the Act as well as the Consumer Protection (The Tribunal for Consumer Claims) Regulations 1999, which the Minister made under Section 122 of the Act. Subject to this Act and the Regulations mentioned above, the Tribunal shall adopt such procedure as it thinks fit and proper. Additionally, to prevent any conflict between the civil court, such as the Small Claims Court, under the Rules of Court, Section 104(1) of the CPA provides that any claims first submitted to the Tribunal shall not be subject to proceedings on the same dispute and between the same parties unless the claim at the Tribunal is withdrawn, abandoned, or struck out.[23]

All claims must be made using Form 1,[24] available for free from any Tribunal office. The claimant must submit four copies along with an RM 5.00 filing fee. Form 1 will be registered, dated, signed by the Secretary of the Tribunal, and sealed. Two sealed copies will be returned to the claimant for service on the respondent, which can be done in person or by pre-paid registered mail. If disputing the claim, the respondent must file a statement of defence and any counterclaim using Form 2,[25] accessible from the Tribunal office. This must be submitted in four copies within 14 days, with an RM 5.00 filing fee. Form 2 will be registered, dated, signed, and sealed, with two sealed copies returned to the respondent and one to the claimant. If there is a counterclaim, the claimant must file a defence using Form 3[26] within 14 days, with no filing fee required. Form 3 will be registered, dated, signed, and sealed, with two sealed copies returned to the claimant for service on the respondent.

23 Naemah (n 16) 173

24 'Form 1 Can Be Found at Official Portal Ministry of Domestic Trade and Cost of Living' <https://www.kpdn.gov.my/en/consumerism/consumer-rights/tribunal-for-consumer-claim/claim-form> accessed 25 May 2024

25 'Form 2 Can Be Found at Official Portal Ministry of Domestic Trade and Cost of Living' <https://www.kpdn.gov.my/en/consumerism/consumer-rights/tribunal-for-consumer-claim/claim-form> accessed 25 May 2024

26 Form 3 Can Be Found at <https://www.kpdn.gov.my/en/consumerism/consumer-rights/tribunal-for-consumer-claim/claim-form> accessed 25 May 2024

Hearing Procedures and Process[27]

The Secretary to the Tribunal shall give notice of the details of the day, time, and place of the hearing in the prescribed form to both the claimant and the respondent.[28] Upon a claim being filed with the Tribunal, a notice of hearing will be issued by the Secretary or Assistant Secretary to the Tribunal in Form 4, stating the date, time, and place of the hearing.[29] This notice will be provided to both the Claimant and the Respondent at least 14 days before the scheduled hearing date. At the hearing, neither the Claimant nor the Respondent may be represented by a lawyer; they must conduct the hearing independently. If the Claimant is a minor or a person with a disability, they may be represented by their next friend or guardian *ad litem*. Where the Respondent is a firm or company, it may be represented by its full-time paid employee.

The setting of the Tribunal[30] can be exercised by the Chairman, Deputy Chairman, or any member chosen by the Chairman, sitting alone. The Tribunal may hold multiple sittings on the same day at times and places decided by the Chairman. If the person presiding over a claim cannot complete the hearing due to death, incapacity, or other reasons, a new member will hear the case unless both parties agree to continue with another member. If a member's term ends while a claim is ongoing, their term will be extended until the claim is resolved.

The hearing of a claim at the Tribunal will be conducted before a member of the Tribunal, referred to as the 'President' during the hearing, who sits alone. The President may at any time assist both parties in conducting their cases. During the hearing, the Tribunal shall, where appropriate, assist both parties in settling the claim by consent. Both parties are entitled to adduce evidence, call witnesses, and produce any document, record, or item supporting their cases.

All hearings before the Tribunal shall be open to the public.[31] This transparency ensures that the proceedings are conducted fairly and that both parties have the opportunity to present their cases comprehensively. The Tribunal's role is to facilitate a fair hearing and, where possible, to help the parties reach a mutually agreeable resolution.

Enforcement of Award and Reason for Decision

Every award made by the Tribunal under Subsections 112(2) and 107(3) of CPA is final and binding on all parties involved in the proceedings, as stipulated under

27 *Hearing Procedures* (Official Portal of Tribunal for Consumer Claims) <https://www.kpdn.gov.my/en/consumerism/consumer-rights/tribunal-for-consumer-claim/hearing-procedure> accessed 16 May 2024

28 Section 107 of Consumer Protection Act 1999 (Act 5999)

29 Section 106 of Consumer Protection Act 1999 (Act 5999)

30 Section 92 of the Consumer Protection Act 1999 (Act 5999)

31 *Filing and Registration Procedure* (Official Portal Ministry of Domestic Trade and Cost of Living) <https://www.kpdn.gov.my/en/consumerism/consumer-rights/tribunal-for-consumer-claim/filing-and-registration-procedure > accessed 16 May 2024

Section 116 of CPA. This means that once an award is issued, it cannot be contested or appealed by the parties, ensuring a conclusive resolution to the dispute. The finality of the Tribunal's awards underscores the importance of the Tribunal's role in providing decisive and authoritative judgements. Every award made by the Tribunal shall be deemed an order of a Magistrate's Court and enforced accordingly by any party to the proceedings in a Magistrate's Court having jurisdiction in the place where the award was made.[32]

The Tribunal shall, where practicable, make its award within sixty days from the first day of the hearing before the Tribunal.[33] At a hearing, the Tribunal may make any one or more of the following awards[34]:

1. A party to the proceedings pays money to any other party.
2. Goods be supplied or resupplied.
3. The goods supplied or resupplied to the consumer are replaced or repaired.
4. The price or other consideration paid or supplied by the consumer or any other person will be refunded to the consumer or that person.
5. A party complies with the guarantee.
6. Money will be awarded to compensate for any loss or damage suffered by the claimant
7. The contract may be varied or set aside, wholly or in part.
8. Costs to or against any party be paid.
9. Interest be paid on any sum or monetary award.
10. The claim is dismissed.

In all proceedings, the Tribunal is required to provide reasons for its award. This ensures transparency and accountability in the decision-making process.[35] By articulating its rationale, the Tribunal enables the parties involved to understand why a particular decision was reached. Moreover, providing reasons allows for informed scrutiny and, if necessary, enables the parties to challenge the decision through appropriate legal channels. This practice upholds the principles of fairness and justice, ensuring that all parties clearly understand the basis on which the Tribunal has made its award.

Judicial Review

Under Subsection 116(1) of Act 599, each award made by the Tribunal is final and binding on all parties to the proceedings. However, any party not satisfied with an award of the Tribunal can apply for judicial review in the High Court for the

32 *Enforcement Award* (Official Portal of Tribunal for Consumer Claims) <https://www.kpdn.gov.my/en/consumerism/consumer-rights/tribunal-for-consumer-claim/enforcement-award> accessed 16 May 2024
33 Section 112(1) of the Consumer protection Act 1999 (Act 599)
34 ibid Section 112(2)
35 Section 114 of the Consumer protection Act 1999 (Act 599)

High Court to reconsider the award. The Tribunal is not involved in the process of judicial review.

By Subsection 116(1) of Act 599, every award issued by the Tribunal is considered final and binding upon all parties involved in the proceedings. Nevertheless, should any party find themselves dissatisfied with an award from the Tribunal, they have the option to apply for judicial review to the High Court. This application allows the High Court to review and reconsider the Tribunal's decision. Notably, the Tribunal itself does not participate in the judicial review process.

Alternative Dispute Resolution for Consumer Disputes

Negotiation at Tribunal Consumer Claims

The provision governing ADR in the context of the Tribunal for Consumer Claims (TCC) is Section 107 of the Consumer Protection Act 1999 (CPA). This section enables the TCC to assess whether assisting parties in negotiating an agreed settlement about the claim is appropriate. However, the section is somewhat unclear and does not define the specific type of ADR that the TCC may use to help parties negotiate, whether it is a non-binding form such as mediation or conciliation or a binding one such as arbitration. This ambiguity has led to deficiencies in the ADR process at the TCC, as it leaves the method of assisting parties at the discretion of the individual President of the TCC, resulting in varying practices across different Presidents. Therefore, the document proposes a new legal framework for ADR at the TCC to address these deficiencies and provide a structured approach to ADR processes.

Section 107(1) of the CPA mandates the TCC to assess whether it is appropriate to assist the parties in negotiating an agreed settlement for every claim within its jurisdiction.[36] The Tribunal considers all circumstances of the claim and factors that may impair the ability of either or both parties to negotiate an agreed settlement.[37] This includes any factors that the Tribunal deems relevant to the negotiation process. If the parties are able to reach an agreed settlement, the Tribunal must approve and record the settlement.[38] This recorded settlement then takes effect as if it were an award issued by the Tribunal.

However, if the Tribunal determines that it would not be appropriate to assist with negotiation,[39] or if the parties are unable to reach an agreement,[40] the Tribunal will proceed to determine the dispute through its usual adjudicative process. This means that the Tribunal will decide on the dispute based on the evidence and arguments presented by both parties. The goal of Section 107 is to provide a mechanism for resolving consumer disputes through negotiated settlements, when possible,

36 Section 107(1) of the Consumer Protection Act 1999 (Act 599)
37 Section 107(2) of the Consumer Protection Act 1999 (Act 599)
38 Section 107(3) of the Consumer Protection Act 1999 (Act 599)
39 Section 107(4)(a) of the Consumer Protection Act 1999 (Act 599)
40 Section 107(4)(b) of the Consumer Protection Act 1999 (Act 599)

but also to ensure that disputes can be resolved effectively when negotiation is not feasible or successful.

Mediation

Negotiation is the only ADR method available at the TCC, whereby parties who file a case are obliged to use negotiation. However, to date, mediation or any other types of ADR are not available at the TCC. Hence, the discussion on the use of mediation for consumer claims will focus on the scope and types of disputes that are suitable for mediation either under the civil court or outside the court.

The Legal Aid Department (LAD) provides mediation services for all Malaysian citizens, offering a voluntary and peaceful way to resolve disputes with the assistance of a mediator.[41] This service mainly benefits consumer claims, allowing parties to settle their issues amicably within 30 days without undergoing a complicated court trial. Mediation is a time-saving method designed to achieve a win-win situation for both parties involved in the dispute.[42] Consumer claims are among the various types of cases suitable for mediation. By opting for mediation, consumers can effectively address their grievances about purchases, services, and other consumer-related issues.[43] This approach helps resolve disputes swiftly and ensures that both parties reach a mutually satisfactory agreement, avoiding the need for prolonged litigation.

Besides LAD, mediation for consumer claims is also applicable at mediation centres in civil courts in each state in Malaysia. According to Practice Direction No. 2 of 2022,[44] which applies to both the Lower Court and the High Court; mediation can be used for civil disputes in two circumstances: when judges instruct parties to use mediation or when parties request to use mediation.[45] Under Practice Direction No. 2 of 2022, there is no restriction or limitation on the type of civil claims. This means court-annexed mediation can also apply to consumer claims. Therefore, parties will resolve consumer claims if judges instruct them to use mediation or if the parties request to use mediation. The law governing mediation at civil court under pre-trial case management when directed by the Court (O. 34, r. 2) of Rules of Court 2012 (ROC).

Meanwhile, under mediation outside the court, parties may seek to resolve consumer disputes at the Asian International Arbitration Centre (AIAC). According to AIAC's Mediation Rules 2023,[46] Any dispute, controversy or claim arising out of or relating to this contract, or the breach, termination, or invalidity thereof, shall be

41 *Mediation* (Official Portal Legal Aid Department Malaysia) <https://www.jbg.gov.my/index.php/en/services/mediation> accessed 20 May 2024

42 *Mediation* (Official Portal Legal Aid Department Malaysia) <https://www.jbg.gov.my/index.php/en/services/mediation> accessed 20 May 2024

43 *Mediation* (Official Portal Legal Aid Department Malaysia) <https://www.jbg.gov.my/index.php/en/services/mediation> accessed 20 May 2024

44 This Practice Direction issued by Chief Justice Federal Court Malaysia on 24 March 2022

45 Mediation for Civil Case No. 5(a) and (b) under Direction No. 2, 2022

46 *Model Mediation Clauset* (Mediation Rules of AIAC 2023) <https://www.aiac.world/Mediation-Mediation> accessed 21 May 2024 'Any dispute, controversy or claim arising out of or relating to

submitted to mediation in accordance with the AIAC Mediation Rules. Mediation under these rules provides a structured process facilitated by a neutral mediator. This option is also available for consumer disputes and claims, offering an efficient and cost-effective alternative to resolve issues outside court. Consumer disputes related to purchases, services, or other consumer-related issues can be effectively mediated under the AIAC Mediation Rules. The parties must appoint a mediator within 30 days of the mediation agreement; if they cannot agree, the Director of the AIAC will appoint one. The language and location of the mediation will be determined by mutual agreement.

Role of Technology in Consumer ADR – Online Dispute Resolution for Consumer Disputes

In Malaysia, online dispute resolution (ODR) is not a common practice; although ADR via negotiation is available at TCC, the use of ADR at the tribunal is not available online.[47] However, despite having consumer tribunals and dispute resolution centres, many Malaysians prefer to complain about products and services on social media, believing companies value their online reputation.[48] Malaysia has strong consumer protection through the Malaysia Communications and Multimedia Commission (MCMC) and the TTC. Still, many consumers are unaware of these options, and increasing awareness and access to ODR could provide safer and more effective ways for consumers to resolve their issues.[49]

Challenges and Opportunities

Challenges

Section 51 of the CPA limits the right of redress against the manufacturer if the goods fail to comply with implied guarantees, potentially leaving consumers without contractual remedies and enabling manufacturers to escape liability. The Act also faces challenges in the interpretation of defectiveness, as the test of defectiveness under Part X is based on a vague safety concept, leading to potential debates over questions of fact, degree, and standard in deciding whether a product is unsafe and defective.[50]

---

this contract, or the breach, termination, or invalidity thereof, shall be submitted to mediation in accordance with the AIAC Mediation Rules (a) (b) (c)'

47 Section 106 of Consumer Protection Act 1999 (Act 5999) which stated the Secretary to the Tribunal shall give notice of the details of the day, time, and place of hearing

48 Sodoq Omoola, 'Provide Online Dispute Resolutions for Consumers' (*News Straits Times*, Malaysia, 22 November 2019) <https://www.nst.com.my/opinion/letters/2019/11/540927/provide-online-dispute-resolutions-consumers> accessed 5 June 2024

49 Sodoq Omoola, 'Provide Online Dispute Resolutions for Consumers' (*News Straits Times*, Malaysia, 22 November 2019) <https://www.nst.com.my/opinion/letters/2019/11/540927/provide-online-dispute-resolutions-consumers> accessed 5 June 2024

50 Sodoq Omoola, 'Provide Online Dispute Resolutions for Consumers' (*News Straits Times*, Malaysia, 22 November 2019) <https://www.nst.com.my/opinion/letters/2019/11/540927/provide-online-dispute-resolutions-consumers> accessed 5 June 2024

Furthermore, the CPA does not allow public interest groups to take action on behalf of aggrieved consumers, unlike in other jurisdictions such as Thailand, India, and China, where consumers can obtain legal aid and representation from consumer organisations.[51] This means that in Malaysia, consumers lack the support of these groups in pursuing their claims. Consequently, individual consumers may face significant challenges when seeking justice, as they must navigate the legal process on their own without the expertise and resources that consumer organisations can offer. This can limit their ability to effectively address grievances, obtain redress, and hold businesses accountable for unfair practices or violations of consumer rights.

Vagueness in the provision of ADR under Section 107 of the Consumer Protection Act 1999, which does not specify the type of ADR to be applied at the TCC, leading to ambiguity in the negotiation process and decision-making by the President of the TCC. The unequal ability of parties to negotiate their disputes without the supervision of the TCC President results in an imbalance of negotiating power, particularly disadvantaging consumers.[52] Besides that, there is a lack of comprehensive discussions on the legal framework of the TCC in existing literature, contributing to the absence of a specific ADR method for the TCC to follow in assisting parties to negotiate mutually acceptable solutions to their disputes.[53] Furthermore, a limited number of cases at the TCC where an award by consent is issued, indicating a need for more effective ADR methods to facilitate mutually acceptable solutions and reduce the number of cases requiring a full hearing.[54] These weaknesses and challenges highlight the need for a more structured and effective ADR framework at the TCC to address the issues faced in the current ADR processes.

'Technology waits for no one, including the law'[55] whereby many internet users in Malaysia prefer to voice complaints about products and services on social media, believing that companies value their online reputation, but these complaints can carry legal risks if found to be false or malicious under the Defamation Act 1957.[56] This indicates that consumers prefer to use online platforms to voice their dissatisfaction over consumerism matters. However, there is no specific, proper

51 Sodoq Omoola, 'Provide Online Dispute Resolutions for Consumers' (*News Straits Times*, Malaysia, 22 November 2019) <https://www.nst.com.my/opinion/letters/2019/11/540927/provide-online-dispute-resolutions-consumers> accessed 5 June 2024

52 Rahmah Ismail and Zamani Osman, 'Alternative Dispute Resolution Process in the Tribunal for Consumer Claims of Malaysia: A Way Forward' (2019) 9(5) *International Journal of Asian Social Science* 342–351

53 Su'aida Safei and Nuraisyah Chua Abdullah, 'Mediation as a Pre-Trial Process at the Tribunal for Consumer Claims, Malaysia: The Way Forward' (2022) 12(10) *International Journal of Academic Research in Business and Social Sciences* 3040–3050 <https://hrmars.com/papers_submitted/14942/mediation-as-a-pre-trial-process-at-the-tribunal-for-consumer-claims-malaysia-the-way-forward.pdf> accessed 3 March 2024

54 Rahmah (n 52) 343

55 Quoting Syed Naqiz Shahabudin in his paper presentation 'Technology Communications and Media in the Face of Globalisation – A Lawyer's Perspective' (Malaysian Law Conference organized by the Malaysian Bar, Kuala Lumpur, 16 November 2005)

56 Sodoq (n 48)

online method that consumers are aware of to resolve consumer claims amicably without any risk of other legal actions such as defamation.

Opportunities

Recognising the limitations of negotiation, the authors of this chapter propose mediation as a more practical alternative.[57] In mediation, a neutral third party (mediator) facilitates communication between the parties, assists them in understanding their respective interests, and helps to find a mutually acceptable resolution without imposing a solution.[58] Moreover, in mediation, the mediator not only helps disputants to remain focused on the dispute but also ensures that the process remains professional, free from personal interests and emotional involvement between parties, unlike the negotiation process, where there is no third party to control the disputants.

Arbitration at the TCC offers a unique approach to resolving consumer disputes that is both efficient and specialised. Unlike traditional court proceedings, arbitration is known for its speed and efficiency. This is particularly important for consumers, as disputes can be resolved quickly, preventing prolonged legal battles that disrupt their lives or businesses. Arbitration also tends to be more cost-effective than litigation in court, reducing legal fees and expenses and making it accessible to consumers with limited financial resources.

Moreover, arbitration at the TCC provides expertise and specialisation in consumer law matters. The Tribunal appoints arbitrators knowledgeable about consumer protection laws and related issues. These arbitrators understand the nuances of consumer rights and responsibilities, ensuring that disputes are handled by experts who can make informed decisions. This specialised approach helps to resolve consumer disputes effectively, providing consumers with access to justice in a timely and knowledgeable manner.

As discussed above, using ODR to resolve disputes is not widely adopted. Therefore, it is crucial to implement ODR as a mechanism to resolve consumer disputes and claims effectively. In 2022, former Prime Minister Datuk Seri Ismail Sabri Yaakob announced plans to establish a new ODR mechanism for small and medium enterprises to resolve minor disputes and enhance cross-border e-commerce activities.[59]

Conclusion

This chapter provides an in-depth analysis of Malaysia's legal framework and mechanisms for consumer protection and dispute resolution, focusing on statutes

57 Rahmah (n 52) 344

58 Rahmah (n 52) 344

59 Adib Povera and Dhesegaan Bala Krishnan, 'New Online Dispute Resolution Mechanism for SMEs Soon, Says PM' (*News Straits Times*, 6 September 2022) <https://www.nst.com.my/news/nation/2022/09/828964/new-online-dispute-resolution-mechanism-smes-soon-says-pm> accessed 5 June 2024

such as the 1999 CPA. These statutes form the foundation of consumer rights and provide avenues for redress in disputes. The enforcement mechanism includes the Tribunal for Consumer Claims and civil courts. The Tribunal for Consumer Claims offers a streamlined and user-friendly approach to resolving minor disputes, while civil courts handle more significant and complex cases. Despite these mechanisms, there are challenges in the current consumer dispute resolution landscape, including the complexity of litigation processes, which may deter consumers from pursuing claims, and the underutilisation of ADR mechanisms at the Tribunal for Consumer Claims.

To address these challenges and capitalise on opportunities, several recommendations are proposed. They are, firstly, enhancing the provisions of the CPA 1999 to provide stronger protections and more precise guidelines for consumers and, secondly, promoting and implementing the use of mediation and arbitration at the Tribunal for Consumer Claims to encourage quicker and more cost-effective resolutions. Thirdly, exploring and implementing ODR mechanisms that are user-friendly and accessible and ensure fairness and transparency in resolving consumer disputes. While Malaysia has made significant strides in consumer protection and dispute resolution, there is room for improvement to meet the evolving needs of consumers, particularly in a digital and interconnected world. By implementing these recommendations, Malaysia can strengthen its consumer protection framework and ensure accessible and effective dispute resolution mechanisms for all consumers.

References

Abd Karim J and Wan Talaat WA, 'Instituting Consumer Claims for Defective Product Against Manufacturers Under the Malaysian Laws' (2011) 1(15) International Journal of Humanities and Social Science 153

Amin N, 'Strict Liability for Defective Products: Balancing of Interests Between Consumers and Producers' (2007) 10 Malaysian Journal of Consumers and Family Economics 30, 39 <https://majcafe.com/wp-content/uploads/2022/11/artikel-4–2007.pdf> accessed 3 March 2024

Amin N and Abu Bakar E, 'ADR for Consumers: An Appraisal of the Tribunal for Consumer Claims Malaysia' in Mohammad Naqib Ishan Jan and Ashgar Ali Ali Mohammad (eds) *Mediation in Malaysia: The Law and Practice* (Lexis Nexis 2010)

Amrhein A, 'The Medical Malpractice Crisis: Why Damage Caps Will Not Solve the Problem and Who Is Really to Blame' (2006) 4(1) The Dartmouth Law Journal 1

'Background of Tribunal: Who Is Consumer' (*Official Portal Ministry of Domestic Trade and Cost of Living*) <https://www.kpdn.gov.my/en/consumerism/consumer-rights/tribunal-for-consumer-claim/background-of-the-tribunal> accessed 23 March 2024

'Consumer Claim' (*Official Portal Ministry of Domestic Trade and Cost of Living*) <https://www.kpdn.gov.my/en/consumerism/hak-pengguna/consumer-complaints> accessed 10 March 2024

Consumer Protection 1999 (Act 599) (Malaysia Federal Law)

'Consumerism' (*Official Portal Ministry of Domestic Trade and Cost of Living*) <https://www.kpdn.gov.my/en/faq/consumerism> accessed 12 April 2024

Donoghue v Stevenson (1932) A.C. 562

'Enforcement Award' (*Official Portal of Tribunal for Consumer Claims*) <https://www.kpdn.gov.my/en/consumerism/consumer-rights/tribunal-for-consumer-claim/enforcement-award> accessed 16 May 2024

'Filing and Registration Procedure' (*Official Portal Ministry of Domestic Trade and Cost of Living*) <https://www.kpdn.gov.my/en/consumerism/consumer-rights/tribunal-for-consumer-claim/filing-and-registration-procedure > accessed 16 May 2024

Hall PC, 'Medical Malpractice Problem' [1979] Annals of the American Academy of Political and Social Science 443

'Hearing Procedures' (*Official Portal of Tribunal for Consumer Claims*) <https://www.kpdn.gov.my/en/consumerism/consumer-rights/tribunal-for-consumer-claim/hearing-procedure> accessed 16 May 2024

Ismail R and Osman Z, 'Alternative Dispute Resolution Process in the Tribunal for Consumer Claims of Malaysia: A Way Forward' (2019) 9(5) International Journal of Asian Social Science 342, 351

Jahn Kassim PN, *Medical Negligence Law in Malaysia* (First Published 2003, Revised, International Law Books Services 2008)

Jayabalan S and Kaur Randawar D, 'The Role of the Modern Contract Law in the Purview of Consumer Protection' (2017) 12(1) Jurnal Intelek, Special Issue: The 2015 International Conference on the Future of ASEAN (ICoFA 2015) 21

Landsman S, 'A Brief Survey of the Development of the Adversary System' (1983) 44(3) Ohio State Law Journal

Masud J and Haron SA, 'Consumer Understanding of Year 2009 Consumer Month Celebration Theme: Consumer Power: I Consumer I Power' (2013) 16(1) Malaysian Journal of Consumer and Family Economics 20, 28

Masum A, et al., 'Consumer Protection for Sale of Goods Under the Malaysian Sale of Goods Act 1957 and the Consumer Protection Act 1999: With Particular Reference to Quality and Fitness of Goods' (2018) 2 AJHSSR 44 <https://www.researchgate.net/publication/325892799_Consumer_Protection_for_Sale_of_Goods_under_the_Malaysian_Sale_of_Goods_Act_1957_and_the_Consumer_Protection_Act_1999_With_Special_Reference_to_Quality_and_Fitness_of_Goods> accessed 5 June 2024

Matang Plastik & Metal Work Industries Sdn Bhd v Daimler Chrysler Malaysia Sdn Bhd & Ors (2014) MLJU 674

Mazirow A, 'The Advantages and Disadvantages of Arbitration as Compared to Litigation' (*Mazirow Real Estate Dispute Resolution*, 2008) <https://www.international-arbitration-attorney.com/wp-content/uploads/796608–1-2008-arthur-mazirowthe-advantages-and-disadvantages-of-arbitrationas-compared-to-lit.pdf> accessed 2 June 2024

'Mediation' (*Official Portal Legal Aid Department Malaysia*) <https://www.jbg.gov.my/index.php/en/services/mediation> accessed 20 May 2024

Meng TP, 'The Legal Saga of Exclusion Clauses in Malaysia' (2019) 1(1) Review of Politics and Public Policy in Emerging Economies 43

'Model Mediation Clauset' (*Mediation Rules of AIAC 2023)* <https://www.aiac.world/Mediation-Mediation> accessed 21 May 2024

Mohd Zakuan ZZ, Hassan SA and Abdul Rashid R, 'Protection of Buyers for Goods Purchased by Description Under the Sale of Goods Act 1957' (2022) 7(8) Malaysian Journal of Social Sciences and Humanities <https://msocialsciences.com/index.php/mjssh/article/view/1697> accessed 3 March 2024

Mohd Zakuan ZZ and Ismail R, 'Health Institution as a Consumer Protection Framework in Malaysia' (2014) 2(3) Global Journal of Politics and Law 77, 83 <https://majcafe.com/wp-content/uploads/2022/11/2019-Vol-23-S1-Paper-3.pdf> accessed 3 March 2024

'National Consumer Policy' (*Official Portal Ministry of Domestic Trade and Cost of Living*) <https://kpdnkk-gov-my.page.tl/NATIONAL-CONSUMER-POLICY.htm> accessed 10 April 2024

Omoola S, 'Provide Online Dispute Resolutions for Consumers' (*News Straits Times, Malaysia*, 22 November 2019) <https://www.nst.com.my/opinion/letters/2019/11/540927/provide-online-dispute-resolutions-consumers> accessed 5 June 2024

Povera A and Bala Krishnan D, 'New Online Dispute Resolution Mechanism for SMEs Soon, Says PM' (*News Straits Times*, 6 September 2022) <https://www.nst.com.my/news/

nation/2022/09/828964/new-online-dispute-resolution-mechanism-smes-soon-says-pm> accessed 5 June 2024

Practice Direction (*Chief Justice Federal Court Malaysia*) Issued on 24th of March 2022

Rules of Court 2012 (P.U. (A) 205/2012) (Malaysia Federal Law)

Sabri MF, 'The Development of Consumer Protection Policies in Malaysia' (2014) 4(6) International Journal of Business and Social Research

Safei S and Chua Abdullah N, 'Mediation as a Pre-Trial Process at the Tribunal for Consumer Claims, Malaysia: The Way Forward' (2022) 12(10) International Journal of Academic Research in Business and Social Sciences 3040, 3050 <https://hrmars.com/papers_submitted/14942/mediation-as-a-pre-trial-process-at-the-tribunal-for-consumer-claims-malaysia-the-way-forward.pdf> accessed 3 March 2024

Sale of Goods Act 1957 (Act 382) (Malaysia Federal Law)

Shahabudin SN, 'Technology Communications and Media in the Face of Globalisation – A Lawyer's Perspective' (Malaysian Law Conference organised by the Malaysian Bar, Kuala Lumpur, 16 November 2005)

'Statistic of Ministry of Domestic Trade and Cost of Living for Year 2021' (*Ministry of Domestic Trade and Cost of Living*) <https://www.kpdn.gov.my/en/media-kpdnhep/arkib/statistik-utama-kpdn/2021> accessed 25 May 2024

'Statistic of Ministry of Domestic Trade and Cost of Living for Year 2022' (*Ministry of Domestic Trade and Cost of Living*, 2022) <https://www.kpdn.gov.my/en/media-kpdnhep/arkib/statistik-utama-kpdn/2022> accessed 25 May 2024

'Statistic of Ministry of Domestic Trade and Cost of Living for Year 2023' (*Ministry of Domestic Trade and Cost of Living*, 2023) <https://www.kpdn.gov.my/en/media-kpdnhep/arkib/statistik-utama-kpdn/2023-arkib-statistik> accessed 25 May 2024

'Statistic of Ministry of Domestic Trade and Cost of Living for Year 2024' (Until 31st March 2024) (*Ministry of Domestic Trade and Cost of Living*, 2024) <https://www.kpdn.gov.my/ms/media-kpdnhep/penerbitan/statistik-utama-kpdn/statistiks-utama-kpdn-20232> accessed 25 May 2024

Tan Chee Wah v Sri Damansara Sdn Bhd (2006) 6 MLJ 752; (2006) 7 CLJ 66 (HC)

'Tribunal for Consumer Claims' (*Official Portal of Tribunal for Consumer Claims*) <https://ttpm.kpdn.gov.my/portal/home> accessed 14 May 2024

Tupper D, 'Litigation Vs. Arbitration' (Back to School Symposium Cle – ACC, Houston, 25 August 2011)

Woolf L, 'Chapter 15: Medical Negligence' in *Access to Justice: Final Report* (HMSO 1996) paras 37, 38, 50, 62

Yaqin A, *Law and Society in Malaysia* (International Law Book Services 1996)

Yean Joon CD and Ahmad Yusoff SS, 'Development of Consumer Protection: Challenges and the Way Forward for Consumer Protection Institution in Malaysia' (2016) 20 JUUM Journal of Law and Society 71

14 Consumer ADR in the United Arab Emirates

Fatih Buğra Erdem

Introduction

Consumer protection in the Arab world has been relatively recent, with specific legislation regarding consumer rights only introduced in 1992.[1] The United Arab Emirates (UAE) took a significant step in this direction by enacting Federal Law No. 15 on Consumer Protection in 2020, replacing the previous Consumer Protection Law of 2006. This new law aimed to safeguard consumer rights and established a regulatory framework to combat fraudulent practices in the UAE markets. Both internal and external pressures, including concerns over commercial fraud and rising commodity prices, influenced the government's decision to strengthen consumer protection laws. The need for updated legislation in the UAE is evident, particularly in areas such as online consumer protection, which currently lacks comprehensive coverage. Al-Hassan highlights the importance of enhancing consumer protection laws to ensure a fair balance between consumers and vendors in online transactions, ultimately benefiting both parties and the economy as a whole.[2]

The UAE has consistently been a leader in consumer protection within the Middle East region. The nation has established a sophisticated legal framework to oversee and safeguard consumer interests in the market of goods and services exchanged within the state's economic system as a member of the global community.[3] The primary objectives behind this initiative by the UAE government were twofold. Firstly, it aimed to elevate the prestigious image of the UAE as a top-tier country in the region regarding business and open markets. Secondly, it sought to formalise the position of consumers, which was previously unregulated in a traditional market, to attract foreign investors and tourists. Consequently, the UAE government seized every opportunity to transform the UAE markets into a secure

1 Tunisia became the pioneer among Arab nations in implementing consumer protection laws in 1992. To achieve this, Tunisia modified the existing French legislation to suit its specific requirements. For further details, refer to the work of A Ibrahim and Hemayiat Al-Mustahlik, Dirasah Muqarenah (Manshorat al-Halabi 2007) 46

2 K Al-Hassan, *Consumer Confidence in E-Commerce: The Need for Reform in the UAE* (PhD Thesis, University of Aberdeen 2007) 267

3 Y Zobair, 'Doing Business in The United Arab Emirates' (1999) 41 *Thunderbird International Review* 215; M Wallman, *Consumer Protection in the UAE* (Al Tamimi & Company 2010) 15

DOI: 10.4324/9781032689739-14

and reliable environment for commercial transactions, whether through traditional means or electronically.

This chapter will offer a brief legal synopsis of the UAE by exploring the various laws enacted by the UAE government to protect the rights of consumers. The conversation will clarify how unfair and dishonest business practices affect the UAE's economic development. In addition, the importance of civil and criminal judicial enforcement will be examined, and the rules governing the admissibility of evidence, the conduct of court cases, and litigation in both types of judicial redress that have been put into place in instances of consumer rights violations will be examined. After that, the section will highlight the legal and civil remedies available under consumer protection laws and assess the advantages and disadvantages of the legislation.

Legal Framework for Consumer Protection

The legal landscape of consumer protection in the UAE has evolved significantly over the years, particularly in response to the country's economic transformation and growth. Initially reliant on traditional sectors like fishing and agriculture, the UAE transitioned to a more diversified economy with a strong emphasis on investment and tourism. However, this shift brought challenges, including the influx of counterfeit goods into the market, posing risks to consumer health and safety.

Before specific consumer protection laws were enacted, the absence of regulations governing international trade left consumers vulnerable to substandard products. The lack of legal recourse further exacerbated issues such as inflated prices of essential goods, impacting both individuals and the overall economy. These challenges underscored the need for comprehensive consumer protection legislation in the UAE.

Pre-2006, the legal framework for commercial disputes in the UAE was characterised by a reliance on general civil and criminal codes, which often fell short of addressing the complexities of commercial law. This led to a lack of effective enforcement mechanisms, allowing perpetrators of commercial crimes to evade accountability. The subsequent development of dedicated consumer protection laws aimed to address these shortcomings and provide consumers with the necessary legal safeguards.

The Federal Law No. 15 of 2020, known as the Consumer Protection Act (CPA), was implemented in 2020 to encompass the sale and purchase of goods and services within the consumer context in the UAE. This law also applies to e-commerce platforms that are registered in the UAE. This new legislation's primary objective is to ensure consumer protection and maintain price stability. It aims to guarantee that goods and services are delivered in accordance with the consumers' needs while also limiting practices that could have a detrimental impact on consumers and controlling price increases. Additionally, the law promotes sustainable consumption and provides adequate protection to consumers, considering the technological advancements witnessed in the field of e-commerce. It also regulates the activities of suppliers, advertisers, and commercial agents in relation to consumer protection.

Furthermore, the law strives to create a free-market environment where consumers are free to choose and are offered fair prices. Lastly, it encourages the establishment of a code of ethics for producers and distributors of goods and services. Notably, the definition of "Supplier" has been expanded to include e-commerce service providers registered in the UAE, which is particularly significant considering the substantial growth of e-commerce during the COVID-19 pandemic, leading to an acceleration of e-commerce activities in the UAE.[4]

The General Design of the Enforcement Mechanism

The enforcement of consumer protection laws in the UAE is an area that requires careful examination and improvement. The existing consumer protection framework lacks effectiveness and needs a rigorous review. Additionally, there is a need to establish a legal framework for resolving disputes between consumers and businesses. While the UAE has implemented various measures to enforce consumer protection, some of these methods are insufficient to achieve significant results that would gain international recognition. However, the UAE has made commendable efforts to strengthen its consumer protection framework, which has started to yield positive outcomes.

The UAE legislature has passed several laws to create a reliable and secure market where companies and traders uphold the rights of consumers, building on earlier attempts to guarantee sufficient consumer protection.[5] It was, therefore, anticipated that government agencies would step in to support and formalise the consumer protection movement. The creation of public entities tasked with protecting consumer interests was demanded, as were additional rules to oversee and guarantee the correct use of the CPA. The aim was to establish a favourable legislative and administrative framework by implementing diverse tactics to surmount impediments that may impede the rights of consumers. This entailed putting in place extensive safeguards for consumers and involving key organisations and government agencies in implementing and upholding consumer protection legislation. In addition, the goal was to set up legal and administrative processes that would lessen the cost consumers would have to pay to protect their rights, including the possibility of efficient legal remedies.

However, it should be highlighted that, compared to pursuing legal action, the initiatives and procedures the pertinent ministries and agencies put in place have shown to be more effective in terms of time. Administrative proceedings in the UAE should be readily available and suitably supplied, like civil and criminal procedures. This aims to evaluate if and how consumer organisations have successfully decreased the incidence of violations of consumer rights. This chapter will

4 Christopher R. Williams, 'Consumer Protection Law in the UAE' (2021) 11(220) *National Law Review* <https://www.natlawreview.com/article/consumer-protection-law-uae> accessed 7 June 2024

5 C Adamson, 'Complaint Handling: Its Rationale and Function in Well-Managed Companies' in R John (ed) *The Consumer Revolution: Redressing the Balance* (Hodder & Stoughton 1999) 138; E Al-Tamimi, 'Current UAE Copyright Law and How It Compares With WTO's TRIPs Agreement and the Berne Convention' (1999) 2(3) *Journal of World Intellectual Property* 371, 374

look at the processes the UAE uses to settle consumer complaints, starting with the roles of the courts and the involvement of different government agencies.

Current Consumer Dispute Resolution Processes

The legal framework for consumer protection in the UAE operates on two levels, federal and local, in accordance with the country's federal system. Federal authorities, including institutions, bodies, and laws, adhere to the federal system and are enforced in the Emirates that follow this system. Conversely, local authorities are specific to Emirates following the local system and do not apply to others. According to Recital 34 of Regulation (EU) 2017/2394 of the EU Parliament, consumer organisations are pivotal in educating consumers about their rights, providing information, and safeguarding their interests, particularly in dispute resolution. Consumers are urged to collaborate with competent authorities to enhance the implementation of this Regulation.

In the UAE, consumers have access to advice and support from consumer protection organisations, often called administrative authorities, when seeking recourse for defective products or harm caused by faulty goods and services. These authorities serve as an intermediary between formal legal action, which can be expensive and stigmatising, and informal methods like guidance and persuasion to ensure businesses comply with regulations. There is an apparent necessity for administrative authorities to step in and establish more streamlined, cost-effective, and efficient procedures for addressing complaints and offering appropriate remedies to consumers. In the UAE, two categories of administrative bodies can take action independently of the judicial system, with the decision to pursue administrative solutions resting with the relevant government department. Both federal and local administrative entities have the authority to address violations of consumer protection laws.

Furthermore, complaints submitted to administrative departments must be written and accompanied by relevant supporting documentation. However, in urgent situations, administrative bodies may act upon verbal complaints. Nevertheless, a formal complaint supported by evidence and documentation should be submitted promptly. Following raids, seizures, or the imposition of fines, the entire case is typically referred to the relevant authority. This authority is empowered to determine the most appropriate course of action to resolve the complaint based on product characteristics and other pertinent factors.[6]

In its commitment to fostering a conducive environment for consumers and a fair market grounded in integrity and transparency, the UAE government has designated various administrative bodies to ensure adequate consumer protection. It has delegated specific responsibilities to these governmental institutions and authorities, granting them sufficient power to oversee and regulate the quality of goods and services in accordance with international standards and specifications. Consequently, multiple institutions and departments have been entrusted with the

6 A Al-Muaini, *The Enforcement of Copyright Law in the United Arab Emirates* (PhD Thesis, University of Aberdeen 2009) 140

task of collaborating to safeguard consumer rights and establish effective mechanisms for dispute prevention.[7]

Consumer protection law enforcement employs various mechanisms based on the responsibilities delegated to relevant authorities. These mechanisms are categorised into two types – prior inspection and subsequent inspection. Prior inspection involves supervisory tasks assigned by the legislator to prevent counterfeit goods from entering the country. On the other hand, subsequent inspection grants authority to government employees to combat counterfeit goods already present in markets and commercial establishments.

It should also be noted that the UAE's existing federal consumer protection legislation lacks provisions addressing the involvement of customs authorities in promoting consistency and collaboration among all customs entities to combat counterfeit goods and products effectively. Customs authorities are not authorised to handle confiscated items until a court verdict has been reached. However, scholars have pointed out that various factors have impacted the role of customs authorities in certain Emirates. Herein, the shortage of specialised personnel in detecting counterfeit goods within relevant authorities should be highlighted, thereby reducing the effectiveness of customs in the UAE. There is an absence of a coordinated network among stakeholders involved in combating this issue, as well as the lengthy investigative procedures related to commercial fraud cases, which have hindered the effectiveness of customs operations.[8]

The court system is often not the preferred choice for many litigants, as ADR lacks the necessary structure to provide adequate redress for those impacted. Hawkins and Thomas emphasise that prosecution should be a last resort, with the primary objective being the achievement of legislative goals rather than the punishment of breaches. One key focus of remedies is to address the delays in the enforcement process within the court system, which can be protracted, involve multiple procedures, and be subject to lengthy appeal processes. In contrast, ADR methods like mediation offer expedited procedures for resolving disputes. Despite the availability of both court adjudication and mediation for consumer dispute resolution, individuals tend to favour mediation over court proceedings. This preference is mainly due to the prolonged duration of cases in UAE federal courts, which can exceed 559 days. Consequently, UAE consumer protection laws include provisions that encourage disputing parties to opt for mediation to settle their conflicts.

Alternative Dispute Resolution for Consumer Disputes

Overview

Consumer protection and the enforcement of consumer rights encompass various aspects, including dispute resolution. For consumer protection measures to be

7 UAE Consumer Protection Law, Article 4, Para 2

8 UAE Consumer Law No. 24 of 2006, Article 20 and UAE Consumer Executive Regulation No. 12 of 2007, Article 21

truly effective, it is crucial to establish a robust mechanism for resolving disputes. However, the UAE law appears to lack adequate provisions for safeguarding consumer interests in this regard.[9] While resorting to the court system may not be the most desirable option for litigants, the ADR method also falls short in its structure and ability to provide effective remedies for affected individuals.[10] Hawkins and Thomas emphasise that prosecution should be considered a last resort, with the primary objective being the fulfilment of legislative goals rather than merely punishing breaches of the law.

One of the critical objectives in addressing this issue is to minimise the delays caused by the court system during the enforcement process. Court proceedings are often protracted, involving multiple procedures and potential appeals. On the other hand, ADR methods, such as mediation, offer expedited procedures for resolving disputes. Consequently, although the law provides consumers with two avenues for adjudicating disputes – the courts and mediation – the preference tends to lean towards mediation. This preference is influenced mainly by the significant time it takes for cases to be resolved in UAE federal courts, which averages between six to 12 months.[11] In comparison, other countries like Tunisia, Jordan, Saudi Arabia, Egypt, Yemen, and Syria have considerably shorter durations of seven, 147, 195, 202, 240, and 559 days, respectively.[12] As a result, UAE consumer protection laws include a provision that encourages conflicting parties to opt for mediation as a means to settle their disputes.[13]

Furthermore, the CPA has utilised mediation as a means of resolving most conflicts within the department. According to Article 17 of the CPA, mediation has been assigned to the Ministry of Economy employees to settle disputes between conflicting parties. It is important to note that the Minister has the authority to review and potentially overturn the decision made through mediation within fifteen days. However, Ahmed discovered that while the Ministry referred parties to mediation, there were no clear guidelines regarding settling cases.[14] This lack of clarity included determining who would be responsible for overseeing the case and which cases should be referred to mediation. This issue arises because the current

9 K Hawkins and J Thomas (eds), *Enforcing Regulation* (Kluwer-Nijhoff 1984) 23; K Hawkins, *Law as Last Resort: Prosecution Decision-Making in a Regulating Agency* (Oxford University Press 2003)

10 M Doyle, K Ritters, and S Brooker, *Seeking Resolution: The Availability and Usage of Consumer to Business Alternative Dispute Resolution in the United Kingdom* (National Consumer Council 2004) 5–6; H Edwards, 'Alternative Dispute Resolution: Panacea or Anathema?' (1986) 99(3) *Harvard Law Review* 668

11 G Anis, 'Q&A: Judicial Review in United Arab Emirates' (*Lexology*, 22 December 2023) <https://www.lexology.com/library/detail.aspx?g=d7203fe4-b317–4359-b064-f49bc8eb28d6> accessed 20 July 2024

12 Y Al-Yosouf, 'Dirasat Halat Dowlat al-Emarat al-Arabiyah al-Motahedah' in *al-Fasad Wa-lhukm al-Saleh Fi al-Bilad al-Arabiyah* (2nd edn, Markez dirasat alwehdah alarabiyah 2007) 582

13 B Ahmed, 'United Arab Emirates' in Richard Clark (ed) *The Dispute Resolution Review* (3rd edn, Law Business Research 2011) 845

14 B Ahmed, 'United Arab Emirates' in Richard Clark (ed) *The Dispute Resolution Review* (3rd edn, Law Business Research 2011) 845

consumer protection law does not contain any provisions regarding the mediation mechanism.[15]

Lebanon's Consumer Protection Law No. 659 of 2005 outlines a more effective structure for consumer protection in order to remedy this. The following guidelines ought to be included in this mechanism: (i) Resolutions involving amounts under three million LBP (7,500 AED) must be settled through mediation; (ii) Cases within the department should be referred to mediation; (iii) A neutral individual or individuals at least three grades above within the relevant ministry should serve as the mediator; (iv) The mediator must get in touch with the disputing parties within three days of receiving approval to begin mediation and set up a session; (v) All parties involved in the dispute, or their representatives, must attend all stages of the mediation process; (vi) The mediator may choose to enlist the aid of experts; (v) The parties to the dispute, or their representatives, must be present at all mediation sessions; (vi) The mediator may choose to enlist the aid of experts; and (vii) The mediation must be completed within fifteen days of the first session, though this time frame may be extended with the consent of all parties.

A straightforward comparison between mediation under the UAE and Lebanese consumer protection laws highlights the lack of clarity in the UAE legislation and the comprehensive provisions provided by the Lebanese legislation regarding mediation.[16] This paper contends that when the legislature clearly defines mediation procedures, parties are more likely to opt for this method as a quick way to protect their rights in the short term. Conversely, if mediation is costly and difficult to access, consumers may be deterred from seeking resolution. One may maintain that in the absence of ADR regulations, there should be provisions that parties can rely on to facilitate the process. He emphasises that mediation is an effective method for resolving consumer protection conflicts due to its time and cost-saving benefits compared to formal dispute resolution methods. Rabah asserts that UAE consumer protection legislation should encompass provisions for mediation and other ADR mechanisms. It is worth noting that cases in UAE federal courts typically last over 559 days, highlighting the urgent need to streamline the enforcement process and reduce delays, which can be achieved through ADR methods like mediation.

Some companies prefer arbitration to resolve consumer disputes instead of resorting to the courts. Nevertheless, Al-Hassan raises concerns about the objectivity of the company-provided arbitration scheme, as its free-of-charge nature may impact its quality. Conversely, if the ADR scheme were solely funded by the company, it would compromise its impartiality. In the UAE, the government encourages consumers to seek mediation to settle their disputes initially. However, the law does not specify the exact mechanism that parties must adhere to in order to reach an agreement. Consequently, it is imperative for the UAE legislator to introduce provisions that outline the types of cases eligible for transfer to ADR and the procedures that parties should follow.

15 K Mahmoud et al., 'Dispute Resolution: United Arab Emirates' (*Lexology*, 30 January 2024) <https://www.lexology.com/indepth/dispute-resolution/united-arab-emirates> accessed 20 July 2024

16 Articles 82–96 of Lebanese Consumer Protection Law No. 659 of 2005

In the UAE, ADR is generally considered a substitute for litigation, with arbitration being the most commonly used ADR technique.[17] However, there is no consistent definition of ADR among experts in the UAE or the broader Middle East region. Some commentators hesitate to classify arbitration and even mediation as an "alternative" due to their extensive use in contractual agreements, such as those in the United Kingdom. More than any operational or legal issue, the UAE's economic structure and cultural norms present the biggest obstacles to the general adoption of ADR. Both the non-confrontational Arabic culture and the previously defined idea of "wasta" are important in settling disputes. When faced with a disagreement, parties in the Middle East and the United Arab Emirates frequently choose to pursue informal remedies based on personal relationships over formal dispute resolution procedures.

The economic framework of the UAE revolves around state-owned enterprises and influential trading dynasties, both of which foster a hesitancy to utilise conflict resolution methods that may be perceived as slightly confrontational. While structured negotiations like mediation are considered less adversarial, there remains a general reluctance to adopt them as a preferred approach. A lack of awareness regarding ADR mechanisms, coupled with apprehensions (albeit unfounded) about the absence of a "without prejudice" rule in UAE legislation, which would safeguard settlement discussions from being used as evidence of liability, contributes to the sluggish progress of ADR in the region. Nevertheless, these challenges can be effectively addressed and should not impede the growth of ADR practices.[18]

The promotion of financial services is greatly aided by the DIFC, a free zone created in the United Arab Emirates. The DIFC has been given the power to enact its own laws, which are based on the common law system, as opposed to the civil law model that oversees the remainder of the UAE. The DIFC has set up its own judicial system in order to administer and execute these laws efficiently. A legal framework for the administration of arbitration and the enforceability of arbitral rulings within the DIFC has also been established by the DIFC through the enactment of the DIFC Arbitration Law, commonly known as DIFC Law No. 1 of 2008. Interestingly, parties not residing in the DIFC may nevertheless sign arbitration agreements with the DIFC, which serves as the arbitration's seat. As a result, they have the advantage of using the DIFC courts' authority to handle cases involving award enforcement and interim measures. Notably, cases can even be heard in English at the DIFC courts, which are staffed by seasoned international judges.

Dubai Law No. 6 of 1997, which governs contracts with the Dubai government, imposes restrictions on the utilisation of arbitration in contracts related to the Dubai government. Article 36 specifically prohibits the inclusion of any dispute resolution provisions outside of Dubai courts or any laws/rules other than those of

17 AR Lodder and J Zeleznikow, *Enhanced Dispute Resolution Through the Use of Information Technology* (Cambridge University Press 2010)

18 P Norman, 'Overview of Alternative Dispute Resolution in the UAE' (Simmons & Simmons Lexica, 2009) <http://www.elexica.com/en/legal-topics/dispute-resolution-commercial/16-overview-of-alternative-dispute-resolution-in-the-uae> accessed 20 July 2024

Dubai in contracts with the Dubai government or its departments. However, there is a provision for a public interest exemption that allows the Dubai government to agree to arbitration in some instances, such as through the Dubai International Arbitration Centre (DIAC).

It is widely acknowledged that one of the primary drawbacks of adjudication in the UAE is the provision of what is often referred to as "rough justice". Additionally, due to the tight time constraints, the decisions made through adjudication may not always be entirely accurate or thoroughly reasoned. The fact that these decisions are not ultimately binding and can be appealed further adds to the disadvantages of this method. The statutory timeframes that must be followed also make it susceptible to being used as an 'ambush tactic' or a "fishing expedition". Several obstacles need to be overcome before adjudication can be widely used in the UAE. The main obstacle is the lack of a recognised enforcement mechanism and statutory framework like those for arbitration. Other obstacles include the fact that adjudication is typically non-binding, that it is not widely used as a method of dispute settlement, and that people are reluctant to employ such an unfamiliar process. The parties' relationship will likely suffer when a conflict escalates to the point where an official dispute-resolution process is required. In certain situations, both sides have solidified their positions to the point where they are hesitant or even incapable of considering a novel or non-binding resolution. Additionally, parties may be reluctant to engage in a process that does not allow for a comprehensive presentation of their respective cases and the opportunity to provide necessary rebuttals.

Substantive Law Changes

Initially, in all legal and commercial disputes that can be resolved without violating the existing laws in force in the UAE or public order and morality, the Mediation and Conciliation Centre (the "Centre") has the exclusive authority to settle legal and business disputes in accordance with Article 8 of the Decree on the Rule of Law, and Article 27 of the Law Decree states that: (i) At a value exceeding five million dirhams; and (ii) Between spouses or relatives up to the fourth degree, regardless of their value. Competitors may agree to refer to the Conciliation Centre in legal and commercial disputes exceeding five million dirhams before the initiation of proceedings or during the hearing.

However, as stated in Article 28 of the Decree, some disputes do not fall within the scope of the Centre's mandate. (i) Urgent and provisional orders and actions; (ii) Proceedings to which the State is a party; (iii) Lease cases before special lease dispute committees; (iv) Business cases, personal cases; and (vi) Other cases decided to be brought before a centre, committee, or other body with similar jurisdiction.

Article 4 of the Rule of Law Decree also authorises mediators and conciliators to conduct the Mediation and Conciliation meetings electronically and remotely, with the approval of the Board or the local council chairman and in accordance with regulations and procedures issued by the Minister of Justice. In disputes submitted for mediation or conciliation, as a whole, the documents and information provided by the parties ("Parties") or the agreements or arrangements made, the mediation and conciliation procedures shall be dealt with with the utmost confidentiality as provided for in Article 5 of the Decision. Article 6 prohibits the Mediator and the Conciliator from acting as arbitrators or counsellors in a dispute or from accepting to be lawyers in any dispute against any of the Parties relating to the subject of the dispute concerning the mediation or conciliation.

Procedural Developments

A new consumer protection law was introduced in the UAE to enhance the rights and protections that consumers have in the nation. In an effort to strengthen UAE consumer rights and improve safeguards. Federal Law No. 15 of 2020 on consumer protection was decided to enact. The old Consumer Protection Law, which is replaced by this historic legislation, introduces a number of significant changes designed to protect the interests of consumers and promote an equitable and open market.

The proposed law upholds and expands consumer rights in the UAE in line with worldwide benchmarks. Some of these rights are the freedom of choice and the right to consumer education. The UAE hopes to empower consumers and guarantee honest and open trading activities by putting all such privileges into law. The proposed legislation unveils consolidated ADR to aid in the resolution of consumer disputes. Additionally, prior to actually filing lawsuits, consumers are urged to pursue redress through alternative dispute resolution procedures like arbitration or mediation. The legislation also creates specialist consumer protection tribunals to settle disputes quickly and fairly. These steps are intended to give customers quick and easy access to alternative options.

Role of Technology in Consumer ADR: Online Dispute Resolution for Consumer Disputes

Since the introduction of the 2021 Mediation Law, conflicting parties have been furnished with a way to choose "onshore courts" provided that the parties come to mutual consent (*consensus ad idem*). Currently, mediation processes are governed by the Federal Decree Law No. 40 of 2023 on mediation and conciliation in civil and commercial disputes. With the enactment of this law, the UAE got a look at connecting parties with expert mediators via Wasata, which serves as a mediation platform launched by the Ministry of Justice to provide an online alternative to the traditional litigation process.[19] The platform's main objective is to facilitate the resolution of civil and commercial disputes by connecting users with registered mediators who specialise in conducting proceedings in either Arabic or English. It encompasses a comprehensive set of procedures, including mediator registration, renewal, and delisting, as well as non-judicial and judicial mediation processes.

19 N Sharratt and A Field, 'The Middle East Becomes Increasingly Pro-Mediation' (2024) <https://www.nortonrosefulbright.com/en/knowledge/publications/ef32e642/the-middle-east-becomes-increasing-pro-mediation> accessed 20 July 2024

Additionally, it manages mediator-related tasks, requests, and sessions, facilitates the payment of mediation expenses and mediator's fees, and assists in the preparation of the final mediation report. The primary purpose of this platform is to expedite dispute resolution and reduce the burden on the courts' systems. In 2022, the utilisation of ADR methods for civil and commercial disputes resulted in a settlement rate of 61.3%.[20]

Challenges and Opportunities

Consumer protection and the enforcement of consumer rights encompass various aspects, including dispute resolution. In order for consumer protection to be genuinely adequate, it is crucial to have a well-functioning mechanism for resolving disputes. However, it is unfortunate that the UAE has not fully embraced Online Dispute Resolution (ODR) principles and ideals, which is why this research is being conducted. Nevertheless, traditional methods of dispute resolution still persist. When contracts are made, carried out, or intended to be carried out in the UAE, the default method for resolving disputes is through the local courts, much like in previous countries. The language of these court proceedings is Arabic, and all court documents must be translated into Arabic by a translator licensed by the Ministry of Justice. Unfortunately, this obligation also applies to consumer-related issues, which has affected the UAE's efforts to uphold consumer rights.

The effective implementation of ODR techniques can be observed in the resolution of consumer disputes arising from commercial transactions conducted through electronic communication. This approach involves the establishment of a system that facilitates the resolution of disputes between consumers and traders using the same medium through which the transaction took place, namely the Internet. This logical extension of e-commerce allows for the resolution of non-personal e-commerce disputes without the need for direct interactions, making ODR techniques valuable tools in achieving effective dispute resolution.

Consumer disputes have been a primary focus for service providers like SquareTrade and CyberSettle, whose customers include popular auction portals. This trend persists today, as some disputes arising from transactions conducted on platforms like eBay are still resolved by external entities offering ODR services, such as Modria.com. Additionally, autonomous systems like eBay's Resolution Centre have been established to address these disputes. Each auction platform utilises its own ODR system or collaborates with other platforms to implement finished solutions.

The implementation of an ODR platform in the UAE will face various obstacles. One of the primary and most significant factors hindering the progress of ODR is the lack of awareness. This issue has been frequently cited as a reason for the limited adoption of ODR, both in the European Union and in relation to ADR. Consumers with unresolved legal issues are often unaware of where to seek

20 See Litigation Procedures <https://u.ae/en/information-and-services/justice-safety-and-the-law/litigation-procedures/mediation> accessed 20 July 2024

assistance after encountering problems with an online transaction. Additionally, businesses are unaware of the potential benefits ODR systems can offer in improving consumer redress. Another contributing factor to the limited success of ODR is the scarcity of credible trust marks. Trustmarks are online labels that assist users in identifying traders who adhere to a specific code of conduct. When a consumer believes that a code breach has occurred, external dispute resolution methods are made available.[21] Secondly, a lack of regulation and legal standards is a significant factor that hinders the progress of ODR. Currently, no accreditation services exist for the ODR field, which also applies to ADR.[22] This absence of established standards leaves potential users uncertain about what to expect. The absence of proper due process guarantees further impacts the trust potential users have in ODR services when they are implemented in the UAE. Thirdly, the development of ad hoc ODR technology poses another significant challenge, as it can be quite costly. This factor is crucial due to the high expenses associated with researching and creating customised ODR software. It is important to recognise that while online ADR can utilise existing software like email and Skype, generic software may not fully unlock the potential of ODR, such as identifying behavioural patterns that can lead to dispute resolution without the need for a neutral third party.[23] Creating user-friendly and effective ODR software is indeed a complex task.[24]

Additionally, for an ODR programme to be effective, the parties involved must be sufficiently motivated to participate in the ODR process rather than going to court. This is a problem since traders can be reluctant to use ODR in the absence of incentives. Given that the trader has already rejected a customer's complaint, why would the trader voluntarily engage in an ODR procedure when the customer is not likely to take legal action? eBay realised that effectively resolving disputes between its users, especially within the European Union, is in their own best interest, which is why the redress system works so well.[25] However, encouraging other traders to participate in ODR schemes becomes more difficult if they do not operate on a third-party auction site where unhappy customers can give negative feedback that could affect future sales.[26] However, the fundamental idea stays the same:

21 P Cortes and AR Lodder, 'Consumer Protection Goes Online: Reflections on the Revolution of European Law for Out-of-Court Redress' (2014) 21 *Maastricht Journal of European and Comparative Law* 14

22 P Cortes, 'Developing Online Dispute Resolution for Consumers in the EU: A Proposal for the Regulation of Accredited Providers' (2010) 19 *International Journal of Law and Information Technology* 1

23 O Rabinovich-Einy, 'Technology's Impact: The Quest for a New Paradigm for Accountability in Mediation' (2006) 11 *Harvard Negotiation Law Review* 253

24 GAW Vreeswijk and AR Lodder, 'Gearbi: Towards an Online Arbitration Environment Based on the Design Principles Simplicity, Awareness, Orientation, and Timeliness' (2005) 13 *Artificial Intelligence and Law* 297

25 L Edwards and A Theunissen, 'Creating Trust and Satisfaction Online: How Important is ADR? The eBay Experience' (2007) 5 *Web Journal of Current Legal Issues*

26 L Webb, 'International BBB Ratings á la eBay: A Proposal for an Improved Online Better Business Bureau to Facilitate International Business Transactions' (2004) 35 *California Western International Law Journal* 127

traders and potential responders need to either be given financial incentives (like reviews or a Trustmark) or forced to participate in a dispute resolution process (by market forces or government rules). Lastly, the lack of enforceability of agreements to utilise ODR and the uncertainty surrounding final outcomes continue to present significant barriers to the widespread adoption of consensual ODR methods, particularly in cases involving domestic negotiation and mediation (excluding cross-border disputes, which are covered by directive).[27]

Conclusion

The long-awaited regulation of the Consumer Protection Act in the UAE came into force in October 2023. Accordingly, radical obligations (including criminal ones) are imposed on all companies providing services or goods in the UAE. Due to the rising trade volume in the UAE, disputes have increased daily. The use of a more consensual order rather than the usual judicial methods has been necessary to resolve these disputes. This led to the need to incorporate ADR models, which have become increasingly popular globally. The UAE has recently introduced ADR models to its legal system. After agreeing to sign the Singapore Mediation Convention in March 2022, the Dubai International Arbitration Centre's mediation rules were published in October 2023.

In conclusion, the UAE has made significant strides in enhancing consumer protection through the adoption of comprehensive legal frameworks and the integration of ADR mechanisms. The recent legislative developments, including the Federal Legislative Decree No. 40 of 2023 and the introduction of the Wasata online mediation platform, reflect the UAE's commitment to providing efficient and accessible dispute resolution options for consumers. While the UAE has established a robust foundation for consumer protection, challenges such as limited consumer awareness, cultural reluctance towards formal dispute resolution methods, and the need for clearer guidelines and enforcement mechanisms remain. By addressing these challenges and continuing to refine its ADR processes, the UAE can further strengthen consumer confidence and create a fairer marketplace. The ongoing efforts to align with international standards and best practices will be crucial in ensuring that the UAE's consumer protection system remains effective and responsive to the evolving needs of its consumers.

References

Adamson C, 'Complaint Handling: Its Rationale and Function in Well-Managed Companies' in R John (ed) *The Consumer Revolution: Redressing the Balance* (Hodder & Stoughton 1999) 138

Ahmed B, 'United Arab Emirates' in Richard Clark (ed) *The Dispute Resolution Review* (3rd edn, Law Business Research 2011)

27 G Lázsló Szöke, 'The Possibility of Online Mediation Under the Hungarian Mediation Act in Comparison with a Number of International, Including European, Documents on Mediation' (2006) 15 *Information and Communications Technology Law* 129

Al-Hassan K, *Consumer Confidence in E-Commerce: The Need for Reform in the UAE* (PhD Thesis, University of Aberdeen 2007) 267
Al-Muaini A, *The Enforcement of Copyright Law in the United Arab Emirates* (PhD Thesis, University of Aberdeen 2009)
Al-Tamimi E, 'Current UAE Copyright Law and How It Compares With WTO's TRIPs Agreement and the Berne Convention' (1999) 2(3) Journal of World Intellectual Property 371, 374
Al-Yosouf Y, 'Dirasat Halat Dowlat al-Emarat al-Arabiyah al-Motahedah' in *al-Fasad Wa-lhukm al-Saleh Fi al-Bilad al-Arabiyah* (Markez dirasat alwehdah alarabiyah 2007)
Anis G, 'Q&A: Judicial Review in United Arab Emirates' (*Lexology*, 22 December 2023) <https://www.lexology.com/library/detail.aspx?g=d7203fe4-b317-4359-b064-f49bc8eb28d6>
Cortes P and Lodder AR, 'Consumer Protection Goes Online: Reflections on the Revolution of European Law for Out-of-Court Redress' (2014) 21 Maastricht Journal of European and Comparative Law 14
Doyle M, Ritters K and Brooker S, *Seeking Resolution: The Availability and Usage of Consumer to Business Alternative Dispute Resolution in the United Kingdom* (National Consumer Council 2004)
Edwards H, 'Alternative Dispute Resolution: Panacea or Anathema?' (1986) 99(3) Harvard Law Review 668
Edwards L and Theunissen A, 'Creating Trust and Satisfaction Online: How Important Is ADR? The eBay Experience' (2007) 5 Web Journal of Current Legal Issues
Hawkins K, *Law as Last Resort: Prosecution Decision-Making in a Regulating Agency* (Oxford University Press 2003)
Hawkins K and Thomas J (eds), *Enforcing Regulation* (Kluwer-Nijhoff 1984)
Ibrahim A and Al-Mustahlik H, *Dirasah Muqarenah* (Manshorat al-Halabi 2007)
Lázsló Szöke G, 'The Possibility of Online Mediation Under the Hungarian Mediation Act in Comparison with a Number of International, Including European, Documents on Mediation' (2006) 15 Information and Communications Technology Law 129
Lebanese Consumer Protection Law No 659 of 2005
Lodder A and Zeleznikow J, *Enhanced Dispute Resolution Through the Use of Information Technology* (Cambridge University Press 2010)
Mahmoud K, Lezala M, Mian A and McLaughlin H, 'Dispute Resolution: United Arab Emirates' (*Lexology*, 30 January 2024) <https://www.lexology.com/indepth/dispute-resolution/united-arab-emirates> accessed 20 July 2024
Norman P, *Overview of Alternative Dispute Resolution in the UAE* (Simmons & Simmon Elexica 2009)
Rabinovich-Einy O, 'Technology's Impact: The Quest for a New Paradigm for Accountability in Mediation' (2006) 11 Harvard Negotiation Law Review 253
Sharratt N and Field A, 'The Middle East Becomes İncreasingly Pro-Mediation' (2024) <https://www.nortonrosefulbright.com/en/knowledge/publications/ef32e642/the-middle-east-becomes-increasing-pro-mediation> accessed 20 July 2024
Vreeswijk G and Lodder A, 'Gearbi: Towards an Online Arbitration Environment Based on the Design Principles Simplicity, Awareness, Orientation, and Timeliness' (2005) 13 Artificial Intelligence and Law 297
Wallman M, *Consumer Protection in the UAE* (Al Tamimi & Company 2010)
Webb L, 'International BBB Ratings á la eBay: A Proposal for an Improved Online Better Business Bureau to Facilitate International Business Transactions' (2004) 35 California Western International Law Journal
Williams C, 'Consumer Protection Law in the UAE' (2021) 11(220) National Law Review
Zobair Y, 'Doing Business in the United Arab Emirates' (1999) 41 Thunderbird International Review 215, 215

15 Consumer ADR in Nigeria

Henry C. Uzokwe

Introduction

Nigeria is a large country, and even now, the precise population is often contested.[1] It comprises different states, ethnic groups, languages, cultures, and many other "legal certainties." While wealthy urban dwellers might be willing to make complaints or go to court when their consumer rights are violated, rural Nigerians may not be suitable for this. The growth of Nigeria's legal system, including ADR, has emphasised the potential to empower rural dwellers and help Nigeria meet its local and international obligations by leveraging its growth potential and providing a lasting solution to the rural population with an effective dispute resolution mechanism. Nearly 48% of Nigerians live in rural areas, and these people depend on the traditional judicial system to resolve disputes.[2] In today's high-tech world, the rural population and the urban dwellers need their rights and remedies protected in a simple and cheap redress mechanism.

With globalisation and continuous technological developments, the changes in the needs and tastes of many rural and urban dwellers in Nigeria have become more apparent. Technological developments made it easier for these people to buy goods and services across different states and borders. When these goods and services are exchanged, there should be obligations and responsibilities to maintain the quality and quantity of the goods and services. Many of these goods sometimes have defects or weaknesses in services, causing the exploitation of consumers. To safeguard the interest of the consumers, the Nigerian government passed legislation called the Consumer Protection Council (CPC) Act of 1992. The CPC Act[3] defines

1 Lysonski, Steven and Durvasula Srinivas, 'Nigeria in Transition: Acculturation to Global Consumer Culture' (2013) 30(6) *Journal of Consumer Marketing* 493–508

2 The term Urban population refers to people living in Urban areas. The figure in this chapter is calculated using World Bank population estimates and urban ratios from the United Nations World Urbanization Prospects

3 Cap C25 Laws of Federation of Nigeria (LFN), 2004. See Felicia Monye, *The Consumer Protection in Nigeria: Struggles, Burdens, and Hopes* (Inaugural Lecture of the University of Nigeria, 26 May 2011)

DOI: 10.4324/9781032689739-15

a consumer as any person who purchases or offers to purchase goods otherwise than for the purpose of resale or to whom a service is rendered.[4]

Nigeria's move towards establishing consumer protection measures can be traced back to the political independence and oil boom in the 1970s.[5] As the country gained independence in 1960 from British colonial rule, it began to enact laws to protect all citizens' rights.[6] While the consumer regime has existed in many developed countries for centuries, it was not until the 1980s and 1990s that Nigeria promulgated the first consumer legislation that established the regulatory agencies. The origin of consumer Protection in Nigeria is the Consumer Protection Council (CPC) Act of 1992.[7] The Act established the CPC[8] and empowered it to carry out various functions, ranging from investigating consumer complaints to prosecuting offenders. Recently, the regulatory landscape of the CPC Act was merged with the CPC to form the Competition and Consumer Protection Commission (CCPC) when the Federal Competition and Consumer Protection Commission (FCCPC) Act of 2018, repealed the CPC Act of 1992, in a consolidation attempt. Consumer protection and policy in Nigeria have undergone significant development over the years, reflecting the government's commitment to protecting the rights and interests of its citizens in the marketplace. Current consumer ADR options available in Nigeria include arbitration, mediation, conciliation, court-arranged ADR, and administrative agencies.

In today's Nigeria, the growing consumer market and increased consumer awareness have constantly led to more consumer-related disputes.[9] The buying and selling of goods and services are rapidly growing; however, under the previous consumer protection regime[10]; there were no easy procedures for resolving civil or commercial disputes without resorting to litigation. This is because Nigeria has not completely embraced the digitalisation of consumer protection.[11] Courts have failed to be a liberator of last resort when approached by aggrieved consumers due to bureaucracy and the absence of suitable legislation.[12] Dispute resolution poses

4 Section 32, Decree No. 66 of 1992, Consumer Protection Council Act and Section 167 Federal Competition and Consumer Protection Act, 2018

5 Benedict Kanyip, *Consumer Protection in Nigeria: Law, Theory and Policy* (Rekon Books Limited Abuja 2005)

6 Section 36 Constitution of the Federal Republic of Nigeria, 1999

7 The first Consumer Protection Council Act was enacted in 1992 and this established the Consumer Protection Commission (CPC)

8 The Consumer Protection Council Act, CAP C25 LFN 2004

9 In the Electricity sector, NERC, Second Quarter 2020 Report shows that the Forum Office (Fos) across the 36 states of the federation reportedly received 203,116 consumer complaints for 2020 approximately 2232 cases per day. See NERC Second <https://nerc.gov.ng/resources/nerc-second-quarter-report-2020/> accessed 20 July 2024; Usman DJ, 'Consumer Protection in the Nigerian Electric Power Sector' in F Monye (ed) *Compendium of Consumer Protection Law in Nigeria* (Princeton & Associates Publishing Co. Ltd 2022) 250–280

10 The Consumer Protection Council Act, Cap 25, 2004 Laws of the Federation of Nigeria

11 Ugbe R et al., 'Consumer Redress Channels Under Nigerian Laws: Comparative Analysis' (2020) 104 *Journal of Law, Policy, and Globalization* 18–30

12 Ekanem EE, 'Institutional Framework for Consumer Protection in Nigeria' (2011) 2(1) *International Journal of Advanced Legal Studies and Governance* 2

many challenges, especially when consumers are ignorant of their rights. Nigeria law provides for all major types of consumer redress. Yet there remain gaps, problems, and other complexities.

This chapter will examine the evolution of consumer policy and consumer ADR mechanisms in Nigeria. The chapter investigates much of the legislative framework and dispute resolution processes, thus offering efficient and accessible mechanisms for resolving disputes beyond the traditional court channel. It also explores the role of technology, especially the Online Dispute Resolution (ODR), in enhancing ADR mechanisms, addressing the various dispute resolution processes, such as mediation and arbitration and emerging challenges and opportunities. This study underscores the importance of consumer ADR in promoting a fair and conducive business environment for commerce and protecting consumer rights in Nigeria.

Legal Framework for Consumer Protection

The National Consumer Policy of Nigeria plays a central role as it aims to protect the rights and interests of all consumers. It clearly outlines the fundamental principles, objectives, and strategies needed to ensure fair and equitable treatment of consumers in all sectors of the economy.[13] Therefore, an excellent grasp of this policy's principles and objectives is most useful for consumers engaged in commercial transactions as well as legal officers who adjudicate matters in court. This policy fosters sustainable economic development, enhances consumer confidence, and promotes consumer welfare. There are, broadly speaking, six types of principles advocated in Nigeria's National Consumer Policy.[14] These are consumer protection, information and education, redress, choice and competition, health and safety, and sustainability.

As can be seen from the principles enumerated above, the objectives of the policy clearly point out the need to improve consumers' well-being through enhanced protection and empowerment. The objectives of the policy are: (I) establishing and updating the existing legal and regulatory framework for consumer protection, (II) empowering consumers through public awareness campaigns and education by informing them of their rights and responsibilities, (III) providing effective and efficient redress mechanism for consumer protection issues, (IV) preventing unfair business practices by offering consumers variety of choices and ensuring adequate competition among suppliers in the marketplace, (V) ensuring that the consumers have the right to health products and services that meet their needs, and (VI) encouraging consumers to make environmentally sustainable choices. Notably, the overall aim of the policy is to improve the consumer's well-being and ensure that they participate effectively in all sectors of the economy. The Federal Competition

13 See the mandate of the Federal Competition and Consumer Protection Commission, <https://fccpc.gov.ng/about-us/our-mandate/> accessed 20 July 2024

14 For detailed explanations of the six key principles advocated in the National Consumer Policy, see the provisions in the Consumer Protection Framework for Bank and Other Financial Institutions Regulated by the Central Bank of Nigeria

and Consumer Protection Commission is responsible for developing, implementing, monitoring, and evaluating the national consumer policy in Nigeria.[15]

The General Design of the Enforcement Mechanism

Having dealt with virtually all the national consumer policy issues, from the objectives to strategy, it is essential to understand how consumer rights and remedies are governed in Nigeria. There are about six notable legal instruments in relation to consumer rights and remedies.

Relevant Legislation

The Consumer Protection Council Act of 1992 is now repealed.[16] The Consumer Protection Council (CPC) was established by this statute in 1992.[17] The enactment of the CPC Act and the establishment of the Consumer Protection Council automatically provided the legal framework for the protection of consumer rights in Nigeria.[18] As the primary regulatory agency, the CPC was vested with several duties and powers, including resolving consumer disputes, encouraging the development of industry codes of conduct, and undertaking enforcement actions against those who fail to comply with the rules. In addition to its statutory role, it conducts investigations, facilitates dispute settlements, and educates consumers about their rights and other available ADR options.[19] The Council collaborates with other ADR entities, regulatory bodies, industry stakeholders, and consumer rights advocacy groups to enforce consumer protection laws and enhance ADR mechanisms. The CPC is an active member of the Consumer International and International Consumer Protection and Enforcement Network.[20]

The Federal Competition and Consumer Protection Act of 2018 (hereafter referred to as FCCPA) repealed the old Consumer Protection Act.[21] This federal statute governing consumer protection and competition law was signed into law by President Muhammadu Buhari in February 2019 with the mandate to administer and enforce all the provisions of the Act and any other enactment with respect to competition and protection of consumers.[22] To help achieve these objectives, the Federal Competition and Consumer Protection Commission[23] and the Competition and Consumer

15 Federal Competition and Consumer Protection Commission Act of 2018

16 Section 165 of the Federal Competition and Consumer Protection Act of 2018 repealed the Consumer Protection Council Act, CAP C25 LFN 2004

17 Decree No. 66 of 1992, Consumer Protection Council Act

18 Apinega SA, 'Consumer Protection and Remedies in Nigeria: An Appraisal' in Adekunle Adedeji and Shankyula T Samuel (eds) *Law and Principles of Consumer Protection* (National Institute of Advanced Legal Studies 2013)

19 Section 8 CPC Act of 1992

20 See Reports on the Legal Framework for E-Commerce in ECOWAS Countries, <https://unctad.org/system/files/official-document/dtlstict2015d2_en.pdf> accessed 10 May 2024

21 Cap. C25, Laws of the Federation of Nigeria, 2004

22 Section 17(a) FCCP Act of 2018

23 Section 3(1) FCCP Act of 2018

Protection Tribunal were established.[24] The primary objective of the Competition and Consumer Protection Tribunal is to ensure that consumer disputes are handled fairly and effectively through the adjudication process.[25] The FCCPC has various duties and powers, including enforcement of competition and consumer laws, and promotion of fair and regulating market conduct to improve consumer welfare.[26]

The Sale of Goods Act is the primary statute that governs the sale of goods in Nigeria. It exhaustively outlined the rights and remedies available to consumers when there is a breach of contract or defective products. Under this statute, consumers have legal recourse, including the right to reject faulty goods and request replacement or repair. Additionally, the consumers have the right to seek damages in court.[27]

The enactment of the Food and Drugs Act (as amended) received enthusiasm in the 1970s.[28] This federal law was enacted to regulate the production, distribution, and sale of food, drugs, and related products in Nigeria.[29] Also, the Act established standards for labelling, advertising, and product safety to protect consumers from harmful or adulterated goods in the marketplace.

The Standard Organisation of Nigeria Act established the Standard Organisation of Nigeria (SON) administrative agency.[30] This is one of the most notable government agencies that is charged with the responsibility of developing and enforcing product standards, quality control measures, and certificates for businesses.[31]

The National Industrial Court (NIC) Act introduced an internal case management system as an alternative method for resolving issues between parties. The NIC Act established the National Industrial Court, which has jurisdiction over disputes arising from employment-related contracts, industrial relations, consumer-related matters, and consumer rights.

Regulatory Models That Inspired Nigeria's National Regime of Consumer Protection

Dealing with unfair business practices is complex and necessary; however, it also means that collaborative efforts from international organisations and partners cannot be overemphasised. Much of the inspiration for the development of the consumer protection framework in the 1980s and 1990s came primarily from the United Nations. The Nigerian Government's collaboration with international organisations to benchmark its national consumer protection regime has undoubtedly helped adopt international frameworks and best practices.[32]

24 Section 39(1) FCCP Act of 2018
25 Section 39(2) FCCP Act of 2018
26 Section 17(a)(I) FCCP Act of 2018
27 Sale of Goods Act
28 See the Preamble of the Food and Drugs Act of 1976
29 Food and Drugs Act Cap. F. 32 LFN 2004
30 Standards Organisation of Nigeria Act of 2015
31 Standards Organisation of Nigeria Act of 2015
32 The notable United Nations Guidelines for Consumer Protection (2016) provided the bedrock for Nigeria national regime of consumer protection. See United Nations Conference on Trade and

Nigeria's influence from the European Union (involving model, international frameworks, and best practices) was high in the majority of the consumer protection legislation, the enforcement mechanisms, and the promotion of consumer rights across the nation.[33] Furthermore, the results show that influence from the regulatory models from other jurisdictions, including South Africa, the United Kingdom, Canada, the United States, and Australia, served as a model for ensuring a high level of consumer protection within the country. All these models seem to have helped Nigeria adapt and modify its consumer protection institutions and laws to suit its unique legal and socioeconomic context.

Current Consumer Dispute Resolution Processes

In Nigeria, things have changed over time. The consumer's model of transactions has changed drastically since the country gained independence from British colonial rule in 1960. The Federal Competition and Consumer Protection Commission (FCCPC) is a statutory body empowered to promote fair competition and protect consumer rights across Nigeria.[34] The FCCPC, established by the Federal Competition and Consumer Protection Act, has the power to enforce consumer law in Nigeria. Today's consumers are more receptive to outside influences such as social media influencers, mass media, celebrity culture, and media education than before. Relationships between the consumers and the service providers are of continued importance even though the mode of transaction may have changed. In a situation where consumer issues are attended to and allowed to influence, it is likely that consumers will yield and will contribute and become part of the economic community when compared to the type that is limiting consumer participation.

The FCCPC, through its different departments, play a vital role in enforcing consumer protection laws and regulations in Nigeria. As can be seen from the FCCPC mandate, it investigates anti-competitive practices, promotes fair competition, and oversees market conduct.[35] Regarding protecting consumer interests through enforcement actions, public awareness campaigns, and advocacy, the FCCPC performs these tasks through its various departments, including consumer protection, enforcement, competition, and legal services.

Overview of the Structure and Main Characteristics of the FCCPC

In Nigeria, government agencies are often divided into various departments, and the FCCPC is no exception. The FCCPC is generally divided into five departments, namely the Office of the Director-General, the Consumer Protection Department,

Development: UN Guidelines for Consumer Protection (2015) <https://unctad.org/system/files/official-document/dtlstict2015d2en.pdf> accessed 10 May 2024

33 See, European Union, 'Consumer Rights and Consumer Protection' <https://europa.eu/yourerope/business/dealing-with-customers/consumer-rights-andcustomer-service/index_en.htm> accessed 10 May 2024

34 Section 17 (a) (e) (g) (I) FCCP Act of 2018

35 Sections 17 and 18 FCCP Act of 2018

the Legal and Enforcement Department, the Corporate Service Department and the Competition and Market Analysis Department. Many of these departments are structured to effectively enforce consumer protection and competition laws across various sectors of the economy.

A fundamental characteristic of the FCCPC is that it is independent, transparent, collaborative,[36] and proactive in all its operations. With respect to FCCPC operations, whether an investigation or inquiry,[37] the FCCPC always acts as a leader while the government is obliged to provide support through funding and an annual budget. Thus far, the FCCPC is endowed with immeasurable competencies to effectively carry out the enforcement, advocacy, dispute resolution, and regulatory oversight mandate.

Structure of the Nigerian Judicial System

The Nigerian judicial system consists of both federal and state courts. The Supreme Court is the highest and final appellate court.[38] This is the only court with the power to interpret the Constitution and hear appeals from lower courts. It also has original jurisdiction in certain matters, like disputes between federal and state governments.[39] Below the Supreme Court are the Court of Appeal, Federal High Court, and National Industrial Court, which handles both civil and criminal cases. In the same order, specialised courts have been established across the six geopolitical zones to address specific legal matters. These courts are as follows: Customary Court of Appeal and Sharia Court of Appeal. Practically, the Nigerian judicial system has three major tasks: protecting individual rights, interpreting laws, and resolving disputes.[40] One of the significant characteristics and a challenge of the Nigerian judicial system is judicial independence.

The law requires that the Supreme Court and its judges be independent and separate from the executive and legislative branches of government. Other unique features of the Nigerian judicial system are constitutional supremacy, the hierarchy of courts, and access to justice. There is a growing interest in court championing ADR. ADR may include mediation or adjudication, and both suit consumer disputes. A well-functioning judicial system is critical to Nigeria's economic growth.

Courts and Consumer Disputes in Nigeria

Consumer disputes are an inevitable part of Nigeria's thriving economy. The legal system has provided a robust framework that regulates consumer protection and establishes competent courts that handle consumer-related disputes. There is no specialised court in charge of consumer disputes in Nigeria. Although the

36 Section 17(r) FCCP Act of 2018
37 Section 17(e) FCCP Act of 2018
38 Section 230 of the Constitution of the Federal Republic of Nigeria (CFRN), 1999 (as amended)
39 Section 232 of the Constitution of the Federal Republic of Nigeria (CFRN), 1999 (as amended)
40 Section 231 of the Constitution of the Federal Republic of Nigeria (CFRN), 1999 (as amended)

Magistrate Courts play a crucial role in resolving consumer disputes, they are not the only court with such jurisdiction. In most rural areas, the Area Courts hold jurisdiction over consumer disputes.[41] The Federal High Courts hold jurisdiction over civil causes and matters, including consumer disputes.[42] It is noted that various courts in Nigeria have jurisdiction to handle consumer disputes. While Magistrate Courts handle small claims, the High Courts deal with more complex cases.[43]

Legal Aid

The establishment of free legal aid services for indigent individuals, including consumers, was one of the two key developments in the history of ADR across different states in Nigeria.[44] Tribunals and small claim courts have been established in different states across Nigeria since the 1990s. The Federal Government of Nigeria, through the Legal Aid Council Act of 1976 (amended in 2011), established the Legal Aid Council. Still, consumer claims are not included in the cases for legal aid.[45] While some limited aspects of consumer disputes may be covered by legal aid, individuals may be required to meet specific criteria by demonstrating their inability to pay for legal representation.

Alternative Dispute Resolution for Consumer Disputes

Nigeria is a federation comprising 36 States and the Federal Capital Territory (FCT) Abuja. Each is a semi-autonomous political unit with its own court system that shares powers with the federal government as enshrined in the Federal Republic of Nigeria.[46] The constitution allows the state legislative assembly to domesticate the federal laws or make laws in diverse areas, including consumer protection.[47] Some of these laws may also inspire other states within the country. Generally, the Nigerian constitution does not provide outright constitutional provisions on consumer protection. The Constitution of the Federal Republic of Nigeria 1999(as amended) was not partially silent on the aspect of consumer protection as it gives constitutional backing to ADR in section 19, which provides for the settlement of international disputes by arbitration, mediation, conciliation, negotiation, and adjudication.[48] Consumer ADR is not a term commonly used in Nigerian laws. The term "consumer ADR" is not used anywhere in the Federal Constitution. Legal

41 Section 16 Area Courts Act
42 Section 251(1) CFRN, 1999
43 In Nigeria, Magistrate Court are lower Courts within the High Court of the Federal Capital Territory. Magistrate Courts exercise jurisdiction both in criminal and civil matters, for mor information on Magistrate see: <https://www.fcthighcourt.gov.ng/magistrate/> accessed 10 May 2024
44 Notably, the establishment of National Industrial courts, tribunals, and small claim courts were some of the developments that took place withing the judicial system
45 See Second Schedule – Legal Aid Council Act of 1976 (as amended in 2011)
46 Laws of the Federation of Nigeria (LFN), 2004
47 Section 90 of the Constitution of Federal Republic of Nigeria (as amended)
48 See Section 19(d) The Constitution of the Federal Republic of Nigeria 1999

provisions on regulating the settlement of commercial disputes by arbitration and conciliation in Nigeria are disseminated in various Acts. The Arbitration and Conciliation Act is the most known Federal law on arbitration and conciliation.

There is no specific law for regulating Consumer Alternative Dispute Resolution. The Arbitration and Conciliation Act of 1988 (the "ACA") or Arbitration and Mediation Act 2023 ('AMA') tried to provide a framework for laws in this regard. However, a critical analysis of the consumer protection-related laws reveals that there is no law for monitoring commercial disputes which involve Consumer ADR at the federal level. The Consumer Protection Council (CPC) Act, the Federal Competition and Consumer Protection Act of 2018 (FCCPA), and different sector-specific regulations now provide some legal basis for consumer ADR in Nigeria. None of these statutes incorporated the term consumer ADR explicitly. Hosts of different sector legislation that govern the conduct of those sectors in Nigeria also address the settlement of consumer disputes.

There is no known history of Consumer ADR in Nigeria. Before enacting the foremost Consumer Protection legislation, many consumers direct their grievances to the consumer protection unit, a section established in the Federal Ministry of Trade and Industry in Lagos, to address the deficiencies and challenges in business practices. Possibly, this reflects a lack of attention towards consumer law and policy in Nigeria at that time. Recently, in Nigeria, laws, acts, rules, and guidelines have made practical provisions to enhance the adoption of ADR and specify procedures to follow when any organisations adopt the ADR method in disputes involving commercial transactions.

Since the mid-1980s, however, the focus has gradually been on consumer-to-business dispute resolution. The federal government, led by the military, did pay much attention to this plight of consumers, although their consumer decree revealed serious gaps and complications in the country's consumer law.

Since 1992, the government of the Federal Republic of Nigeria has been implementing different consumer reform programmes on consumer protection[49] and consumer alternative dispute resolution. The role of consumer watchdog was assigned to the CPC, which was established in 1992 and operated under the umbrella of the enabling legislation, the Consumer Protection Council Act.[50] Section 2(a) of the Consumer Protection Act (as amended), clearly provides speedy redress to consumers' complaints through negotiation, mediation, and conciliation.[51]

This is the most important legislation for consumer protection in Nigeria – Consumer Protection Council Act No. 66 of 1992 (as CPC Act – amended). The CPC Act established the Consumer Protection Council, Nigeria (CPC).[52] The CPC under

49 The repeal of the 26-year-old Consumer Protection Council Act of 1992 (the 'CPC' or 'Old Act') by The Federal Competition and Consumer Protection Act (the 'FCCPA' or 'New Act') signifies an important legal change

50 Cap 25, Laws of the Federation of Nigeria 2004

51 See CPC, s 2(a), Cap 25, 2004 Laws of the Federation of Nigeria

52 The Consumer Protection Council (CPC) is established under the Consumer Protection Council Act, Cap 25, 2004 Laws of the Federation of Nigeria. They were statutorily mandated to promote the interest of consumers over all products and services

the Consumer Protection Council Act, Cap 25, 2004 Laws of the Federation of Nigeria enforced the consumer protection legislation and served as a template for legislation enacted by each state of the Federation and the Capital Territory Abuja. Notably, this Act was repealed in 2018 and replaced with the new Federal Competition and Consumer Protection Act (FCCP). The new federal legislation on consumer protection was signed into law by President Muhammadu Buhari on 5 February 2019. This Act established a new Federal Competition and Consumer Protection Commission as the latest consumer watchdog.

The Consumer Protection Council Act of 1992 made provisions for establishing the Consumer Protection Council (CPC) as a parastatal of the Federal Government of Nigeria and establishing state committees (for each state), which became non-existent in most states before the Act was repealed in 2018. Through the CPC enabling Act, and as shown previously, the consumers are also empowered to seek redress through state committees and for civil actions for restitution or compensation in a court of competent jurisdiction. Nonetheless, the institution did not commence operations until 1999, when its institutional framework was installed; these institutions were meant to protect consumers and make the marketplace more efficient. Their duties included provisions for the speedy redress of consumers' complaints through negotiation, mediation, and conciliation.[53] However, the Consumer Protection Act of 1992 made provisions for consumers to have speedy redress through the Alternative Dispute Resolution.[54] The CPC was also widely celebrated because it laid the foundation for the consumer protection framework, which has undergone several amendments to reflect evolving global practices.

ADR in Nigeria has evolved significantly in recent years, prompted by the need to provide cost-effective and accessible paths for consumers to redress grievances. Commercial disputes have a distinct characteristic, especially when they involve consumers and retailers (producers) who have unique business relationships that need to be sustained even after the dispute is resolved. Resorting to ADR to settle such disputes becomes more appropriate than going through the courts.[55] When it involves consumers and retailers living in rural communities, resolving such a dispute is essential if the retailer's reputation is to be maintained. The ADR processes could help the parties to preserve their existing relationship and promote reconciliation.[56]

Role of Technology in Consumer ADR

Apart from the substantive effort of the government to expand other forms of ADR processes, the use of ICT in various sectors has also received a significant boost from the Nigerian Communication Commission (NCC). These platforms are often seen as a technological leap forward, showing a streamlined, accessible, and

53 Section 2(a) of CPC Act of 1992
54 Section 2(a) of CPC Act of 1992
55 Chioke AN, *Professional Ethics and Skills in Law* (2nd edn, Kingdom Age Publications 2022) 225
56 Chioke AN, *Professional Ethics and Skills in Law* (2nd edn, Kingdom Age Publications 2022) 226

efficient means of resolving disputes outside the traditional court system. The rise of ODR in Nigeria perhaps typifies why the legal and judicial landscapes have leveraged technology to facilitate the resolution of disputes through digital means. The ODR process includes a variety of methods, including arbitration, mediation, and negotiation, which are conducted mainly online. Several factors can be attributed to the rise of ODR in Nigeria:

It is, of course, not a new observation that things like the COVID-19 pandemic and increased internet penetration necessitated a shift towards remote and digital solutions across many sectors. To facilitate the resolution of consumer disputes in Nigeria, people need to have access to online services through internet penetration. There is also a growing number of internet users in the country, which, according to the Nigeria Communications Commission (NCC), has exceeded 100 million as of 2021.[57] More recently, however, the ODR platforms offered a more efficient alternative to resolving disputes in different court processes.

ADR channels offered another option for consumer redress, especially during the COVID-19 pandemic. In most states in Nigeria, ADR has become a pre-condition for bringing suits before the courts. Nigerian courts grant legal value to electronic communications and virtual hearings, and most mediation sessions have embraced this video conferencing technology in resolving consumer disputes. These innovations are most practical in relation to electricity consumers. The Electricity Act 2023 established the Nigerian Electricity Regulatory Commission (NERC). NERC has established Forum Offices (FOs) in many states of the Federation and FCT Abuja to resolve consumer complaints. Under NERC's Customer Complaints Handling Standards and Procedures Regulations, dissatisfied consumers must submit written complaints either through email or physical presentation to the Customer Complaint Unit (CCU). The regulations require consumer complaints to be resolved expeditiously. The NERC's Second Quarter 2020 report illustrated that the FOs received 1,883 cases plus 932 pending cases from the first quarter of 2020.[58] With these recent developments, parties can save time or overcome logistical challenges by remotely participating in hearings and mediation sessions.

Challenges and Opportunities

Despite the remarkable impact and input of government and non-governmental organisations on the introduction of alternative dispute resolution mechanisms in Nigeria, there are still some challenges and prospects. Since the COVID-19 pandemic, Nigeria has gradually embraced ODR for consumer disputes, but this is not without challenges. It is clear that practical consumer complaints resolution is highly required to ensure that the various complaints brought by consumers in different industries are speedily attended to. While the country has torched new hope among consumers by using ODR for dispute resolution, several factors need to be addressed to ensure the readiness and effectiveness of these platforms.

57 The Consumer Affairs Bureau (2023), <https://consumer.ncc.gov.ng> accessed 20 July 2024>
58 NERC Second Quarter 2020 Report

First, public awareness and sensitivity of consumers regarding the use and benefit of the ADR mechanism. The Government, non-governmental organisations, and the Federal Competition and Consumer Protection Council (FCCPC) should regularly organise public awareness programmes to educate consumers products and services on their rights and the various channels of redress when those rights are breached.

Second, legal and regulatory reform should be implemented. The regulatory regime should be amended to ensure that the various laws on consumer protection are adequately harmonised to cater for new emerging areas of consumer protection in the e-commerce industry. More relevant agencies should be established to undertake administrative and enforcement roles in various consumer protection laws in Nigeria. This positive step will help some agencies to focus more on consumer protection and prevent overlaps in the discharge of statutory duties. For many years, the state, in pursuance of its statutory responsibilities, sought to play a role in consumer protection regulation, though usually this was done indirectly through guidelines and regulations. Reviewing and updating the legal framework has been rare. There have been incidents of legislative inadequacies which need to be updated to accommodate ODR mechanisms and address issues such as enforceability and recognition of digital signatures.

Third, enforcement mechanisms and redress: This is necessary to ensure that regulatory agencies not only serve as watchdogs but also help to encourage internet penetration in Nigeria. Although much has been done to promote internet penetration in Nigeria, there are still gaps in access to reliable internet connectivity, especially in rural areas. These involve adequate infrastructure and connectivity to aid the smooth operations of ODR platforms and ensure equal access for all Nigerian consumers.

Another factor that often slows Nigeria's readiness to move to ODR is that the consumers lack the digital skills to navigate ODR processes. Consumers or litigants could complain of breach of their consumer rights to producers who would want them to lodge their complaint through the digital processes. Many consumers may lack the necessary digital skills or not be familiar with online platforms. The state ought to promote digital literacy and provide user-friendly approaches to ensure consumers' meaningful participation in online dispute resolution.

Although the introduction of ODR platforms for consumer disputes in the last few years was the honouring of an important commitment by the Nigerian government, the rate at which the overlooked training and capacity-building initiatives were substantially below what is usually commendable. Legal professionals or ADR practitioners with limited skills and knowledge required to facilitate ODR processes may not perform effectively. In order to determine whether these professionals will perform effectively, it is, of course, necessary to engage in continuous professional development programs to enhance their competence and confidence in handling online disputes.

Finally, data security issues are one aspect of integrating technology in ADR processes in Nigeria, which has given rise to much concern among consumers. Two preliminary points may be made on this subject. The first paramount issue is ensuring the security and confidentiality of consumers' sensitive information exchanged during online ADR proceedings. The second point is that many consumers have experienced one form of data breach or fraud and, in general, it should not be another process that could put them at online privacy risks that might undermine their trust in online platforms. There is, however, no necessary link-up in ODR platforms between the cybersecurity threats and issues that compromise the integrity of the ADR processes in any established institutions, although it would not usually be reasonable to dismiss the issue of trust and security.

It will be apparent from the previous discussion that technology-driven ADR solutions can enhance access to justice by removing barriers and making dispute resolution more accessible to all consumers. Similar opportunities can be seen when ADR procedures are automated with administrative tasks, reducing the time and resources required to resolve disputes.

Conclusion

Consumer ADR in Nigeria has undergone a series of significant transformations, adapting to modify the consumer landscape. While these phases continue to embrace challenges, efforts are being made to overhaul and strengthen the system, making it more accessible and efficient for all consumers. Equally, consumer ADR has proved to be one of the most effective ways of providing adequate protection for consumers and promoting a conducive business environment for commerce. The enactment of the FCCPA and the establishment of the Commission means that Nigerian consumers will increasingly see an updated consumer protection framework that will strengthen enforcement mechanisms to ensure the adequate protection of consumer rights in the country.

This chapter underscores ADR's critical role in resolving consumer disputes through different agencies in Nigeria. It also highlighted the benefits of ODR platforms, practical challenges, and potential ways to strengthen consumer ADR mechanisms and ensure equitable access to justice for all consumers in Nigeria. Making consumer ADR work in Nigeria requires a collaborative approach involving stakeholders from consumer organisations, the legal community, and the Government. To confront unfair business practices and counter the criticism of various access to justice, the Government needs to work together to ensure fair dispute resolution and adequate protection of consumer rights. With the continued reforms, increased consumer awareness, adoption of technology, and empowerment, the future of Consumer ADR in Nigeria has the potential to improve consumer protection and foster a fair marketplace.

References

Ajetunmobi AO, *Alternative Dispute Resolution & Arbitration in Nigeria, Law, Theory and Practice* (Princeton & Associates Publishing Co. Ltd 2017)

Apinega SA, 'Consumer Protection and Remedies in Nigeria: An Appraisal' in Adekunle Adedeji and Shankyula T. Samuel (eds) *Law and Principles of Consumer Protection* (National Institute of Advanced Legal Studies 2013)

Chioke AN, *Professional Ethics and Skills in Law Practice* (2nd edn, Kingdom Age Publications 2022)
Constitution of the Federal Republic of Nigeria, 1999
Consumer International, <https://www.consumersinternational.org/> accessed 20 July 2024
Consumer Protection Council Act, Cap C25, Laws of the Federation of Nigeria, 2004
Ekanem EE, 'Institutional Framework for Consumer Protection in Nigeria' (2011) 2(1) International Journal of Advanced Legal Studies and Governance
Electricity Act, Laws of the Federation of Nigeria, 2023
Federal Competition and Consumer Protection Commission Act, 2018
Food and Drugs Act, Cap F32, Laws of the Federation of Nigeria, 2004
Institute of Chartered Mediators and Conciliators, <https://www.icmcng.org/> accessed 20 July 2024
Kanyip BB, *Consumer Protection in Nigeria: Law, Theory and Policy* (Rekon Books Limited Abuja 2005)
Lysonski S and Durvasula S, 'Nigeria in Transition: Acculturation to Global Consumer Culture' (2013) 30(6) Journal of Consumer Marketing 493, 508
Monye F (ed), *Compendium of Consumer Protection Law in Nigeria* (Princeton & Associates Publishing Co. Ltd 2022)
Monye F, *Law of Consumer Protection* (Spectrum Books Ltd 2003)
Monye FN, *The Consumer Protection in Nigeria: Struggles, Burdens, and Hopes*. An Inaugural Lecture of the University of Nigeria; delivered on 26 May 2011
National Policy on Consumer Protection, Federal Ministry of Trade and Investment, 2019
Reports on the Legal Framework for E-Commerce in ECOWAS Countries, <https://unctad.org/system/files/official-document/dtlstict2015d2_en.pdf> accessed 10 May 2024
Sale of Goods Act, Laws of the Federation of Nigeria, 1893
Standards Organisation of Nigeria Act, Cap S9, Laws of the Federation of Nigeria
The Consumer Affairs Bureau, (2023) <https://consumer.ncc.gov.ng> accessed 20 July 2024
The Global State of Financial Inclusion and Consumer Protection, 2022, <https://documents.worldbank.org/en/publication/documents-reports/documentdetail/099013124180517721/p16239315d0da60591bd9c1b6325ce5c6ef> accessed 20 July 2024
The Lagos Multi-Door Courthouse, <https://lagosmultidoor.org.ng> accessed 20 July 2024
The Mandate of the Federal Competition and Consumer Protection Commission, <https://fccpc.gov.ng/about-us/our-mandate/> accessed 20 July 2024
The National Industrial Court of Nigeria ADR Centre, <https://nicnadr.gov.ng/adr/about.php> accessed 20 July 2024
The Nigerian Communications Commission, <https://consumer.ncc.gov.ng/> accessed 20 July 2024
The Nigerian Institute of Chartered Arbitrators (NICArb), <https://www.nicarb.org/> accessed 20 July 2024
Ugbe R, Anyatang BF, Kooffreh BB and Agi A, 'Consumer Redress Channels Under Nigerian Laws: Comparative Analysis' (2020) 104 Journal of Law, Policy, and Globalization 18, 30
United Nations Guidelines for Consumer Protection, (2016) UNCTAD/DITC/CPLP/MISC/2016/1

16 Consumer ADR in Pakistan

Muhammad Danyal Khan

Introduction

The lengthy case duration and the unbearable burden of political cases are persistent problems Pakistan faces. Thus, there is a dire need to revolutionise the legal processes and switch the legal system to ADR, which is a viable solution. The implementation of the Alternate Dispute Resolution Act 2017 is a crucial step in this regard, as it was implemented to provide speedy and less expensive alternatives. This chapter deals with ADR's growth, implementation, and impacts in Pakistan, particularly on consumer disputes and litigation alternatives. It enlists hurdles to the effective adoption of ADR in Pakistan and examines the role of technology in curbing those obstacles. It highlights the need for legislative reforms necessary to fully mainstream ADR into Pakistan's legal framework. This chapter will explore the role of ADR in transforming the judicial system of Pakistan into a speedier, more accessible, and just system.

Legal Framework for Consumer Protection

The Constitution of the Islamic Republic of Pakistan establishes a federal form of government. It outlines the administrative structure, which includes four provinces: Balochistan, Khyber Pakhtunkhwa, Punjab, and Sindh.[1] Additionally, the administrative setup comprises the Islamabad Capital Territory and two parts of Pakistan-administered Kashmir: Azad Jammu and Kashmir and Gilgit-Baltistan.[2] The federal structure has to divide power and authority in such a manner that there is a balance between central and provincial governments.[3] Article 18 of the

1 Constitution of Islamic Republic of Pakistan 1973, Article 1; Iram Khalid, 'Politics of Federalism in Pakistan: Problems and Prospects' (2020) 28(1) *South Asian Studies* 199, 212

2 Bakhtiar Khan, Arif Khan and Sajjad Ali, 'Reforms in the Erstwhile Federally Administered Tribal Areas of Pakistan: A Critical Analysis' (2022) 3(3) *Journal of Humanities, Social and Management Sciences (JHSMS)* 104–115

3 Muhammad Ahsan Rana, 'Decentralization Experience in Pakistan: The 18th Constitutional Amendment' (2020) 17(1) *Asian Journal of Management Cases* 61–84

DOI: 10.4324/9781032689739-16

Constitution of the Islamic Republic of Pakistan guarantees all and sundry an inalienable right to carry on lawful trade, business, and profession.[4]

The 18th Amendment, dated 19 April 2010, is a benchmark in Pakistan's history towards decentralisation.[5] This was the key amendment that guaranteed the separation of powers among federation and provinces, creating a significant amount of decentralisation. The powers given to the provinces include consumer protection, education, and health.[6] The separation of legislative power impeded local issues and the needs at the provincial government level.[7] Consumer protection is a significant aspect of governance and has attracted a lot of attention from legislation both at the federal and provincial levels.[8] It also highlighted the demand for clear and effective consumer protection laws at both levels. The Islamabad Capital Territory and the provinces have thus framed their own sets of laws that aim to protect consumers' rights and interests.

In a country like Pakistan, where the rule of law is depleting, terrorism is a constant threat, and the economy remains fractured, the emergence of consumer protection laws can be seen as quite a notable development.[9] During the past two decades, the situation in Pakistan has considerably changed regarding consumer rights protection due to the tenacity of archaic statutes like the [Punjab] Weights and Measures Ordinance of 1965.[10] The importance of strong consumer rights and interest protection mechanisms arose with the intricate socio-political environment and unpredictable economic conditions.[11] The consumer issues were first slowly recognised by early legislation such as The Price Control and Prevention of Profiteering and Hoarding Act of 1997[12] and the Monopolies and Restrictive Trade Practices Ordinance of 1970.[13] However, these were inadequate remedies and did not cover the level where a legislative frame was addressed for the multifarious challenges consumers face in a dynamic marketplace. Although Pakistan faces several

4 Saima Bazmi, 'Politico-Judicial Activism in Pakistan: A Historical Overview' (2022) 4(3) *Pakistan Journal of Social Research* 97, 104

5 Constitution of Islamic Republic of Pakistan 1973, Article 18

6 SA Khan, 'Situation Analysis of Health Care System of Pakistan: Post 18 Amendments' (2019) 7(3) *Health Care Current Reviews* 244

7 Adeel Ahmad et al., 'A Synthesis of Spatial Forest Assessment Studies Using Remote Sensing Data and Techniques in Pakistan' (2021) 12(9) Forests 1211

8 Ms Sohni Siddiqui, Zahid Ahmed and Aneeta Memon, 'Impact of Devolution on Education in Pakistan in the Light of 18th Amendment: A Review Article' (2021) 10 *The Government-Annual Research Journal of Political Science* 82, 93

9 Haider Mahmood, Muhammad Tanveer and Maham Furqan, 'Rule of Law, Corruption Control, Governance, and Economic Growth in Managing Renewable and Non-Renewable Energy Consumption in South Asia' (2021) 18(20) *International Journal of Environmental Research and Public Health* 10637

10 The Punjab Weights and Measures Ordinance of 1965 (W.P. Ord. XXXIII of 1965)

11 Nazneen Durrani, Kaneez Fatima, and Jamil Ahmed, 'The Role of Economic and Political Factors in Shaping Consumers' Confidence in Pakistan' (2023) 3(2) *Journal of Social Sciences Review* 718, 735

12 Price Control and Prevention of Profiteering and Hoarding Act, 1977

13 The Monopolies and Restrictive Trade Practices (Control and Prevention) Ordinance of 1970 (Ordinance NO. V OF 1970)

challenges, the development of consumer protection legislation certainly attests to the regard in which the country holds the promotion of a fair and transparent business environment.[14] Such laws not only bring rigidity in the measures of unfair trade practices but also open paths for consumers to seek compensation against their grievances.[15] As now, the country faces these daunting challenges, the development of consumer protection laws would go a long way toward safeguarding the rights and welfare of the people in the conduct of business and trade.

The ADR has long been recognised as a workable and culturally acceptable conflict resolution system in Pakistan.[16] ADR consisted of different forms, particularly community-based efforts such as Panchayats and Jirgas. The experienced people and notables of the community come together to resolve disputes through mutual consensus and use mediation in these practices.[17] Such forums have always played a significant role in maintaining social harmony and resolving disputes at the local level, which is often accepted by all parties involved in a conflict. During the reign of the British, the ADR got formal recognition and was institutionally established in Pakistan in the 1940s.[18] The British government recognised the potential of ADR in resolving disputes. Thus, they tried to institutionalise ADR in the legal system by formal arbitration structures. This process was carried on with a special focus on local customs, traditions, and common law norms.[19] Henceforth, ADR has proven an impetus in shaping the legal system of Pakistan without resorting to formal court procedures.[20] It gives people and groups an affordable, effective, and speedy way to resolve disputes. The adaptability of ADR to the needs of Pakistan made it a universally accepted and workable method of resolving disputes. Soon after the acceptance of the ADR Act of 2017 by the federal government, similar acts were enacted in Punjab in 2019 and in Khyber Pakhtunkhwa in 2020.

The Islamabad Consumer Protection Act of 1995 adopted ADR as the first move by the federal capital towards a proper legal framework for consumers to address complaints. The Khyber Pakhtunkhwa Consumer Protection Law of 1997[21] followed this, and it extended consumer protection measures to its province. In 2003, Balochistan enacted the Balochistan Consumer Protection Act; the two followed

14 Aatir Rizvi et al., 'Consumer Protection and Protectionism in Pakistan: Regulatory Framework, Issues and Solutions' (2023) *Journal of Positive School Psychology* 1339, 1355

15 Sajid Hussain Qureshi, Asif Shahzad, and Naima Saeed, 'White-Collar Crimes in Pakistan: A Comprehensive Study of Nature, Laws, and Enforcement Mechanisms' (2023) *International Journal of Social Science and Entrepreneurship* 45, 63

16 Ikram Ullah, 'Interim Measures in Arbitration Under the Pakistani Legal Regime' (2013) 29(4) *Arbitration International* 653, 670

17 S Muhktar and M Khan, 'Remedies to Challenge Arbitral Awards in Pakistan' (2017) 1(1) *Journal of Asian Research* 14, 28

18 Jan Paulsson, 'Arbitration in Three Dimensions' (2011) 60(2) *International and Comparative Law Quarterly* 291, 323

19 Samza Fatima, 'Alternative Dispute Resolution in the Light of Arbitration Laws' (2022) 4(3) *Pakistan Journal of Social Research* 831, 838

20 Samza Fatima, 'Alternative Dispute Resolution in the Light of Arbitration Laws' (2022) 4(3) *Pakistan Journal of Social Research* 831, 838

21 The [Khyber Pakhtunkhwa] Consumers Protection Act of 1997

suit in 2005 with The Punjab Consumer Protection Act and The Sindh Consumer Protection Act of 2015.[22] These provincial acts are general and will have as their object the provision of a comprehensive framework for all matters related to consumer rights, quality of goods and services, misleading advertisements, and unfair trade practices.[23] The legislative efforts clearly attempt to create an environment in which consumers can make informed choices and find remedies for the injury of their rights. In this particular context, the Punjab Consumer Protection Act 2005 and the Sindh Consumer Protection Act 2015 have already established consumer protection courts, further showing their seriousness in establishing an expedited and economical system of justice for all consumers.[24] This is a positive outcome of the devolution of power through the 18th Amendment, which opened up opportunities for provinces to make laws on their own regarding consumer protection. Pakistan has a comprehensive legal framework for the protection of the rights and interests of consumers.

The General Design of the Enforcement Mechanism

Pakistan has officially moved to take critical steps towards safeguarding consumers' rights by signing UN Resolution No. 39/248 of 1985.[25] This resolution sets the legitimate needs of consumers globally and serves as an advisory document for nations. It highlights the importance of protecting consumer rights. This resolution majorly covers three fundamental consumer needs: promotion and protection of economic interests, protection from hazards to health and safety, and the availability of effective compensation methods for consumers.[26] It also covers subsequent rights. The Government of Pakistan must ensure that all consumers enjoy their fundamental rights as enshrined in this resolution and also recognise the significance of consumer protection.

These policies must focus on fundamental consumer rights, including protection, representation, compensation, information, education, freedom of choice, access to necessities, and a healthy environment.[27] There is a dire need to establish and maintain a refined infrastructure for the development, implementation, and monitoring of consumer protection policies. This infrastructure is essential

22 The Sindh Consumer Protection Act of 2014. Sindh Act No. XVII of 2015

23 Maheen Masood and Mehrukh Salman, 'The Role of Deceptive Advertisements and Ethical Decision Outcomes in Determining Buying Behavior' (2023) 14(2) *The Business and Management Review* 23, 35

24 Love Kumar et al., 'Opportunities and Constraints for Cleaner Production Policy in the Developing World: A Case Study of Sindh Region, Pakistan' [2023] *Environment, Development and Sustainability* 1, 44

25 Abid Ahasan Rupam, 'Consumer Legal Forum of Bangladesh: A Comparative Study with India and Pakistan' (2023) 1(1) *Law and Society Students' Journal* 12

26 Abid Ahasan Rupam, 'Consumer Legal Forum of Bangladesh: A Comparative Study with India and Pakistan' (2023) 1(1) *Law and Society Students' Journal* 12

27 Muhammad Saad Masud Khan et al., 'Philanthropy and Socio-economic Development: The Role of Large Indigenous Voluntary Organizations in Bridging Social Divides in Pakistan' [2023] *Voluntas: International Journal of Voluntary and Nonprofit Organizations* 1, 12

for protecting and promoting consumers' economic rights. This will also ensure effective mechanisms for the compensation of their grievances.[28] Following UN guidelines, the government should establish consumer courts and consumer protection councils. These forums will assist consumers in claiming compensation in case of disputes, violations, or harm caused by products or services.[29] The resolution enumerates many subsequent rights, including the right to protection from hazardous products, the right to claim damages, the right to information, freedom of choice, and the right to a healthy environment.[30] This resolution thus creates a framework that protects and empowers consumers in the marketplace.[31] Pakistan can streamline itself with international standards by implementing these laws and mechanisms. This will also make a just and safe economic zone where consumers' rights will be respected and protected.

The ideal scenario in market dynamics is often considered one of perfect competition. In a perfectly competitive market, individual sellers have no control over the price of the commodity. They act as price takers and sell a negligible portion of the total output. This market structure ensures that consumers have a variety of choices and can purchase goods at prevailing market prices. However, in reality, this ideal is often not met, necessitating robust consumer protection measures. The UN resolution and Pakistan's commitment to it acknowledge the challenges consumers face and emphasise the importance of creating a marketplace that safeguards their rights. This commitment reflects not only a legal obligation but also a moral imperative to ensure that consumers are treated fairly, have access to essential information, and are protected from any risks to their well-being.[32] By adopting these measures, Pakistan can create a marketplace that serves the best interests of consumers and thus promotes economic fairness and stability.

Current Consumer Dispute Resolution Processes

To formally materialise its commitment to safeguarding the interests and rights of citizens and consumers from all walks of life, Pakistan established the Consumer

28 Yasir Jehan et al., 'Socio-Economic and Environmental Impacts of Tourism on Local Community in Gilgit Baltistan, Pakistan: A Local Community Prospective' (2023) 14(1) *Journal of the Knowledge Economy* 180, 199

29 Nazneen Durrani, Kaneez Fatima, and Jamil Ahmed (n 12)

30 Erum Shaikh et al., 'Customer Satisfaction and Customer Loyalty: An Empirical Case Study on the Impact of Benefits Generated Through Smartphone Applications' (2023) 12(1–2) *International Journal of Public Sector Performance Management* 119, 139

31 Mirza Huzaifa Asif et al., 'Determining the Influencing Factors of Consumers' Attitude Toward Renewable Energy Adoption in Developing Countries: A Roadmap Toward Environmental Sustainability and Green Energy Technologies' (2023) 30(16) *Environmental Science and Pollution Research* 47861, 47872

32 Mirza Huzaifa Asif et al., 'Assessing Eco-Label Knowledge and Sustainable Consumption Behavior in Energy Sector of Pakistan: An Environmental Sustainability Paradigm' (2023) 30(14) *Environmental Science and Pollution Research* 413, 432

Rights Commission of Pakistan (CRCP) in 1998.[33] CRCP focuses on those underprivileged groups within the society to bring about positive change and a culture of consumer rights awareness in Pakistan. The CRCP was designed as a game changer and a platform that protects and empowers consumers. It mainly focuses on the protection of those who may be at the margins or are voiceless within the socio-economic setup.[34] The commission acknowledges that there is still a strong need for targeted efforts to protect those whose interests are threatened by systemic challenges in asserting their rights within the marketplace. The mission of CRCP is remarkable in the sense that it proceeds with the agenda to help an organised movement in Pakistan. To transform single cases into collective pressure for consumer rights at the national level, the commission will commit itself to this end.[35] Thus, unity will prove to be the strength and multiply the impact of consumer protection campaigns. This aims to ensure that all the citizens of Pakistan benefit equally from legally enforceable rights.

The CRCP has played an integral role in sensitising the public regarding consumer rights, educating them on their rights, and giving citizens a platform to address their concerns.[36] This paves the way for informed and empowered consumers who create accountability on the side of businesses and service providers. Moreover, the CRCP is designed to apply legal rights, not merely through theories but through practical means. The commission advocates for and partook in making laws and regulations that protect consumers by helping create a solid legal framework that addresses the challenges in today's marketplace. The establishment of the Consumer Rights Commission of Pakistan in 1998 depicts the institution's dedication to social justice and empowerment.[37] The CRCP has played a vital role in making the landscape of Pakistan consumer-friendly by empowering underprivileged groups through an organised movement and advocacy of legally enforceable rights, such as those created under the new law. Consequently, citizens can ensure their rights and interests in the market irrespective of their socio-economic background.

Before the enactment of specific legislation such as the Islamabad Consumer Protection Act 1995, a study conducted on consumer protection laws in the pre-modern age revealed that general contract and tort principles were applied.[38] In this age, consumers had little protection from unprincipled commercial practices and concomitant product problems. In contrast, the post-modern legislation

33 Asmara Farzand and Adnan Rahman, 'Analysis of the Legislation Pertaining to Consumer Protection in Punjab: A Legal Perspective With Case Laws' (2023) 5(2) *Journal of Law and Social Studies (JLSS)* 192, 202

34 Consumer Rights Commission of Pakistan in 1998 <https://crcp.org.pk/> accessed 17 April 2024

35 Consumer Rights Commission of Pakistan in 1998 <https://crcp.org.pk/> accessed 17 April 2024

36 Iram A Khan and Muhammad Waqas, 'What Ails Thee Knight Sans Arms: Status of Consumer Protection in Pakistan' (2011) 2(2) *International Journal of Business and Social Science* 242, 248

37 Iram A Khan and Muhammad Waqas, 'What Ails Thee Knight Sans Arms: Status of Consumer Protection in Pakistan' (2011) 2(2) *International Journal of Business and Social Science* 242, 248

38 Kishwar Khan and Sarwat Aftab, 'Consumer Protection in Islam: The Case of Pakistan' (2000) 39(4) Australian Economic Papers 483

provided by the Islamabad Consumer Protection Act, which was subsequently replicated at the provincial level, takes a broader and more detailed view of consumer rights.[39] Due to their flexibility, pre-modern laws often brought many inadvertent decisions with inconsistent protection. This paper tries to analyse the possibility and limitations of both the frameworks of the pre-modern laws against a possible robust pre-modernist consumer protection regime in the post-modern laws. Consumer protection laws of Pakistan are in line with international standards, and that underscores the fact that it is a matter of urgency for any country to take the measures necessary to protect the rights and interests of the population. Though academic discussion supports a Shariah-based formula for consumer protection laws, the review of federal and provincial laws establishes that they largely follow international statutes and hardly rely on religious doctrine.[40]

By drawing from other global models and conventions, the laws provide for fair business practice, product safety, and dispute settlement. However, cultural and religious considerations can never be ignored completely. Regarding the consumer protection laws in Pakistan, the foundation of Shariah is not directly amalgamated into the framework of laws.[41] This fact reflects a conscious effort to bring out these laws in alignment with broader international norms and standards, thereby making them of a more secular nature. For their part, consumer protection laws in Pakistan trace from the doctrines enunciated on product liability under the common law. The legal regime, thus, translates the direction set for other countries under the leading case of *Donoghue v Stevenson* (1932).[42] These came along with various other legislations enacted by former West Pakistan and were given fresh impetus by placing a couple of new laws directly to protect the rights of the consumers. For instance, the earlier legislations were the Pure Food Ordinance of 1960,[43] which provided for the safety and quality of consumables, and the Pakistan Hotels and Restaurants Act of 1976,[44] which provided minimum standards for the hospitality industry. Though the primary scope of the PSQCA Act 1996[45] is the safety of products, and it does not specifically deal with product liability, the very enactment of this piece of law goes a long way to reflect an overall commitment to the cause of quality assurance.

The legislative setup broadened by the following enactment, the Pharmacy Act of 1967 and the Drugs Act of 1976.[46] To bring effective control over pricing and prevent undue profiteering, regulatory authorities were created, which include the Pakistan Telecommunication Authority (PTA), Natural Gas Regulatory Authority,

39 Khan and Waqas (n 36) 245

40 Nur Hikmah Yahya and Rosmawati Mohamad Rasit, 'Muslim Consumer Rights Based on Islamic Advertising Principles' (2019) 41(1) *Islamiyyat* 83, 92

41 Fatima Khaleel, Pervez Zamurrad Janjua, and Mumtaz Ahmed, 'Ethical Consideration of Islamic Banks in Pakistan: An Empirical Analysis' (2022) 13(6) *Journal of Islamic Marketing* 1351, 1372

42 Fatima Khaleel, Pervez Zamurrad Janjua, and Mumtaz Ahmed, 'Ethical Consideration of Islamic Banks in Pakistan: An Empirical Analysis' (2022) 13(6) *Journal of Islamic Marketing* 1351, 1372

43 The Punjab Pure Food Ordinance of 1960 (Ordinance VII, 1960)

44 The Pakistan Hotels and Restaurants Act of 1976 Act No. LXXXI, 1976

45 Pakistan Standards and Quality Control Authority (PSQCA) Act of 1996

46 Pharmacy Act of 1967

and National Electric Power Regulatory Authority. The legal cover is provided through the Federal Ombudsman Order of 1983,[47] the Price Control and Prevention of Profiteering and Hoarding Act of 1997,[48] and the Pakistan Penal Code (1860). However, they were not consumer rights orientated at the first instance. The breakthrough finally came in 1994 when the National Assembly of Pakistan and the Senate began a detailed debate on consumer rights legislation. In 1995 the Islamabad Consumer Protection Act was promulgated – a great step forward. This act established a more advanced legal framework to protect the rights and interests of consumers in the country of Pakistan. It was aimed at deceptions in marketing and matters of unfair trade under the Islamabad Consumer Protection Act, thus offering a way of redress to the consumers and handling disputes. This legislative milestone paved the way for all other consumer laws at federal and provincial levels and emphasised further detailed and direct guidance to safeguard the rights of consumers. One can trace the development of consumer protection in Pakistan from indirect safeguards present throughout the disparate statutes to a more concentrated legal framework devised to protect consumers, along with ensuring accountability within commercial transactions.

Alternative Dispute Resolution for Consumer Disputes

Overview

Pakistan has taken a great leap in arbitration by promulgating the Alternate Dispute Resolution Act 2017.[49] The said enactment reflects a step more significant for the specific court within the legal system under subordination to either amendment to Order X, Rule 1, of the Code of Civil Procedure 1908[50] or provision of discretion by the court for offering ADR to litigating parties. The Alternate Dispute Resolution Act 2017 has, in essence, been one that aimed at the reduction of the burden on the civil courts through court-driven cases transfer to ADR systems.[51] According to Article 3, courts have the right to make an order regarding any matter to ADR if satisfied that the case can most effectively be determined by resorting to such a method. Further, Article 10(5) discusses that the parties must establish evidence through which the legitimacy of the award is achieved before issuing an enforcement plea to the court.[52] Additionally, the ADR engagement is notified before the legal proceeding is pursued in the court.[53] The whole purpose of this legislative framework in its enactment is to promote the use of ADR to speed up conflict

47 Federal Ombudsman Order of 1983
48 Price Control and Prevention of Profiteering and Hoarding Act of 1997
49 Sung-Kwon Won, 'Overview of Alternate Dispute Resolution With Special Reference to Arbitration Laws in Pakistan' (2013) 23 *Journal of Arbitration Studies* 149
50 Alternate Dispute Resolution Act 2017
51 Alternate Dispute Resolution Act 2017
52 Alternate Dispute Resolution Act 2017, section 3
53 Alternate Dispute Resolution Act 2017, section 10(1)

resolution deliberately while, at the same time, relieving the official court system from the associated burden in Pakistan.[54]

The level of achievement of this ADR Act in Pakistan remains in the early stages of practice, with fluctuating levels of development and achievement in various regions. ADR is also observed to be faster in areas with a high concentration of education. The prevalence of ADR in Islamabad has been relatively higher than in places where literacy has proved challenging. This success was due to higher levels of education, advanced comprehension of ADR processes, establishment of ADR structures, availability of highly skilled professionals, supported legal framework, and effective government support. Implementation of the ADR Act faces various challenges in Punjab and KPK.[55] These issues include limited access to the services, lack of experience among the service providers, weak infrastructure, financial constraints, inadequate resources, and relatively weaker legislative frameworks. Furthermore, deeply rooted customary practices like Jirgas and cultural norms may deter people from participating in formal ADR processes.[56] Thus, overcoming these barriers and proactively sensitising the masses about ADR techniques is essentially required if the ADR Act in Punjab and KPK is to be meaningfully enforced. Beyond that, a successful, effective, and extensive acceptance of ADR at a national level can only be achieved through concerted efforts among the government, civil society, and other stakeholders to make it accessible. While the ADR Act is an encouraging step towards the promotion of ADR in Pakistan, there is still a lot that needs to be done if ADR has to reach its maximum potential in terms of fostering a more amicable and just society. Legal impediments should also be removed to make ADR more effective in KPK by making it less dependent on traditional methods of dispute settlement such as Jirgas and Panchayats. The establishment of specialised ADR centres is another crucial step. Moreover, due to a lack of information and understanding of the role of ADR in resolving disputes, it is vital to enlighten and increase awareness of the importance of ADR among the people of Pakistan to put this into practice effectively. Pakistan can remove these barriers and take full advantage of ADR for dispute resolution by implementing a targeted, coordinated strategy.

Modern Consumer ADR Challenges in Pakistan

On a note of the concept of ADR in Pakistan, there is a growing consensus that there is a pressing requirement for thorough training of mediators and arbitrators.[57] This involves fostering a deep understanding of the local socio-cultural dynamics. Although ADR has the potential to resolve disputes efficiently, it is opposed by some organisations and individuals, mainly lawyers, who fear that its usage would

54 Alternate Dispute Resolution Act 2017, section 13

55 Fatima (n 21) 836

56 Fatima (n 21) 836

57 Muhammad Ramzan and Kashif Mahmood, 'Rationalizing Alternate Dispute Resolution in Pakistan' (2016) 6(1) *International Journal of Research in Social Sciences* 88, 95

deprive them of work.[58] This is, however, not the case because the widespread use of ADR tools will not only ensure a reduction in the backlog faced by the courts currently but also create new opportunities for lawyers or legal professionals to specialise in this field, which is expanding fast.[59] Through mediation, the parties can easily cut through the long and complex procedure of litigation and settle for just a couple of weeks instead of spending years within the courts. The issues of ADR and arbitration in Pakistan, on the other hand, are deeply rooted within the framework of the state. The Arbitration Act of 1940, while it is valid and enforceable, is quite archaic in practical application and could use some serious amendments or serious revamping.[60] This law involves heavy court intervention, which renders the arbitration process as cumbersome as common litigation. Although some steps forward in the way of recent legislation have been made in the form of the ADR Act of 2017 and its linked provincial acts, there is still a long way to go.[61] A party that elects to arbitrate will frequently apply to a court to intervene in various administrative and procedural matters. As a result, the entire process might render it inactive for a long time or there could be a lot of delay in the process of arbitration.

Moreover, many misconceptions and myths are still attached, discouraging the efficient implementation of ADR in Pakistan. The idea that there can be any universal application of ADR ignores several modes of ADR and how each enforces the decision. Moreover, patriarchal tendencies adhere to the concept of over-governmental control over the ADR systems and, therefore, ruin their independence and power. Uncertainty in the current legislation raises a couple more issues that hamper the effective use of the ADR mechanisms. Moreover, the commonest understanding is that ADR increases costs and is solely responsible for all the ills of the legal system. Here, it is pertinent to appreciate that while ADR is a flexible toolkit for conflict management at every stage, its application today is not prevalent in Pakistan's legal setup. Even though there are established benefits of both ADR and arbitration in other societies, this credibility has primarily been unnoticed in its effectiveness at enhancing the judicial system in Pakistan due to various limitations. To place Pakistan in a position to take full benefit of ADR, there is an indispensable need for far-reaching reformation in the area of judiciary, legislation, and the legal profession.

Overcoming such challenges would invariably call for systematic changes in the mode of the country's legal system. Also, there is a need to create awareness of the benefits of ADR for legal practitioners, litigants, and particularly the public. Mediation training programs for mediators, along with arbitrators' programs, should

58 Ali Khan and Muhammad Mumtaz, 'Justice Delayed is Justice Denied: Access to Speedy Justice and Alternative Dispute Resolution System in Pakistan' *Journal of Law and Social Policy* 80

59 Majid Ali and Li Lu Geng, 'Alternative Dispute Resolution (ADR) in Pakistan: The Role of Lawyers in Mediation Procedure' (2019) 6(4) *International Journal of Research* 421, 430

60 Ramsha Iftekhar, Dua Wajid Khan, and Fatima Wattoo, 'Critical Analysis of Mediation Law of Islamabad (Alternative Dispute Resolution Act, 2017)' (2022) 6(1) *Islamabad Law Review* 40, 56

61 Ramsha Iftekhar, Dua Wajid Khan, and Fatima Wattoo, 'Critical Analysis of Mediation Law of Islamabad (Alternative Dispute Resolution Act, 2017)' (2022) 6(1) *Islamabad Law Review* 40, 56

encompass local settings and cultural norms to ensure better the effectiveness of dispute resolution within changing socio-cultural contexts. Though ADR has the potential to reduce the burden of Pakistan's legal system, its mass implementation faces many barriers. However, these are just issues that can be dealt with vigorously pursuing changes in law, skills and knowledge, and public understanding. Pakistan will be adept at handling them and harnessing the transformative power of ADR to lay down a system effectively, easily, and most importantly, equitably, settling their disputes.

Role of Technology in Consumer ADR – Online Dispute Resolution for Consumer Disputes

Pakistan is currently experiencing a surge in online trading activities. However, the country's legal landscape needs a dedicated legal framework for online dispute resolution (ODR), and a conspicuous gap needs to be addressed.[62] Although online trade has experienced a significant increase at the private level due to the growing prevalence of e-commerce platforms, the need for state-level regulation for online trade raises concerns about the effectiveness and fairness of dispute resolution mechanisms in this burgeoning sector.[63] Online trading has become an integral part of Pakistan's economic landscape, with a growing number of businesses and consumers engaging in digital transactions. The rapid growth of the online sector is undeniable.[64] Therefore, it is necessary to implement a comprehensive legal framework to address the inevitable disputes that arise during online transactions.

The reality of online trade in Pakistan highlights the need for a robust legal framework for online dispute resolution. Although private entities have made progress in implementing ODR systems, the need for a standardised and legally mandated structure at the state level presents a significant challenge.[65] State-level regulation for online trade is not only an inevitable reality but also a pressing need to ensure that the rights of both consumers and businesses are adequately protected in the digital sphere. Online trade has prominently integrated ODR systems rooted in the broader framework of ADR.[66] Multinational vendors such as Amazon and Alibaba have successfully adopted ODR mechanisms, streamlining trade

62 Naureen Akhtar et al., "Online Dispute Resolution as a Solution to E-Commerce Disputes: A Comparative Study of Pakistan and UK' (2022) 28(3) *Journal of Contemporary Issues in Business and Government* 150, 159

63 Serkan Kaya and Muhammad Danyal Khan, 'Online Dispute Resolution in Pakistan: Challenges and Opportunities' (2022) 7(2) *Journal of Nusantara Studies (JONUS)* 103, 119

64 Serkan Kaya and Muhammad Danyal Khan, 'Online Dispute Resolution in Pakistan: Challenges and Opportunities' (2022) 7(2) *Journal of Nusantara Studies (JONUS)* 103, 119

65 Zafar lqbal Kalanauri, 'Electronic Filing System, Virtual Courts and Online Dispute Resolution-Need of the Hour for Pakistan Legal System' (2021) 5(1) *International Journal for Electronic Crime Investigation* 17, 30

66 Sohail Ahmad Phatak et al., 'Alternate Dispute Resolution-Free and Speedy Complaints Redressal Framework Using Technology: Ombudsmanship at Proverbial Doorsteps in Pakistan' (2022) 22(3) *IJCSNS* 223, 344

processes, and reducing dependence on traditional remedial systems governed by civil laws and the often-cumbersome procedures of classical courts.

However, Pakistan's progressing online trade sector is not immune to challenges, especially in dispute resolution. Disputes arising from online transactions require a nuanced and efficient resolution mechanism that aligns with the dynamic nature of e-commerce and provides a quick and accessible means for dispute resolution. To cope with these challenges, Pakistan needs to establish a legislative and policy framework for online dispute resolution, adhering to the principles laid down by the United Nations Commission on International Trade Law (UNCITRAL).[67] These guidelines provide a comprehensive and international foundation for establishing the ODR system to ensure that the legal framework aligns with global standards and practices.

This development of a solid legislative and policy framework for ODR in Pakistan would greatly benefit the growth and sustainability of the online trade sector. Such a framework would boost confidence in consumers and businesses and ensure a just and efficient mechanism to resolve disputes arising from online transactions.[68] In addition, this would establish Pakistan as a progressive participant in the worldwide digital economy, promoting confidence and attracting foreign investment in the rapidly expanding online trade sector. Despite the remarkable growth of online trade in Pakistan, the lack of a legal framework for resolving online disputes creates a major obstacle. Pakistan must act promptly to develop a legislative and policy framework for ODR in line with UNCITRAL guidelines, as state-level regulation is the only viable solution.[69] This strategic move will not only resolve the current challenges faced by the online trade sector but also make Pakistan a leader in adopting innovative and globally recognised solutions in the current era.

Challenges and Opportunities

Pakistan's consumer ADR system heavily relies on courts, primarily due to the complex legal structure emerging from decentralising legislative powers after the 18th Amendment to the Constitution. As consumer protection laws continue to increase throughout provinces, consumers and businesses face the challenge of navigating through a complex web of legislation.

This kind of complex system causes serious hazardous implications for the people demanding their rights. Such a legal system, which contains difficult and unknown legal terminology, creates obstacles for anyone attempting to seek remedies for their grievances. Moreover, there is a division of legislation among different provinces, which further worsens this system. This system makes it difficult

67 Asif Khan and Advocate Babar Ali, 'Electronic Court System and Speedy Justice: A Comparative Critical Analysis of Legal Systems in Pakistan, Malaysia, and India' (2021) *Journal of Law and Social Policy* 26

68 Colin Anderson et al., 'Everyday Governance in Areas of Contested Power: Insights From Mozambique, Myanmar, and Pakistan' (2023) 41 *Development Policy Review* 12683

69 Ronald A Brand, 'UNCITRAL, Access to Justice, and the Future of Online Dispute Resolution' (2021) 8(1) *BCDR International Arbitration Review* 87, 102

for consumers to understand and resolve legal issues and seek compensation for their complaints. Therefore, there is an urgent requirement for a more effective and easily accessible alternative dispute resolution system for consumers. The system, which comprises a unified consumer ADR statute applicable nationwide, will significantly reduce the grievances of consumers and businesses. It will thus provide a guide in a single book, making it easy to understand and claim rights. The legislation that will establish a unified and standardised legal framework would harmonise the consumer protection process and facilitate the resolution of conflicts between parties without resorting to judicial proceedings. Moreover, this method is mostly confidential, and thus, businesses and classified materials will not be made public.

Furthermore, through the synchronisation of consumer ADR regulations on a national scale, Pakistan will conform to the ideals of a consolidated market and ensure consumer advocacy. It will enable individuals to confidently exercise their rights, irrespective of their geographical location or linguistic background. It will also promote a just and transparent marketplace for all parties involved. The intention behind implementing provincial consumer protection legislation in Pakistan was undoubtedly to distribute legislative authorities. However, it has unintentionally resulted in a legal system that heavily relies on court-based methods for ADR in consumer cases. Given many laws, it is pertinent to establish a single and standardised consumer ADR law that can be used nationwide. Implementing such a shift will streamline the legal procedure and promote consumer involvement, which will result in a just and transparent marketplace for everyone.

Conclusion

In conclusion, the evolution and adoption of ADR in Pakistan proves to be a key step towards alleviating the burdens on the judiciary. This is possible by providing a more streamlined and efficient forum for resolving disputes. The Alternate Dispute Resolution Act of 2017 and subsequent regional initiatives offer a framework in this regard. This framework could potentially transform dispute resolution across the nation. Many factors exist that hamper the successful implementation of ADR. It includes but is not limited to regional differences, cultural resistance, outdated legal structures, and a lack of awareness. Challenges erupted from the fractured legal system, especially after the decentralisation of the 18th Amendment, particularly in consumer disputes. This creates a dire need for a unified system for consumer ADR legislation.

Pakistan must pave the way for the full potential of ADR by overcoming these obstacles. This includes reforms in the outdated laws like the Arbitration Act of 1940. Additionally, it involves the need to create the necessary infrastructure for the proper functioning of ADR. Investing in advanced training programs that respect socio-cultural norms is much needed in this regard. Moreover, due to the shift towards online trading, there is an urgent need for robust ODR frameworks. These frameworks should adhere to international standards to ensure fair and effective methods to deal with digital commerce disputes.

Pakistan can create a more just, efficient, and accessible dispute resolution structure by implementing these reforms and promoting an understanding of ADR. This shift will reduce the judicial backlog and create a more secure environment for businesses and investors. Consequently, this will result in the socio-economic development of the country. Although the journey towards a fully designed ADR system in Pakistan is challenging, it is undoubtedly mandatory for the future of its legal and commercial sectors.

References

Ahmad, A, Rashid Ahmad, S, Gilani, H, Tariq, A, Zhao, N, Waqar Aslam, R and Mumtaz, F, 'A Synthesis of Spatial Forest Assessment Studies Using Remote Sensing Data and Techniques in Pakistan' (2021) 12(9) Forests 1211

Akhtar N, et al., 'Online Dispute Resolution as a Solution to E-Commerce Disputes: A Comparative Study of Pakistan and UK' (2022) 28(3) Journal of Contemporary Issues in Business and Government 149

Ali M and Lu Geng L, 'Alternative Dispute Resolution (ADR) in Pakistan: The Role of Lawyers in Mediation Procedure' (2019) 6(4) International Journal of Research 421

Alternative Dispute Resolution Act, 2017 (XX of 2017) Pakistan

Anderson, C, Joshi, A, Barnes, K, Ahmed, A, Ali, M, Chaimite, E, Forquilha, S, Khan, D, Khan, R, Loureiro, M, Myanmar Research Team, Posse, L, Rowlands, J and Shankland, A, 'Everyday Governance in Areas of Contested Power: Insights From Mozambique, Myanmar, and Pakistan' (2023) 41 Development Policy Review 12683

Asif, MH, Zhongfu, T, Irfan, M, Ahmad, B and Ali, M, 'Assessing Eco-Label Knowledge and Sustainable Consumption Behavior in the Energy Sector of Pakistan: An Environmental Sustainability Paradigm' (2023) 30(14) Environmental Science and Pollution Research 41319

Asif MH, Zhongfu T, Dilanchiev A, Irfan M, Eyvazov E and Ahmad B, 'Determining the Influencing Factors of Consumers' Attitude Toward Renewable Energy Adoption in Developing Countries: A Roadmap Toward Environmental Sustainability and Green Energy Technologies' (2023) 30(16) Environmental Science and Pollution Research 47861

Bashir S, Khan AS and Khan FS, 'The Role of Consumer Education in Strengthening Consumer Protection Laws' (2023) 5(2) Pakistan Journal of Social Resolution 85

Bazmi S, 'Politico-Judicial Activism in Pakistan: A Historical Overview' (2022) 4(3) Pakistan Journal of Social Research 97

Brand RA, 'UNCITRAL, Access to Justice, and the Future of Online Dispute Resolution' (2021) 8(1) BCDR International Arbitration Review 87

Constitution of Islamic Republic of Pakistan 1973

Consumer Rights Commission of Pakistan in 1998, <https://crcp.org.pk/> accessed 17 July 2024

Donoghue v Stevenson [1932] AC 562

Durrani N, Fatima K and Ahmed J, 'The Role of Economic and Political Factors in Shaping Consumers' Confidence in Pakistan' (2023) 3(2) Journal of Social Sciences Review 718

Farzand A and Rahman A, 'Analysis of the Legislation About Consumer Protection in Punjab: A Legal Perspective With Case Laws' (2023) 5(2) Journal of Law & Social Studies (JLSS) 192

Fatima S, 'Alternative Dispute Resolution in the Light of Arbitration Laws' (2022) 4(3) Pakistan Journal of Social Research 831

Federal Ombudsman Order 1983

Iftekhar R, Khan DW and Wattoo F, 'Critical Analysis of Mediation Law of Islamabad (Alternative Dispute Resolution Act, 2017)' (2022) 6(1) Islamabad Law Review 40

Jehan, Y, Batool, M, Hayat, N and Hussain, D, 'Socio-Economic and Environmental Impacts of Tourism on the Local Community in Gilgit Baltistan, Pakistan: A Local Community Perspective' (2023) 14(1) Journal of the Knowledge Economy 1

Kalanauri ZI, 'Electronic Filing System, Virtual Courts & Online Dispute Resolution-Need of the Hour for Pakistan Legal System' (2021) 5(1) International Journal for Electronic Crime Investigation 1

Kaya S and Khan MD, 'Online Dispute Resolution in Pakistan: Challenges and Opportunities' (2022) 7(2) Journal of Nusantara Studies (JONUS) 103

Khaleel F, Janjua PZ and Ahmed M, 'Ethical Consideration of Islamic Banks in Pakistan: An Empirical Analysis' (2022) 13(6) Journal of Islamic Marketing 1

Khalid I, 'Politics of Federalism in Pakistan: Problems and Prospects' (2020) 28(1) South Asian Studies 199

Khan A and Ali B, 'Electronic Court System and Speedy Justice: A Comparative Critical Analysis of Legal Systems in Pakistan, Malaysia, and India' (2021) Journal of Law & Social Policy 26

Khan A and Mumtaz M, 'Justice Delayed Is Justice Denied: Access to Speedy Justice and Alternative Dispute Resolution System in Pakistan' (2020) Journal of Law and Social Policy 80

Khan B, Khan A and Ali S, 'Reforms in the Erstwhile Federally Administered Tribal Areas of Pakistan: A Critical Analysis' (2022) 3(3) Journal of Humanities, Social and Management Sciences (JHSMS) 104

Khan IA and Waqas M, 'What Ails Thee Knight Sans Arms: Status of Consumer Protection in Pakistan' (2011) 2(2) International Journal of Business and Social Science 242

Khan K and Aftab S, 'Consumer Protection in Islam: The Case of Pakistan' (2000) 39(4) Australian Economic Papers 483

Khan MB and Fatima M, 'English Law of Torts and Product Liability' [2020] Journal of Law & Social Policy 14

Khan MSM, Harvey, C, Price, M and Maclean, M, 'Philanthropy and Socio-Economic Development: The Role of Large Indigenous Voluntary Organizations in Bridging Social Divides in Pakistan' [2023] VOLUNTAS: International Journal of Voluntary and Nonprofit Organizations 1335

Khan SA, 'Situation Analysis of Health Care System of Pakistan: Post 18 Amendments' (2019) 7(3) Health Care Current Reviews 1

Kumar L, Naqvi, SA, Deitch, MJ, Khalid, MJ, Naeem, K, Amjad, AQ, Kumar, A, Gebremicael, TG, and Arshad, M, 'Opportunities and Constraints for Cleaner Production Policy in the Developing World: A Case Study of Sindh Region, Pakistan' [2023] Environment, Development and Sustainability 4391

Mahmood H, Tanveer M and Furqan M, 'Rule of Law, Corruption Control, Governance, and Economic Growth in Managing Renewable and Nonrenewable Energy Consumption in South Asia' (2021) 18(20) International Journal of Environmental Research and Public Health 10637

Masood M and Salman M, 'The Role of Deceptive Advertisements and Ethical Decision Outcomes in Determining Buying Behavior' (2023) 14(2) The Business & Management Review 23

Muhktar S and Khan M, 'Remedies to Challenge Arbitral Awards in Pakistan' (2017) 1(1) Journal of Asian Research 14

Pakistan Standards and Quality Control Authority (PSQCA) Act 1996

Paulsson J, 'Arbitration in Three Dimensions' (2011) 60(2) International & Comparative Law Quarterly 1

Pharmacy Act 1967

Phatak SA, Chaudhary, MAI, Khattak, MS and Naveed, A, 'Alternate Dispute Resolution-Free and Speedy Complaints Redressal Framework Using Technology: Ombudsmanship at Proverbial Doorsteps in Pakistan' (2022) 22(3) IJCSNS 344
Price Control and Prevention of Profiteering and Hoarding Act 1997
Qureshi SH, Shahzad A and Saeed N, 'White-Collar Crimes in Pakistan: A Comprehensive Study of Nature, Laws, and Enforcement Mechanisms' [2023] International Journal of Social Science And Entrepreneurship 45
Ramzan M and Mahmood K, 'Rationalizing Alternate Dispute Resolution in Pakistan' (2016) 6(1) International Journal of Research in Social Sciences 88
Rana MA, 'Decentralization Experience in Pakistan: The 18th Constitutional Amendment' (2020) 17(1) Asian Journal of Management Cases 61
Rizvi A, et al., 'Consumer Protection and Protectionism in Pakistan: Regulatory Framework, Issues and Solutions' [2023] Journal of Positive School Psychology 1339
Rupam AS, 'Consumer Legal Forum of Bangladesh: A Comparative Study with India and Pakistan' (2023) 1(1) Law and Society Students' Journal 12
Shaikh E, et al., 'Customer Satisfaction and Customer Loyalty: An Empirical Case Study on the Impact of Benefits Generated Through Smartphone Applications' (2023) 12(1–2) International Journal of Public Sector Performance Management 1
Siddiqui MS, Ahmed Z and Memon A, 'Impact of Devolution on Education in Pakistan in the Light of 18th Amendment: A Review Article' (2021) 10 The Government-Annual Research Journal of Political Science 82
The Balochistan Consumer Protection Act, 2003
The Islamabad Consumers Protection Act, 1995
The [Khyber Pakhtunkhwa] Consumers Protection Act, 1997
The Monopolies and Restrictive Trade Practices (Control and Prevention) Ordinance, 1970 (Ordinance NO. V OF 1970)
The Pakistan Hotels and Restaurants Act, 1976 Act No. LXXXI 1976
The Punjab Consumer Protection Act 2005 (Pb. Act II of 2005)
The Punjab Pure Food Ordinance, 1960 (Ordinance VII of 1960)
The Punjab Weights and Measures Ordinance, 1965 (W.P. Ord. XXXIII of 1965)
The Sindh Consumer Protection Act, 2014. SINDH ACT NO. XVII OF 2015
Ullah I, 'Interim Measures in Arbitration Under the Pakistani Legal Regime' (2013) 29(4) Arbitration International 653
Won S, 'Overview of Alternate Dispute Resolution With Special Reference to Arbitration Laws in Pakistan' (2013) 23 Journal of Arbitration Studies 149
Yahya NH and Rasit RM, 'Muslim Consumer Rights Based on Islamic Advertising Principles' (2019) 41(1) Islamiyyat 83

17 Concluding Remarks and the Way Forward

Eda Sahin-Sengül and Serkan Kaya

I. Overview of the Chapters

Consumers with low-value claims are often the weaker party and require institutional protection. Initially, while consumer rights were recognised, little attention was given to enforcing these rights. This is especially true in emerging economies, where legal systems are ill-equipped to protect consumer rights. ADR systems are emerging as a potentially effective way to provide consumers with access to justice globally. The rise in digital transactions has increased consumer disputes, necessitating the development of substantive consumer rights, especially online transactions. However, these rights are only meaningful if they can be practically enforced. Traditional litigation is expensive, time-consuming, and complex, making ADR systems a more viable option in our digital society. Over the past few decades, ADR systems have gained popularity for resolving consumer complaints. Mechanisms such as arbitration, mediation, and ombudsman services offer efficient, faster, less formal, and often more cost-effective dispute resolution compared to traditional legal procedures.

In emerging economies, courts remain the primary forum for resolving consumer disputes. Challenges persist despite numerous procedural reforms and positive outcomes from the consumer redress system and other legislative measures. To provide adequate legal protection for consumers in today's digital world, it is essential not only to enhance the effectiveness of the traditional litigation system but also to establish and develop an extrajudicial system that allows consumers to access justice.

This book examines and assesses the present ADR practices and legislative changes in emerging economies, highlighting the potential of ADR/ODR methods to provide legal certainty in consumer dispute resolution. The primary focus is on identifying the challenges within the consumer redress system in emerging economies that hinder access to justice and cause delays. By drawing on the extensive experience of developed nations, this book seeks to highlight the necessary legal amendments in emerging economies to establish and accelerate the growth of ADR for consumer disputes. This approach aims to solve problems, offer more secure solutions, and build consumer confidence and trust.

DOI: 10.4324/9781032689739-17

Throughout the book, the authors analyse consumer ADR systems first in developed and then in developing nations. Following the same approach, the subsequent sections first explain the issue in developed nations and then in developing nations to offer a comparative analysis of the jurisdictions discussed in the book. The chapter concludes by identifying and reflecting on common challenges facing emerging economies in promoting consumer ADR. Examining the 15 jurisdictions allows us to derive general conclusions despite the substantial differences in their legal, political, and economic systems. The goal is to emphasise the major findings from the analysis of the law in action in emerging economies.

Developed Nations

Chapter 2 addresses ADR and access to justice for consumers from an EU perspective. It explores the current EU legal framework for resolving consumer disputes, with a particular focus on the ADR Directive and the ODR Regulation as significant steps towards establishing a robust legal framework and supporting the EU internal market. Given their substantial impact on cross-border disputes, it is crucial to assess the potential for harmonisation and evaluate their effectiveness in managing cross-border disputes within the single market. While this chapter highlights the positive aspects of the legal advancements made thus far, it also argues that certain objectives set by the Commission still need to be achieved to enable the ADR Directive and the ODR Regulation to reach their full potential.

Developing countries can draw several valuable lessons from the EU's experience with consumer protection and dispute resolution mechanisms. The EU has established a robust legal framework, including the Consumer ADR Directive and the ODR Regulation, which ensures high-quality, accessible dispute resolution across all economic sectors and introduces a multilingual online platform for resolving cross-border e-commerce disputes. Strong institutional support and enforcement mechanisms, such as national ODR contact points and the CPC Regulation, are crucial for addressing breaches of consumer protection laws collaboratively. Despite these frameworks, the European Union faces challenges in consumer awareness and trader participation, highlighting the importance of raising awareness and simplifying procedures to ensure accessibility. Developing countries can leverage technology to develop user-friendly online platforms for dispute resolution and implement policies that encourage participation of the infringing companies.

Chapter 3 explores how ADR affects consumers' ability to seek legal remedies within the UK. The consumer ADR system in the UK is a robust framework that has evolved over time and has been influenced by both national legislation and EU directives. It includes private, independent, and online arbitration schemes such as Consumer Arbitration, operated by Consumer Dispute Resolution Limited (CDRL), one of the main ADR providers in the UK. The system also employs expert determination procedures for highly technical disputes and adjudication for performance issues. What works well is the adaptability of the system to technological advancements and legislative changes, notably Brexit. The transition towards

ODR is particularly promising, offering potential solutions that are user-friendly, equitable, and capable of handling a diverse range of consumer disputes. However, the system has faced challenges in coherence and accessibility, indicating areas for improvement.

Developing countries can learn several lessons from the UK's experience. Firstly, the importance of a robust and adaptable ADR system that can evolve with changing consumer transactions and digital advancements. Secondly, the value of having diverse dispute resolution methods to cater to different types of disputes. Lastly, there is the necessity for continuous evaluation and adaptation of ADR mechanisms to ensure they meet consumers' specific needs while maintaining high standards of fairness and efficiency. This includes the potential of ODR as a promising avenue for dispute resolution in the digital age. Developed nations have well-established consumer redress systems and advanced mechanisms for handling disputes across various fields. In contrast, emerging countries lag behind in consumer dispute resolution, often not fully leveraging the advancements in information and communication technology.

Developing Nations

Chapter 4 examines the consumer ADR system in Turkey, governed by the Consumer Protection Law (CPL) of 2013, which aims to safeguard consumers' interests and provide redress for losses. The system includes consumer arbitration boards for disputes below TRY 104,000 and consumer courts for higher-value disputes, with mandatory mediation for claims above this threshold. Technological integration through the National Judiciary Informatics System (UYAP) and electronic submission systems has improved accessibility and efficiency, while binding decisions by arbitration boards ensure resolutions are respected. However, the system faces challenges such as lengthy resolution times, delays due to the requirement for five-member arbitration boards, and a lack of consumer awareness about ADR processes. Turkey can learn from developed nations by aiming for swifter resolution times, simplifying board structures, and increasing consumer awareness, similar to the EU's ODR Regulation, to enhance the efficiency and accessibility of its consumer ADR system.

Chapter 5 looks into the consumer ADR system in Chile, primarily governed by the Consumer Protection Act (CPA) of 1997, with significant reforms in 2018 introducing the Collective Voluntary Procedures (PVC). The National Service of the Consumer (SERNAC) plays a central role in enforcing consumer law, promoting consumer rights, and handling complaints. The system includes mechanisms like SERNAC's Seal, individual complaints, and PVCs, which aim to resolve disputes without court involvement. Technological integration, such as online complaint submissions and the "I Want to Get Out" platform, has improved accessibility and efficiency. However, challenges include lengthy resolution times, limited enforcement power of SERNAC, and the need for more institutionalised ADR mechanisms for individual complaints. Chile can learn from developed nations by improving the efficiency and accessibility of consumer dispute resolution processes.

Chapter 6 analyses the consumer ADR system in Georgia, governed by the law on the Protection of Consumer Rights, including mechanisms like consumer arbitration and mediation. The system benefits from a strong legal framework and the involvement of the Georgian National Competition Agency in handling disputes. Therefore, Georgia's Consumer ADR system has made strides in providing mechanisms for resolving disputes, but there are areas that require further development. The system includes various ADR methods, yet it faces challenges in accessibility, coherence, and adaptability to technological advancements. These aspects need improvement to ensure broader and more effective consumer access to justice. On the positive side, some aspects of the system, such as its foundational structure and the incorporation of diverse dispute-resolution methods, work well. However, challenges include limited consumer awareness, insufficient differentiation between consumer and commercial arbitration, and a lack of streamlined procedures for small disputes. Georgia can learn from developed nations by enhancing consumer awareness, simplifying arbitration procedures, and ensuring the independence and impartiality of arbitration bodies. Additionally, adopting EU standards for ADR and ODR could improve the efficiency and fairness of the system.

Chapter 7 discusses China's consumer ADR system, which has seen significant development and is characterised by a comprehensive framework that includes both non-judicial and judicial ADR channels. The non-judicial ADR channels, which include negotiation, mediation, administrative appeals, and arbitration, are utilised most frequently. The Consumer Rights Protection Law (CRPL) serves as the primary law for consumer protection, and the Chinese government continues to refine and enhance systems for protecting consumer rights and interests. ODR has also been rapidly developed to facilitate ADR. What works well is the variety of options available to consumers and the rapid development of ODR. However, the system could benefit from improvements in coherence and accessibility, similar to the UK's ADR system. The distinct characteristics of China's consumer ADR, primarily shaped by public power, also present unique challenges and opportunities for improvement.

Chapter 8 scrutinises the consumer ADR system in Romania, governed by Government Ordinance 38/2015, which transposes the ADR Directive into national law. Key entities include the ADR Directorate within the National Authority for Consumer Protection (NACP), the Alternative Banking Dispute Resolution Centre (ABDRC), and ADR-Fin within the Authority for Financial Supervision. The system benefits from a strong legal framework and the involvement of specialised ADR bodies, which offer quicker and more cost-effective dispute resolution compared to traditional courts. However, challenges include limited consumer awareness, reluctance of traders to participate, and a lack of qualified staff within ADR entities. Romania can learn from developed nations by enhancing consumer awareness, simplifying ADR procedures, and ensuring the independence and impartiality of ADR bodies. Additionally, adopting more robust technological solutions for ODR could improve the system's accessibility and efficiency.

Chapter 9 examines the consumer ADR system in Saudi Arabia, including mechanisms like arbitration and mediation, governed by the Saudi Centre for Commercial Arbitration (SCCA) and supported by legislative reforms in 2012 and

2016. The system benefits from a strong legal framework and the recent introduction of ODR during the COVID-19 pandemic, which has improved accessibility and efficiency. However, challenges remain, such as a lack of public trust in alternative mechanisms, cultural barriers in ADR systems, the risk of the outcome and potential delays in court proceedings. Saudi Arabia can enhance its consumer dispute resolution system by making the ADR processes easily accessible and utilising technology to make the process more efficient.

Chapter 10 focuses on the consumer ADR system in South Africa, governed by the Consumer Protection Act (CPA) of 2008, which promotes alternative dispute resolution through mechanisms like industry ombuds, provincial consumer protection authorities, and mediation. The system benefits from a strong legal framework and the involvement of specialised ADR bodies, which offer quicker and more cost-effective dispute resolution compared to traditional courts. However, challenges include unawareness of the ombuds, lack of cultural and linguistic diversity in the legal framework, and enforcement issues, particularly with provincial consumer tribunals. South Africa can learn from developed nations by enhancing access to justice for low-income consumers and making ADR procedures more accessible and affordable.

Chapter 11 explains the consumer ADR system in India, governed by the Consumer Protection Act of 2019, which emphasises expeditious and effective dispute resolution through mechanisms like consumer courts, mediation, and ODR. The system benefits from a strong legal framework, the establishment of the Central Consumer Protection Authority (CCPA), and the integration of technology for online complaint filing and mediation. The system works well in offering a formalised process and has had success in handling a significant number of cases. However, challenges include a significant backlog of cases, limited consumer awareness, and inconsistencies in the application of ADR mechanisms. India can learn from developed nations by enhancing digitalisation, increasing public awareness of ADR mechanisms, and ensuring more streamlined and user-friendly processes to reduce delays and improve access to justice for consumers.

Chapter 12 studies the consumer ADR system in Brazil, governed by the Consumer Protection and Defence Code (CDC) of 1990, which provides a robust legal framework for consumer rights. Fundamental mechanisms include PROCONs (Programa de Proteção e Defesa do Consumidor) for extrajudicial dispute resolution, special civil courts for simplified procedures, and the Consumidor.gov.br platform for online dispute resolution (ODR). The system benefits from strong legal backing, technological integration, and the involvement of specialised ADR bodies, which offer quicker and more cost-effective dispute resolution compared to traditional courts. However, challenges include limited consumer awareness, lengthy resolution times, and the need for more data to assess the effectiveness of ODR platforms. Brazil can learn from developed nations by increasing consumer knowledge through focused campaigns, streamlining alternative dispute resolution processes, guaranteeing the autonomy and unbiasedness of ADR bodies, and implementing more advanced technological solutions for online dispute resolution to improve accessibility and efficiency.

Chapter 13 explores the consumer ADR system in Malaysia, governed by the Consumer Protection Act 1999 (CPA 1999), which includes mechanisms like the Tribunal for Consumer Claims (TCC) and civil courts. The system benefits from a strong legal framework, the establishment of the TCC for efficient and cost-effective dispute resolution, and the integration of technology for online complaint submissions. However, challenges include the complexity of litigation processes, underutilisation of ADR mechanisms like mediation and arbitration, and limited consumer knowledge of legal matters and processes. Malaysia can learn from developed nations by enhancing mediation and arbitration where mediators and arbitrators understand the nuances of consumer rights and responsibilities, ensuring that disputes are handled by experts who can make informed decisions, and implementing ODR to effectively resolve consumer disputes and claims.

Chapter 14 addresses the consumer ADR system in the United Arab Emirates (UAE), which has recently incorporated ADR models into its legal framework, particularly following the adoption of Federal Legislative Decree No. 40 in December 2023. This decree expanded conciliation and mediation methods to cover various legal disputes, including consumer disputes. The system benefits from a strong legal framework, the involvement of administrative bodies, and the integration of technology through platforms like Wasata for online mediation. However, challenges include a lack of clear guidelines for mediation, a lack of ODR, and cultural reluctance towards formal dispute resolution methods. The UAE can take cues from developed countries by fully embracing an ODR system, ensuring the enforceability of agreements to utilise ODR, and removing the uncertainty surrounding final outcomes.

Chapter 15 discusses the consumer ADR system in Nigeria, governed by the Federal Competition and Consumer Protection Act (FCCPA) of 2018, which established the Federal Competition and Consumer Protection Commission (FCCPC) to handle consumer disputes through mechanisms like arbitration, mediation, and conciliation. The system benefits from a strong legal framework and the integration of technology for ODR. However, challenges include limited consumer awareness, lengthy resolution times, and the need for more robust enforcement mechanisms. Nigeria can learn from developed nations by providing adequate infrastructure and internet connectivity to aid the smooth operations of ODR platforms and ensure equal access for all Nigerian consumers, increasing consumers' digital skills to navigate ODR processes, and organising professional development programs to enhance legal professionals' competence and confidence in handling online disputes.

Chapter 16 focuses on the consumer ADR system in Pakistan, governed by various provincial laws and the Alternate Dispute Resolution Act of 2017, which aims to provide speedy and cost-effective dispute resolution. The system benefits from a strong legal framework, the involvement of community-based efforts like Panchayats and Jirgas, and the establishment of consumer protection courts in some provinces. However, challenges include the complex legal structure and division of legislation among different provinces, which makes it difficult for consumers to understand and resolve legal issues and seek compensation for their complaints.

Pakistan can learn from developed nations by having an effective and easily accessible alternative dispute resolution system for consumers in place and synchronising consumer ADR regulations on a national scale. Therefore, adopting a unified national consumer protection framework could streamline processes and improve accessibility and efficiency.

II. The Way Forward

The promotion of consumer ADR in emerging economies faces several common challenges that need to be addressed to enhance access to justice for consumers. One of the primary issues is the limited awareness and education about ADR mechanisms among both consumers and businesses. In many emerging markets, there is a lack of understanding regarding the benefits of ADR, leading to the underutilisation of these mechanisms. Educating consumers and traders about the availability and advantages of ADR is crucial for fostering a culture where alternative dispute resolution is seen as a viable and preferable option to litigation. Also, lengthy resolution times and procedural complexities can deter consumers from seeking redress. Simplifying ADR procedures and ensuring timely resolutions are crucial steps.

Accessibility remains another significant challenge, particularly for those living in rural areas or regions with limited digital infrastructure. ADR mechanisms, especially those relying on online platforms, can be difficult to access for populations with low digital literacy or without regular access to the internet. Addressing these accessibility issues requires tailored strategies to ensure that all segments of the population can benefit from these mechanisms.

Legal and institutional barriers also hinder the effective promotion of consumer ADR in emerging economies. Outdated laws, diverse or inadequate enforcement mechanisms, and the limited capacity of ADR institutions can all contribute to a system that is unable to fully support the needs of consumers. Reforming legal frameworks to better accommodate ADR, alongside strengthening the institutions that oversee these processes, is essential for creating a more supportive environment for alternative dispute resolution.

Cultural resistance to ADR presents another hurdle. In many emerging economies, formal litigation is often seen as the more legitimate or trusted method of resolving disputes, which can result in a reluctance to use ADR. Overcoming this resistance involves building trust in ADR processes through transparent and fair practices, and by highlighting the successful resolution of disputes through ADR.

The integration of technology into ADR systems, particularly through ODR, offers a promising solution to many of these challenges. However, technological integration is not without its difficulties, particularly in regions with low digital literacy or insufficient technological infrastructure. Learning from the experiences of developed nations, emerging economies can focus on adopting scalable and user-friendly ODR platforms that are accessible to all, regardless of their technological proficiency.

To move forward, it is crucial for emerging economies to enhance their legal frameworks to better support consumer ADR mechanisms. This includes updating outdated laws and ensuring that enforcement mechanisms are in place to give ADR outcomes the necessary authority throughout the country regardless of where consumers live. Additionally, investing in capacity building and training for ADR professionals is essential to improve the quality and consistency of dispute resolution. Public-private partnerships can play a key role in developing the necessary infrastructure and promoting ADR as a mainstream method for resolving consumer disputes.

Continuous monitoring and evaluation of ADR systems are also vital. This allows for the ongoing adaptation of ADR processes to meet the changing needs of consumers and to integrate technological advancements effectively. By learning from the experiences of developed nations – such as implementing consumer education campaigns, simplifying, and standardising ADR processes, ensuring the independence of ADR bodies, and leveraging technology – emerging economies can create robust and accessible ADR systems that provide fair and efficient resolutions for consumer disputes.

In conclusion, while emerging economies face significant challenges in promoting consumer ADR, there are clear strategies that can be adopted to overcome these barriers. By focusing on education, accessibility, legal reforms, and technological integration, these countries can build ADR systems that effectively serve their populations and contribute to broader access to justice for consumers.

Index

Note: Page numbers in *italics* indicate figures, **bold** indicate tables in the text, and references following "n" refer notes.

Kolibri 360 GmbH
Ferdinand-Jühlke-Straße 7
99095 Erfurt, Deutschland
produktsicherheit@kolibri360.de